Luminos is the Open Access monograph publishing program from UC Press. Luminos provides a framework for preserving and reinvigorating monograph publishing for the future and increases the reach and visibility of important scholarly work. Titles published in the UC Press Luminos model are published with the same high standards for selection, peer review, production, and marketing as those in our traditional program. www.luminosoa.org

This publication is openly available online thanks to generous support from Arcadia, a charitable fund of Lisbet Rausing and Peter Baldwin.

Until the Storm Passes

Until the Storm Passes

Politicians, Democracy, and the Demise of Brazil's Military Dictatorship

Bryan Pitts

UNIVERSITY OF CALIFORNIA PRESS

University of California Press
Oakland, California

© 2023 by Bryan Pitts

This work is licensed under a Creative Commons CC BY-NC-ND license.
To view a copy of the license, visit http://creativecommons.org/licenses.

Suggested citation: Pitts, B. *Until the Storm Passes: Politicians, Democracy, and the Demise of Brazil's Military Dictatorship*. Oakland: University of California Press, 2023. DOI: https://doi.org/10.1525/luminos.142

Names: Pitts, Montie Bryan, author.
Title: Until the storm passes : politicians, democracy, and the demise of Brazil's military dictatorship / Bryan Pitts.
Description: Oakland, California : University of California Press, [2023] | Includes bibliographical references and index. | Contents: Introduction : a nation for all or a few? : the political class, the people, and the rise and fall of Brazil's military dictatorship—"The blood of the youth is flowing" : the political class and its children take on the military in 1968—"The funeral of democracy" : the showdown with the military and Institutional Act No. 5—"The political class has learned nothing" : the military punishes the political class—"Sheltered under the tree" : the everyday practice of politics under dictatorial rule—"We aren't a flock of little sheep" : the political class and the limits of liberalization—"We cannot think about democracy the way we used to" : the ABC strikes and the challenge of popular mobilization—"I want to vote for President" : Diretas Já, the political class, and the demise of the military dictatorship—Conclusion : freedom, justice, and solidarity for Brazil? : the political class under dictatorship and democracy.
Identifiers: LCCN 2022021160 | ISBN 9780520388352 (paperback) | ISBN 9780520388369 (ebook)
Subjects: LCSH: Government, Resistance to—Brazil—History—20th century. | Brazil—Politics and government—1964–1985.
Classification: LCC F2538.25 .P585 2023 | DDC 981.06/3—dc23/eng/20220525

LC record available at https://lccn.loc.gov/2022021160

32 31 30 29 28 27 26 25 24 23
10 9 8 7 6 5 4 3 2 1

CONTENTS

List of Figures viii
List of Media Files ix
Acknowledgments xi
List of Abbreviations xvi

Introduction: A Nation for All or a Few? The Political Class, the People, and the Rise and Fall of Brazil's Military Dictatorship 1
   A (Political) Class That Rules 4
   Structure versus Rational Choice and Generals versus Civil Society 7
   Sources and Chapter Outline 10

1. "The Blood of the Youth Is Flowing": The Political Class and Its Children Take on the Military in 1968 14
   From Jubilation to Disillusion: A "Revolution" Gone Astray 15
   "I Stand in Solidarity with the Students": Politicians and the Student Movement 18
   "It Is Our Children Who Are There": The Invasion of the Universidade de Brasília 22
   Conclusions 31

2. "The Funeral of Democracy": The Showdown with the Military and Institutional Act No. 5 33
   Weighing Benefits and Risks: The Political Class and Military Maneuver under Duress 35
   "To the King, I Give All, Except My Honor": The Congressional Debate 41
   "History Alone Will Judge Us": The Closing Arguments and Vote 46
   Conclusions 50

3. "The Political Class Has Learned Nothing": The Military Punishes the Political Class   53
   "The Resumption of the Revolution": The Aftermath of AI-5   54
   "You Become a Leper": Purging the Political Class   65
   "Zeal for the Collective Interest": Reshaping the Political Class through Reform   74
   Conclusions   79

4. "Sheltered under the Tree": The Everyday Practice of Politics under Dictatorial Rule   81
   "It Is Not Necessary to Live": The Autênticos and the Anti-Candidacy   83
   Building a Party from the Bottom Up: The Rise of Orestes Quércia in São Paulo   89
   "Our People Are Still at a Very Low Level": Détente and "Relative Democracy"   92
   Conclusions   96

5. "We Aren't a Flock of Little Sheep": The Political Class and the Limits of Liberalization   98
   "Brazil Is Doing Well. Are You?": 1974 and the Rebirth of the MDB   99
   The Limits of Détente: The Military Overreacts to the 1974 Elections   110
   The Audacity to Strong-Arm the Generals: Paulo Maluf Runs for Governor of São Paulo   114
   Conclusions   123

6. "We Cannot Think about Democracy the Way We Used To": The ABC Strikes and the Challenge of Popular Mobilization   125
   1978: "The Most Peaceful Strike Ever Seen in São Paulo"   126
   1979: "It Is up to the Workers to Change the Rules of the Game"   132
   1980: The Republic of São Bernardo   139
   Conclusions   147

7. "I Want to Vote for President": Diretas Já, the Political Class, and the Demise of the Military Dictatorship   149
   Hanging on by Their Fingernails: The Military Attempts to Retain Power   150
   "Democracy within Reach": The Political Class and Mass Mobilization in Diretas Já   152
   "I Saw the People Born of the Masses": The Promise and Limits of Popular Mobilization   158
   "Only Good Politics Can Save Them": The Political Class and the 1985 Election   161
   Conclusions   170

Conclusion: Freedom, Justice, and Solidarity for Brazil? The Political
    Class under Dictatorship and Democracy   173

Notes   181
Bibliography   229
Index   243

LIST OF FIGURES

1. Federal deputies scuffle with police at UnB   25
2. Deputy Santilli Sobrinho fights with police to prevent the arrest of his son   25

LIST OF MEDIA FILES

1. Tumult during the speech of Haroldo Leon Peres, March 29, 1968   *21*
2. Clip of Nísia Carone speech, December 12, 1968   *42*
3. Clip of President Artur da Costa e Silva speaking to the CSN, December 13, 1968   *57*
4. Clip of Vice President Pedro Aleixo speaking to the CSN, December 13, 1968   *57*
5. Clip of Augusto Rademaker speaking to the CSN, December 13, 1968   *58*
6. Clip of Jarbas Passarinho speaking to the CSN, December 13, 1968   *59*
7. Clip of Ulysses Guimarães speech before the electoral college, January 15, 1974   *87*
8. Clip of individual autêntico vote declarations, January 15, 1974   *88*
9. Clip of João Cunha speech criticizing attacks on legislators, April 28, 1980   *146*
10. Clip of Ulysses Guimarães speech, April 24, 1984   *160*
11. João Cunha electoral college vote, January 15, 1985   *170*
12. Clip of Tancredo Neves speech before the electoral college, January 15, 1985   *172*

ACKNOWLEDGMENTS

I used to joke that when I finished my book I wanted my acknowledgments to echo Bilbo Baggins, who, as he celebrates his eleventy-first birthday, quips, "I don't know half of you half as well as I should like, and I like less half of you half as well as you deserve." But that's not the best way to approach these acknowledgments, for as a process that has spanned a decade and a half winds down, I find myself overwhelmed with gratitude for those who supported me along the way, not just as scholars and colleagues, but as friends and confidants. Most acknowledgments start with the professional and conclude with the personal; here I do the opposite, for without the support I've received through profoundly trying times personally, I would have found little success professionally. Above all, I want to thank the family members, friends, therapists, and fellow travelers on the road to recovery who have supported me through a decade of addiction, from which I have only recently begun to emerge. Change became possible when I began to accept how much you care for me and to see in myself the things you saw in me all along. My journey to finishing this book has been difficult, the trials along the way largely self-inflicted. I would never have survived this long without all of you. Though you are too many to name, I would like to specifically acknowledge Justin Smith; my parents, Montie and Brenda Pitts, and brothers, Jordan and Adam; Michael Burden Jr.; Nick Branock; Emily Brinegar; my sponsors, Richard B. and Richard F.; Alvaro Jarrin; Bruno Brolezzi; Dat Nguyen; Heather Everett; Leigh Campoamor; Brian Mier; Pete Sigal; Alejandro Velasco; and Erica Giesbrecht.

I am proud not only to have had John D. French as an adviser but also to count him and Jan Hoffman French among my friends. The emails John and I have exchanged bouncing ideas about the dictatorship off each other and sharing exciting sources could fill half a dozen books. And then there were the hours-long meetings in his dining room and innumerable phone calls in which he provided line-by-line feedback, the breakfasts at Elmo's, the intensive workshops, and more. His mentorship has gone well beyond this book; over the years, John has taught me much about navigating academic politics, dealing with rejection, and picking one's battles. As friends, he and Jan have been there for me during my darkest moments. After years of my using substances and sex to rebel and cope, it was John who started me on the road to recovery when he told me, "Sometimes we expend so much effort rebelling against the unjust rules of our childhood that we wind up letting them define us as much as if we had followed them to the letter." Those words may have saved my life, for which I will be forever grateful.

I came to Duke in 2006 with no idea what it meant to be a historian but well prepared to be a scholar. As a New Testament major at Oral Roberts University, I learned from James B. Shelton what it means to engage with a text closely, examine its biases, and ascribe it meaning. I also took a summer course on Mexican history at the University of Oklahoma, and Terry Rugeley, with his encyclopedic knowledge of Mexico, served as an inspiration as I fell in love with Brazil two years later. During my MA at Vanderbilt, I was privileged to learn from Latin Americanists such as Edward Wright-Rios, John Janusek, Jane Landers, and Marshall Eakin, who would later serve on my dissertation committee. As a PhD student at Duke, I learned how to be a historian not only from John French but also from Pete Sigal and Jocelyn Olcott, who both have the uncommon gift of being both formidable scholars and wonderful people, as well as from Kathryn Burns and Louis Pérez at UNC Chapel Hill. Ara Wilson provided an anthropologist's perspective for my prelim defense. Special thanks to Natalie Hartman at the Center for Latin American and Caribbean Studies for her tireless dedication and generous support, along with the many lunches we enjoyed together.

When asked if I regret my decision to get a PhD in light of the collapse of the academic job market, I am sometimes tempted to say yes—until I think about the lifelong friends I met along the way. Liz Shesko and Alejandro Velasco have provided feedback at nearly every stage of this project, most recently the introduction and conclusion. Just as important, they are friends of the sort who don't come along often—the colleagues I turn to first when overjoyed or devastated with the unexpected twists and turns of academia and life. David Romine and his spouse, Lis Tyroler, were there for me on June 18, 2013, the darkest day of my life, and I am forever in their debt. I also appreciate the friendship and intellectual engagement of Erin Parish, Alvaro Jarrín, Anne-Marie Angelo, Anne Phillips, Kristin Wintersteen, Kelly Kennington, Katharine French-Fuller, Jeff Richey, Martin Repinecz, Vanessa Freije, Daniel Bessner, Orion Teal, Pam Lach, and, after I graduated, Gray Kidd and Travis Knoll.

The research for this book was only possible due to generous financial support from many sources. At Duke, my research was funded by the Duke Graduate School, the Department of History, the James B. Duke 100th Anniversary Fund, the Center for Latin American and Caribbean Studies, and the Mellon Foundation. A Fulbright-Hays Doctoral Dissertation Research Abroad Fellowship from the US Department of Education supported a year in Brazil in 2009–10. A Fulbright Scholars Postdoctoral Award (US Department of State) funded an additional seven months of research for this book in Brasília in 2015, and a 2017 research trip to Rio de Janeiro was supported by both the Global Brazil Humanities Lab at Duke and the Latin American and Caribbean Studies Institute at the University of Georgia (UGA). Much of the writing of this book was completed during a postdoc at UGA, funded by the Portuguese Flagship (US Department of Defense) and UGA's Title VI National Resource Center grant (US Department of Education).

In Brazil, I spent months at the Arquivo Público do Estado de São Paulo, where the staff were gracious and patient as I spent months requesting one set of bound newspapers after another. At the Centro de Memória Eleitoral of the Tribunal Regional Eleitoral de São Paulo, I was deeply moved by the friendliness of the entire staff but especially Alex Brasil and José "Zezinho" D'Amico Bauab, who invited me to contribute a chapter to a 2011 edited volume on São Paulo politics. Also in São Paulo, the staff at the Fundação Mário Covas were remarkably generous with their knowledge of one of São Paulo's iconic politicians. Director Osvaldo Martins was kind enough to sit down and talk about his memories of Covas. In the Cidade Maravilhosa of Rio de Janeiro, I enjoyed productive research at the Centro de Documentação de História Contemporânea do Brasil, Brazil's greatest archive of political history and a trailblazer in oral history, and Paulo Fontes of CPDOC was kind enough to provide a letter of affiliation when I was applying for research grants. The staff of the Arquivo Nacional were also helpful as I consulted the documentation of the dictatorship's intelligence-gathering agencies in both 2010 and 2017. And in Campinas, Fernando Teixeira da Silva at the Arquivo Edgard Leuenroth (AEL) provided invaluable information about the archive's holdings. During my postdoc in Brasília, thanks to Júlio Pinto, I found a home among the faculty at the Centro de Formação of the Câmara dos Deputados, and I am especially grateful to André Sahtler Guimarães and Malena Rehbein Rodrigues for providing me with office space and facilitating introductions to archival staff and politicians in the lower house of Brazil's Congress. Staff at the Centro de Documentação e Informação (CEDI) of the Câmara and Secretaria de Arquivo of the Senate also generously digitized and emailed me valuable congressional print sources. The entire staff of the Câmara's Coordenação de Engenharia de Telecomunicações e Audiovisual (COAUD) welcomed me as they explained, with justified pride, their remarkable efforts to preserve, digitize, and make publicly available five decades of recordings of congressional sessions. Finally, I thank all the former politicians and their family members, allies and adversaries of the military regime alike, who welcomed me into their offices and homes to share their memories of those days.

From the moment I began this project, I have wanted one thing: for Brazilians to think I have offered a useful contribution to knowledge about their country.

Over the years, scholars such as Paulo Fontes, Rafael Ioris, Larissa Corrêa, Diego Galeano (an Argentine but practically a Brazilian by now), Erica Giesbrecht, David Fleischer, and Philippe Arthur dos Reis have offered input, mentorship, and friendship. Above all, I have profited from the erudition and collegiality of Alexandre Fortes, who served on both my prelim and dissertation committees. I have also had wonderful interactions with the community of North American Brazilianists, especially James Green, Jan Hoffman French, Marshall Eakin, Tom Rogers, Brian Mier, Sean Mitchell, Jeffrey Lesser, Colin Snider, Erika Robb-Larkins, and Robert Moser.

I have worked at three universities since returning from my postdoc in Brazil, picking up valued colleagues and friends at every stop. During my postdoc at UGA, I was fortunate to develop a friendship with the inimitable, irascible Thom Whigham, who provided excellent feedback on chapter drafts and a sympathetic ear as I grappled with the tribulations of the job market. Emily McGinn and Derek Bentley became dear friends as we transitioned to alt-ac careers. And Richard Gordon generously shared the secrets of writing a winning Title VI grant application, which set me on the road to my new career helping run Latin American Studies programs. At Indiana University (IU), I benefited immensely from the intellectual and personal generosity of Jeffrey Gould, Daniel James, Peter Guardino, Rebecca Dirksen, Micol Seigel, Luciana Namorato, and William Mello, who welcomed me as a colleague with open arms. I am particularly grateful to Anke Birkenmaier, who encouraged me to continue writing even though research wasn't part of my job description. I also profited from IU's Faculty Writing Groups, which allowed me to nearly finish this book as I exchanged ideas about balancing research, teaching, service, and life with scholars such as Arlene Diaz and Judah Cohen. I was also privileged to work with many promising scholars in IU's MA program in Latin American Studies and grew especially close to Matt Cesnik, Nate Young, and John "Monty" Montgomery, who was kind enough to provide feedback on the introduction to this book. During my moments of frustration with my alt-ac position, Sam Dwinell offered his sympathy and solidarity. After my arrival at UCLA, I developed close relationships with the Latin American Institute directors Kevin Terraciano and Rubén Hernández-León, both of whom have provided encouragement and advice during the final push to finish this project. Thanks also to William Summerhill and the students in his Fall 2020 HIST 201I graduate seminar for their helpful suggestions on the final chapter of the manuscript. And Daniel Schoorl trained me in the art of union organizing and became a valued friend as we protested our way across Los Angeles together in June 2020.

Finally, my deep gratitude goes to Kate Marshall, my editor at the University of California Press. From the moment I met her at the 2014 meeting of the American Historical Association, I knew that UC Press was where I wanted to publish this book. Thanks also to the external readers, Rafael Ioris and Lucia Grinberg, for insightful reports that have made this a vastly better book. I also appreciate all the help provided by Enrique Ochoa-Kaup, who as editorial assistant has patiently guided me through the bureaucratic maze of publishing.

But above all I wish to acknowledge the powerful role that Brazil and my multitude of Brazilian friends have played in shaping me. When I went to Rio on a Foreign Language and Area Studies (FLAS) fellowship in 2005, it was the first time I was completely and unashamedly out of the closet to everyone I met. In other words, it was the first time I was unapologetically myself, with no need to perform or pretend. Brazil has always been the place where I am my truest self; as a result, I have developed friendships with people who like me for who I am, not for any facade I might put up. I connect with Brazil in a way I have never connected with anywhere else. My life there has been an unending dance, both figuratively and literally—*litrão* beers to the sound of rock at Pôr do Sol in 408/409 Norte in Brasília, dancing the night away in dive bars on São Paulo's Rua Augusta, and trying to samba on Rua dos Ouvidores in Rio at midnight, belting out with all my strength, "Viver e não ter a vergonha de ser feliz." The greatest compliment of my life came when a friend called me "o gringo mais brasileiro de todos os tempos"—the most Brazilian gringo ever. It is to this remarkable country and its people, so many of whom have enriched my life more than words can ever express, that I dedicate this book. Entre outras mil, és tu, Brasil. Agora e sempre.

LIST OF ABBREVIATIONS

POLITICAL PARTIES

ARENA	Aliança Renovadora Nacional
MDB	Movimento Democrático Brasileiro
PCB	Partido Comunista Brasileiro
PcdoB	Partido Comunista do Brasil
PDS	Partido Democrático Social
PDT	Partido Democrático Trabalhista
PL	Partido Libertador
PMDB	Partido do Movimento Democrático Brasileiro
PSD	Partido Social Democrático
PSP	Partido Social Progressista
PT	Partido dos Trabalhadores
PTB	Partido Trabalhista Brasileiro (1945–1965)
PTB	Partido Trabalhista Brasileiro (1980–)
UDN	União Democrática Nacional

STATES

AC	Acre
AL	Alagoas
AM	Amazonas
BA	Bahia
CE	Ceará

ES	Espírito Santo
GB	Guanabara
GO	Goiás
MG	Minas Gerais
PA	Pará
PB	Paraíba
PE	Pernambuco
PI	Piauí
PR	Paraná
RJ	Rio de Janeiro
RN	Rio Grande do Norte
RO	Rondônia
RS	Rio Grande do Sul
SC	Santa Catarina
SP	São Paulo

OTHER

ABC	Santo André, São Bernardo, and São Caetano
AI	Ato Institucional
CEBRAP	Centro Brasileiro de Análise e Planejamento
CGI	Comissão Geral de Investigações
CLT	Consolidação das Leis do Trabalho
CSN	Conselho de Segurança Nacional
DOI-CODI	Departamento de Operações de Informações—Cento de Operações de Defesa Interna
DOPS	Departamento de Ordem e Política Social
DCD	*Diário da Câmara dos Deputados*
DCN	*Diário do Congresso Nacional*
DSF	*Diário do Senado Federal*
FIESP	Federação das Indústrias do Estado de São Paulo
FL	Frente Liberal
IBOBE	Instituto Brasileiro de Opinião e Estatística
IMF	International Monetary Fund
JB	*Jornal do Brasil*
JT	*Jornal da Tarde*
OAB	Ordem de Advogados Brasileiros
SNI	Serviço Nacional de Informações
STF	Supremo Tribunal Federal
TRE	Tribunal Regional Eleitoral

TRT	Tribunal Regional do Trabalho
TSE	Tribunal Superior Eleitoral
TST	Tribunal Superior do Trabalho
UnB	Universidade de Brasília
UNE	União Nacional dos Estudantes
USP	Universidade de São Paulo

Introduction

A Nation for All or a Few? The Political Class, the People, and the Rise and Fall of Brazil's Military Dictatorship

On January 1, 2003, Brazil inaugurated a former shoeshine boy turned democratic socialist politician as president. A union leader with a fourth-grade education, Luiz Inácio Lula da Silva stood before Congress and offered a daring new vision for a country that for centuries had been a global leader in social inequality: "We are starting a new chapter in Brazil's history, not as a submissive nation, handing over its sovereignty, not as an unjust nation, passively standing by while the poorest suffer, but as an active, noble nation, courageously presenting itself to the world as a nation for everyone."[1] Congress offered its enthusiastic applause.

On January 1, 2019, Brazil inaugurated a former military captain turned Far Right politician as president. A congressman infamous for his attacks on women, LGBTQ+ people, Afro-Brazilians, and Indigenous people, Jair Bolsonaro stood before Congress and offered another vision for a country that, over the past decade and a half, had become a global leader in expanding opportunity: "We shall unite our people, value the family, respect religions and our Judeo-Christian tradition, combat the ideology of gender, and preserve our values. Brazil will return to being a country free of ideological bonds."[2] Congress offered its enthusiastic applause.

How could the Brazilian political elite support Lula's vision to reduce class- and race-based inequalities and then, only a few years later, support Bolsonaro's Far Right agenda? This book argues that the answer lies in understanding the dispositions of Brazil's "political class," especially the way it approached democracy, during the 1964–85 military dictatorship.[3] The dictatorship, during which the trauma of military tutelage led politicians to embrace new possibilities for popular mobilization, was when a national political elite always defined by its fear, even hatred, of the working class began to accept that ordinary people had some role in setting the course of the nation. This was due not simply to a commitment to democracy but also because they needed the collaboration of the popular classes to escape military tutelage. This book tells the story of how the dictatorship reshaped Brazil's political class, as a new relationship between politicians, the military, and the people was forged. The changes the political class experienced—and did not experience—have shaped Brazil to the present.

But what is the political class? It is universally acknowledged in Brazil that the country has always been ruled by an overwhelmingly white and male "political oligarchy" whose "numbers are relatively small, its ranks relatively closed, and its power concentrated in a few hands."[4] United not by control of the means of production but rather by a common socialization that produces shared attitudes and behaviors, this group has shared since the colonial period a "common identity as legitimate leaders of their society" by virtue of wealth, education, occupation, or, most commonly, heredity.[5] It is known to its members, as well as to the intellectuals, businesspeople, professionals, clergy, and military officers who may join its ranks, as the "political class." Its control of political institutions in pursuit of patronage and personal gain has been enjoyed by few, lamented by many, and, until recently, effectively challenged by no one, despite fruitless attempts—including those by the military regime—that altered political practice and replaced some members but left the political class as a group intact.[6]

On March 31, 1964, a coalition of conservative military officers and politicians overthrew the left-leaning government of President João Goulart, in what the military would call the "Revolution" of 1964.[7] For the officers who helped plot it, this "Revolution" had three objectives: to eliminate leftist "subversion," promote economic development, and impose reforms on politicians, many of whom, they believed, were shamelessly corrupt.[8] Aware that all three of these objectives could founder in the face of Brazil's deeply engrained regionalism, they sought to achieve them through one overarching strategy: the centralization of power at the federal level, specifically, the executive branch. Everyone involved expected that this would take longer than a traditional military intervention, as had happened in 1945 and 1954, when the military promptly handed power back to civilians.[9] No one expected the Armed Forces to govern for twenty-one years. For their part, politicians were shocked to discover that the military saw them as a problem for the "Revolution" to fix and were ambivalent at best to a centralization of power that would necessarily impinge on their own. Over the next two decades, politicians saw hundreds of their colleagues removed from office. They saw their own children in the student movement persecuted. They saw Congress closed three times and election law shamelessly manipulated. Most humiliating, they saw their presumed right to rule Brazil called into question.

For the military factions that triumphed in 1964, underlying these measures was the belief that if the most "subversive" and "venal" politicians could be removed, the remainder would collaborate to build a modern, moral Brazil.

Although it only became clear gradually, they had miscalculated. Time and again, the political class—ostensible allies and foes of the regime alike—pushed back. Sometimes this was because they had sincere democratic ideals; sometimes they simply wanted to regain the power they had enjoyed for generations. Regardless, the changes wrought on politicians were profound, and the regime ended in 1985 with their embrace of a level of popular mobilization that few would have countenanced in 1964.

Departing from the prevailing understandings about the Brazilian transition to democracy, which emphasize the contributions of "civil society" or the initiative of the generals, this book explores how the often-inadvertent opposition of the Brazilian political class helped precipitate the military regime's demise. It answers unresolved questions about Brazil's democratic transition and contributes to a global conversation about the role of elites in political and social transformation. How did the internal dynamics and shared dispositions of the political class change and remain the same under military rule? What impact did popular mobilization have on the political class? And what effect would these transformations have on both Brazil's democratization and that democracy's crisis starting with the 2016 parliamentary coup that removed President Dilma Rousseff? I argue that shifts in Brazil's political class and its relationship with the rest of society contributed decisively to the demise of military rule and the consolidation of the most inclusive democracy Brazil has ever seen. In rejecting military tutelage, politicians reconciled themselves to heightened popular participation. In one sense this signified a profound shift in their dispositions, but in another it was only a strategic calculation that could—and did—reverse itself when the opportunity came in 2016 to return Brazil to something like the elite-dominated semidemocracy that had governed Brazil before 1964.

This focus on the political class's role in Brazil's democratization does not imply a questioning of the roles played by labor, movements against the cost of living, the Catholic Church, and the women's, Black, and LGBTQ+ movements. Indeed, as this book demonstrates in its final two chapters, it was precisely these social movements that forced the political class to reluctantly embrace mass mobilization. Rather, this book argues that the existing scholarship has, with few exceptions, underestimated the importance of the political class in this process.[10] I do not assert that the political class was solely responsible for the regime's fall, but I do argue that its discontent with military rule would prove decisive. Students demonstrated, workers struck, business elites grumbled, and still the regime endured. It only fell when its remaining allies in the political class finally decided they had had enough.

Looking beyond Brazil, this book invites scholars to rethink how Cold War authoritarian regimes coped with conflict and competition from civilian elites, depending on the formal and informal rules governing the system. Among South America's bureaucratic authoritarian military regimes, Brazil's stands out for its attempts to justify its rule through electoral politics and the appearance of constitutional legality.[11] In Chile and Argentina, the election of Salvador Allende and Juan Perón served as proof to the military that liberal democracy was the problem. But for the Brazilian military in 1964, Goulart had threatened democracy with his talk of leftist reforms; the "Revolution" was thus not democracy's collapse but its salvation. Although the regime placed drastic limits on liberal institutions, the military continued to believe that the controlled collaboration of the political class, via parties, was vital to the legitimation of its reformist project. Unlike in Chile and Argentina, where the military dissolved Congress, in Brazil Congress was closed three times, for a total of eleven and a half months. While in the Southern Cone elections were suspended until the twilight of military rule, in Brazil they continued uninterrupted for nearly all offices. While the Brazilian generals reformed parties, in Chile and Argentina parties were banned for years.[12] The Brazilian generals saw civilian politicians and liberal institutions as vital to their project in a way their Southern Cone counterparts did not.

This did not mean that the military regime trusted the political class. Virtually all Brazilian elites since independence in 1822 had held that the unlettered popular classes, easily swayed by religious or populist demagogues, were not qualified to participate directly in politics. Instead, they required elite tutelage. The generals and the political class shared this basic mistrust of the popular classes. However, unlike the political class, which was almost exclusively drawn from Brazil's upper class, military officers overwhelmingly came from the middle class. Officers' class background combined with their intensified professional and technical training meant that by 1964 a great many officers looked down not only on the unlettered masses but also on the elites who ruled by birthright instead of merit.[13] For the military, a fundamental transformation in political behavior was needed; after 1968, this was intensified to include overt tutelage of politicians. No longer would their perceived corruption, rivalries, and regionalism be allowed to retard Brazil's development; rather, the nation would patriotically march toward modernity, guided by the military. Politicians could participate to the extent that they accepted these changes as permanent. Yet politicians believed that although they had the duty to exercise tutelage over the rest of Brazil, the imposition of tutelage on them by middle-class officers was a fundamental violation of how the world should work.

A (POLITICAL) CLASS THAT RULES

The term "political class" arose from a century of "elite theory" that originated near the turn of the twentieth century with Italian and German theorists.[14] They challenged both the Marxist vision of a classless society and liberal democracy on the grounds that both were unsustainable.[15] Rather, the domination of the many by the few was an immutable law.[16] The few, who Gaetano Mosca called the "political class," are distinguished not only by control of the means of production but also by political power and socialization, and they work to protect their collective interests. For classical elite theorists, "the most that can be hoped for is a relatively liberal but still quite unequal political order governed by capable, cooperative, and enlightened elites."[17] Ultimately the incompetence "of the masses" keeps oligarchies in power. "The masses are content to employ all their energies to effecting a change of masters."[18]

In the wake of World War II, classical elite theorists fell into disrepute due to their appropriation by fascism.[19] Yet postwar scholars did not challenge the thesis that a political class should inevitably dominate human societies; after all, Hitler and Mussolini had initially achieved power through democratic mechanisms, proving that the masses were untrustworthy. Other scholars lamented elite rule but accepted it as unalterable, even in "advanced democracies." Rather than a class in the Marxist sense, elites were seen as the people who occupied the most influential decision-making positions, many times because of their own merit and not as a result of wealth or privilege.[20] These scholars developed convenient means of conceptualizing the elite and its various subgroups, and the generation of political scientists and sociologists they influenced left rich empirical studies of the composition of elite groups.[21]

Pierre Bourdieu's concept of *habitus* added much-needed clarity. Bourdieu argues that the "dominant class" is united not by conspiracy or cohesion but rather by habitus, a set of "structured [and] structuring structures" that are "collectively orchestrated without being the product of . . . a conductor" and do not require a conscious "obedience to rules."[22] A habitus is *unconscious*. Predicated on membership in the "dominant class," it "is a set of dispositions, a general, basic stance which determines a person's perception, feeling, thinking, behavior, and which, more than anything else, marks the boundaries drawn for every individual by his social origin and position."[23] United by a habitus based on their position among the economically dominant class, those who exercise power can disagree on nearly anything without undermining their group consciousness and presumed right to exercise political power. Moreover, since a habitus should be known without having been consciously learned, the dominant class tends to reproduce itself, since it is difficult for nonmembers to acquire the proper socialization.[24]

Elite theorists, then, have shown that there is a politically active subset of the upper class (the so-called *classes conservadoras* or *dirigentes*, conservative or directing classes) that is united by a set of dispositions and behaviors that produce a habitus. Though members of the Brazilian political class may or may not own land, factories, or banks, they are united by a common way of seeing the world that is reinforced by education and socialization. New members enter and old ones leave, but the term describes a group whose members see themselves as sharing interests that distinguish them from not only the middle and lower classes but also the rest of the upper class. The political class encompasses civilian elites who due to pedigree, wealth, profession, or education choose to participate in political decision making at the local, state, or national level, particularly by being elected or appointed to public office. This may include career politicians; industrial, business, and landholding elites; media moguls; and lawyers, doctors, engineers, university professors, and other members of the "liberal professions." As a result of long-standing regional divides, the federal political class is effectively made up of delegates from the twenty-six state political classes.[25] These state political classes are small, probably no more than a few hundred men (and, only recently, women) in number. They attend the same social functions, send their children to the same schools, dine at the same restaurants, and negotiate marriages and alliances among themselves. Subregional power brokers and members of the industrial, business, professional, and intellectual classes of large cities together make up the state political class. In turn, each town has its own political class, often composed largely of landowning families.

Still, not all members of the upper strata identify with the political class. Despite their wealth and power, many intellectuals, businesspeople, and professionals, along with virtually all high-ranking military officers, are contemptuous of the political class. The disdain with which many military officers regard politicians is shown again and again throughout this book. This divide between the political class and the military is not a simple result of differing class origins. For while it is true that the political class tends to be drawn from higher social strata than the military,[26] the self-perceived interests of the middle and upper classes in Brazil (and indeed throughout Latin America) have long been recognized as coinciding. Rather, the political class and military clashed because of their socialization into distinct habitus. Politicians, on the one hand, saw themselves as Brazil's rightful rulers based on their pedigree, wealth, and education, legitimated by the institutions of liberal electoral democracy (however restricted in practice). Military officers, meanwhile, saw themselves as heading a national institution that did not merely represent the people; rather, it *was* the people—*o povo fardado*, the people in uniform. As leaders of this institution, officers saw themselves and the men they led as a "moderating power" that had the right (or duty) to overrule the executive, legislative, and judicial powers in defense of the nation—a belief used to justify numerous interventions across the twentieth century. Along with representativity and the duty to moderate national politics, the habitus of the officers who led the coup was based on values related to hierarchy, professionalization, and modernization.[27] At its core, the conflict between the military and the political class between 1964 and 1985 was a result of each group's conviction that it alone had the right and ability to lead Brazil.

I focus heavily, particularly in the second half of the book, on São Paulo, Brazil's most populous and powerful state. With 25 million residents in 1980, São Paulo was home to 21 percent of Brazilians. Since the 1950s its population had skyrocketed, as migrants from Brazil's Northeast came to work in its expanding manufacturing sector.[28] In the 1970s, the state produced between 30 and 40 percent of the nation's gross domestic product (GDP), and São Paulo and its political, commercial, and industrial elites benefited most from the 1968-74 "economic miracle," when Brazil's economy grew by an average annual rate of 10.9 percent.²⁹ Yet this stubbornly independent state had long been a thorn in the side of the federal government, most notably, during its 1932 armed revolt against the centralizing regime of Getúlio Vargas. Then, in 1964, São Paulo played a key political and military role in the coup that deposed Goulart. Demographic muscle, a dynamic economy, and rapid urbanization combined with vocal opposition, regionalism, and political marginalization set São Paulo apart from the rest of Brazil and rendered it especially problematic for the regime. It was in this singularly powerful and volatile state that politicians' support was most vital for the generals, but it was here that they failed most spectacularly.

STRUCTURE VERSUS RATIONAL CHOICE AND GENERALS VERSUS CIVIL SOCIETY

In ascribing a decisive role in the dictatorship's demise to the political class, this book departs from most social science scholarship on the military regime. The twenty-one years of military rule are probably the most exhaustively studied period of Brazilian history, with contributions from economists, political scientists, sociologists, historians, and anthropologists. Although this body of work spanning five decades has responded to varying political, methodological, and theoretical imperatives, certain debates have remained constant. In particular, explanations for the regime's rise, consolidation, weakening, and fall have centered on questions of agency (who) and causality (what). Who deserved more credit for the regime's fall, the generals who permitted liberalization and willingly stepped aside or the civil society that pressured them at every turn? Were the political and social changes unleashed by the two decades of military rule the product of structural factors or of the decisions of key actors?

Some of the most respected studies of the dictatorship have ascribed the power to effect political change primarily to the military, particularly the generals who occupied top posts in the Armed Forces and executive. Alfred Stepan's classic study of the military between 1945 and 1964 does this for the coup, and many of the contributions to his enormously influential 1973 edited volume reproduced this approach as they debated whether the military had succeeded at creating a lasting political model.³⁰ Thomas Skidmore and Leslie Bethell and Celso Castro, writing in 1989 and 2008, respectively, gave primary credit to the military for the move to a more democratic political system.³¹ Elio Gaspari's elegantly written five-volume history of the regime, based largely on the private archives of Ernesto Geisel (1974-79) (the fourth general-president) and the papers of his personal secretary, reproduces this pattern.³²

This emphasis on key military actors is counterbalanced by a vast body of scholarship on the role of "civil society" in the regime's liberalization and collapse. Beginning in 1974, when the opposition stunned the generals with a decisive victory in legislative elections, sociologists and political scientists produced a flurry of studies of voter behavior.[33] Over the next decade, as opposition to the generals' project surged among organized labor, students, the progressive Catholic Church, and the nascent Black, women's, and LGBTQ+ movements, a regime that had once seemed nearly unassailable suddenly appeared vulnerable to popular demands.[34] The studies of these new and resurgent social movements were part of a burgeoning political science literature on democratization globally. Overall, the picture that emerged was of a heroic civil society collectively toppling military rule. Jean Rossiaud put it rather bluntly when he said that the "process of democratization [was] constructed by . . . social movements and civil society organizations," but he was not far off from the general view.[35]

The narrative that was consolidated was of a process characterized by a dichotomous relationship between the military-dominated state and civil society. As Maria Helena Moreira Alves put it, state and opposition had an "essentially dialectical" relationship in which each sought to "control, check, or modify the other."[36] But of course this formulation leaves out the political class. The cabal that has ruled Brazil for its own benefit for over five centuries has been nearly forgotten in accounts of the military regime's demise. This is all the more surprising in light of near-universal recognition among scholars that the support of the political class was vital to the success of the 1964 coup, so much that Brazilian scholars have recently taken to labeling it a "civilian-military" coup and regime.[37] One possibility is that when narratives about the fall of the regime were consolidated in the late 1980s, historians had been shaped by two decades of "history from below" that actively pushed back against studying elites; similarly, political scientists at the time were eager to research the role of civil society (beyond political institutions and parties) in political change. Either way, the role of the political class in the regime's fall remained largely unexplored. The present book tells for the first time the story of the political class's decisive role in the demise of the military regime.

To be sure, politicians have not been completely ignored, and there are several excellent studies of political parties by political scientists and historians. Lucia Grinberg's recent study of the military-allied party, the Alliance of National Renovation (ARENA) stands out for highlighting how the regime's civilian allies chafed under the yoke of military tutelage.[38] And Célia Melhem's book on the São Paulo branch of the legal opposition party, the Brazilian Democratic Movement (MDB) reveals how its growth in the state was due not only to electoral strategy but also to the time-honored Brazilian traditions of clientelism and personalism.[39] The one scholar who studied the political class as a whole, independent of party, was Frances Hagopian. Her *Traditional Politics and Regime Change in Brazil* shows that as the regime crumbled, the state and local political classes in Minas Gerais were motivated primarily by their desire to hang onto power amid the pressures of democratization. Still, Hagopian privileges the rational choices made by politicians in pursuit of self-interest; she has much less to say about political culture and socialization. In addition, she studied elites in the largely rural state of Minas Gerais, whose political class is very different from that of São Paulo, the highly diverse, urbanized hub of Brazilian industrialization, with large populations of foreign-born immigrants and internal migrants.[40]

Hagopian's book is illustrative of another debate that has animated much of the scholarship on the military regime. If the answer to the question of agency has been posed in terms of a dichotomous choice between generals and civil society or state and opposition, the question of causality has been answered with functionalist explanations based on structure (dependent development, economic inequality, political institutions) or interest (rational choice). The ascription of causality to individual cost-benefit calculations reflected broader methodological trends in political science; such an approach is familiar to historians too, with their emphasis on the contingent nature of historical change. As Bolivar Lamounier puts it, "In fact, [the regime's liberalization] involves a *calculus* of decompression, that is, an interactive model in which the various actors, whatever their ideologies, calculate the costs and benefits of the status quo and of alternative solutions."[41] Rational choice rejects any claim that structural factors are so powerful "that political agents are not free to pursue strategies to revise those relations and institutions and that they cannot be effective in doing so."[42] Yet just as the generals/civil society binary fails to account for the political class, structure/interest does not adequately account for a third causal factor: culture, specifically, political culture.

John D. French defines political culture as a set of "overlapping discourses" that constitute "recurrent and readily identifiable motifs and gestures that cross differences in education, geography, socioeconomic roles, and occupations and professional specializations."[43] For French, political culture is *discursive*, as individuals deploy common symbols to advance their political goals. While anthropologists have produced a rich literature on contemporary Brazilian culture, political science, the field that has contributed the most to the study of the military regime until very recently, had little interest in culture and other hard-to-quantify variables.[44] As for historians, since the 1960s, the "social turn" toward "history from below" has generated vast interest in subaltern political consciousness and struggles for citizenship while largely ignoring elite political culture. Yet as Emília Viotti da Costa writes, "It is impossible to understand the history of the powerless without understanding the history of the powerful."[45] The Brazilian voters, workers, clerics, and demonstrators who have so captivated scholars cannot be understood without a more nuanced investigation of the political culture and habitus of politicians whose beliefs and practices conditioned and responded to their actions.

Both the political class and Brazilian political culture have received little attention in studies of the military dictatorship's demise. But the problem is not simply that the dichotomies employed by earlier scholars leave them out; it is also that dichotomies, whether state/opposition, military/civil society, or structure/rational choice, oversimplify the always contingent nature of historical change. The lived experience of human beings, with all the messy intersections of structure, interest, culture, identity, values, and personality and the contingencies of the moment, cannot be easily fit into dichotomous boxes. Categories are vital to historical and social scientific analysis, but they can never fully capture the lived experiences of which history and culture are made. After all, many politicians in the 1960s and 1970s had served in the military when they were younger or had relatives in the Armed Forces; it is difficult to place them in either the military or the political class. Whether they had a military background or not, individual politicians' relationship with the regime could change with shifting public opinion, electoral law, intramilitary conflicts, state and local politics, patron-client relationships, and personal vendettas. And many leftist activists had parents in the political class, often regime allies. With party boundaries fluid, ideology at the margins, and interpersonal relationships tantamount, it is essential to acknowledge that dichotomies, including "political class/military," do not supersede historical contingency.

This book thus destabilizes dichotomies and privileges contingency while bringing back into focus the words and dispositions of political elites. In doing so, it is indebted to the French historian Maud Chirio, who applies a similar approach to the study of the military between 1964 and 1985. She argues that as the regime evolved, the terms of the debates within the military shifted as well; at the same time, military factions were based not only on disputes about the duration and severity of military rule but also on the same personalism and rivalries that they so reviled in civilian politicians.[46] Furthermore, military factions all built alliances with sympathetic groups within the civilian political class. The military/civilian dichotomy tells little about an actor's ideology or relationship with the regime, and overreliance on it obscures the ever-shifting loyalties and in-between spaces that define the day-to-day practice of politics.

SOURCES AND CHAPTER OUTLINE

This book utilizes sources gleaned from nineteen archives in Brazil, the United States, the United Kingdom, Portugal, and Spain. The most important source is newspapers, which offer rich possibilities for achieving a textured reading of the culture of the political class. Controlled by powerful families with an extensive network of political connections, Brazil's dailies contain a wealth of political analysis. Political reporters enjoyed access to politicians and often knew more about alliances, rumors, and vendettas than politicians themselves.[47] Biography, memoir, and oral history also shed much light on politics under the regime. They contain detailed and often contradictory behind-the-scenes accounts of closed-door meetings, personal conflicts and slights, and innuendos that newspapers often only hint at.

Legislative and electoral records also provide a wealth of insight. In particular, the archive and technical staff of the federal Chamber of Deputies have organized and digitized a staggering amount of material. This includes both the daily transcript of the Chamber's proceedings (the Diário da Câmara dos Deputados) and audio recordings of sessions from the 1960s to the present. Comparisons of the written transcripts with the recordings often reveal telling editing of the former designed to soften the speeches before the generals could read them. Even more important, the rare opportunity to listen to historical sources facilitates the analysis of not only words but also tone, applause, accent, and shouting matches among the deputies.[48] In addition, this project made extensive use of the archive of the São Paulo state electoral court, which contains candidate registries, electoral prosecutions and appeals, and election results.

This book also relies heavily on more private sources. One particularly intriguing source is correspondence from embassies in Brazil to their home foreign ministries. Politicians often hid their true feelings from the press but not from foreign diplomats hungry for information about a rapidly changing political situation. The most extensive records were produced by the US State Department, but the British National Archives and the archives of the Spanish and Portuguese foreign ministries contain similar documents. The military regime also maintained a network of intelligence services whose archives reveal the behaviors that the military found laudable and threatening among politicians. These include the state-level political and social police (Department of Social Order and Policy [DOPS] and its successor, the Department of Social Communication [DCS]); the information-gathering arm of the federal Justice Ministry, the Division of Security and Information (DSI-MJ); and the recently opened records of the regime's primary intelligence gathering service, the National Information Service (SNI).[49] Finally, I was also privileged to conduct oral histories with prominent surviving politicians from the military period, including former governors, finance ministers, and congressmen.

This book starts not in 1964 but in 1968. For although the military had stripped hundreds of politicians of their political rights, instituted indirect elections, abolished the old political parties, and, in 1967, imposed a new constitution, by 1968 it appeared that these reforms were drawing to a close. Politicians hoped that with its goals accomplished, the military would now permit a return to civilian rule. The year 1968 is when the uneasy truce was shattered, the stage set for seventeen years of conflict between the political class and the military. First, as chapter 1 describes, the military and the political class clashed over the demands of a revitalized leftist student movement, in which politicians' own children were often prominent players. In the face of politicians' vicious denunciations of the military's repression of their children, the military demanded that the Chamber of Deputies grant them permission to prosecute an opposition deputy for insulting the Armed Forces in a congressional speech. Chapter 2 analyzes the drama that followed, as the Chamber of Deputies debated whether—and ultimately refused—to revoke the parliamentary immunity of the offending deputy. After four years of military infringement on their prerogatives, the political class would tolerate no more. In response, an infuriated military closed Congress for nearly a year and suspended civil liberties.

Chapter 3 analyzes this period of open dictatorship, in which the military resolved to punish the political class. In 1969 over three hundred politicians were removed from office. The military also reformed the constitution to ensure that the parliamentary rebellion of 1968 would never repeat itself. Politicians had refused to collaborate with the Armed Forces for the good of Brazil; now they would be forced to collaborate. As chapter 4 shows, although some young members of the opposition were determined to challenge the regime frontally, most preferred to, as one put it, "wait under the tree for the storm to pass," hoping to survive until the regime collapsed. Other politicians worked within the system to win elections, emphasizing everyday issues that mattered to voters. Except for a few noisy dissidents, it appeared that the politicians had acquiesced to military tutelage, convincing the generals that their political model was succeeding. In order to secure politicians' continued cooperation, the new general-president, Ernesto Geisel, resolved to allow a limited relaxation of the political system.

Chapter 5 shows how this liberalization backfired. In the 1974 legislative elections, the MDB stunned the generals by winning sixteen of twenty-two open Senate seats, nearly half of the seats in the Chamber of Deputies, and control of six state legislative assemblies. In response the military launched a campaign of violence against the banned Brazilian Communist Party (PCB), whose infiltration they believed had played a decisive role in the MDB's victory. And in 1977 Geisel briefly closed Congress again and decreed another set of humiliating electoral reforms designed to cement the regime's hold on power. Yet this backfired too, as even the regime's own allies took offense at the repression and intensified military tutelage. Their discontent was exemplified by the 1978 São Paulo gubernatorial contest, as ARENA rejected the regime's anointed candidate and nominated the former São Paulo city mayor, Paulo Maluf.

This was the beginning of the end for the regime. Chapter 6 analyzes politicians' response to massive strikes in suburban São Paulo that were led by future president, Luiz Inácio Lula da Silva. The strikes forced some politicians to accept expanded popular political participation, as opposition politicians defended striking workers in Congress in the streets and thereby crafted an alliance with the working class that held the potential to transform Brazilian social relations by rejecting both military rule and elite-dominated liberalism. The promises and limits of this coalition became clear during the presidential succession of 1984. Chapter 7 shows how, via the famed Diretas Já demonstrations, opposition (and some regime-allied) politicians endorsed popular mobilization on an unprecedented scale. Yet when Diretas Já failed to pressure Congress into ratifying a constitutional amendment to reinstate direct elections, politicians defaulted to the backroom deals that remained their preferred way to resolve conflict. A pact between dissident members of the regime-allied party and the opposition led to the indirect election of Tancredo Neves as president of the republic. With the election of this moderate oppositionist, the regime came to a close. The "Revolution" ended not because of any commitment to democracy on the part of the military, or as a direct result of popular mobilization, but because it lost its base of support in the political class.

1

"The Blood of the Youth Is Flowing"

The Political Class and Its Children Take on the Military in 1968

On the morning of August 29, 1968, hundreds of heavily armed policemen descended on the campus of the University of Brasília (UnB), located barely two miles from Brazil's futuristic Congress. Brandishing arrest warrants for leftist student activists, they kicked in classroom doors, smashed laboratory equipment, and marched the children of Brazil's elites across campus at gunpoint to be held in a basketball court for processing. When politicians arrived to intervene, they were met with insults and even beatings. The political class had largely supported or tolerated a "Revolution" to save the country from leftist subversion, economic ruin, and political malfeasance; the few who protested had been removed from office. Yet four years later it was clear that the military sought not a passing intervention but a profound transformation of Brazil's political system and the political class with it. Although the military was adamant that it desired a partnership with politicians, politicians were to be the junior partners. In 1968, politicians' mounting frustration reached a breaking point.

After explaining politicians' reaction to the changes imposed after 1964, this chapter analyzes the first act in the showdown of 1968: the political class's reaction to repression of the leftist-dominated student movement. Given the social and family ties between politicians and students, both regime allies and opponents were furious when the military attacked them with unprecedented (at least for them) levels of violence. Frustrated by their inability to stop it, they could only hurl denunciations at the police, the military, and the regime. How had a "Revolution" to save the country from communism devolved into Soviet-style repression? Regime allies had never dreamed that their "Revolution" would one day turn on their own children, and even the opposition was shocked at the ferocity of the violence.

FROM JUBILATION TO DISILLUSION: A "REVOLUTION" GONE ASTRAY

On March 31, 1964, a military uprising drove the left-leaning president, João Goulart, into exile. Ten days later, Congress selected General Humberto Castelo Branco to serve the remainder of Goulart's term. A significant portion of the political, landowning, and business classes was overjoyed. Goulart's talk of leftist reforms was threatening to an elite that had been shaken by the Cuban Revolution, and his friendliness to labor, openness to land reform, and encouragement of popular mobilization challenged ingrained hierarchies. Moreover, Goulart was "the beloved disciple of the dead dictator" Getúlio Vargas,[1] whose centralizing rule was recalled with horror by regional elites.[2] For its protagonists, the coup represented not democracy's collapse but its salvation. This message resonated strongly in São Paulo, which in 1932 had waged a brief war—the Constitutionalist Revolution—against Vargas. An *Estado de S. Paulo* editorial crowed, "As one man, São Paulo finds itself today fully mobilized, and, with the same spirit as three decades ago, rises up in defense of the present Constitution."[3]

The most enthusiastic supporters came from the National Democratic Union (UDN), the right-leaning party established in 1945 to oppose Vargas. São Paulo federal deputy Herbert Levy applauded Brazil for "vigorously repelling its Cubanization and demonstrating its democratic maturity."[4] Yet it was not only the UDN that cheered. Governor Adhemar de Barros, of the Social Progressive Party (PSP), congratulated *paulistas* (residents of São Paulo) for "ris[ing] up . . . once more in defense of democratic ideals, safeguarding the supreme values of our Christian civilization."[5] Even future leaders of the opposition such as federal deputies Ulysses Guimarães and André Franco Montoro remained silent when Goulart was deposed.

It did not take long for the coup's civilian collaborators to begin worrying that they might have made a mistake. Paulo Egydio Martins, a businessman and aspiring politician who had participated in the conspiracy, later complained, "Days after the Revolution, we civilians in São Paulo felt that our role had ended, that . . . we became totally forgotten. . . . We felt literally dismissed; we realized that power was in the hands of the Army and that we would have nothing more to do with it."[6] Sure enough, the military soon decreed an "Institutional Act" that, among other measures, granted the president sixty days to *cassar* (summarily remove from office) politicians, fire public employees, and suspend the political rights of both for ten years.[7] Still, the act stopped short of the sweeping intervention some coup supporters had urged, and rather than an attack on the political class as a whole, it was a temporary measure enabling the new government to rid itself of communists, *getulista* (Vargas-allied) holdovers, and assorted "subversives."

The next sixty days saw the *cassação* (removal) of 3 former presidents (one of whom, Juscelino Kubitschek, was currently a senator), 3 governors, 62 current and former federal deputies and substitutes, 53 current and former state deputies and substitutes, 15 current and former mayors and vice mayors, and 12 municipal councilors. The act mainly targeted allies of Goulart; his home state, Rio Grande do Sul, bore the worst of the punishment, with a quarter of the removals. As Montoro pointed out later, the act had not gone very far; it had an expiration date and left untouched the October 1965 presidential election.[8] Even after June, when Kubitschek was cassado and Castelo Branco's term was extended by a year via a constitutional amendment, it seemed that by 1966 the "revolutionary process" would end, and direct elections would pick Castelo Branco's successor after an unprecedented two-year military intervention.

A crisis in October 1965 shattered this illusion and began to turn some of the political class against the regime. In response to the victory of Kubitschek-allied candidates for governor in two states, Castelo Branco decreed a new institutional act. The first act had had eleven articles; this one had thirty-three. In addition to renewing the president's right to cassar politicians and public employees (for seventeen months instead of sixty days), AI-2 (Ato Institucional no. 2) made presidential elections indirect, decided by a simple majority in Congress; allowed the president to place Congress in recess; packed the Supreme Court; and transferred jurisdiction over crimes against national security to military courts. Most traumatically for politicians, in an expression of military frustration with their factionalism, AI-2 abolished the existing political parties.[9]

Thirty-five years later, Montoro identified AI-2 as "the watershed of Brazilian political life," when "the government renounced all its promises of redemocratization and plunged the country into the night of the discretionary regime."[10] Similarly, Paulo Egydio Martins later argued that by caving to military pressure, Castelo Branco had chosen the unity of the military over the good of the nation.[11] Yet at the time neither voiced his disagreement publicly. Those who did react did so cautiously, although their discontent often shone through. Upon receiving a call with news of AI-2, São Paulo's governor, Adhemar de Barros, was overheard remarking, "May God our Father help us to endure this crude blow." Yet later, when a telegram offering the justice minister's justification for the act arrived, the governor sent a reply expressing "the full trust of . . . São Paulo in the patriotic action of our President Castelo Branco."[12] The paulista UDN released a statement that applauded most of the act's measures but condemned, "with all vehemence," the abolition of the old party system while stating while that the UDN could not "applaud indirect elections, which abruptly alter the tradition of our republican life."[13] A Social Democratic Party (PSD) statement explained that the party was "surprised by this discretionary manifestation" and promised "to fight for the full recuperation of the normality and tranquility of democratic life in our country."[14] Deputy Doutel de Andrade, president of the Brazilian Labor Party (PTB), remarked that Castelo Branco had "dealt a mortal blow to what remained of republican institutions" and called on Congress to push back, lest Brazil suffer "the irremediable liquidation of the democratic regime."[15]

While AI-2 abolished the old parties, it also stipulated that the president could set rules for forming new ones. A one-party system; a two-party system with a government-allied party and an opposition; and a three-party system with a government-allied party, an opposition, and an "independent" party were all considered. Ultimately, a "complementary act" permitted three parties, each with a minimum of 20 senators and 120 federal deputies.[16] Yet politicians were so eager to join the new government-allied party, ARENA, that there were barely enough legislators remaining to form even one more party. The few legislators who wished to risk open opposition (or who were unable to tolerate coexisting with enemies who had joined ARENA) formed the rival MDB.[17] Some joined the MDB because they were unable to stomach the regime's attacks on democracy; when asked in our interview whether he joined the party because it opposed the regime, former deputy José de Lurtz Sabiá (MDB-SP) exclaimed, "Obviously!"[18] But he was in the minority. According to one oft-repeated legend, Castelo Branco had to intervene personally to convince Paraíba's Rui Carneiro to join the MDB so that the party could manage twenty senators.[19] Others simply picked whatever side their political rival had not chosen. After Pedro Ludovico, who had dominated Goiás politics for over three decades as appointed interventor, elected governor, and senator, chose the MDB, the state's factions that opposed him joined ARENA, not because they were loyal to the regime, but because it represented their best chance to displace the state's godfather.[20]

Still, AI-2 did not go as far as many politicians feared it might. Castelo Branco used the act to remove only sixty-two politicians, including only six at the federal level. The most notable casualty was Adhemar de Barros, who despite his initial support had begun to spar with the generals publicly. In 1966, AI-3 extended indirect elections to governorships and authorized governors to nominate mayors of state capitals, to be confirmed by the state legislatures. Several months later, Castelo Branco chose General Artur da Costa e Silva as his successor, and the nomination was ratified by Congress in October. Castelo Branco and his legal experts also drafted a new constitution that expanded presidential and reduced legislative power and institutionalized many of the provisions of AI-2, such as indirect presidential elections.[21] Congress rubber-stamped it in January 1967. The MDB complained that the new constitution had institutionalized military rule and suffocated basic liberties, yet MDB secretary general, José Martins Rodrigues, confided to US diplomats that the statement was "more a declaration of position than [a] call to sabotage [the] Constitution" and that the MDB would wait and see how Costa e Silva applied it before deciding whether to try to amend it (a move doomed to failure since ARENA enjoyed a commanding congressional majority).[22]

Rodrigues's position was typical. While they were displeased with new parties, indirect elections, and curtailed legislative powers, politicians were uncertain how to express their discontent. Vocal opposition was one option. Unconditional public support despite private disagreement was another. Yet another was measured criticism of specific measures without challenging military rule. Or a politician may have shifted positions depending on the winds at the moment, the instructions of a prominent ally, or the cassação of a friend or mentor. Criticism thus sometimes came from unexpected sources. In a January 1968 interview, ARENA senator Carlos Carvalho Pinto, a former paulista governor, complained that the two-party system and indirect elections were "retarding dangerously" Brazil's return to full democracy. He also argued that the military as an institution should have no political role beyond defending democratic institutions. Now that the military had saved Brazil from anarchy, civilian politicians must prove that they were responsible enough for power to be returned to them.[23] His discontent was representative. In January 1968, the magazine *Realidade* published the results of a survey of 246 federal deputies and senators (over half of Congress). An overwhelming 85 percent supported a multiparty system, 84 percent believed states did not have sufficient autonomy, 80 percent preferred direct presidential elections, and 65 percent thought the executive branch had taken over too many powers rightfully belonging to the legislature. Only 11 percent believed that the new Constitution reflected the aspirations of the Brazilian people. The regime's encroachment on the prerogatives of the political class had provoked deep discontent in both parties.[24]

Yet despite the curtailment of legislative powers and the enshrinement of indirect elections in an authoritarian constitution, things were looking up as 1968 began. AI-2 had expired on March 15, 1967, when Costa e Silva took office. The act had been used only sparingly; Costa e Silva began his term with talk of a "humanization" of the "Revolution"; and the new constitution, if it limited the powers of Congress, theoretically gave the regime the power it needed to transform Brazil without new institutional acts while stipulating that cassações could only be carried out via a Supreme Court trial, with congressional approval. The "Revolution's" legitimacy was based on the claim that it had saved democratic institutions from dictatorship; it was thus essential for the military to collaborate, however one-sidedly, with politicians. In 1964, the UDN, never able to win power via elections, had conspired with the military to overthrow Goulart. Now they found themselves running Congress, and UDN stalwarts like Senator Daniel Krieger (president of ARENA) and federal deputy Rondon Pacheco (the president's civilian chief of staff) enjoyed ready access to the president. Even in the MDB politicians remained free to criticize the government. By early 1968, then, the political class had reached an uneasy truce with the military, with hope that the "revolutionary" cycle would soon draw to a close.

"I STAND IN SOLIDARITY WITH THE STUDENTS": POLITICIANS AND THE STUDENT MOVEMENT

Yet in 1968 this truce began to collapse as the military violently repressed the student movement. On March 28, Edson Luís, a Rio de Janeiro secondary student, was killed by police during a protest over cafeteria food. Previously student demonstrations had focused on issues like the number of admissions slots and university governance; other than the most politically active, few cared about overthrowing the regime.²⁵ Now Luís's death galvanized students to take to the streets. The largest demonstration occurred in June when students marched in Rio de Janeiro in the famous March of the 100,000. As the size and political tone of the protests increased, so too did the repression, culminating in the arrest of hundreds of student activists at the clandestine congress of the banned National Student Union (UNE) in October.

All the members of the MDB took the students' side, and they were joined by a significant minority of arenistas. For in a country where a university education was the privilege of a tiny elite, the protesting students were "our children, our brothers, our relatives."²⁶ Guanabara deputy Breno da Silveira had a son attending UnB who was arrested in March; his other son was part of the army force sent to break up the demonstration.²⁷ One of the organizers of the March of the 100,000, Vladimir Palmeira, was the son of ARENA senator Rui Palmeira. And the student activist son of deputy Pedro Celestino Filho (MDB-GO), Paulo de Tarso, would be "disappeared" by the regime in 1971.²⁸ As former colonel and ARENA deputy Paulo Nunes Leal said, "When we have children in school, we . . . [imagine] that the parents who cry today at the disappearance of their beloved child could be us, since no one can presume to claim that their child will never participate in a student demonstration."²⁹ Mário Piva put it more pointedly: "Those who today try to defend the ones responsible [for the death of Luís] or who overlook the graveness of the problem were either never young themselves, or don't have children studying in university like I do."³⁰

Politicians saw younger versions of themselves in students, who one deputy called "the vanguard of the people's conscience."³¹ It was natural that the deputies, over 80 percent of whom had attended university, would identify with students; in them they saw "future economic, political, and financial leaders," the "new elite of an ignorant country."³² José Mandelli explained, "The youth of today will be the men of tomorrow. It is they who should take our place in public affairs, as professors, in the liberal professions, in trade.³³ Mário Covas, Chamber minority leader, was particularly impressed with Honestino Guimarães, a student leader at UnB, once remarking to his wife, "He's going to be a great politician. . . . I was overcome when I heard that born leader."³⁴ Regime allies such as Júlio de Mesquita Neto (son of the owner of *O Estado de S. Paulo*) and São Paulo governor Roberto de Abreu Sodré had fought as students against the Vargas regime decades before. Their activities generated a file with the São Paulo political police and earned the latter more arrests than he could count.³⁵ Although Miguel Feu Rosa was too young to have opposed Vargas, he spoke for many who had when he said, "Whatever my party affiliation, I cannot deny my origins. It was in student politics that I forged my personality as a public man. . . . I stand in solidarity with the students of my country; I participate in their sufferings and in their pain."³⁶ As former deputy Léo de Almeida Neves explained in 2015, "It was a serious error for the dictatorship to ban student organizations because that is where the country's political leaders were shaped."³⁷

As university graduates in a country where most did not complete primary school, members of Congress could identify with student activists in ways that they could not with members of other social movements. Idealistic by nature, students were "generous, impulsive, noble, and patriotic," and their elders owed them "a little bit of understanding."[38] They were "the most enlightened segment of the Brazilian population, . . . citizens who have a cultural and humanistic refinement far above the average."[39] While many deputies may have frowned upon the repression of labor unions and peasant movements, repression of students was different because it pitted uneducated, lower-class, often Black and Brown police against students who reminded politicians of themselves.[40] Their denunciation of violence against students was the indignant cry, "How dare you do this to people like us!"

The reality was that most Brazilian university students had little in common with the politicians whose families had walked the halls of power since at least the Proclamation of the Republic in 1889. As Brazil industrialized in the 1950s and a growing middle class demanded access to higher education, the populist governments of Vargas and Kubitschek had greatly expanded the university system, and in the 1960s the military regime accelerated this trend. University enrollments grew from 27,253 in 1945 to 93,202 in 1960 to 278,295 in 1968.[41] Most of these students came not from the political elite but from the growing and largely immigrant-descended middle classes in the industrializing Southeast and South.

Yet none of this mattered to politicians who were nostalgic about their own activism of yesteryear; whatever the actual composition of Brazilian universities in 1968, politicians viewed those involved in the student movement as similar to themselves and deserving of deferential treatment from their "inferiors." Anecdotal evidence indicates that the student movement was largely made up of upper-class students for, unlike middle-class students, who often had to work while they studied, the children of the elite enjoyed financial support from their parents, leaving plenty of time for activism.[42] And even if they did not come from the same social class, chances are they looked a lot like politicians. Although data on the racial composition of Brazilian universities in the 1960s are difficult to obtain, if the vast majority of students did indeed come from the middle and upper classes, it is almost certain that the vast majority were also white, according to Brazilian standards.[43]

In the wake of each new confrontation, senators and deputies denounced the violence, nearly invariably blaming the police and, occasionally, the military. Márcio Moreira Alves was perhaps the most forceful: "What this military regime has done in Brazil is transform every uniform into the object of the people's execration. . . . [The government] has turned [the Armed Forces] into a shelter of bandits."[44] Antônio Cunha Bueno, who during his studies at the São Paulo Law School had been active in student politics, offered his "vehement protest" of police repression of students, which, "if not restrained, will inevitably create the climate necessary for the implantation of a dictatorship."[45] The protests came most frequently from younger, vocal members of the MDB, but they were joined by *arenistas* (ARENA members) who were aghast at the attacks on students. Others, while deploring police violence and defending the students, argued that nefarious, communist subversives were exploiting students' "enthusiasm, good faith, and excitement" in order to advance their own "criminal and unspeakable objectives."[46] When student protests included the burning of American flags or throwing rocks at the American embassy, according to Nazir Miguel, "that is communist infiltration. And communists belong in jail, because they are subversives. Students should be in school studying, not starting street riots."[47] Still, few arenistas defended the police or attempted to shift the debate to violence committed by students.[48] Most government allies kept silent, joined by more prudent oppositionists.

Other politicians, particularly from the opposition, left the halls of Congress and joined students in the streets. Such activities were controversial; ARENA's Haroldo Leon Peres provoked a shouting match when he implied that MDB deputies were inciting students and thus shared responsibility for the violence.[49] The image of politicians standing alongside "subversives" who were often related to them must have infuriated those in the military who already resented the political class. As Costa e Silva's military chief of staff, General Jayme Portella, complained, opposition deputies, "using their immunities, were inciting agitation."[50]

MEDIA FILE 1. Tumult during the speech of Haroldo Leon Peres, March 29, 1968.
SOURCE: Câmara dos Deputados, Coordenação de Audiovisual (COAUD), Arquivo Sonoro, http://imagem.camara.gov.br/internet/audio/default.asp.

However, there were limits to politicians' involvement. Covas insisted that his respect for the autonomy of the student movement would not permit him to interfere in its internal functioning; his role was limited to dialogue and mediation.[51] Moreira Alves hit closer to the truth when he argued that the real barrier to deeper involvement was that leftist student activists were suspicious of even opposition politicians, whose attempts to oppose the regime through legal channels, they believed, were insufficiently revolutionary.[52] In a meeting of MDB leadership, deputy Edgar Godoy da Mata Machado (MDB-MG) admitted, "Students and workers want nothing to do with the MDB because they believe that the current political system is artificial and inauthentic."[53] The former student leader Franklin Martins, writing in 2002, argued that a chasm separated the student movement from opposition politicians: "They had been defeated in 1964 without putting up any resistance. . . . Why, then, should the youth take their advice into account?" Their very presence in Congress was a betrayal that proved how tepid their opposition was. The MDB was merely "a plaything in the hands of the military whose sole objective was to prop up a simulacrum of a Congress and a mimicry of democracy."[54]

Students heaped even more scorn upon politicians who supported the regime; even if they stood up to the military, "it was . . . because they had been thrown overboard by those who held power."[55] In São Paulo, students' anger was vividly illustrated on May Day, when Sodré attempted to speak to ten thousand workers and students but was drowned out with cries of "Murderer!" Soon the jeers were accompanied by eggs, wood, and rocks, and after he was hit in the head by a rock (or in his account, a nail-studded potato), the governor retreated to the safety of a cathedral.[56] Students and workers took over the stage and unfurled a banner with an image of Ché Guevara.[57] Although Sodré—not inaccurately—blamed communist infiltrators, the event strikingly demonstrated the disgust student activists felt for regime-allied politicians.[58] If politicians could look back on their own militancy with nostalgia, the very students with whom they sympathized were determined not to grow up to be like them.

"IT IS OUR CHILDREN WHO ARE THERE": THE INVASION OF THE UNIVERSIDADE DE BRASÍLIA

Although the largest marches took place in Rio and repression occurred across the country, federal legislators were most directly involved in Brasília.[59] In part this was because of the capital's isolation. Though Brazilians had long dreamed of establishing a capital in the sparsely populated interior, it was only during Kubitschek's administration that it came to fruition. Designed in the shape of an airplane, its modernist buildings drawn up by the communist architect Oscar Niemeyer, Brasília potently symbolized Brazil as the "country of the future." But the city had been rushed to completion in 1960, barely in time for Kubitschek to inaugurate it, and even by 1968 many government agencies had yet to relocate from Rio. Located over a thousand kilometers from Rio and São Paulo, its isolation was exacerbated by poor roads and unreliable telephone service. As one deputy lamented, "We live in a capital that most of the time is poorly informed about the reality of events, due to its distance from the large cities where news is made."[60] The metropolitan area's population was only 400,000 in 1968; many were migrant laborers who had little in common with legislators and federal employees. Its symbolism as the harbinger of a modernizing Brazil combined with its isolation meant that events in Brasília were enormously relevant to politicians forced to spend time there.

This was particularly true for events at UnB, where politicians' children often studied. The University of Brasília was part of the city's original "pilot plan"—a national university for the new capital of a modernizing nation. In the vision of its first rector, the anthropologist Darcy Ribeiro, UnB would challenge outmoded ideas about admissions, pedagogy, and university governance. The university was also unique at the time in that it united all its academic programs on a single campus—an arrangement that not only facilitated intellectual exchange but also heightened opportunities for mobilization.[61] Yet only two years after he began to implement his plan, the coup brought to power the enemies of Ribeiro, who had been Goulart's minister of education and culture and later his civilian chief of staff, and the generals fired him almost immediately. After all, academics who held progressive ideas about education may have also been subversive. UnB's location at the center of political power and its unorthodox approach placed it squarely in the regime's gaze. The campus, barely six years old in 1968, was only four kilometers from Congress. Demonstrations nearly always occurred on weekdays, when it was easiest to assemble a crowd and when Congress was in session.[62] Thus while politicians stayed informed about events in their home states, their proximity to UnB during the week meant that they were always aware of events there, often more than at universities back home.

UnB students knew that their deputy or senator fathers (or friends' fathers) enjoyed a measure of security because of their parliamentary immunity, which protected them from arrest. After all, Covas and other deputies had demanded an explanation from the justice minister and visited students in the hospital in April 1967 after police invaded the UnB library and beat students protesting the visit of the US ambassador. When Edson Luís was killed in March, UnB students again mobilized, and a group of opposition deputies attended their protest march. When the police began attacking the students, Covas and fellow deputies attempted to intervene, but the police ignored their pleas, and in the melee deputy José Martins Rodrigues was hit in the head with a truncheon. A few days later, after students captured a plainclothes National Information Service (SNI) agent and confiscated his revolver, at the urging of their professors they agreed to give it back—but only if they could hand it over to an opposition deputy. Then, at a Mass to commemorate the death of Luís, police arrived to arrest Honestino Guimarães; he fled into the sacristy, and while the bishop held the police at bay, students rushed to Congress, where the congressional leadership was in the midst of a meeting with other student leaders to negotiate the end of the military occupation of the campus. Covas and ARENA vice-leader Peres—who had accused opposition deputies of inciting student violence—rushed to the church and saved Guimarães from arrest, and Guimarães and other student leaders left in official cars of the Chamber.[63] On another occasion, students took refuge in Congress after a demonstration; after twelve hours of negotiations, politicians used their private cars to take the students home.[64] And at a march at the end of June, Covas and several other MDB deputies marched at the head of the students' procession. Later Covas hid Guimarães and five other students in his apartment with his family for days while the police searched for them.[65]

On the morning of August 29, the long-standing tension between the regime and UnB erupted into open conflict. With arrest warrants for Guimarães and four other "subversives," officers of the political and social police (DOPS) and federal police, backed up by two hundred military police officers, descended on the campus "as though they were Russians entering Prague" and arrested Guimarães.[66]

Students fought back, a patrol car was tipped over and set on fire, and police began a brutal sweep, kicking in doors, smashing lab equipment, and using tear gas, truncheons, rifles, and machine guns to round up students and herd them to a basketball court for processing. One student was shot in the head, another in the knee, and others suffered broken bones, either at the hands of the police or when they fell attempting to flee.[67]

Congress was in the midst of its morning session when the invasion began. In the Senate, Aurélio Vianna (MDB-GB) announced that he had just heard news of a confrontation at UnB and would be leaving with a group of senators to find out what was happening. Celestino Filho made a similar announcement in the Chamber. At the urging of ARENA leader Ernani Sátiro and Chamber president José Bonifácio Lafayette de Andrada (great-great nephew of the famed patriarch of Brazilian independence, José Bonifácio de Andrada e Silva), a group of deputies rushed to their cars and departed for UnB, a short drive down Brasília's broad avenues. All told, at least twenty deputies and three senators converged on the campus.[68] São Paulo deputy José Santilli Sobrinho rushed to UnB with his son to pick up his daughter. When they exited their car, police surrounded them and began to beat the son with a truncheon. Santilli Sobrinho attempted to intervene, waving his congressional identification and crying out that he was a deputy, but the police knocked the ID out of his hand and began to beat him too, shouting, "That's why we're doing this!"[69] They were only saved from arrest when other legislators intervened as they were being dragged to a police car, with Santilli Sobrinho shouting, "You're beating a federal deputy! I protest!" The police tried to arrest them too, until Senator Argemiro de Figueiredo (MDB-PB), whose own son was in the basketball court, stated that if the officers attempted to arrest legislators, they wouldn't go without a fight.[70]

The university was in chaos. Politicians saw hundreds of students marched across the campus at machine gun point. The police refused to allow wounded students to leave for the hospital before receiving higher orders.[71] The press noted indignantly that women students and faculty had fainted under the stress and that the police had entered restrooms where women were hiding.[72] An ARENA deputy gave an impromptu speech calling for reductions in funding for DOPS and the SNI, and Rodrigues told a federal police commander, "General, I'm proud to be on the side of the students and the people, and against these bandits," to which the commander shot back, "You're the bandit!"[73] Even ARENA deputy Clovis Stenzel, a UnB professor and enthusiastic supporter of the regime, was overheard exclaiming, "I, who am identified as belonging to the hard line, think all of this is an atrocity."[74]

Eventually the police let most students leave, arresting only a few "ringleaders." They left behind bloodstained floors, spent shell casings, and shattered lab equipment. Politicians were in shock, and all who maintained a home in Brasília had a story to tell. Oswaldo Zanello feared for his daughter, who had received

IMAGE 1. Federal deputies scuffle with police at UnB. SOURCE: Arquivo Central da UnB.

IMAGE 2. Federal deputy José Santilli Sobrinho attempting to protect his children from arrest. SOURCE: Arquivo Central da UnB.

threats from DOPS. Aniz Badra was stung when his son accused him of serving a Nazi government.[75] Deputies' children and their friends' children had been treated like common criminals, and they themselves had suffered violence and threats of arrest by the police, who respected neither congressional credentials nor social class. Few had any doubts as to the source of the invasion. It may have been the police who conducted it, but the orders had obviously come from above. The most likely source appeared to be the hated Justice Minister Luis Antônio da Gama e Silva, to whom the federal police were subordinate.[76]

Reaction from Congress was immediate and outraged. After the announcement of the invasion, sixteen of the remaining thirty-three deputies on the docket discarded their prepared remarks to denounce it. Nearly all questioned why hundreds of police were necessary to arrest one student. Two deputies compared it to the Soviet crackdown on Czechoslovakia's Prague Spring the week before.[77] Others took the opportunity to inveigh against those who gave the police their orders (by implication, the military). Getúlio Moura (MDB-RJ), for example, stated, "We protest against those who ordered these poor, incompetent, completely unlettered and incapable policemen to commit these acts of violence."[78] Before rushing to UnB, the MDB's Rodrigues expressed feelings likely shared by many deputies: "It is our children who are there, and we find ourselves powerless."[79]

Emotions were raw during the tumultuous afternoon session; it nearly had to be suspended five times amid hostile confrontations.[80] Wilson Martins lamented, "Those of us who have children in university, instead of being content, expecting that tomorrow we'll have a doctor, an engineer, a liberal professional in our home, [now] fear at every moment that we'll find their corpse in their own classrooms."[81] Seven deputies, including two from ARENA, gave speeches decrying the invasion, and eleven more, including three arenistas, offered sympathetic rejoinders to a speech by paulista Gastone Righi Cuoghi excoriating the police. Moreira Alves inveighed, "We don't have a government in this country; we have a mob in power, a gang, a group that uses its hired guns against the nation."[82] Another deputy argued that it was clear that the police had received their orders from the army and that the arrest warrants were but a pretext for an operation of psychological warfare designed to demoralize the university. Righi agreed, claiming that the factions of the military now in power had opposed placing a university in Brasília out of fear of the unrest fifteen thousand students could generate.[83] Only paulista Cantídio Sampaio supported the police, claiming that the students attacked them first. When fellow paulista David Lerer called him a liar, Sampaio punched him in the face.[84]

But not everyone was incensed. For although many arenistas defended the students, a significant minority sided enthusiastically with the military. Despite both parties' lack of ideological cohesion, ARENA was more likely to attract politicians with a deeply conservative worldview that venerated authority, eschewed disorder, and loathed leftist politics. ARENA vice-leader Peres spoke for these when he begged the deputies to suspend judgment until all the facts were known. After all, abuses were unavoidable in a tense atmosphere. Deputies should know this, since they had all been involved in rallies or protests that had gotten out of hand. What right did they have to cast stones when they had similarly repressed unruly mobs?[85] ARENA's Carlos de Brito Velho (a physician by training) interrupted, to thunderous applause, "I'll cast the first stone! . . . I have committed many acts of violence against the strong and the powerful, but against the weak, never."[86] Regardless, Peres emphasized, if the police committed excesses, the students had too; after all, a police car had been set afire, and an officer had allegedly been shot in the arm.[87] When Ernani Sátiro, ARENA's leader, defended Peres for his "equilibrium and serenity," he was roundly booed, as Uniro Machado exclaimed, "How can you be so callous? Let heaven be astonished!" When Bonifácio charged the deputies to listen "with tranquility," Machado cried, "Tranquility? When the blood of the youth is flowing? I want to see how tranquil some of you are when it's your children in this situation!"[88]

Mário Covas gave the MDB's official position in a speech sufficiently vehement that he withheld it from publication in the *Diário da Câmara dos Deputados*, the daily record of the Chamber's proceedings. He began with a blow-by-blow account of events at UnB, emphasizing that unlike Peres's "police version," his account contained the eyewitness testimonies of deputies and professors. Other deputies added details as he went along. Moreira Alves reported that the student shot in the head had been left lying atop a table for an hour before the police would allow him to be taken to the hospital. Mário Maia, a practicing physician, arrived from the hospital where he had just served as the anesthesiologist for the brain surgery that saved the student's life. An ARENA deputy received lengthy applause when he proposed that the Brazilian flag above Congress be lowered to half-mast in mourning.[89]

For Covas, the police's boorish behavior was the result of a society "that did not educate them . . . to have the human reactions worthy of a civilized people." The real fault for the repression lay with the government, which had still not held anyone responsible for the killing of Edson Luís, a "dictatorship" that used the "magic word" "subversive" as an "excuse for all sorts of violence." He stated that if he thought that resigning from Congress could help the students' cause, he would do it in instantly and promised that if he found himself in a similar situation again, he would offer himself for the police to beat instead. Although he had no children in college, after a day like this he suspected that he may not want them to go when they grew up; "a lack of knowledge and culture" might be preferable to "one day having to pass through the grievance and humiliation" that students in Brasília had experienced today.[90]

The invasion was hotly discussed into the next week. Behind the scenes, some arenistas were infuriated. Although Sampaio had punched Lerer for questioning his claim that the students had attacked first, his wife was rumored to belong to a group of women preparing a letter to Costa e Silva demanding that he stop ordering their husbands to defend lies. And it was later claimed that Jorge Curi had proposed that ARENA vice-leaders refrain from giving speeches defending the government: "No one can violate their conscience to defend the indefensible. I've had it with tolerance and swallowing toads."[91] Over the next three weekdays, forty-seven deputies gave speeches condemning the invasion. The first two days, Thursday and Friday, they maintained a degree of caution by focusing their attacks on the the police and the Costa e Silva administration rather than the military as an institution. But as days passed without any explanation for the assault on UnB, frustration among the deputies began to mount. Rumor had it that ARENA leader Sátiro had gone to the presidential palace on Friday seeking an explanation but had been denied an audience.[92] On Monday MDB deputies, especially younger ones known for their vehement criticisms of the government, went on the attack.

Hermano Alves complained that five days had passed with no investigation or identification of those responsible and speculated that the silence was because those who had issued the orders were "shielding themselves with Army officers' uniforms."[93] Rodrigues interjected that he had heard that the police and DOPS officers who ordered the invasion were actually army officers assigned to the police forces, noting sarcastically, "All the honors for this exceptional military operation go to those who make up . . . the 'glorious Army of Caxias.'"[94] Everyone conceded that the invasion was not the fault of the entire army but rather of "militarist" extremists whose paranoid obsession with subversion threatened to distract the Armed Forces from their true mission.[95] The result of this alienation of the military from the people, Jairo Brum warned, could be "a blood-soaked tragedy," because "one day Brazilians will . . . take to the streets with weapons in hand to defend themselves from the police who . . . threaten us and wound our children."[96] Yet amid these terrible events Congress was powerless, its leadership shirking its duty to demand an explanation. Arenista Paulo d'Araújo Freire, who had criticized students for supposed acts of violence in March, now exclaimed, "I will by no means give my modest vote to support the government as long as they refuse to punish these bandits and criminals who want to implant Hitler's system in Brazil."[97]

It was then the turn of Márcio Moreira Alves. No one could have imagined that his speeches this day and the next would spark a showdown between the military and the political class. Indeed, the tone of his September 2 speech was much like those that preceded it. Moreira Alves complained that there were no answers, only questions, about events at UnB. Who had ordered the invasion? To what extent were Gama e Silva and the justice ministry responsible? How would the government respond? The crescendo came in a series of rhetorical questions:

> When will the nation's hemorrhage be stanched? When will troops stop machine-gunning the people in the streets? When will a boot kicking in a lab door cease to be the government's proposal for university reform? When will we, . . . when we see

our children leave for school, be sure that they will not return carried on a stretcher, cudgeled, or machine-gunned? When will we be able to trust those who ought to execute and carry out the law? When will the police stop being a band of criminals? *When will the Army stop serving as shelter for torturers?*[98]

Mariano Beck broke in to read a letter signed by 175 "Mothers and Wives of Brasília," at least 30 of whom were married to deputies and senators. The letter decried the "scenes of savagery and indescribable violence that once again have bloodied the University of Brasília. . . . What we mothers and wives want is only to see our children and husbands studying and working in peace and security."[99] While the mothers and wives may or may not have had children at UnB (the wife of the thirty-two-year old Moreira Alves, for example, had neither a husband young enough nor children old enough to be in college), the discursive kinship that they invoked illustrates just how much politicians identified with students.

Moreira Alves's speech the next day added fuel to the fire. This time he proposed that to protest the military's refusal to investigate its role in the UnB invasion, parents keep their children away from military-sponsored Independence Day festivities on September 7 and that young women "who dance with the cadets and date the young officers" withhold sexual favors. Tying his tongue-in-cheek proposal, which he later dubbed "Operation Lysistrata," to the manifesto from the "wives and mothers of Brasília," he suggested that the boycott could serve as part of a wider movement of women's resistance.[100] As he pointed out later, his suggestion (which he said he hoped the girlfriends had taken) was a thinly veiled attack on the military's manhood: "Here was this spoiled brat, scion of a long line of politicians[,] . . . not only calling them a gang of torturers, but going to the groin and attacking their machismo!"[101] Questioning the military's morality and patriotism was bad; challenging its manhood was worse.

Born in Rio de Janeiro, Moreira Alves came from a Minas Gerais family in which "politics was lived intensely." His paternal grandfather had served for nearly three decades as a federal deputy during the First Republic, a brother of his paternal grandmother was foreign relations minister for Vargas, and his father was an appointed mayor of Petrópolis under Vargas.[102] After several years as a political reporter for the left-leaning *Correio da Manhã*, where he won the Brazilian equivalent of the Pulitzer Prize for his coverage of a shootout in the Alagoas legislative assembly (written from a hospital bed after being wounded in the melee), he parlayed his journalistic accomplishments into a successful run for Congress in 1966.[103] From the beginning, he was a vociferous opponent of the regime; his 1967 book denouncing torture won him no friends in the military.[104] In Brasília, he initially rented a house on Lake Paranoá with three other left-leaning MDB deputies that was humorously dubbed the "Socialist Republic on the Lake." He had been born into politics, was fluent in English and French, and was married to a French woman; in many respects he personified the ideal member of the political class.

Moreira Alves and twenty to thirty other young deputies comprised a bloc in Congress notorious for its impassioned speeches reprehending the government for its attacks on democratic institutions, torture, and insufficiently nationalist economic policies. São Paulo's Ivette Vargas derisively dubbed the group the *imaturos* (immature ones). The ideal "public man" (*homem público*) was assumed (at least discursively) to be stately and dignified, firm in his convictions but measured in his reactions, willing to defend his honor but knowing when to turn the other cheek. The imaturos, with their fiery speeches and brash behavior, were more akin to impulsive students than homens públicos. As Moreira Alves complained later, "Every conservative body calls those who represent rebellious forces of change 'immature,' 'hasty,' 'insane,' 'infantile,' as if adjectives could stop time."[105] The imaturos delighted in interrupting arenistas' speeches with attacks on the government; Moreira Alves later ruefully recalled a time when one of the "little bastards who tried to make a career of kissing the military's ass" complained that they had ruined the speech he had paid someone to write and intended to distribute to his constituents.[106] The imaturos were not well liked, and Moreira Alves attracted little sympathy. One ARENA deputy described him as "very radical, intolerant in his ideas, and not very amenable to democratic dialogue. He has an enraged disposition and is almost always full of resentment."[107]

The first speech, taken alone, might not have had further repercussions. After all, he had gotten away with calling the army a "shelter of bandits" in March—an expression almost identical to his "shelter of torturers" comment now. Once Moreira Alves gave the speech, if the Chamber leadership had been more attentive, the offending phrases might have been stricken before the *Diário da Câmara* was published, or the *Diário da Câmara* could have been withheld from circulation. Indeed, after he had called the government "bandits and gangsters" on August 29, the Chamber leadership had censored "bandits," leaving only "gangsters," which he had uttered in English.[108] Something similar may have happened on September 3. A comparison of the typed transcript of the second speech with the published version reveals minor edits, made by the Chamber leadership or Moreira Alves himself, in an effort to soften the harsh language. The version in the typed notes urged young women who *freqüentam* young officers to boycott them. *Freqüentar*, which translates into English as "to frequent," can also mean "to have relations with," or, euphemistically, "to have sexual relations with." In the notes, however, *freqüentar* is crossed out and replaced with a handwritten *namorar*, meaning "to date"; its substitution for the sexually charged *freqüentar* was likely an attempt to render the speech less objectionable.[109]

Another way to limit the fallout would have been for ARENA deputies to give speeches of their own defending the military. But none did. Their silence indicates that Jorge Curi, who had urged ARENA vice-leaders to refrain from defending the government, spoke for many. Even the majority leader, Sátiro, had been tepid in his defense of the regime. He had remained absent for days, hoping to avoid explaining why he had not yet wrangled an explanation for the invasion from Costa e Silva; he briefly entered during Moreira Alves's first speech, only to leave abruptly when he realized its subject. When he finally spoke that afternoon, he promised that he would offer an explanation once he had one.[110]

Published on September 3–4 in the *Diário da Câmara*, the speeches were distributed in the barracks as an example of the contempt in which the political class held the military.[111] Military critics of Moreira Alves seized on three passages—the reference to a "shelter for torturers," the proposal to boycott Independence Day, and, above all, the suggestion that young women should "boycott" their soldier companions. On September 5, Army Minister Lyra Tavares requested that Costa e Silva take measures to prevent more attacks like these and repair the damage done to the military's honor.[112] The stage was set for an unprecedented showdown.

CONCLUSIONS

In 1968, the indignities that had been heaped on politicians since 1964 culminated in the repression of the student movement. Politicians had watched, even collaborated, as colleagues were removed, institutional acts were decreed, and a new constitution was imposed. Yet now the military had targeted their children and their friends, the privileged elite who despite their youthful rebellion would one day assume their place as leaders of Brazil. These attacks on their children and their social class were more than many politicians could bear, and they showed their displeasure by protecting students from arrest, joining their marches, and blasting the regime for its ham-fisted handling of a situation that, in their eyes, should have been handled with understanding.

On the surface, this sympathy is surprising. Few politicians, even on the Left, found much in common ideologically with students who read Marx and Mao, idolized Fidel and Ché, and dreamed of a revolution to overturn the structures that facilitated the dominance of the political class (and the students themselves). Former leaders of the student movement have emphasized these differences. Students would never dream of becoming politicians themselves; for them, politics were only useful when "directed toward transforming society, not gaining posts or positions."[113] Scholars have similarly highlighted the divergences between the students of 1968 and parliamentary politics.[114] In part, this is because scholars have focused on Rio de Janeiro and São Paulo, where politicians took a less prominent role than in Brasília. But this oversight is also due to their assimilation of the students' antipolitician rhetoric.

Yet these differences were not enough to overcome ties of family and class. Indeed, several prominent student leaders were the sons of politicians. Politicians sympathized with the students because they were their own children, because they remembered their own days as student activists with nostalgia, or because students belonged to their social class. Perhaps they were communists; perhaps they were "subversive." But that was of no account, for they were politicians' children. When students were harassed by unlettered soldiers and policemen, it was a fundamental violation of the way the political class believed the world should work.

When students appealed for politicians' assistance, it was because they recognized that they were members of the same class and could expect aid. It is difficult to imagine many politicians from either party inviting trade unionists or rural workers to hide in Congress from the police. Despite their Marxist ideology, student activists were cut from the same cloth as their parents, and many, like Franklin Martins, São Paulo student leaders José Dirceu, José Serra, and Aloysio Nunes Ferreira Filho, and most notably, student and armed militant Dilma Rousseff, would go on to have political careers of their own. Time has proven that Covas was correct when he equated Honestino Guimarães's leadership of students with preparation for politics.[115]

In 1968, however, the military had little patience for leftist students or their politician parents. Though there are few sources relating the military's reaction, it is not difficult to imagine. The "Revolution" had been necessary, in their eyes, to root out subversion, wherever it might be found. If communist "subversion" came from the children of Brazil's political elites, the response should be no different than if they were rural workers, trade unionists, or leftist priests. But instead of recognizing the danger and repudiating their children's errors, politicians, including supposed allies, were seeking to shield them. To the military, suspicious of civilian politicians from the outset, it must have looked as though they tolerated such behavior because they secretly wished that they too could fight the regime. Adding insult to injury, out-of-control oppositionists like Moreira Alves were recasting the military doing its duty as torture, questioning their patriotism, and challenging their manhood. The time had come to send a message to the political class once and for all, and the regime resolved to do so by demanding that Congress revoke Moreira Alves's immunity so that he could be tried for his insults to military honor. The next chapter turns to the dramatic confrontation that ensued.

2

"The Funeral of Democracy"
The Showdown with the Military and Institutional Act No. 5

"Brazil is watching the decision we will make. But history alone will judge us."[1] With this weighty line, Márcio Moreira Alves stepped away from the rostrum in the Chamber of Deputies on December 12, 1968. For the past two months, he had stood at the center of Brazil's direst crisis since 1964. In response to his speeches criticizing the UnB invasion, military leadership had demanded the revocation of his parliamentary immunity so that he could be tried for "subversion." Now Congress was poised to vote. Would the 369 deputies present, two-thirds of whom belonged to ARENA, cave in to military pressure? Or would they take the perhaps politically suicidal step of defying the generals and sending a message that the military had gone too far in its efforts to reform the political class? The 1967 constitution had theoretically given the "Revolution" the tools to effect its transformation of Brazil while promising that legislators were inviolable in the exercise of their office. Now the military was attempting to extend its repression to Congress. For many politicians, this was the last straw. The showdown that ensued would fundamentally alter the relationship between politicians and the military.

Although it is widely recognized that the Moreira Alves case was a pivotal moment for the military regime, key questions remain about this second act in the 1968 showdown between politicians and the military. Why, despite the "chaos" the student movement unleashed, was it a congressional speech that incited the military? Why, after four years of tolerating the erosion of their influence, did politicians choose now to take a stand? What were they taking a stand for? By analyzing the military's response to Moreira Alves's speeches, the frantic attempts to find a compromise, politicians' efforts to guess the military's reaction to disobedience, and the final debate, this chapter answers these questions, which have remained unresolved after five decades of reflections.

In the wake of Moreira Alves's speeches on September 2 and 3, vague "lower military echelons" complained to Army Minister Lyra Tavares.² In a letter to Costa e Silva, Tavares emphasized that the deputy's speech was his "right as an adversary of the government." However, since the military existed to defend Brazil's institutions, the "restraining of such unjustifiable violence and verbal aggression against the Military Institution" would constitute a "measure to defend the regime itself." Although Tavares never suggested that Moreira Alves be prosecuted, he hinted that the military would not look kindly on a failure to restrain him: "Notwithstanding the manifest gravity of the insults . . . the Army continues to make every effort to contain them within the bounds of the discipline and serenity of its attitudes, obedient to the civilian authorities and confident in the steps that you decide to take."³

What ensued over the next three months illustrates the regime's concern with legality (as the military saw it). If an Argentine politician a few years later had made a similar attack on the military, that individual probably would have been abducted, beaten, and likely never seen again. But in Brazil the new constitution had institutionalized the "Revolution," returning Brazil (in theory) to a full democracy. Costa e Silva could not simply arrest Moreira Alves; there were legal procedures. He thus forwarded Tavares's letter to the justice minister, who concocted a legal argument to allow the Supreme Federal Court (STF) to try Moreira Alves.

The fifty-five-year-old justice minister, Luís Antônio da Gama e Silva, was one of the regime's most polarizing figures. A graduate of the São Paulo Law School, in 1939 he lost his job as political editor for a newspaper due to his opposition to Vargas. After the Estado Novo fell, he was hired as a law professor at the University of São Paulo (USP), and in 1963 he was named USP's rector. He wholeheartedly supported the coup and in 1967 was appointed Costa e Silva's justice minister.⁴ His unconditional support for the regime, enthusiastic repression of the student movement, and petty vindictiveness made him one of the regime's most "radical" figures and earned him a host of enemies. General Olympio Mourão Filho, one of the architects of the coup, described him as someone "lacking character, who confuses . . . violence with authority."⁵

Gama e Silva immediately received (or solicited) letters from the navy and air force ministers that echoed Tavares but in stronger terms. The air force minister asked him to take the "legal steps capable of restraining the repetition of these verbal aggressions that deliberately aim to disparage" the military.⁶ The navy minister asked Gama e Silva to prosecute Moreira Alves for attempting to "place the Armed Forces in conflict with the people with the clear intention of attacking the democratic order."⁷ After a "meticulous study," Gama e Silva submitted a report to Costa e Silva recommending prosecution.⁸ Costa e Silva approved it, and on October 11 a federal prosecutor, Décio Miranda, forwarded the case to the STF, which if it decided to pursue a trial would have to request the revocation of Moreira Alves's parliamentary immunity.

Gama e Silva's argument was based on article 151 of the constitution, which stated that freedom of expression did not apply in cases involving "an attack on the democratic order" or corruption. Should the person violating this article be a federal legislator, the applicable house of Congress would have to grant permission for a trial. Yet article 34 guaranteed that deputies and senators were "inviolable in the exercise of their office, for their opinions, words, and votes." Parliamentary immunity was a hallowed principle of Brazilian law, enshrined in five of Brazil's six constitutions (the sole exception was Vargas's 1937 constitution). There were two questions. First, did the exceptions to free speech in article 151 override the parliamentary immunity enshrined in article 34? And second, did Moreira Alves's comments constitute an "attack on the democratic order"? Gama e Silva argued strenuously that the answer to both questions was yes.[9] If the Chamber agreed, it could give permission for the STF to try him, and the STF (which AI-2 had packed by increasing the number of justices from eleven to sixteen) could then remove him from office. If the exceptions did not supersede immunity or if his speeches had not constituted an attack on democracy, Moreira Alves could not be tried.

WEIGHING BENEFITS AND RISKS: THE POLITICAL CLASS AND MILITARY MANEUVER UNDER DURESS

Once the chief prosecutor requested that the STF try Moreira Alves and the case went public, politicians realized that it could spark a dangerous confrontation. They thus searched for a way to keep Congress from having to vote on the matter. Perhaps the STF would decline to prosecute Moreira Alves.[10] Or maybe a flurry of meetings and letters between the ARENA leadership, Costa e Silva, and military leaders could defuse the crisis. In early November the government agreed to a 30 percent salary increase for military and civilian public employees.[11] Other proposals included a special Chamber session in tribute to the Armed Forces; censure for deputies who insulted the military, with repeat offenders forfeiting up to a month's pay; and a constitutional amendment limiting immunity for insults to the Armed Forces.[12] Yet all these solutions came to naught. When no one in the military responded, a showdown became likely.

Although the press and the political class were paying avid attention, most Brazilians were not. A poll in the *Jornal do Brasil* revealed that 40 percent of Guanabara respondents approved of the case against their native son, while 38 percent had no opinion; only 22 percent were opposed.[13] Of course, the government saw these polls and realized that Moreira Alves would not receive public sympathy; as a US embassy report put it, "It is doubtful that many Brazilians perceive any important relationship between their own lives and the political intrigues at the federal level."[14]

Still, "intrigues at the federal level" were highly relevant to Moreira Alves, whose career, and possibly life, was in danger. After several threatening phone calls and a report from a military contact that several officers planned to kidnap, beat, and possibly castrate him, he installed floodlights around his home, hired a bodyguard, and purchased a stockpile of guns.[15] His experience as a correspondent in the Suez Canal Zone and wounding during the 1957 shootout in Alagoas had earned him a reputation as a marksman, though he had not fired a gun in either Egypt or Maceió. A fellow deputy experienced in violent political disputes ridiculed his precautions; this sort of situation, he explained, required at least two machine guns, five rifles, three thousand rounds of ammunition, and five seasoned bodyguards.[16]

In late October, the STF agreed to take the case.[17] The court now requested that the Chamber grant permission to try Moreira Alves.[18] For the next five weeks, while the case was examined by the Constitution and Justice Committee, the Chamber weighed its options. There were compelling reasons to believe that the deputies would grant the request to try an unpopular colleague.[19] Moreira Alves did nothing to help himself when in late October he castigated Rio de Janeiro police as "bandits" and "crazy sadists" after they shot demonstrating students.[20] ARENA leadership and Covas convinced him to authorize the exclusion of the most offensive lines from the *Diário da Câmara*. Many deputies were incensed that he spoke so aggressively at this sensitive moment. As one newspaper mused, "If he . . . aggravates the threat that also hangs over the entire institution, it would be better for the institution to throw him overboard to try to avoid a shipwreck."[21] Deputies also feared that the military might retaliate, even close Congress, if they refused to hand over Moreira Alves. ARENA's Clovis Stenzel, who enjoyed close military contacts, warned that the MDB's involvement with "subversion" could lead to a new institutional act and further cassações.[22] As the speaker of the Chamber put it to ARENA vice-leader Geraldo Freire, "No one's going to trade their place in Congress for Márcio's."[23]

Still, if the deputies set this precedent, who would be next? What would happen to Congress's remaining power and prestige? As it stood, Congress had lost many of its legislative functions, but it was still free to speak its mind. Now even that right to serve as a moral check was threatened. As Covas pointed out years later, "If you approved that [request], everyone [else] who was inconvenient for the regime would be successively removed from parliamentary life."[24] Deputy Fr. Antonio Godinho put it starkly but accurately: "If the Chamber hands over one head, it will automatically be putting its own neck on the guillotine."[25]

Indeed, rumors circulated that the government was targeting several outspoken São Paulo MDB deputies, and government allies were sent into a panic over a rumor that four arenistas would be next.[26] When another rumor had it that the regime was preparing a list of Guanabara state deputies to remove, Gama e Silva offered the tenuous reassurance that nothing was planned—for now.[27] But in mid-November a military court asked the Chamber to grant permission to try Hermano

Alves for violating the national security law in newspaper articles.²⁸ It was clear that the witch-hunt would not stop with Moreira Alves and that no one was safe.

The request was dealt a serious blow by its failure to win the support of key ARENA leaders, in particular, its national president, Rio Grande do Sul senator Daniel Krieger. A foe of Vargas who was thrice imprisoned under the Estado Novo, Krieger was first elected to the Senate for the UDN in 1954. He supported the regime from the beginning, and he had accepted many of its most controversial extralegal measures.²⁹ When ARENA was formed in early 1966, Castelo Branco asked Krieger to lead the new party. Still, disagreements emerged. After the coup, he helped author a proposal for an institutional act that the military rejected as too timid, instead adopting AI-1. In late 1966 he declined Costa e Silva's invitation to serve as justice minister and criticized the new constitution's restrictions on civil liberties.³⁰ From the beginning he opposed the prosecution of Moreira Alves, and in early October, before the case went public, he sent Costa e Silva a letter explaining his disagreement. He also refused to have the party take a formal position and declined to pressure deputies to vote in favor of the request. As he put it a decade later, "I could not permit myself to cooperate, out of fear of reprisals, with the castration of Congress and the rape of the Constitution."³¹ Publicly, however, when asked his opinion by reporters, the ARENA president maintained a prudent silence, limiting himself to quoting an Arab proverb, "Saying little is worth silver; saying nothing is worth gold."³²

Krieger's position was a slap in the face to the military because it felt like a violation of their trust. He had supported the coup, accepted extralegal measures, and delivered key votes in Congress. He was untouched by accusations of corruption, and though he could stand on principle, he avoided embarrassing the regime. If the military could not trust Krieger, who could they trust? For members of the military committed to the dream of reshaping political practice, Krieger was acting as though politicians could revert to their old habits. Costa e Silva's military chief of staff, General Jayme Portella, fumed that he "refused to understand that a case like this could not be handled with amiability. . . . There had to be a formula or a measure to hold [Moreira Alves] accountable, because the Revolution had not extinguished itself."³³

Such intransigence was alien to politicians accustomed to compromise, and they searched frantically for a solution that would leave both the military's honor and their own intact. Krieger proposed that the Chamber apply an "unprecedented" penalty, suspension of Moreira Alves from Congress, a solution he claimed MDB leaders were prepared to support.³⁴ For politicians, there was no reason why such a compromise could not resolve the impasse. Should it not be enough to demonstrate that Congress regretted the speeches and discipline Moreira Alves itself? If politics was "the art of swallowing toads"—and the political class had swallowed many since 1964—surely the military could swallow one now.

The problems went beyond Krieger. Chamber majority leader Ernani Sátiro had taken a leave of absence due to heart trouble, leaving the ARENA vice-leader Geraldo Freire to defend the case.[35] Freire later recalled that when Gama e Silva informed ARENA leadership of the request (after it had already been sent to the STF), Sátiro warned him, "You're bringing a storm onto our heads; this is going to bring us serious problems."[36] Why would Gama e Silva and the military stir a hornets' nest? Could they not see the threat that the request posed to politicians' honor? With Krieger unwilling to defend the request and Sátiro ill, that left only Freire, an obedient but less known and respected deputy, to marshal the ARENA troops.

If the attempts at compromise bore no fruit and the Chamber refused to permit the prosecution, what would the military do? In the best-case scenario, they would accept Congress's decision, and political life would continue as before. But in the worst case, so-called military hardliners would overthrow Costa e Silva or force him to sign a new institutional act, close Congress, and reinstitute cassações. Yet no one knew how likely this was. If there really was a movement afoot to "radicalize" the regime would it do any good to hand Moreira Alves over? After all, in 1937 the Chamber had revoked the immunity of deputies opposed to Vargas, and it had done nothing to stop the establishment of the Estado Novo a few months later.[37] Who were the military ministers speaking for when they demanded prosecution? How invested was Costa e Silva in prosecuting Moreira Alves? Even if he accepted compromise, what would happen if fellow officers and the rank and file were dissatisfied with his decision?

Even the US embassy, usually well informed because of the cozy relationship between the two countries' militaries, was confused. A telegram worried that the "President [is] finding it increasingly difficult to balance the 'needs' of the Revolution as expressed by the military who brought him to office against his constitutional responsibility toward civilian institutions," yet concluded that comparisons to the tense atmosphere in October 1965, when military pressure had led a reluctant Castelo Branco to sign AI-2, were "overly alarmist."[38] As late as December 4, the Americans noted that "senior Army contacts in Rio and Brasília" did not appear to be in crisis mode.[39] This was probably because they never expected Congress to actually say no.

Politicians were not as well informed as the Americans and, unless they had their own military connections, were reliant on the press, always a key source of rumor and gossip for Brazilian elites. Reporters expended considerable effort attempting to ascertain the attitudes of Costa e Silva, top military brass, and the rank and file. Reports from an October meeting with the military high command claimed that Costa e Silva had called Moreira Alves's comments "inconsequential stupidity" and argued that the "rules of the game" would have to be maintained.[40] Transportation Minister Mário Andreazza (whose thirty-year military career gave him close contacts) claimed, "There is no possibility that [Costa e Silva] will stand back from [the constitution's] text and destroy the regime."[41] Also encouragingly, the *Folha* cited "measurable sectors" in the army that opposed the prosecution on the grounds that it made them look "intolerant and antidemocratic."[42] Yet nine days later the *Jornal do Brasil* cited equally vague "military sectors" that expected from politicians "flexibility . . . to heed the necessities of the moment," arguing, "The Revolution . . . cannot hinder itself with laws that hamper its efficiency."[43] Another source claimed that the military ministers might accept a congressional refusal but that they were being pressured by "lower echelons," who demanded the restoration of military honor.[44] After all, politicians' speeches were only one symptom of growing "subversion." Interior Minister Afonso Albuquerque Lima, a general with a large following who had open pretensions of succeeding Costa e Silva, declared:

> [The military will not remain silent faced with] groups who, having forgotten their duty to the Pátria, hurl themselves against those who have devoted themselves to her and give even their very lives to defend her. . . . All sorts of injustice are committed against the military, who at this moment are in the backlands opening up roads, digging wells, while these melodious singers get rich at pompous festivals, singing hymns of subversion.[45]

While the targets of this threat were surely students and the singer Geraldo Vandré, whose thinly veiled call for armed resistance against the regime had become a hit song, Albuquerque Lima's comments reflected a deeper sense of betrayal.[46] The pampered middle and upper classes—singers, students, and the political class—whose fortunes had been preserved when the military saved Brazil from communism were now committing "injustices" against their rescuers.

Even with the high stakes, the opposition of powerful arenistas, and hope that the military would act democratically, passage of the request seemed likely, given ARENA's 282–127 majority in the Chamber. Even with a unanimous MDB vote, it would take seventy-eight ARENA defections to defeat it. Yet first the request would be reviewed by the Constitution and Justice Committee, composed of twenty-one arenistas and ten oppositionists, all experts in constitutional law. The chair, Djalma Marinho, a UDN stalwart from Rio Grande do Norte, held a law degree and was a thirteen-year veteran of the committee. Like Krieger, he opposed the request and moved it through the committee slowly, hoping for a compromise.

The first order of business for the committee was to review Moreira Alves's defense, which was made in a forty-one-page document that brilliantly dismantled Gama e Silva's case. Turning the accusations against him on their head, Moreira Alves argued that the case was being brought not against one deputy but against the democratic order itself. Unlike a legislator's immunity from criminal charges, the "inviolability of the rostrum" was not a personal prerogative but an "essential attribute of the Chamber of Deputies itself"; a threat against it represented "an attack on the prerogatives of all Brazilians."[47] The centerpiece of the argument cited the West German constitution and nine French and Italian legal authorities, all backed up by an impressive array of Latin legal terms. And through a close reading of both articles in question, it convincingly demonstrated that the inviolability promised in article 34 superseded the exceptions to freedom of expression in article 151. Finally, in an attempt to extend an olive branch, Moreira Alves and his lawyer suggested, "Only the Chamber, through its regimental norms, is able to punish its members who possibly abuse their inviolability."[48] If Moreira Alves had done something wrong, the Chamber could discipline him internally.

Next, Lauro Leitão, the ARENA member assigned to examine the case (*relator*), submitted an unconventional opinion that laid out the legal arguments but refrained from taking a position.[49] In response, Oscar Pedroso Horta (MDB-SP) submitted a brief citing a host of legal scholars and thirteen dictionary definitions of *inviolable* to argue against the government's case.[50] In light of Moreira Alves's eloquent defense, Leitão's refusal to endorse the request, and Pedroso Horta's meticulous refutation of the case, eight of the committee's arenistas quietly made it known that they were not disposed to vote for the request. If the request were defeated in committee, it would still go to the full Chamber, but its passage would be in jeopardy. The top legal minds in a Chamber of lawyers found Gama e Silva's convoluted justifications absurd.

Costa e Silva, Gama e Silva, and Freire thus began to pressure deputies with "the classic resources for such situations—threats and compromises."[51] Costa e Silva met quietly with Marinho and several ARENA committee members. While acknowledging their misgivings, he argued that the final decision should be based on "political," not legal, criteria.[52] Deputies were "terrified." The pressure indicated that the president was either deeply invested or under irresistible pressure, making it hard "to believe ... that it could be possible [for Congress] to maintain any spirit of resistance."[53] Of course, such personal outreach could work both ways, as when former Pernambuco governor, Paulo Guerra, met with ARENA deputies from his state at the Congressional Country Club to urge them to vote against the request.[54]

Meanwhile, Covas instructed MDB deputies to give lengthy speeches in the Constitution and Justice Committee, hoping to delay the vote until Congress's summer recess began on December 1. This would buy time to find a compromise before the recess ended in March.[55] Marinho collaborated by refusing to enforce the twenty-minute time limit on speeches[56] Meanwhile, Marinho met with Costa e Silva and his civilian chief of staff, Rondon Pacheco, to suggest putting off the vote until the new year, and they appeared amenable.[57] Here was the beginning, politicians hoped, of a negotiated solution. But that night Costa e Silva dashed their expectations by asking the ARENA leadership to reclassify the case as "urgent," thus requiring the committee to vote immediately.[58] He and Gama e Silva instructed Freire to replace nine ARENA committee members opposed to the request with more pliant deputies.[59] Costa e Silva then called a special session of Congress to force an immediate decision. On December 10, the puppet committee predictably recommended that the Chamber hand over Moreira Alves.[60] Afterward, the normally shy Marinho, who became nauseous when forced to speak publicly, took a bold stand. "Rejecting this request is an act of moral courage," he insisted and added, paraphrasing Calderón de la Barca, "To the king [I give] all, except my honor."[61] He quit the committee in protest, along with all ten MDB members. The regime had pulled out all the stops. "Now Márcio's closest friends know that he is doomed, and they've lost hope," mourned one paper.[62] What Congress had desperately sought to avoid was happening: the Chamber would have to choose between shameful capitulation and principled resistance that could see Congress closed.

While the new committee deliberated, Covas and other MDB leaders were reported to have met with an influential colonel, Francisco Boaventura Cavalcanti, who reassured them that if Congress refused the request the military would do nothing.[63] Then on December 4 the army released a statement that denied pressuring Congress.[64] However, this was followed two days later with a "clarification" that the army did not believe that democracy included "impunity for those who abuse their prerogatives to offend an institution that has the right to be respected and is determinedly disposed to defend that right."[65] Rumors swirled that "radical" military factions were pressuring Costa e Silva to issue a new institutional act if Congress did not give up Moreira Alves, although some believed the rumors were a bluff.[66] The stage was set for the final showdown. Congress could take the "political" decision and sacrifice Moreira Alves, hoping that it would placate the military, keep Congress open, and preserve what few of its powers would remain; or it could stand up for principle, send a message that the military had gone too far, and risk the closure of Congress. Which would the deputies choose?

"TO THE KING, I GIVE ALL, EXCEPT MY HONOR": THE CONGRESSIONAL DEBATE

The debate that had raged for two months culminated in nearly one hundred speeches in the two weeks after the packing of the Constitution and Justice Committee. Some deputies advocated capitulation, either because they agreed with the request or because they feared the consequences of a refusal. José de Carvalho Sobrinho (ARENA-SP) argued, "The people don't elect their representatives to be ignorant or corrupt, to mislead [people with] their ideology, to be subversive or degrading toward the institutions or the branch [of government] that they represent."[67] Clovis Stenzel (ARENA-RS) called for an institutional act "to thwart the illegal opposition that is disturbing the country" and predicted that the Chamber, "with many votes from the MDB," would revoke immunity.[68] But opponents drowned out the supporters. The MDB was strident in its opposition; between October 10 and December 12, 62 of the party's 127 deputies spoke 140 times, all against the request. The surprise was the 43 speeches by 22 arenistas who, like the dissidents on the Constitution and Justice Committee, were aghast at this attack. Men who had welcomed the coup, stomached waves of cassações, accepted the dissolution of their parties, and tolerated the erosion of their power finally took a stand. These 84 deputies were from twenty-one of Brazil's twenty-two states. Forty-four (52.4 percent) were from only five states: Rio de Janeiro, Guanabara, Minas Gerais, São Paulo, and Rio Grande do Sul, all urban, industrialized states in the Southeast and South.

The climax came during the final two days of debate, December 11–12, when thirty-six deputies gave emotionally charged speeches against the request and one, Geraldo Freire, defended the measure (as acting leader of ARENA, he was obligated to defend the party's position before the vote).[69] The speeches provide profound insight into not only politicians' motivations for opposing the revocation of immunity but also their political culture. What mattered to the political class was not ideology or party; rather, they were united by a common educational and social background, the sociability of life in an isolated capital, and familial and economic ties that produced a shared way of seeing their place in the world. Their speeches reveal common attitudes toward democracy, law, and representation and repeatedly cite honor, literary and regional heroes, and their legacy—all essential elements of this political culture.

Considering that 54 percent of deputies were law school graduates, the most direct argument was a legal one: Did immunity apply to an "attack on the democratic order"?[70] Brito Velho argued that what was at stake was not free speech but rather the ability to exercise the function of a federal deputy—debating and voting on laws.[71] For his words in Congress, Moreira Alves could never be prosecuted, and revoking immunity would violate the constitution. Nísia Carone, wife of former Belo Horizonte mayor, Jorge Carone, *cassado* (removed from office) in 1965, exclaimed, "It is preferable to be a housewife, where we give the orders, than to be a deputy, be called 'Your Excellency,' and have to vote against the Constitution."[72]

MEDIA FILE 2. Clip of Nísia Carone speech, December 12, 1968.
SOURCE: Câmara dos Deputados, COAUD, Arquivo Sonoro, http://imagem.camara.gov.br/internet/audio/default.asp.

Of course, the constitution was not the real issue. As Benedito Ferreira astutely observed, "I would like to express my astonishment at the regard in which many in the opposition seem to hold our constitution . . . , when not long ago . . . [they said it was] bestowed from above, savage, 'Polish,' imposed by *manu militari*."[73] As for arenistas, their loyalty to the constitution was suspect too, since they had supported a coup that violated the previous constitution. Rather, defending the constitution was attractive because it offered a justification for defying the military. This was probably the thinking of the six paulista arenistas who released this statement: "We consider lucid loyalty to be the best way to serve the government, as opposed to blind subservience. In a government repeatedly placed at the service of the Constitution, the most appropriate way to follow is to obey what the Constitution commands."[74] As Carone stated, "A constitution made by the Revolution should be respected by the Revolution."[75]

Others argued that the prosecution was a distraction from the "Revolution's" objectives. Feu Rosa argued that although the "Revolution" had gotten off track, by standing up for their prerogatives, politicians could put it back on the right path:

> Since April 1964, a group of soldiers and civilians with the most idealistic and purest desires has desired profound and true transformations in national life. And all of us have been permanently frustrated. The same structures, the same systems, the same old habits, and, in many cases, the same men continue disappointing us, vexing us, and even making us nauseous. . . . I hope that the decision of this Chamber today serves as a turning point from the lame, inferior, slack-legged Revolution of paper and of spittle, to the true Revolution for which this country begs, the Revolution . . . of progress and development, of new mentalities and the modernization of customs.[76]

Appeals to the constitution and the "Revolution" were not directed only at fence-sitting colleagues; they were also directed at the military. Politicians thus sought to convince the military that Moreira Alves's speeches were inconsequential or that his prosecution played into a subversive plot. ARENA's Jonas Carlos da Silva argued that Moreira Alves was a "useful innocent, politically immature." His speech had actually done a service by proving how broad the regime's support was: Had anyone boycotted Independence Day, and had women abandoned their officer boyfriends? By prosecuting Moreira Alves, the Armed Forces were falling into a communist trap; leftists would love to provoke a radical military response, proving that the regime was a dictatorship that required a communist revolution to overthrow it.[77]

Others, like Jairo Brum, appealed to the military's honor: "[It is] inadmissible [that the military] could be pressuring [us] to become cowards and assault the institution they are supposed to protect and preserve. . . . No one can accept that! I can't accept it!" How could men willing to give their lives for the Pátria "turn themselves into the torturers of the Brazilian people"?[78] As Covas asked, "How can we believe that the Brazilian Armed Forces, who . . . went to defend liberty and democracy on foreign soil [in World War II], would place as a requirement for their survival the sacrifice of liberty and democracy in Brazil?"[79]

Appeals to the constitution, the "Revolution," and military honor all attempted to influence the military or justify disobedience, but they were not the reasons deputies opposed the revocation of immunity. Eschewing legal debates, several offered a compelling explanation based on the separation of powers and legislative autonomy—principles they understood as fundamental to democracy. For them, revoking immunity would demonstrate unacceptable subservience and the loss of Congress's reputation. Antonio Magalhães argued that the request sought "to establish as a norm of behavior the docility of the legislative branch" and turn Congress into "a mere appendage of the executive, to which it would confer legality."[80] The problem was not that the request trampled the constitution or betrayed the "Revolution"; it was that it trampled the political class. This time the regime was going too far.

Voting against the request could thus be cast as defending democracy. This represented a liberal conception of democracy that the deputies held universally: in a democracy, the three branches of government remained independent, and Congress, legitimized by the popular vote, could speak its mind freely. For Alcides Flores Soares, "If immunity is violated, the [legislative] branch will be destroyed, and with it, democracy itself."[81] Democracy's guardian was an independent legislature, which served as the nation's spokesperson. "The Chamber of Deputies [is] the branch [of government] in which the people deposit all their hopes," proclaimed one deputy; and another stated, "This is the House of the Brazilian people. . . . Here, the Brazilian people appear every day, to discuss and debate their destiny."[82] The fact that these "Brazilian people" were nearly all white, male, educated, and wealthy did not generate much concern; as Brito Velho put it, "Man is the builder of history. . . . However, that role . . . belongs not to everyone, but to the few."[83] Ordinary people (if literate) participated in politics solely by voting. Of course, if the political class was to enjoy a monopoly on political power, it was vital to justify it through their voters. The deputies reminded each other, "The eyes of the people are upon us."[84] Eugênio Doin Vieira affirmed that his vote would be motivated, "out of reverence, admiration, and respect for my voters from Santa Catarina. . . . I would not . . . be worthy to return to my state and present myself before public opinion if I did not take this position."[85]

When deputies justified their disobedience in these ways, some surely hoped to protect themselves from retaliation. In addition, Moreira Alves later claimed that many stood accused of crimes ranging from corruption to murder and feared that if immunity were revoked now, it might soon be weakened to exclude their own crimes.[86] And the refusal to obey the generals was certainly a reaction to the erosion of the political class's prerogatives. Yet politicians were not motivated only by self-preservation; rather, their impassioned defenses of "democracy" were the fruit of nearly a century and a half of elite participation in now-threatened liberal institutions. Moreover, the speeches contain impassioned references to honor, historical heroes, and the judgment of history that were not simply the justifications of people eager to preserve political power, but of people deeply concerned with preserving their honor.

Alfredo de Arruda Câmara, a priest and arenista from Pernambuco, framed his vote as a defense of his reputation: "Old and poor, I possess but one treasure: my name, which I need and want to leave undamaged . . . to posterity."[87] Joel Ferreira explained, "I cannot leave the legacy to my children and the generations that come after me of a man who . . . submitted himself to the weight of despotism and force and failed to do his duty."[88] Honor was related to masculinity. ARENA's Paulo d'Araújo Freire argued that if they capitulated, Congress would become "a group of well-trained high school boys, standing in line."[89] For Getúlio Moura, the committee's endorsement of the case had set the stage for an "already profoundly emasculated" Congress to become a "mere puppet of the executive branch."[90] Rio de Janeiro deputy Júlia Steinbruch, married to a senator, recalled three decades later how she had pressured her fellow deputies, saying, "Look at your wife, how she's . . . someone who admires you. Imagine how she's going to be saddened, embittered, if she sees her husband become feeble now."[91]

Honor lay not only in upholding the law or democracy but also in measuring up to the heroes of yesteryear. Deputies thus frequently invoked the memories of biblical, classical, regional, or ethnic champions who had challenged the powerful, stood for the law, or defended democracy. Mário Maia cited the biblical story of David and Goliath:

> This lesson should serve as an example in the face of all the forces that are being raised up against this House: the weapons that cost the money and sweat of the people, the swords, the guns, the machine guns, and the tanks represent the armor of the army minister. . . . And we must be like David, armed with the stones of dignity, morality, and honor, for only with these shall we defeat brute force.[92]

Yet if the scriptures contained positive examples, they also contained warnings. Feliciano Figueiredo argued that just as God had supposedly punished the "cursed race" of Jews with two millennia of suffering, culminating in the Holocaust, for allowing Jesus's crucifixion, divine judgment would befall the Chamber if it capitulated:

> The simplistic reasoning of the *fisiológicos*, the blind obedience of the cajolers . . . —none of this will save us from the eternal condemnation and degrading afflictions reserved for those who disobey the duties of morality and independence, submissive automatons to the impositions of bayonets, who criminally give service to those who aspire to tyranny.[93]

Bernardo Cabral freely paraphrased Simonides's famed epitaph at the site of the battle of Thermopylae: "Passerby, tell Sparta that you saw us fallen here because we fulfilled the sacred laws of the Pátria." Just as the Spartans had died in defense of the laws of their Pátria, so also should the deputies be willing to sacrifice in the defense of their ideals. Cabral continued, "If this Congress is impeded from functioning . . . for maintaining untouchable the principle of inviolability, let a monument be raised at its entrance with this inscription: 'Visitor, this House is closed because the majority of its members decided to defend its honor, dignity, and decency.'"[94] For Arruda Câmara, granting the request would signify Congress's passive acceptance of a forced suicide: "This is Rommel's cup of poison. It is the '*Ave Caesar, morituri te salutant*' of the gladiators. It is the moral death of the Parliament, like the Gospel writer says: 'You have the appearance of life, but in fact you are dead.'"[95] While the scriptural allusions probably would have been recognized in a devoutly Catholic country, it is noteworthy that Cabral and Arruda Câmara assumed their listeners would recognize—or at least be impressed by—quotations from Simonides and Suetonius, hardly commonplace cultural references for most Brazilians.

Brazilians also had their own heroes to emulate. Nísia Carone invoked the slogan of the Inconfidência Mineira, Brazil's first rebellion against Portugal, "Libertas, quae sera tamen" (Freedom, albeit late).[96] Yukishigue Tamura called on the deputies to "do justice to the glories of our forebears" and cited such heroes as a Japanese legislator who had opposed militarism, the paulista *bandeirantes*, Bonifácio de Andrade e Silva, and Tiradentes.[97] How would history remember this day? Would the deputies join David, the Spartans, Tiradentes, and their local champions in defending their principles? Or would they be reviled for their cowardice? As Unírio Machado prophetically put it, "If we resist, the respect of our contemporaries and of history will be confirmed; if we capitulate, it will be definitively destroyed."[98]

All these themes—defense of the constitution, the prerogatives of Congress, liberal democracy, and the invocation of honor, heroes, and history—were components of a political culture whose roots lay in centuries of rule by a hereditary political class and 150 years of authoritarian imperial and republican liberalism. They were part of a distinct way of looking at the world and the political class's place in it. When the deputies insisted that this was not about Moreira Alves, they were right. The stakes were far higher. The attempt to subordinate Congress to a military-dominated executive represented a fundamental threat to the way the deputies thought the world should work. The time had come to draw a line in the sand.

"HISTORY ALONE WILL JUDGE US": THE CLOSING ARGUMENTS AND VOTE

After two days of debate, Moreira Alves addressed the Chamber. In a speech largely received with silence, he reiterated that he opposed militarism, not the military—a distinction that could give his colleagues a justification to acquit, although it was unlikely to sway the military. "I deny . . . that I have at any time or in any place insulted the Armed Forces," he stated. "The military . . . deserves my respect. Militarism, . . . a criminal deformation that contaminates civilians and members of the military alike—it is this militarism that we repudiate." Most of his speech, however, emphasized the threat to Congress's freedom of expression. "It is not a deputy being judged here; what is being judged is an essential prerogative of the legislative branch." Ultimately, the vote was a test of Congress's honor, an opportunity for the deputies to write their legacy. "The coming generations will not remember the deputy whose right to speak his mind from the rostrum is challenged today, but they will know whether the Parliament that he belonged to maintained its prerogative of inviolability or gave it up."⁹⁹

The brilliance of the speech lay in its reinforcement of the themes that had animated the discourses of his colleagues. Although deputies had other reasons to defend immunity—self-preservation and a desire to defy the regime chief among them—the references to honor and posterity indicate that Moreira Alves believed he could reach them on a deeper, even visceral level. Hardened as they may have been by opportunism and self-interest, the political class still inhabited a world in which appeals to liberal democracy, honor, and the witness of history reverberated strongly. As Moreira Alves put it in his dramatic conclusion:

> I pray to God that the Chamber will deserve Brazilians' respect; that in the future we will be able to walk through the streets with our heads held high and look our children and friends in the eye. Finally, I pray to God that the legislative branch will refuse to hand to a small group of extremists the sword of its own beheading. Brazil is watching the decision we will make. But history alone will judge us.¹⁰⁰

Following Moreira Alves's speech, the leaders of both parties made their appeals. First came Mário Covas, the thirty-eight-year-old leader of the MDB. A native of Santos, São Paulo's port city, and an engineer by training, he started his political career as his city's secretary of public works and ran unsuccessfully for mayor in 1961. In 1962 he was elected federal deputy, with his base of support coming from Santos's militant dockworkers' unions. He had been leader of the MDB in the Chamber since March 1967 and was known as a brilliant orator. While he was by no means a friend of the regime, he had a streak of pragmatism. His eloquent speech, given impromptu with only a few jotted notes, would be remembered as one of the great speeches in Brazilian history. He emphasized that the vote would not be a judgment of the *carioca* deputy but of Congress. "Today this House is being placed on trial," he said. "Having withdrawn to the defendant's chair, it awaits the verdict that its own occupants will return."¹⁰¹ Since 1945 dozens of requests to revoke immunity had come before Congress, and the Chamber had upheld not one.¹⁰² Though taking a stand would bring risks, the preservation of the Chamber's honor outweighed them. "When I die," Covas said, "I would rather it be as a defendant of a crime, but in good faith, instead of as one who has committed the sin of diffidence."¹⁰³ He closed with an affirmation, modeled on the statements of belief contained in the Nicene Creed, which, like the creed, served to remind his listeners of the fundamental beliefs they shared.¹⁰⁴

> I believe in the people, anonymous and collective. . . . I believe that it is from this amalgam, this fusion of earth and emotions, that not only power emanates, but wisdom itself. And since I believe in them, I cannot doubt their delegates. . . . I believe in the democratic regime, which cannot be confused with anarchy, but which can never . . . serve as a mask for tyranny. I believe in the Parliament, even with its excesses and weaknesses, which will only disappear if we maintain it free, sovereign, and

independent. I believe in liberty, . . . this indispensable condition that confers upon the creature the image and likeness of its Creator. . . . I believe . . . in honor, this attribute that cannot be delegated, transferrable only because it is a divine quality. . . . I wish to declare my firm belief that today the legislative branch will be absolved. From the height of this rostrum, . . . from the loftiness of this assembly, the voices of the Spirit of Law and the Goddess of Justice can be heard in their plaintive appeal, "Do not allow an impossible crime to be transformed into the funeral of democracy, the annihilation of a branch of government, and the mournful hymn of lost liberties."[105]

When the applause subsided, it was time for ARENA's Geraldo Freire to take the podium. In Freire's view, opponents of the request had missed the point. Democracy, honor, and the independence of Congress were not the issue; the question was whether the Chamber would grant permission for a deputy to be tried before an impartial STF, whose brilliant legal minds had already concluded that the evidence justified a trial. It was not the Chamber's job to determine whether Moreira Alves had committed a crime because it was not a judicial body but a political one. Freire's argument was based on equality before the law: "It would be utterly incredible if we voted on laws that all Brazilians were obligated to obey while we considered ourselves demigods . . . above good or evil." Everyone was subject to the law—"deputies, rural laborers, factory workers, college graduates, and the unschooled—because in this Pátria, there are no privileges." Parliamentary immunity had limits and could never excuse an "attack on the democratic order," like Moreira Alves's call to boycott Independence Day. "If there is no abuse in this, I ask Brazilians: What is an abuse of rights? From the time we are children . . . we all learn . . . that the Pátria must be placed above all. And if we . . . boycott the commemoration of our own independence, do we not mutilate at the roots the source of our own nationality?"[106]

Freire's argument had holes, the insistence that Moreira Alves had attacked democracy and the trust in the STF foremost among them. After all, it was a massive leap from a call to boycott Independence Day to "denying the authenticity of the very independence of Brazil." And he cited only one legal scholar, an Argentine who was unlikely to impress deputies as much as the litany of Brazilian and European scholars whose opinions the other side had gathered.[107] Nonetheless, the speech constituted a shrewd attempt to shift the terms of the debate—from the legal to the political, from democracy to equality before the law, from prerogatives to responsibilities—and provided justifiable (though uncompelling) reasons to vote in favor of the request. Had Freire swayed enough deputies to win the day?

For three hours, the vote and tally proceeded, as each deputy dropped an envelope containing their ballot into the box. The most vocal opponents of the request were applauded as they cast their votes. Female deputies received applause too, since most had been elected to replace their cassado husbands and now had the courage to stand up against more cassações.[108] Still, not even MDB deputies' votes could be taken for granted. They were politicians too, pragmatic to the core; when the vote was secret, how would they vote? A colleague pulled Covas aside and whispered that he had seen Athiê Coury place a "yes" ballot in his envelope. While Coury, a fellow citizen of Santos, may not have been an "exemplary oppositionist," Covas could not imagine him voting in favor but approached him anyway, joking, "Come on, you tricky Turk, show me your ballot."[109] At this attack on his honor by the leader of his party, Coury "became pale, refused to open the envelope, complained at the lack of trust, and declared himself offended." Covas insisted, "Open it." Coury looked Covas squarely in the eye and delayed opening it. When he finally pulled out the ballot, it was a "no."[110]

Finally, the vote was complete, the ballots counted. By a margin of 216–141, the Chamber rejected the request. The result was met with "extremely prolonged applause" and the spontaneous singing of the national anthem by the deputies and gallery.[111] Covas wept openly, and thirty years later he still became emotional when he spoke of it. "It was a magical moment, a moment when it was difficult to contain one's emotions, a very dramatic, beautiful moment, a moment when the Parliament was affirmed," he recalled.[112] Moreira Alves, though, slipped out, stopping only to make a briefly statement to reporters, acutely conscious of the handgun in his pocket.[113]

The result was shocking. On December 10, the *Jornal do Brasil* had predicted the request would pass by a 190–170 margin.[114] "As late as [the] morning [of] December 12," a US embassy telegram noted, "congressional sources and military observers [were] virtually unanimous in expecting [a] government victory in [a] close vote."[115] All eyes now turned to the military. Would it accept the Chamber's decision? More hopeful observers pointed out that it was still not too late for a congressional censure or a new request to revoke immunity under another legal pretext, either of which would be preferable to "impulsive extra-constitutional [measures] ... [that] would ... create [a] deep division between [the] present government and [the] country's major civilian political leaders."[116] Or perhaps there would be a military power struggle, and "moderates" like Costa e Silva would win. "I want to believe that the President ... will be able to resist the pressure and put an end to this crisis, which ... will only end up benefiting forces that are truly subversive, which is not the case of the Parliament," the Portuguese ambassador telegrammed.[117] Yet when an ARENA vice-leader proposed a statement from both parties clarifying that the vote did not represent an attack on the Armed Forces, he was overruled by Covas and José Bonifácio, who said, "The Chamber has already decided; the decision's been made."[118] Deputies huddled in their offices until after midnight, awaiting news from Rio, where Costa e Silva had traveled the preceding afternoon.[119] He and Gama e Silva ominously refused to comment.[120] The military entered a state of alert. Stenzel, who had predicted that the military was planning an institutional act, reported that the military command was demanding more cassações.[121] "Our colleagues in the opposition thought we were just trying to frighten them with our warnings. Now they'll see that we weren't bluffing," he said.[122]

On December 13, when Congress held its usual session, the same arenistas who had spoken against the revocation of immunity gave speeches attempting to convince the military to avoid a drastic response. Brito Velho warned, "If the armed classes violate the Constitution, I want to declare that they will have committed a felony."[123] The six paulista deputies who had issued a statement justifying their rebellion in constitutional terms issued a new statement. It read, "By consulting Congress, the government showed that it recognizes its autonomy, and having recognized it, it needs to respect its sovereignty."[124] Yet no one was paying attention. Instead, legislators quietly began emptying their accounts in the congressional branch of the Banco do Brasil, perhaps fearing that the regime might try to freeze their assets.[125] Still, Covas tried to remain optimistic: "In this case, I'm like St. Thomas—I'll only believe in this act if I read it."[126]

The evening of December 13, the news arrived: the president would sign an institutional act. Shortly after nine o'clock Gama e Silva read Institutional Act No. 5 over the radio. AI-5 authorized the president to place legislatures in recess and decree laws in their stead, replace governors and mayors with appointed interventors, cassar politicians and suspend any citizens' political rights for ten years, forcibly retire civil servants, and declare a state of siege. Habeas corpus was suspended for several crimes. A complementary act immediately placed Congress in indefinite recess. As a US embassy telegram put it, AI-5 was "a self-issued license authorizing [the] executive to govern without [the] trappings or inconveniences of democracy."[127] The tensions that had simmered between the military and political class for half a decade had boiled over into open conflict, and the military would now rule alone until the political class learned its lesson.

Bonifácio somberly stated, "At this moment, the country goes from the rule of law to the state of fact. . . . Obeying the new regime, I declare [our] mission closed."[128] Conscious of the moment's historical significance, the ARENA leadership posed for a photo. "I wanted to avoid all this, but no one would believe me," Freire lamented. Some *emedebistas* (members of the MDB), certain they would be cassado, cleaned out their offices. By midnight, nearly everyone was gone. Covas stood outside, chatting with journalists as he awaited his ride. The guards turned out the lights. Darkness descended over Congress, and an open military dictatorship descended on Brazil.[129]

CONCLUSIONS

In 1968 Brazil witnessed upheaval on a scale seldom seen in a country whose elites had always managed to keep unrest in check. Yet now it was these very elites who were the source of unrest. Instead of restraining their "subversive" student children, politicians defended them. A few months later, politicians added insult to injury, refusing to sacrifice their freedom of expression and honor to satisfy the military. Politicians' resistance was often motivated more by self-preservation, political aspirations, and a defense of elite privilege than by principled opposition. Yet nonideological motives for resistance do not lessen its significance.

Surprisingly, most scholars have minimized politicians' role in the Moreira Alves affair, arguing that it was but a pretext for a military "hard-line" to institute a dictatorship that they had been planning for months, if not years.[130] AI-5 can be read this way. "Clearly subversive acts originating from the most distinct political and cultural sectors prove that the legal instruments bestowed upon the Nation . . . are serving as a means to combat and destroy [the Revolution]." Among these threats were "subversive processes and revolutionary warfare." Other than the oblique reference to "political and cultural sectors," there was no mention of Moreira Alves or the political class. While AI-5 was decreed in a context of social mobilization and nascent revolutionary struggle, this does not negate the importance of the political crisis sparked by the UnB invasion and Moreira Alves's speeches. Even if elements of the military were planning this earlier, the political class's insubordination is what finally convinced them to carry out a "coup within a coup." After all, organized labor had made a brief comeback, only to disappear after the repression of a June strike near São Paulo. The Far Left's "revolutionary struggle" had claimed the lives of perhaps half a dozen soldiers and police. The student movement, on its own, was not enough to justify an institutional act. The act only came when Congress took a stand that confirmed the military's suspicion that their collaborators in the political class were not truly committed to the "Revolution." Students, workers, and a few armed guerrillas were worrisome to the generals, but in and of themselves they did not represent a fundamental threat. Rebellious and ungrateful politicians did, and for this reason, AI-5 should be understood as a naked attempt to coerce them into submission.

Portella, Costa e Silva's military chief of staff, argued strenuously in his 1979 memoirs that the Moreira Alves case was responsible for the decree of AI-5. While Costa e Silva had expected the MDB to defend its own, "he never could have imagined that the party that gave him support in the Chamber would use the secret vote to respect an insult directed at the Armed Forces by a communist deputy."[131] In Portella's telling, AI-5 became necessary when ARENA politicians let concepts like constitutionality and immunity blind them to the greater importance of preserving the honor of the Armed Forces. While there are problems with Portella's version, his account likely accurately reflects the sense of betrayal many military men experienced when their civilian "allies" stood against them. Such an affront was not a simply a pretext for military "radicals"; rather, the protection of an insolent deputy was a frontal attack on the "Revolution."

Tavares, in the days after the decree of AI-5, explained that it became necessary as a result of a long list of crises. The congressional vote, which he called "one of the blackest pages in the history of Brazilian democracy," made a tense situation unbearable and demanded a response.[132] Similarly, General Ernesto Geisel, who in 1968 was a minister on the Supreme Military Court, argued twenty-five years later:

> In the face of the difficulties created by the students and the politicians, [Costa e Silva] made AI-5. . . . Looking objectively at what happened with Márcio, you have to conclude that it was utterly unimportant nonsense. But when you have responsibility and you're living from one day to the next, you see one thing after another pile up until you reach a breaking point where there must be a reaction.[133]

Veja explained that the months of social unrest had convinced military leaders that they must put their "Revolution" back on the right track, "for ten years, if necessary." The Moreira Alves case was the straw that broke the camel's back, because it revealed that when push came to shove, the government could not count on its own allies in the political class.[134]

At the same time, for many politicians the violent repression of the student movement and the attempt to revoke Moreira Alves's immunity were the most intolerable in a series of attacks on the political class. The attacks on their children showed the depths of the military's scorn for them. And the Moreira Alves affair demonstrated that the military desired an unacceptable level of tutelage over the political class. Faced with the loss of what little prestige remained to them, 216 deputies risked a new institutional act rather than capitulate. For this act of courage, they paid a heavy price. Congress was closed, and the next nine months saw a wave of attacks on the political class, as a host of politicians were *cassado*, had their political rights suspended, and, in a few cases, were imprisoned. It is to these dark months that chapter 3 turns.

3

"The Political Class Has Learned Nothing"

The Military Punishes the Political Class

On December 18, 1968, five days after the decree of AI-5, Mário Covas sat at home with his wife, Lila, when there was a knock at the door. Two federal policemen informed him that they had been sent on a "disagreeable task," showing an arrest warrant signed by the regional military commander. While Lila made coffee, Covas changed clothes. As he recalled in a handwritten prison diary, he ordinarily would have argued that parliamentary immunity precluded his arrest. But in days like these, "when any timidity has been eliminated," resistance was pointless. Besides, many of his colleagues, "estimable and honorable men," had already been jailed. Whether due to "honor . . . or a little bit of vanity," the knock came as a "relief."[1] The arrest was a validation of his stand for principle, a vindication of his honor as a public man.

The ten months following the decree of AI-5 were among the darkest the Brazilian political class had ever known, with the indefinite closure of Congress, the arrest of dozens of politicians, and the cassação of over 330 colleagues at all levels. It was reminiscent of the Estado Novo, so reviled by the masterminds of 1964. Certainly older arenistas must have drawn parallels between themselves and the *tenentes*, the idealistic young officers who had fought to overthrow the First Republic in the 1920s, only to see their dreams dashed by Getúlio Vargas's centralization of power.[2] Like Vargas, the military sought to make regional elites subservient to a centralized government, closed Congress, and persecuted politicians.[3] Unlike Vargas, however, whose Estado Novo had been an ad hoc solution, the military envisioned a profound transformation of politics. To key military figures, the Moreira Alves affair demonstrated that despite nearly five years of the

"Revolution," politicians had learned nothing. The "Revolution" they had refused to accept voluntarily would now be imposed through military tutelage.

How long would this state of affairs last? Would the political class ever recover its power? Politicians found themselves in a frightening, uncertain world, where the foremost concern was surviving amid their drastically curtailed influence. Convincing the generals that they had learned their lesson became politicians' best bet to get Congress reopened. For arenistas, the situation held opportunities: if and when institutional politics recommenced, the military would need trustworthy politicians who would make sure that a fiasco like the Moreira Alves case never happened again. In the MDB, meanwhile, politicians could only keep their heads down to avoid the personal and professional calamity of cassação.

Cassações were always justified by allegations of corruption or subversion. This fit perfectly with the belief, fundamental to military culture, that the Armed Forces were the guardians of Brazil's morality.[4] The military was thus well positioned (in their own minds) to punish "immoral" politicians, in a high-minded defense of the greater good. As Costa e Silva explained, "I have a strong sense of the moderation and experience necessary to evaluate what is sufficient to serve as an example. The punishment should never be applied to harm individuals but rather to defend the collectivity."[5] But in practice cassações were profoundly political, and corruption and subversion were often just excuses to rid the regime of recalcitrant politicians or even to settle personal vendettas.[6] Whatever the precise motivations, what is most striking is that even in the wake of the betrayal represented by the Moreira Alves vote, with Congress closed and Costa e Silva ruling by decree, the generals in power still expected that if the worst troublemakers were removed the rest of the political class could be salvaged.

"THE RESUMPTION OF THE REVOLUTION": THE AFTERMATH OF AI-5

Immediately, a wave of arrests swept up regime opponents, politicians among them. All indications are that the arrests were uncoordinated, ordered by local military commanders or police officials who targeted anyone deemed an enemy of the "Revolution." Moreira Alves first hid in Campinas, in the home of MDB state deputy Francisco Amaral. He then moved to the apartment of federal deputy Pedroso Horta in São Paulo before slipping away to Chile.[7] He later traveled to the United States, where he spoke to Latin Americanist scholars about Brazil's repressive regime.[8] Hermano Alves took refuge in the Mexican embassy before fleeing to Mexico, Algeria, France, and England, where he worked as a correspondent for O Estado.[9]

Some politicians who remained faced even more outrageous treatment. Guanabara's former governor Carlos Lacerda, a member of the former UDN who had been one of the key planners of the coup, was arrested in Rio de Janeiro, as was former president Kubitschek.[10] Their crime was participation in the short-lived Frente Ampla (Broad Front), which, between late 1966 and its banning in early 1968, had called for the restoration of liberal democracy.[11] Within a few days, MDB deputies Henrique Henkin, Martins Rodrigues, and Paulo Campos and ARENA deputy José Carlos Guerra were arrested, and Covas and Righi were picked up soon after. Police stormed David Lerer's apartment and beat him before hauling him to army police headquarters, where he spoke to Covas through a hole in the wall.[12] Hélio Navarro was taken to São Paulo DOPS headquarters to answer questions about antiregime statements and eventually served twenty-one months in prison.[13] Journalists and editors who had criticized the regime were also detained.[14]

The ignominy of arrest notwithstanding, it was politicians' and journalists' class status and connections that could take the sharp edge off the repression. *Jornal do Brasil* executive Manoel do Nascimento Brito escaped arrest when he was tipped off by a military friend who spirited him away from his office before DOPS arrived to arrest him.[15] The seventy-five-year-old lawyer Heráclito Sobral Pinto, who had opposed the regime from the beginning and defended its foes in legal proceedings, was arrested in Goiânia on December 14. The next day, he was taken to the barracks of the army police in Brasília, where he received visitors and spent the night in an apartment reserved for officers. On December 16, he was moved to the army police prison, where he, *Jornal do Brasil* correspondent Carlos Castello Branco, and four deputies were placed in unlocked cells and invited to dine with the officers.[16] In response to an officer's claim that AI-5 would establish "Brazilian-style democracy," he supposedly retorted, "I've heard of Brazilian-style turkey but not Brazilian-style solutions. Democracy is universal, without adjectives."[17]

Covas admitted that he was "flattered" by his treatment. On the way to prison the officers stopped so he could buy cigarettes, and in the car they praised him for his behavior in Congress. When he arrived at the same prison from which Sobral Pinto had been released the night before, the commander, who he had met when visiting deputies arrested earlier, greeted him with a shrug that said, "What can I do? You know my opinion of you." In prison for only a week, he took meals with officers, and his wife brought him books, a chessboard, and newspapers.[18] This was a far cry from the treatment lower-class Brazilians who ran afoul of the law received; despite their disdain for the political class, the military rarely subjected these white men to the torture or prolonged sentences reserved for leftist guerrillas, the poor, and the dark-skinned.

Still, politicians must have been infuriated as they watched colleagues forced to hide in embassies and apartments, former presidents and governors being arrested, and respected journalists being hauled off to jail. This was not how educated, cultured Brazilians were supposed to be treated. As Covas lamented in his handwritten prison diary, "The principal characteristic of this new coup was to attack honest men [*homens de bem*]. Neither subversion nor corruption can any longer serve as an excuse. [Now they] simply [want] to get rid of men who are inclined to speak. Especially if they possess moral authority."[19]

After five days, Covas was questioned. The thirty-question interrogation survived only because he was provided with an eleven-page typed transcript. While Covas suffered no physical mistreatment, the accusations must have been deeply offensive to a "public man." The officers criticized him for his "notorious" ties to communists (and, by implication, being one himself) and supporting students' attempts to launch a "revolutionary war." They accused him of buying votes in his last electoral campaign, seeking to create "artificial crises" for political profit, and committing acts of ideological inconsistency.[20] Throughout the tone was accusatory and condescending. His questioners made mocking references to his intelligence:

> Since you are such an intelligent man, with great mental agility, you couldn't ignore that the lamentable events at the University of Brasília . . . were the result of causes that had long been agitating, demoralizing, and disturbing that university. . . . As leader of the MDB, . . . why didn't you direct those you led to examine the preexisting causes that generated that situation instead of getting stuck on analyzing one episode?[21]

They accused him of supporting "enemies of the Revolution" by endorsing the Frente Ampla and associating himself with former president Jânio Quadros. "Doesn't it appear to you that your attitude . . . is incompatible with the conduct that should be maintained by a parliamentarian whose duty it is to watch over the law and not disrespect it?"[22]

This persecution brought to the fore the social ties that bound politicians together, including arenistas who lent support to arrested colleagues—a courageous gesture, since supporting someone out of favor with the regime could put one's own career in jeopardy. During Covas's days in prison, he received three notes signed by a total of twelve fellow MDB deputies; Rio de Janeiro deputy Adolfo de Oliveira included two sets of playing cards to help him pass the time.[23] Meanwhile fellow politicians, including arenistas like Alagoas senator Teotônio Vilela, rushed to his apartment so that Lila would not have to be alone.[24]

If arrests, interrogations, and beatings terrified the political class, particularly members of the opposition or allies of Kubitschek, Lacerda, or Quadros, public statements from military figures blaming the political class for the regime's dictatorial turn made things worse still. These statements were not mere rhetorical flourishes designed to intimidate politicians; comments made behind closed doors, where none but top military brass and civilian collaborators in the cabinet could hear, also blamed politicians for the crisis.

On December 13, as Costa e Silva prepared to sign AI-5, he called the National Security Council (CSN) to advise him, a meeting whose historical importance was so obvious that its audio was recorded. The CSN was made up of the president, vice president, a secretary general, the seventeen cabinet ministers, the head of the SNI, and the chiefs of staff of the Armed Forces branches. While most of the cabinet ministers were civilians, only eight had ever held elected office. The remaining members held little sympathy for the politicians they now resolved to punish. Costa e Silva opened the two-hour meeting by framing the institutional act as the result of the Moreira Alves vote. "The government," he complained, "counted on the comprehension of the public men of the country, who have as much responsibility as we do for the maintenance of peace, order, and public tranquility.... We counted on their clearly understanding that they could not collaborate with an aggression toward another area [the military], also responsible for the Revolution." In Costa e Silva's telling, he had displayed extraordinary patience, for without harmony between politicians and the military the country would be carried to "material, moral, and political disaggregation." But they had repaid him with an act of "provocation," proving that they aimed to block the "evolutionary process of the Revolution."25

MEDIA FILE 3. Clip of President Artur da Costa e Silva speaking to the CSN, December 13, 1968.
SOURCE: Recording of the 43rd Session of the CSN, https://www1.folha.uol.com.br/folha/treinamento/hotsites/ai5/reuniao/index.html.

When Costa e Silva finished, he passed the microphone to each member of the CSN. Vice President Pedro Aleixo spoke first. A lawyer and former deputy from Minas Gerais, Aleixo expressed his opposition to the act in an almost pleading tone. He explained that it had been unrealistic to ask deputies to make a "political" decision to support the government over Moreira Alves while ignoring the case's legal flaws. "The choice to send the case to the Supreme Court, from the legal point of view, does not seem to me to have been the most advisable one." Perhaps Moreira Alves had committed slander; if so, the Chamber could have expelled him for violating parliamentary decorum.26 Whatever its text might claim to the contrary, the act contained "absolutely nothing that ... characterizes a democratic regime." Why not start with something less drastic? "Understanding ... all the high reasons of state that inspire you and the elaborators of this document, I very humbly, very modestly declare that if we have to take a step like this ... I would start precisely with a state of siege." If that proved ineffective the nation would understand the need for a new act. "I state this with the greatest respect, but certain that I am fulfilling a duty to myself, a duty to you..., a duty to the Council, and a duty to Brazil."27

MEDIA FILE 4. Clip of Vice President Pedro Aleixo speaking to the CSN, December 13, 1968.
SOURCE: Recording of the 43rd Session of the CSN, https://www1.folha.uol.com.br/folha/treinamento/hotsites/ai5/reuniao/index.html.

The ministers of the navy and army scoffed at Aleixo's proposal. Navy Minister Augusto Rademaker retorted, "We don't have to debate this question juridically, legally, or constitutionally because the things that happened in Congress were not just words or offenses against a person; they were offenses against an institution." The Armed Forces had patiently attempted to resolve the problem through legal means, not repression, and what had it gotten them? "What needs to be done now is, in fact, a repression to end these situations that could carry the country not to a crisis, but to a chaos from which we won't be able to escape."[28] Army Minister Lyra Tavares pointedly stated, "If [Aleixo] had the responsibility to maintain this nation in order, he wouldn't get so stuck on extremely respectable texts of law." While the country was once again degenerating into subversion, politicians such as Moreira Alves were inciting the people against the Armed Forces. The military had waited patiently, "convinced . . . that there was no way there would not be a solution." Yet the Chamber had refused to acknowledge the attack on the military's honor or purge subversion from its own ranks.[29]

MEDIA FILE 5. Clip of Navy Minister Augusto Rademaker speaking to the CSN, December 13, 1968.
SOURCE: Recording of the 43rd Session of the CSN, https://www1.folha.uol.com.br/folha/treinamento/hotsites/ai5/reuniao/index.html.

Civilian members of the CSN with no electoral or legal experience took the same position. Finance Minister Antônio Delfim Neto argued, "I believe that the Revolution, very early on, put itself in a straitjacket that impeded it from realizing its objectives." He explained that he was in "full agreement" with AI-5; "It doesn't go far enough," he stated, and argued that they should modify the act to grant Costa e Silva (and by extension himself) the authority to decree constitutional amendments to accelerate Brazil's development.[30] As an ambitious economist serving in the federal government for the first time, Delfim undoubtedly saw in AI-5 a chance to impose his own economic policies without congressional interference. It was a position he has maintained for the rest of his life; in our 2015 interview, he stated emphatically, "I signed it. And if conditions were the same, I would sign it again."[31]

CSN members with a background in electoral politics were more reluctant. Foreign Minister José de Magalhães Pinto, who as governor of Minas Gerais had led the 1964 conspiracy against Goulart in his state, admitted, "It is a terrible situation for all of us. When I took the responsibility to incite the movement [of 1964], I didn't feel as uneasy as I do now; however, I must say that I give all my solidarity ·. . . to the Revolution because . . . I do not want to see it lost."[32] He struck the same tone a few days later with the Portuguese ambassador, saying he had experienced a "dilemma . . . between his democratic convictions and the necessity of impeding the disaggregation of the Revolution, ultimately deciding in favor of the latter by supporting the institutional act. He did not regret it because the danger Brazil was running was incalculable."³³

Labor Minister Jarbas Passarinho expressed similar unease: "I know that you loathe, as do I[,] . . . moving on the path toward a pure and simple dictatorship." Still, he argued, the act was necessary. "But to hell with every scruple of conscience. . . . What matters now isn't that democracy be defined just by the text of a constitution. What matters is that we have the historic courage to recover the [revolutionary] process."³⁴ Strikingly, Passarinho, a former colonel who had entered politics after 1964 as appointed governor of his home state of Pará, expressed more unease with the act than Delfim Neto, a technocrat with no special attachment to democratic forms.

MEDIA FILE 6. Clip of Labor Minister Jarbas Passarinho speaking to the CSN, December 13, 1968.
SOURCE: Recording of the 43rd Session of the CSN, https://www1.folha.uol.com.br/folha/treinamento/hotsites/ai5/reuniao/index.html.

Costa e Silva then summoned his justice minister. In a meeting that morning with Costa e Silva, the military ministers, the head of the SNI, and Rondon Pacheco, Gama e Silva had suggested a far more draconian act, causing Army Minister Lyra Tavares to protest, "Not like this Gama. This way, you'll make a mess of the whole house."³⁵ It was so excessive that Costa e Silva reputedly told a fellow general later, "If you had read that first one, you would have fallen to the floor. It was absurd. It would have closed Congress, made changes to the judicial branch, along with several other ferocious Nazi measures."³⁶ Gama e Silva then presented a second draft, the one submitted to the CSN as AI-5. To explain the reasoning behind the act, he stated:

> I cannot understand the behavior of the Chamber of Deputies, particularly the party . . . that wanted to call itself the "party of the Revolution," as anything other than an authentic act of subversion. . . . The Revolution was made precisely . . . to impede subversion and ensure the democratic order. If this order is at risk, [we must] seek help from suitable revolutionary instruments to restore true, authentic democracy.³⁷

He rejected Aleixo's call for a state of siege. AI-5 was "truly a measure of national salvation." It was not dictatorial, because the man to whom it gave new powers was Costa e Silva, who "due to his attitudes, due to his deliberation, due to his equilibrium, and due to his patriotism" would never allow himself to act as a dictator. It had been a mistake to place a time limit on previous institutional acts, so this one should have no limit. "The Revolution limited itself, and the consequence is the self-destruction that people want to provoke within it now."³⁸

The minutes and recording reveal two key points. First, AI-5 was a response to the behavior of Congress, not the student movement or the guerrilla struggle. Second, for both military and civilian CSN members, commitment to democracy lasted only until it proved inconvenient. Costa e Silva, Gama e Silva, and the others had little stake in preserving the constitution they themselves had established. Apart from Gama e Silva, they did possess a rhetorical attachment to liberal democracy, but their ideal was an authoritarian "democracy" defined by security and public order, not loyalty to legal texts. This understanding was even more limited than the elitist democracy propounded in the congressional debates over Moreira Alves. Certainly AI-5 flew in the face of the conception of democracy that Aleixo and Magalhães Pinto held, but this was not enough to convince them to challenge the military, which had even less compunction about discarding what remained of democracy. Even Aleixo's opposition was qualified by his admission that if a constitutional state of siege proved ineffective, he would endorse a departure from legality. In the end, every member of the CSN, including Aleixo, signed AI-5. By signing the act, they placed a fig leaf of civilian endorsement over the military's naked power grab.

These two points made in private—that the political class was to blame for the new act and that liberal "democracy" needed redefinition—were soon reinforced publicly. Late on December 13, as he prepared to read AI-5 over the air, Gama e Silva explained that while the "months of agitation" had caused concern, a new act was required only when agitation spread to Congress. "The revolutionary war . . . reached the very national parliament through the behavior of members of the party who had the responsibility to defend . . . the Revolution . . . , thus creating this climate of disquietude."[39] The problem was not students, guerrillas, or even Moreira Alves but rather ARENA. Naturally, arenistas bristled at the claim that they were to blame. The next day, twenty-one ARENA senators (nearly a third of the Senate) signed a telegram decrying the act. "Since it is impossible to use the parliamentary lectern . . . ," they wrote, "we manifest to you our disagreement with the solution adopted by the executive branch through AI-5." The act represented a "political regression with unpredictable consequences," and by warning Costa e Silva of the great responsibility he had assumed with such sweeping powers, they were "fulfilling a duty . . . imposed upon [them] by the popular representation with which [they] are invested."[40] Senators were in the best position to oppose the act; other than Krieger, who had taken a public stand against the prosecution of Moreira Alves, they had nothing to do with the problem. The references to duty and their voters were a reminder that they were men of honor representing the Brazilian people.

Costa e Silva's response two days later was deeply worrisome. In a terse reply that was not published in the press, the president wrote:

> I should remind you that it was the lack of political party support . . . that led me to take the decision consolidated in AI-5. . . . I almost begged for the support

of my party in preserving . . . the Revolution. . . . This evolutionary process was disturbed by the lack of understanding of those who did not, perhaps, sincerely desire the rule of law. The revolutionary evolutionary process is thus suspended due to a lack of political support, due to the true hostility of the party that should have been the most interested in the prevalence of "juridical and social values," which would only be truly valid without the demoralization and discrediting of the Armed Forces.[41]

The "revolutionary evolutionary process" referred to the regime's evolution from arbitrary acts to legalized institutionalization, a process the constitution was to have consolidated. For Costa e Silva, politicians had shown that they had not truly accepted the necessary transformation of politics. As a result, the military would rule without them. The president offered this explanation publicly at a military graduation ceremony the same day. He claimed that those "defeated by [the Revolution of] March [1964]" were attempting to defame the "Revolution" and divide the military. "They warned the country about an inexistent militarism and blamed the military for the nation's problems. They offended you, and when you become offended, they claimed you were pressuring the other branches of government." In this version, Kubitschek, Lacerda, Goulart, and Moreira Alves had all been part of a fantastical plot to overthrow the "Revolution." Yet as Costa e Silva stated, "The Revolution is irreversible," and "whenever it is indispensable, like it is now, we will carry out new revolutions within the Revolution!" Politicians, particularly arenistas, had failed to recognize this.

> The entire nation understood that the military could not accept . . . being dishonored with impunity as a class by an enormous insult that would receive the cowardly protection of immunity, which was never intended for such objectives. [The military] gave proof of its tolerance and democratic spirit, and instead of wrongly using the weapons the people entrusted to them, they sought the recourse granted by law. But unfortunately, they did not receive the . . . support of many deputies in the majority party. . . . The government was thus obliged to intervene and take strong measures that could reactivate the Revolution. This is why the new institutional act was approved.[42]

The most ominous aspect of Costa e Silva's response was its ambiguity. Phrases like "recovering the revolutionary process" hinted at an improvisational approach. If Costa e Silva hesitated to specify what this would look like, it was probably because he was under pressure from the military to come down hard on the political class and did not know how far the punishment would go. Might Congress and state legislatures be closed permanently? Might the military decide that the time had come not simply for the reform of politics, but for their end?

Hints of the pressure Costa e Silva faced came in the form of pronouncements from high-ranking officers. The harshest indictment came from General Henrique de Assunção Cardoso, First Army chief of staff, in a remarkable speech at a command transfer ceremony:

> Almost five years escaped without the political class taking advantage of the opportunity March 31 offered them. . . . At first they were remissive, and later they made themselves accomplices of the open enemies of the Revolution. . . .
>
> Except for the patriotic exceptions of a few . . . , the sad truth is that the majority of them have never accomplished anything tangible or sincere. . . . [They] persevered in sullying the already precarious reputation of the legislative branch, particularly with reference to the abuse of their prerogatives and the ostentatious and scandalous enjoyment of innumerable privileges and advantages.
>
> Civilian leaders were never so far removed from reality; they never showed themselves more incapable; they never betrayed so shamelessly the most basic principles of the fight against corruption and subversion.
>
> December 13 marked, however, the resumption of the Revolution. . . . [T]he political class has forgotten nothing and learned nothing. The traitorous vote of the Chamber of Deputies was not an alienation or a mistake! It was a pure and simple attempt to return to the past, a tacit revocation of the Revolution.[43]

Such comments targeted not merely "subversives" or renegade arenistas, but the entire political class; they drew on broad disgust with politicians common across Brazilian society. For a significant swath of the Armed Forces, the Moreira Alves case proved what they had long suspected: despite four years of "Revolution," the political class was more interested in protecting its perks than in the good of the nation. Their shortsighted behavior had held Brazil back for too long. As the military saw it, the time had come to put them in their place.

This opinion was not just a tool of intimidation. The same attitude was manifested privately in São Paulo in October by officers attending a birthday party for an air force officer. The invitees included a US consular officer; a few judges, lawyers, and businessmen; and "hard-line" officers. In a far-reaching conversation about politics, several invitees agreed that the military was "the first lady of the nation"— a curious feminization but one that accurately reflected their understanding of the support the military should provide the executive branch. Although by this time over three hundred politicians had been cassado under AI-5, they believed that to continue the "goals of the Revolution," still more cassações were necessary, along with the temporary closure of all state legislatures and municipal councils. In their ideal scenario, all candidates would have to be "approved by a board or court designed to judge the candidates' fitness." According to the US consular officer, their ideology was based on two principles: "the current crop of Brazilian politicians was unworthy of trust"; and "the responsibility for setting things right in Brazil rested with the Armed Forces."[44] Still, it is significant that even these "radicals" did not advocate the permanent closure of Congress or other legislatures; despite everything, they believed that civilian politicians were needed to rule Brazil (under military tutelage) and that if the bad apples could be eliminated, the rest might be salvaged.

In the face of discouraging public military comments, politicians were at a loss as to how to minimize the threat that lay on the horizon. What was certain was that even before Congress could be reopened new cassações would come. Their responses had to take this into account, for being removed from office, their political rights suspended for a decade, would be devastating not only politically but also financially and socially. For an arenista, particularly one who had voted against the government in the Moreira Alves case, was it safest to enthusiastically praise AI-5? Or was it wiser to lie low? For the MDB, was cassação likely enough that one should boldly speak out and go out in a final blaze of glory? Or might silence enable one to escape?

Politicians' responses thus ran the gamut from forceful condemnation to fawning adulation. It was only a courageous few who opted for the former route. In addition to helping draft the December 14 telegram criticizing the act, Krieger took the bold step on January 5 of submitting to Costa e Silva his resignation as Senate majority leader and president of ARENA, explaining that he had made this decision in November due to his disagreement over the Moreira Alves case.[45] Indeed, in the coming months, Krieger's name was brought up in rumors about who might be purged.[46] Minas Gerais senator Milton Campos, an early supporter of the coup and Castelo Branco's justice minister, issued a statement that surprisingly escaped the press censors: "With this act, we now live under a state of fact, which has substituted the rule of law. . . . I only have words to lament what has occurred and to express my inconformity."[47]

Most members of the MDB opted for a cautious approach. Deputy Jorge Cury urged the collective resignation of all MDB legislators, and other oppositionists called for the party to dissolve itself.[48] Yet the most the party did was issue a statement arguing that Brazil's "liberal traditions are disesteemed by the immoderation of arbitrary [actions], which are also incompatible with the institutional and historical destiny of the Armed Forces."[49] Most MDB politicians chose to "wait and see with passive acceptance of [a] situation in which [there is] no role for [the] opposition."[50] If there was a behind-the-scenes power struggle between "radical" and "moderate" military factions, it was prudent to keep quiet and hope the latter won.[51]

The attitudes of Krieger and Campos notwithstanding, most of ARENA chose to cheer the act. The governors of São Paulo, Minas Gerais, Guanabara, Paraíba, and Rio Grande do Sul called Costa e Silva to "applaud the decision of the government and define it as courageous and necessary to contain the agitation that was trying to demoralize the revolution of 1964 and impede the country's progress." Ten other governors sent telegrams to express their approval.[52] They had good reason to do so; after all, the governors of Guanabara and Minas Gerais were both allies of Kubitschek, and both had to be concerned that they were now targets for cassação.[53] São Paulo's Sodré had at times run afoul of the generals, and there were whispers that he could be cassado as well.[54] Yet he still maintained dreams of succeeding Costa e Silva, which would surely come to naught if he delayed in endorsing the act.[55]

Some legislators were also quick to express their support, perhaps attempting to outdo governors who were rivals back home. Paraná's Alípio de Carvalho, a retired general and ARENA federal deputy, praised AI-5 for "stopping the process of disintegration that was once again taking over Brazil" and pledged his support for the "Revolution's" "great task of cleansing and restoration."[56] On December 26, thirty-four of ARENA's forty-two senators sent a new telegram responding to Costa e Silva's reply to the December 14 telegram. This time the senators expressed confidence in Costa e Silva and his desire for good relations with politicians, who sought only to offer their service to the "Revolution."[57] This second telegram was spearheaded by Piauí senator Petrônio Portella and Rio Grande do Norte senator Dinarte Mariz, while Krieger and several other signatories of the first telegram refused to sign. Thirteen senators signed both, considering it possible both to oppose AI-5 and to support Costa e Silva against "radical" officers. Still, the US ambassador derisively wrote of the double signatories, "Most of them stand for absolutely nothing and are notable only for their well developed instinct to survive." Indeed, it was rumored that some in the military wanted the thirteen double signatories to be cassado, not so much because they opposed AI-5, which was to be expected from politicians, but because their willingness to sign both documents seemed to be a symptom of the lack of principle that the military was seeking to eradicate from the political class.[58] As he read the papers in prison, Covas fumed:

> It is such a totality of announcements saying the same thing that you start to get the impression that someone agrees with this. Alípios, Zezinhos, Geraldos, and other less cited scoundrels, how arrogantly they prepare themselves, assiduously attempting to discover the will of those in power. And how quickly the *camarilla* of governors expresses its solidarity in order to hold onto their jobs.[59]

Behind the scenes, however, politicians were stunned. American diplomats who spoke with them described their mood as "shock and depression," "hopelessness," "deep despair," "apprehension," "cynicism," "uncertain[ty] and fearful[ness]," "gloom and tension," and "dismay and pessimism," all informed by "self-preservation and financial self-interest" and the conviction "that military men are bent upon destroying rather than punishing or reforming the 'political class.'"[60] Still, few were willing to express this publicly. The criteria for cassações were so obscure that with nearly everyone's future in doubt, any criticism might tip the balance. Arenistas in particular had cause for anger, since many had helped bring about the "Revolution," served the government faithfully (in their view), and now witnessed Congress closed and their paychecks suspended for their trouble. Despite his public praise, Alípio de Carvalho confided to a diplomat that he would never have voted to prosecute Moreira Alves if he had known this would happen and that it would be hard to remain in ARENA after this.[61] In public, Carvalho, a career soldier who only entered politics in 1966, toed the party line. Yet he showed a different side in private, one that looked more like a politician than an officer.

"YOU BECOME A LEPER":
PURGING THE POLITICAL CLASS

On December 30, the first of what would become twelve lists of purges was released. Politicians were not only removed from office; in most cases, their right to run for office, join political parties, or even vote was suspended for ten years. Although cassação had been an accepted way since the 1930s to rid the state of troublesome (usually leftist) politicians, the suspension of political rights, with its frontal attack on civil liberties, was an innovation of the military dictatorship. Between December 1968 and October 1969, 335 current or former senators, federal and state deputies, mayors, and municipal councilors were removed—nearly three-fifths of the total purged during military rule.[62] The repression was targeted at the industrialized South and Southeast, above all, São Paulo, Guanabara, Rio de Janeiro, Rio Grande do Sul, and Minas Gerais. The northeastern state of Pernambuco, a hotbed of union and leftist mobilization, was also hit hard, and no state escaped unscathed, but of the 335 politicians affected, 175 (52.2 percent) came from these five states. These states, especially São Paulo, were the center of opposition to the regime, and nearly half of paulista federal deputies fell.

Despite the fact that Gama e Silva had privately recommended the removal of forty-four deputies, the first list contained only thirteen names.[63] Moreira Alves, Hermano Alves, Lerer, Righi, and seven other outspoken deputies were expelled from Congress—a development that surprised none of them since several were imprisoned at the time.[64] Lacerda, the right-wing former governor of Guanabara, had his political rights suspended too, the clearest example of how the regime had alienated its allies. Lacerda had long-standing presidential aspirations; when Costa e Silva was chosen to succeed Castelo Branco, he broke with the regime. His rejection of the "Revolution" was one of the most painful betrayals the regime suffered, and it is unsurprising that the military responded by suspending his political rights.[65] These thirteen would become the first group of many. While Costa e Silva emphasized at the first CSN meeting, "We are not talking about an actual court," the proceedings would in theory be based on evidence gathered by the SNI.[66] But although the SNI was indeed building dossiers, "evidence" consisted largely of comments even more innocuous than the Moreira Alves speeches, and the accused had no right to defense. Like the words *revolution* and *democracy*, the concept of due process was redefined to fit the needs of a regime supposedly threatened by subversion. Legal standards of evidence only distracted from the "more important" concern: national security.

Over the next ten months, new lists appeared about once a month. A "no" vote in the Moreira Alves case was not enough to condemn anyone by itself. Although half of ARENA federal deputies had refused to support the government then, only 7.7 percent were purged, while 33.8 percent of MDB deputies met the same fate.[67] More important factors included belonging to the "radical" faction of the MDB, membership in the now-banned Frente Ampla, and alleged communist sympathies. Accusations of corruption, moral failures, or personal enmity with a member of the CSN could also be damning but were often ignored if a politician was obedient. The real criteria were criticism of the regime or regular votes against it in Congress. Of the ARENA deputies who most frequently voted against the government, 42.9 percent were cassado, while only 0.5 percent of those who most frequently voted with the government were removed; in the MDB, 45 percent of the most consistent opponents of the regime were cassado, while none of the least combative were.[68] As Costa e Silva stated about one of those removed, "He's been systematically against the government, and this is a bad example. If we should or want—and I still don't know if we do—to rebuild the political structure of the country, we need to eliminate these elements."[69]

Initially the lists focused on Congress. Purges were widened later to include state and local politicians. With input from military leaders, Gama e Silva would create a preliminary list of targets, with a dossier on each. The dossier contained information the security and information services had cobbled together from a variety of sources. First came legislative speeches, then newspaper columns or interviews, and finally information from the regime's intelligence services, including statements at rallies and meetings with politicians who were enemies of the regime or had themselves been purged. Gama e Silva then selected names to forward to Costa e Silva, who read the dossiers and decided what punishment if any he felt was appropriate. He then submitted his final list to the CSN. Usually the CSN ratified his decisions. A few times they convinced him to spare someone. Sometimes they debated lightening the penalty by not suspending someone's political rights, and in still other cases they persuaded Costa e Silva to increase the penalty (suspension of political rights when he had proposed only cassação).[70]

The process was seldom straightforward, and vendettas could weigh as heavily as supposed subversion or corruption, both of which were often simply a convenient excuse to sideline an adversary. In the December 30 CSN meeting, Passarinho defended MDB deputy José Lurtz Sabiá, arguing that while he was prone to making violent criticisms of government ministers, that did not justify cassação. Moreover, Passarinho pointed out that Sabiá had defended foreign investment in Brazil—hardly something one would expect of a "subversive." Some of Sabiá's most vicious attacks had been directed at Gama e Silva, and cassação could cast doubt on whether AI-5's purpose was to punish subversion and corruption or to settle scores.[71]

A few months before, Gama e Silva had confided to Krieger that he was considering prosecuting Sabiá for slandering him.[72] Now, however, he claimed that "problems of a personal nature were not taken into consideration" but that Sabiá "did not show interest in preserving the Revolution. . . . We aren't just talking about agitation, subversion, or corruption, since the Revolution seeks the implantation of an authentic democracy in the country. This deputy . . . is completely incompatible with the democratic regime that [the Revolution] wants to establish in Brazil."[73] The health minister, who Sabiá had also criticized, added that he needed to be removed due to "his lack of decorum and personal dignity in attacking indiscriminately someone he doesn't even know."[74] Personal attacks (or antiregime statements) were thus recast as "antirevolutionary" rhetoric. As Costa e Silva put it in another CSN meeting, "Every time a deputy attacks the regime . . . he turns himself into an enemy of the Revolution."[75]

This became clearer as succeeding lists were released. The January 16 list contained names of individuals who were neither blatantly corrupt nor antirevolutionary, including the six São Paulo arenistas who had signed manifestos explaining their "no" vote in the Moreira Alves case. Costa e Silva argued that their votes had been merely the latest in a string of failings. The justification for removing Hary Normanton was almost certainly his ties to organized labor as former president of the São Paulo railroad workers' union, as the military frequently conflated trade unions with communism. Although Normanton had once supported Adhemar de Barros in his crusade to reduce communist influence in the paulista labor movement, Costa e Silva now falsely claimed that he was "known to be a card-carrying communist, who we now have the chance to eliminate from politics."[76] As for Marcos Kertzmann, "He's been disloyal to ARENA," Costa e Silva griped. "Always against, always against." He had "disobeyed party instructions in many votes important for the government" and had worked with labor unions; these offenses showed that he was "an opportunist and a demagogue." To add insult to injury, he had allegedly attended a December 12 party held at a Brasília hotel to celebrate the refusal to grant permission to try Moreira Alves.[77] Both were removed from office and had their political rights suspended.

Israel Novaes had, among other alleged "sins," called for investigations of torture, belonged to an organization expressing sympathy for Cuba, and collaborated with the student movement. "He's been disloyal to his party; he's against everything," Costa e Silva grumbled. When Aleixo pressed Costa e Silva to specify what behavior had been so objectionable, the president retorted, "His behavior has been against the Revolution." Yet after Passarinho admitted that Novaes had written the preface for his forthcoming book and half-jokingly expressed worry that this could provoke the information services to open a file on him, Costa e Silva simply removed him from office without suspending his political rights.[78] The same penalty was applied to the other three deputies who had signed the manifesto, whose similarly trivial sins included supposedly attempting to bribe Costa e Silva with a watch to be taken on a state visit and becoming intoxicated at receptions.[79] The "Revolution" was turning on its own supporters, politicians who initially supported it but grew disillusioned when they realized that the military intended a far more sweeping reform of the political system than they envisioned.

Yet the case that generated the most intense debate was that of Mário Covas. "He is a young man who I know personally, to whom I've taken a liking, but who has gone too far," Costa e Silva said, proposing that he be cassado but without a suspension of his political rights.[80] Aleixo argued that even this was too harsh, reminding Costa e Silva that as leader of the MDB in the Chamber, Covas was obligated to attack the government: "If a measure of this nature is taken against the leader of the opposition party, we will almost be establishing a criterion that no one will be able to exercise a leadership position."[81] Once again Aleixo sought to lend a lawyer's and politician's perspective to a CSN dominated by military officers and civilian technocrats. And, as they frequently did, the officers and technocrats dismissed his arguments.

Gama e Silva and Delfim Neto, both paulistas who stood to profit if the up-and-coming Covas were removed from the picture, argued strenuously in favor of a suspension of political rights. Delfim Neto admitted that Covas was not a communist but argued that his "very active participation" in the "socialist movement in São Paulo" was what had gotten him elected leader of the MDB to begin with.[82] Gama e Silva went further, arguing that Covas was guilty of "communist activity in the Santos region." "His statements against the regime, his actions against the Revolution, are as frank, loyal, and sincere as it is possible for them to be." He made a point of stating that Covas's inclusion had not been his idea but that he received recommendations from the military—a clear reminder that he had military backing.[83]

The entreaties of Gama e Silva and Delfim Neto notwithstanding, the president still wished to decree only Covas's removal from office. "He is a man who can still be recovered for national politics," the president said.[84] However, the navy minister now pointed out that with a simple removal from office, Covas would be able to run again in 1974. (The law governing eligibility to hold office stated that anyone removed from office, even without suspension of political rights, would be unable to run for office for two years, which would prevent Covas from running in 1970.) The year 1974 was the same one that the politicians whose political rights had been suspended in 1964—most notably, Brizola, Kubitschek, Quadros, and Goulart—would be eligible again. More fundamentally, AI-1 and AI-2 had not gone far enough; this time it was necessary to eliminate anyone who stood in the way of the "Revolution." The navy minister argued, "I think it's preferable to err through excess by eliminating these people. . . . We have to tighten the net, because any elements that we spare now will be a threat tomorrow."[85] The army minister added that the continued presence of politicians like Covas would hamper the "implantation of Brazilian democracy, free from disorder and strikes."[86] Finally, the chief of staff of the Armed Forces added, "If we conserve the possibility for this man to be a leader . . . , he will be highly pernicious for the Revolution."[87]

Facing the pressure of the military members of the CSN, Costa e Silva agreed to a ten-year suspension of political rights for Covas. Yet even as he removed him from politics for a decade, the president qualified that he saw Covas as "intelligent, well spoken, and appearing to be sincere in his convictions." The paulista deputy had come to visit him three times before his election as president, supposedly resisting Costa e Silva's entreaties to win him to the "Revolution" by arguing (in Costa e Silva's paraphrase), "I know you're trying to convert me, but I can't come over to your side because I need my constituency to be reelected, and my constituency isn't on your side."[88] It was probably because he knew Covas so well, Costa e Silva admitted, that he felt such reluctance. As the former industry and commerce secretary Paulo Egydio Martins recalled years later, when he was in Castelo Branco's cabinet and Covas was an MDB vice-leader in the Chamber, they would have lunch together every couple of weeks, causing quite a commotion among the regime's intelligence services.[89] Attention to building cordial relationships immune to political disagreement nearly saved Covas from having his political rights suspended.

On occasion the CSN targeted a politician as a result of accusations of serious moral failure. The SNI file on a federal deputy from Alagoas accused of multiple homicides stated, "The fact that he has fled the justice system, shielded by his parliamentary immunities, contradicts the moralizing spirit of the Revolution." Costa e Silva said, "The question we should be answering is the following: Is this man . . . worthy of belonging to Congress?"[90] A substitute deputy was accused of seducing five girls as young as fourteen with promises of marriage or financial benefits, abandoning them, and then bribing the families to drop charges. He was also accused of killing the brother of a victim, who attempted to kill him for destroying his sister's honor. Although Aleixo pointed out that "he is as revolutionary as it is possible to imagine," this could not save him in light of these accusations.[91]

These examples illustrate how removal from office was based on a conjuncture of factors. While "subversion" was often important, it became more dangerous if one had upset a member of the military or the CSN, if one's removal could further the political aspirations of a member of the CSN, or, above all, if one had voted systematically and publicly against the government. On occasion, moral failings could be so severe that even support for the "Revolution" could not save a politician. On still other occasions, the military might be responding to the pressure of allied politicians seeking to remove rivals. "Everyone wanted to get rid of their competitors," Delfim Neto recalled years later.[92] Regime figures were aware that the justifications were tenuous. A Costa e Silva aide told a US diplomat that Covas was cassado for accepting money from a tax-evading tobacco company to make congressional speeches on its behalf. The embassy promptly reviewed congressional records and found no speeches by Covas on the company's behalf and correctly concluded that his removal was due to "political considerations."[93]

As the regime neared the end of its housecleaning of Congress in February, the time arrived for the second phase of its punishment of the political class, which would focus on state legislatures, municipal councils, and civil servants. The first step took place at the end of the February 7 CSN meeting, when Costa e Silva announced the indefinite recess of the legislative assemblies of five states. Chief among these legislatures' sins had been the calling of excessive extraordinary sessions, for which they received salary bonuses—up to seventy such sessions in sixty-six hours.[94] As Costa e Silva remarked with satisfaction, the withholding of state deputies' salaries during the recesses would more than make up for all the bonuses; perhaps this would serve as a warning to the remaining seventeen legislatures, "so they can behave better."[95]

Now the process for purging politicians shifted slightly. Since state and local politicians were largely unknown to the SNI, local military commanders and SNI agents prepared dossiers for review by "higher echelons" (presumably military commanders and Gama e Silva).[96] Yet since officers stationed in far-flung regions might not know local politics well, the process often began with recommendations from local politicians, who might use their advice to settle vendettas.[97] For example, in August a Bolívar Poeta de Siqueira, vice-president of the local ARENA directorate in the São Paulo town of Penápolis, sent a letter to Costa e Silva, Gama e Silva, and the ARENA national directorate accusing local members of a rival ARENA faction of misdeeds against the "Revolution," including defecting to the MDB when their candidate lost the 1968 mayoral elections, only to return to ARENA a few months later. Since the state directorate had proved impervious to his pleas, Siqueira begged the president and justice minister to remove them from office.[98]

The influence of local rivalries is clear in the case of the mayor-elect of Covas's hometown of Santos, Esmeraldo Tarquínio. Voted state deputy of the year by journalists in 1968 for his conscientious representation of working-class people, there was not a whisper of corruption against him. Federal deputy Sabiá later referred to him as "a serious, public, Black, upstanding man who was easy to get along with."[99] Yet a general had never forgiven him for a few speeches he had given criticizing the government, and he had been photographed by DOPS at a student march; the US consulate in São Paulo had also heard that the white Santos political elite could not countenance the idea of a Black mayor and had lobbied for his cassação.[100] None of these reasons appear explicitly in the CSN minutes, but the evidence indicates that the US sources were correct. For example, Tarquínio's file contained all the usual alleged offenses: expressing sympathy for Fidel Castro, inciting strikes, and receiving electoral support from communists. He was also accused of having called the army a racist institution. A terse statement from the São Paulo DOPS summarized the intelligence services' view: "Communist. Antirevolutionary."[101] But the file contained no actual evidence of communism, and "antirevolutionary" could be applied to many politicians who escaped. Before Costa e Silva pronounced sentence, Army Minister Lyra Tavares interjected that he had recently been in Santos, where Tarquínio's "aggressions" against the Armed Forces had led the army garrison there to request his removal.[102] It is not difficult to imagine that Santos politicians who resented Tarquínio's outsider status as a working-class Afro-Brazilian might have brought his "aggressive" comments to the attention of friends in the local garrison.[103]

Something similar happened on April 29, when the fifth list revoked the political rights of 174 people. Although several faced undocumented claims of being "corrupt and a corruptor," they were by no means the most notoriously corrupt legislators. However, two paulistas were closely tied to the governor, Sodré.[104] One, João Mendonça Falcão, was his chosen leader of ARENA in the legislative assembly, and the other was a close friend; rumor had it that the governor broke down in tears at news of their cassação. To make matters worse, Costa e Silva had refused to even consult Sodré about the selection of a new mayor for the city of São Paulo. (Costa e Silva's choice was a family friend, Paulo Maluf, a Lebanese-Brazilian businessman.) Some political observers speculated that all this may have been an attempt to embarrass Sodré into resigning.[105] Ultimately, as the stories of Tarquínio's and Sodré's allies indicate, petty personal rivalries or the desire to put a prominent ally in his place could make a target of an otherwise upstanding or unthreatening politician. To be clear, while leftist sympathies or alleged corruption factored into the regime's decisions, they tended to function more as justifications; the real reasons involved personal rivalries or a history of voting against the government.

If for the regime this process was a way to purify the political class while ridding itself of troublesome opponents, it looked very different for those who were targeted. On the one hand, being cassado for standing up to a dictatorial regime could be a badge of pride. As Léo de Almeida Neves put it when asked if he had worried that he might lose his seat in Congress, "No, I wanted it. We [opposition] deputies hoped we would be cassado."[106] But this affirmation of their honor and the recognition of their resistance were the only bright spots for most, for whom cassação could mean exile or loss of friends, prestige, jobs, or income. Others, like Moreira Alves, Hermano Alves, and others of the regime's most vocal critics remained in exile for up to a decade.

Those who stayed in Brazil perhaps wished they had not. Righi was arrested several times over the next two years. Sometimes he was treated well; during his August 1969 arrest, when he was held in Santos with Tarquínio, they were allowed to play pool in the officers' break room. Other times were more stressful; once he was taken to São Paulo in an unmarked black van, to the infamous headquarters of DOI-CODI (Department of Information Operations—Center for Internal Defense Operations) on Rua Tutóia, where some of the most gruesome torture of regime opponents took place. "It's very hard to describe how we felt right then. You have the impression that this isn't really happening. It is so intense. You are worried about yourself, your family, your affairs, about what could happen, if those guys might beat you up, put you on the 'parrot's perch,' kill you," he told me in 2015. Arrest was also hard on one's family. After one of his arrests, Righi's wife, Luciene, seven months pregnant, gave birth to a stillborn son, which she attributed to the extreme stress she suffered during his eight-day imprisonment when she had no idea whether he was dead or alive.[107] When Covas was arrested again in 1969, Lila, terrified that he would disappear, frantically called everyone she could think of to try to discover where he was being held. In the end, it was Paulo Maluf, the newly appointed mayor of São Paulo and a personal friend of Costa e Silva, who discovered Covas's whereabouts from military contacts and passed the information to Lila[108]

Even for those who were cassado but not arrested, there were psychological, social, professional, and financial repercussions. For many, politics had been their life; when that arbitrarily ended, it was profoundly traumatic. On the day that Almir Turisco d'Araújo was cassado, his family sat with him by the radio; when he heard his name listed, "devastated," he retreated to the bathroom to cry in privacy.[109] "Politics [were] the only stimulus that completely mobilized [Cunha Bueno's] personality," his biographer wrote. "To place himself outside of it, . . . and above all having been punished by the very system he helped establish, shook him to the marrow."[110] As Lila Covas remembered, "I tried many ways to cheer [Mário] up. However, he became very embittered without politics. He grew ever more withdrawn."[111]

One bright spot was the solidarity of friends and colleagues. Juracy Magalhães, a former general, federal deputy, senator, and governor of Bahia who had served in Castelo Branco's cabinet, wrote to Cunha Bueno, "I know your character, and I know that you will not be tormented by the punishment you have received. Such are the vicissitudes of those who serve the people."[112] Cunha Bueno also received a letter from General Olympio Mourão Filho, an architect of the coup who later diverged from Castelo Branco and Costa e Silva over how authoritarian the regime should become. The general wrote, "I still have not recovered from the astonishment your cassação caused me. It is a shame that our country is in this type of situation, without full rights for even those who signed onto your decapitation. Tomorrow they may be victims of the same guillotine."[113] When Sabiá was cassado, his arenista friend Gilberto Azevedo gave him a hug and confided that his fellow *paraense* (Pará resident) Passarinho had defended him before the CSN.[114]

Still, friends had to be careful, lest their gestures of support make them a target. When Maluf found out Covas's whereabouts for Lila, he did so on the condition that she not reveal where she had gotten the information.[115] Cassado politicians understood the difficulties their friendship could cause colleagues. As Covas recalled, "It creates a bit of embarrassment, it makes you police yourself a lot, because you always think that if you go to a meeting of politicians who are still active, it looks like you are refusing to 'leave this world.'"[116] Invitations to cocktail parties, dinners at upscale Brasília restaurants, and calls from foreign diplomats were all curtailed, or ceased altogether. Lila Covas remembered, "Many people who had called themselves our friends distanced themselves from us. I remember well people who would cross the street because they were afraid to greet anyone in my family. Many would dissemble and pretend they didn't know us."[117] Amaury Müller, who was purged seven years later, recalled, "It was without a doubt the most traumatic experience of my life. . . . Back then a politician who had been cassado was a sort of leper, from whom many people fled or kept a safe distance."[118] Removal from office also ruined public reputations cultivated over decades; the city of Adamantina added insult to injury when it renamed an avenue bearing Cunha Bueno's name.[119]

Without their old salaries and generous benefits, the cassados were forced to seek other means of support. The day after his removal from Congress, Cunha Bueno took out a newspaper ad alerting readers that he was reopening his law practice after a twenty-two-year hiatus.[120] After being released from prison in 1970, Hélio Navarro began working as a lawyer for political prisoners, a profession in which he was joined in 1972 by Righi, who had spent much of the previous three years at the University of São Paulo earning graduate degrees in economic, financial, and commercial law.[121] Still, this was a precarious way to make a living, as political prisoners' families were often already in dire financial straits because of legal expenses or perhaps because other members of the family had themselves been targeted by the regime and lost jobs; Righi took most such cases pro bono.[122] Tarquínio, former mayor-elect of Santos, had a hard time attracting clients when he tried to return to law. He found a job in broadcasting, but the offer was withdrawn after military officials informed the station that it would be inappropriate for a purged politician to appear on radio or TV. After being released from military custody in December, Lerer accepted a scholarship offer abroad, but when he tried to leave Brazil, he was detained at the airport and his passport confiscated. He had been a civil servant before becoming a deputy, but on being removed from office he was fired and lost his retirement benefits. He then sought to return to his profession as a doctor but found that employers were afraid to hire him. He eventually found a job via an informal arrangement with another doctor; Lerer did all his work and received part of his salary, without appearing on the payroll.[123]

Even if one was lucky enough to gain employment, removal from politics complicated life in innumerable other ways. Covas was shocked to discover that he would no longer be allowed to have an account at the state-run Banco do Brasil. To get a business loan, he had to become creative. When he wanted to invest in real estate in São Vicente, he approached his boyhood friend Paulo Egydio Martins, former minister of industry and commerce under Castelo Branco, who was currently working as president of a real estate credit bank. Although Martins had supported the regime from the beginning, he granted the loan and even served as the guarantor.[124] With money tight, Covas's wife had to let their maid go and take their children out of private school, and she began to sew and sell clothes to bring in extra income.[125] Together such problems further isolated cassado politicians, who, unless they were independently wealthy, might find themselves deprived of some of the perks that went with their former status.

Nonetheless, some did find ways to dabble in politics. While suspension of political rights prevented a politician from running for office, their family members could run, and several politicians immediately set about getting relatives elected to replace them. Before AI-5 a common approach was to ask one's wife to run for office, but all the wives elected to Congress were cassada in late 1969. While the generals hesitated to eliminate someone from politics due to family ties, their conviction that women deputies were merely their husbands' mouthpieces won out. Indeed, their dossiers provided little evidence of subversion, none of corruption, and scant examples of antiregime statements, but they did invariably highlight the men to whom they were married.[126] Three days after the removal of the last wife of a purged politician, the regime decreed that the spouse of anyone punished by an institutional act was now ineligible to run for office.[127] Yet enterprising politicians simply turned to getting their sons elected. This was a natural next step, since membership in the political class was often, although not exclusively, hereditary; this strategy simply meant that the son's political career would begin sooner than expected. In 1972, twenty-three-year-old Jorge Orlando Carone, son of Nisia Carone, ran successfully for city councilor; in 1974 he was elected to the Minas legislative assembly. His younger brother Antônio was elected to the council in 1976. After Cunha Bueno was cassado, his son Antônio Henrique was promptly elected to the state legislature in 1970. Sons never faced the scrutiny that wives did, and there does not appear to have been any discussion of making them ineligible. For the military, sons were capable of independent political action, while wives were not.

"ZEAL FOR THE COLLECTIVE INTEREST": RESHAPING THE POLITICAL CLASS THROUGH REFORM

Though sporadic cassações would continue until October, by the end of May, 259 of the 335 politicians (77.3 percent) who were cassado in 1968–69 had been removed. At this point, the "reactivation of the Revolution" shifted from exception to normalization. This had not always been a foregone conclusion. Passarinho recalled later that there was military pressure to close Congress permanently, "because the act, above all, was a punishment applied to Congress."[128] Gama e Silva claimed in a meeting with ARENA leadership that he had pressed Costa e Silva to dissolve Congress altogether.[129] Senator Filinto Müller told an American diplomat that Delfim Neto and Planning Minister Hélio Beltrão concurred, since they found it easier to carry out their functions without congressional interference. The president had rejected this idea.[130] Yet much remained uncertain. As Costa e Silva mentioned in the March CSN meeting, "Of course we'll have political reopening . . . , but when, how, and where, I still don't know. . . . Reopening depends on various provisions, including reforms."[131] "Reforms" referred to constitutional changes that would formalize military tutelage of politics. The Spanish ambassador summarized, "What the government and Revolution hope . . . is that along with the legal and constitutional reforms, ARENA reforms its mentality. And its leaders believe that after everything that has happened . . . , politicians will have grasped the true national reality, which they will not be permitted to contest at any moment."[132]

The first reform came in late May, when Costa e Silva decreed a complementary act ordering party reorganization. Previously, local, state, and national party directorates had been organized from the top down; that is, prominent national politicians would maneuver to get their allies placed on state directorates, whose members in turn sought to influence municipal directorates. The new act reversed the process, ordering reorganization from the bottom up, whereby local party members would elect a directorate. Delegates from municipal directorates would select a state directorate, with the process repeating itself at the national level. Potentially, the new procedures could facilitate the "renovation" of politics, with leaders with a base of local support undermining entrenched politicians at the state and national levels. A provision requiring parties to hold conventions in at least a quarter of municipalities in twelve states presented difficulties for the MDB, a small party with tenuous local bases of support, even before the cassações. Worried that the collapse of the opposition would lead to a one-party state, Costa e Silva instructed Gama e Silva to meet with MDB president Oscar Passos to discuss changes to the requirements to help the MDB survive.[133] The generals were cognizant of the need to have an opposition, even if only for show, to combat charges of dictatorship from abroad.

Chastened ARENA leaders were pleased that the military was paying attention to them as for months they had been lobbying for the reestablishment of dialogue. Since continued dialogue would be conditioned on their convincing the military to trust them, the June meeting of the national directorate approved a motion effusively praising Costa e Silva: "The country, under your firm command, understood the necessity of the exceptional instruments [i.e., AI-5] that the government utilized in order to keep the ideals of the Revolution from being frustrated and to be able to ensure the return of the rule of law, without threatening contestations against Peace and Security."[134] The motion interpreted AI-5 as a response to generic "perturbations," conveniently ignoring the fact that the chief perturbation had come from ARENA. While prepared to do nearly anything to get back into the generals' good graces, admitting blame for AI-5 was going too far.

The approach seemed to be working. Party reorganization proceeded as planned, though some arenistas complained that the government failed to pressure politicians to join ARENA; what was the use of supporting the regime if it failed to return the favor?[135] The MDB formed enough directorates to survive, but its future was uncertain. Who wanted to join a party that would have no opportunity to win power and possibly lose one's political rights by doing so? Still, Passos confided to a US diplomat that the party was more united than ever; whatever the flaws of the method, at least the headache of the radical imaturos had been eliminated.[136]

At the same time, Costa e Silva asked Aleixo and a committee of legal scholars to draft constitutional revisions that would incorporate many of the provisions of the institutional acts. This measure was to be accompanied by a host of new reforms designed to facilitate the moralization and control of the political class.

Strict fidelity laws would require party-line votes when party leadership decided that a vote was of vital interest. The end of paid extraordinary sessions would reduce corruption. Reductions in the size of the Chamber of Deputies and the state legislatures would reduce costs and require a higher threshold of votes for a candidate to be elected. In addition, Institutional Act no. 7 (AI-7) capped state deputies' salaries, limited state legislatures to eight paid extra sessions per month, imposed restrictions on living allowances, and eliminated salaries for municipal councilors in cities with fewer than three hundred thousand residents.

The Brazilian generals' approach differed radically from their counterparts in the Southern Cone. In Argentina, the 1966–73 dictatorship dominated by General Juan Carlos Onganía banned political activity outright. By 1976, when a second coup launched the bloody Proceso de Reorganización Nacional, leading figures in the military worried that Onganía's ban on political activity had created pent-up tensions that contributed to the violence from Right and Left that had characterized the three-year Peronist interlude. They thus determined to suspend politics rather than ban them. This more "moderate" posture still entailed the closure of Congress, the banning of left-wing and Peronist parties, and the strict circumscription of right-wing and centrist party activity. The Chilean generals imagined an even more drastic break with the past. Parties that had opposed the 1973 coup were immediately disbanded; four years later, even sympathetic parties were dissolved.[137] When the Pinochet dictatorship finally sought to legitimize itself via the plebiscite of 1980, neither parties nor Congress entered the equation; instead, the generals hoped to foster civilian political participation through right-wing Catholic-inspired corporatist groups called *gremios*.[138] In Argentina, politics had to be suspended until an undefined moment in the future. In Chile, corrupt civilian institutions had to be destroyed and replaced with something new.[139] Meanwhile, in Brazil, even at the regime's most repressive moment, appropriate reforms sought to ensure that they would work for the good of the nation.

By the end of August, the reforms were complete, and Costa e Silva prepared to reopen Congress to approve them on September 7, Brazil's independence day.[140] The punishment of the political class had come to a close, and politicians, firmly under military tutelage, could once again offer their collaboration to the "Revolution." But on August 29, an unexpected development derailed Costa e Silva's plans and definitively changed the course of the military regime. The president suffered a debilitating stroke that left him bedridden. Constitutionally, Aleixo should have assumed the presidency until Costa e Silva recovered and if he did not recover, become president. Yet in the most drastic departure from legality the regime would ever make, the ministers of the army, navy, and air force unilaterally issued Institutional Act no. 12 (AI-12), declaring that until Costa e Silva recovered, they would govern as a junta. Given Aleixo's opposition to AI-5, it was impossible for the military ministers to accept him.[141]

The decree of AI-12 marked an even more grotesque break with legality than AI-5. AI-5 had superseded a constitution that politicians' "subversion" had supposedly revealed as inadequate. AI-12 simply ignored the constitution altogether. As Costa e Silva's health deteriorated, politicians watched nervously, hoping that if the military selected a new general-president, at least Congress might be reconvened to "elect" him. Rio Grande do Sul deputy Brito Velho, one of the most vocal arenistas opposed to the request to prosecute Moreira Alves, decided that he was willing to wait no longer, and on September 13, nine months after the decree of AI-5, he resigned from the Chamber with a dramatic statement: "Nine months is the longest a human being can wait for anything. Anything more belongs to the field of zoology."[142]

Freed from Costa e Silva's insistence that relative tolerance should govern the punishments meted out, the junta reopened the process of cassações. Costa e Silva had not called a meeting of the CSN since July 1, when six state deputies and thirty-six local politicians had been removed, but now the junta called six meetings in seven weeks, at which an additional thirty-four politicians, ranging from senators to city councilors, were removed from office and had their political rights suspended. Meanwhile, the junta began polling army generals, who would in turn poll their subordinate officers, to select a new president. In October, they settled on Emílio Garrastazu Médici, head of the SNI under Costa e Silva, and, to the relief of many observers, someone known as a "moderate," in contrast to the other likely candidate, Interior Minister Albuquerque Lima, who was known as an extreme nationalist who some feared might move Brazil toward the Peruvian model of a left-leaning populist military regime.[143]

In a characteristic nod to legality—out of place after the Aleixo fiasco—the junta reconvened Congress to "elect" Médici to a full five-year term, not simply fulfill the remainder of Costa e Silva's.[144] Yet in further disregard for democratic norms, the junta decreed its own set of constitutional changes, incorporated into the constitution as Amendment 1. In addition to implementing many of the reforms Costa e Silva and Aleixo had planned, the amendment decreed sweeping changes designed to solidify the executive's power over the political class. The troublesome article 34, which the Chamber had used to justify its rejection of the request to try Moreira Alves, was rewritten to drastically limit parliamentary immunity. As under the 1967 constitution, legislators could not be imprisoned unless caught in the act of committing a crime, but whereas the old constitution had only included offenses for which there was no bail, the new one allowed imprisonment if they were caught committing *any* crime or if they "disturbed public order." They could also be tried before the STF without legislative approval.

What would happen to the political class now? Certainly there could be no hope of a quick return to the less dictatorial regime prior to the decree of AI-5. But even within these constraints, politics would continue. Amendment 1 had established that in 1970 the governors would be chosen by the ARENA-dominated state legislatures; arenistas could thus begin jockeying to gain the military's favor. And elections for the Chamber of Deputies, two-thirds of the Senate, and the state legislatures were still scheduled for 1970. However, the same question as ever remained: How much would politicians truly change? With weapons like AI-5 and party fidelity laws, the military could force them to change behavior, but would politicians accept the permanent military tutelage implied by a "reform of mentality"?

Both the security services and Médici professed confidence that they could change. In a confidential report widely disseminated among the security services and the Armed Forces, the Army Information Center opined:

> [Party leaders] understand that it is necessary to correct the behavior of the parties and political factions, with the goal of integrating themselves into the country's process of transformation and becoming vehicles for the transmission of the aspirations of the masses. . . . . Both ARENA and the MDB . . . want to be attuned to reality, and thus begin to act in a way that preserves civilian politics.[145]

Médici, in his October 25 inaugural address, elaborated his vision for the political class thus:

> I believe that political parties have value . . . when the dynamic of ideas prevails over the smallness of personal interests. And I feel that I should urge the party of the Revolution . . . to be a true school of national politics, in harmony with revolutionary thought. And I expect the opposition will honor us by fulfilling its role, pointing out errors, accepting it when we get things right, indicating paths [to be followed], acting as a check, and also making its own school of democracy, dignity, and respect.[146]

Similarly, in a December meeting with US ambassador Charles Elbrick, he claimed that Congress "had 'learned its lesson' . . . and was profiting from [its] experience" under AI-5.[147] In a February 1970 interview, Médici made it clear that the road back to meaningful participation would not be easy, emphasizing that a return of "democracy" depended on "the collaboration of all Brazilians, of every class and from every corner," but especially the political class:

> The perfection of the democratic regime . . . demands first and foremost a profound change in mentality on the part of those who directly or indirectly influence the political process. . . . Unless zeal for the collective interest begins to prevail over the machinations of individuals or groups, the vices that perverted political-administrative habits and took the country to the brink of . . . catastrophe will persist.[148]

Médici claimed that he accepted that the opposition could someday win power but emphasized, "What will by no means be tolerated . . . is that the battle between parties be carried out with the purpose of subverting the regime, nor that the opposition try to win power in order to reestablish the situation that threatened to throw the country into . . . chaos."[149] His aggressive comment left no room for doubt: the military would hold a tight rein until it felt confident that the political class had abandoned dreams of a return to the past. For ARENA, this meant unquestioning acceptance of the regime's dictates. For the MDB, it meant "constructive" opposition that would respectfully point out mistakes and offer suggestions while avoiding the "subversion" of 1968. If the country was "pacified" by the end of his term, his son claimed later, Médici planned to hand power over to a civilian successor.[150]

CONCLUSIONS

By the end of 1969, the political class had experienced its most trying crisis since Vargas imposed his Estado Novo in 1937. A year before, in the Moreira Alves vote, the Chamber of Deputies had sought to reassert its independence from the military. That gamble had failed spectacularly. Politicians had been imprisoned and forced into exile. Over three hundred had been banished from politics, their lives thrown into disarray. Congress had spent ten months in recess, and several state legislatures remained closed. And when Costa e Silva fell ill, the military had illegally shoved aside the vice president in favor of another general. Although in public most politicians coped by supporting the regime or simply remaining quiet, 1969 was a pivotal year in the evolution of the political class's disillusionment with military rule. Throughout the year, every indication was that the Armed Forces were united in their belief that "the political class has learned nothing" and would now require military tutelage to force them to put aside "the machinations of individuals or groups" in favor of "zeal for the collective interest." The implementation of a sweeping military-engineered project to not only defeat "subversion" and remake Brazil's economy and administrative structure but also discipline the political class had begun. This was not intended as a temporary solution. Rather, Costa e Silva, Médici, and officers from across the "moderate" and "hard-line" spectrum envisioned a dramatic transformation of politics that would convince politicians, by force if necessary, to set aside self-interest and work under military tutelage for Brazil's development. Now Congress would exist to carry out the will of the "Revolution." As federal deputy Clovis Stenzel, the regime's eternally zealous defender, put it, "Either [Congress] will join the Revolution, and there will be a Congress, or it won't, and there won't be a Congress."[151]

At the time, with military regimes in control of much of Latin America, it appeared legitimate to those who led the regime to question whether liberal democracy was adequate to meet the challenges of national security. Perhaps democracy needed to be subjugated to a centralized executive empowered to cut through political wrangling and red tape to ensure security and development. If this solution ran counter to the mundane interests of the political class, so what? Perhaps this was the wave of the future. As Senator Milton Campos pointed out after Congress reopened, the Italian political scientists Gaetano Mosca and Vilfredo Pareto had shown that it was natural for a new political class—in this case, the military and technocrats—to replace old leaders, in an endless "circulation of elites." Although Campos worried that "circulation" by result of force was "eroding democracy," the phenomenon was inevitable.[152] Perhaps the old political class was obsolete, to be replaced by a military-dominated technocracy.

Yet this project contained a fundamental contradiction: while mistrusting politicians, it refused to completely push them aside. Despite the subordination of the political class to the military, the generals had been shaped by a century and a half of Brazilian liberal discourse that made them unwilling to forgo the semblance of the "democratic" legitimacy elected civilian politicians provided. Hence there was never any serious consideration of closing Congress permanently; even avowedly "hard-line" officers took for granted that legislatures and elections would endure. By refusing to govern without civilian political elites, the Brazilian military's actions kept alive politicians' hopes that they might someday regain their power and privileges.

Over the next five years, the generals would nearly convince themselves that the political class had been transformed into the enlightened, pliant ruling elites of whom they dreamed, lending a democratic facade to military rule by participating in elections, voting on bills, and doing as they were told. Although a few young politicians would opt for a more militant posture against the regime, the response of most of their colleagues would be to wait out the dictatorial storm—or to take advantage of it to build their own careers.

4

"Sheltered under the Tree"

The Everyday Practice of Politics under Dictatorial Rule

On September 22, 1973, federal deputy Ulysses Guimarães, national president of the MDB, stood at the rostrum of the Senate in Brasília. The party had just nominated him as its "anti-candidate" to run for president against General Ernesto Geisel, the regime's anointed candidate, in the 1974 electoral college vote, where ARENA would enjoy a massive advantage. Gazing over the heads of the delegates, Guimarães gave a grandiloquent acceptance speech filled with allusions to Portuguese poetry and Greek mythology that would have been incomprehensible to working-class Brazilians. At its crescendo, he declared, "'It is necessary to navigate. It is not necessary to live.' Stationed today in the crow's nest, I hope to God that soon I will be able to shout to the Brazilian people, 'Good news, my Captain! Land in sight!' Without shadow, without fear, without nightmares, the pure and blessed land of liberty is in sight!"[1]

Guimarães was saying that the MDB was driven by the desire to take a stand. In the audience there was a new generation of deputies dubbed *autênticos* (authentics) who agreed; no matter the risks, the opposition should fearlessly stand up to tyranny. Yet many of those assembled were less interested in taking a stand than surviving. As Minas Gerais deputy Tancredo Neves warned the Bahian autêntico Francisco Pinto, "Son, don't put your chest on the tip of the bayonet! Let's just stay sheltered under the tree and wait for the storm to pass."[2] But in the years following the decree of AI-5, it looked as though the storm might never pass. Congress had become a rubber stamp for the regime. Leftist university students had been driven into exile or opted for armed resistance, and the military was marshaling all its firepower to annihilate them. Meanwhile, under the guidance of Finance Minister Delfim Neto, the economy grew at an annual clip of nearly 11 percent between 1969 and 1974, and the "Brazilian miracle" generated an approval rating of over 80 percent for Médici in São Paulo, whose political and economic elites benefited most from accelerating industrialization.³ Amid repression, economic growth, and the regime's popularity, members of the opposition were forced to make their peace with the situation to which they were subjected. Most remained sheltered under the tree, waiting. The autênticos took courageous stands but had little to show for it. Yet there was a third path, embodied by Campinas mayor Orestes Quércia, that proved most effective: building a machine at the state level while emphasizing the day-to-day issues that matterered to voters. No matter the constraints, Quércia and those like him had campaigns to plan, alliances to build. There were party leadership posts to win, privileges (however limited) to be enjoyed, and funds to be procured for one's municipality. There were friends to help and enemies to win over or thwart.

These three paths demonstrate that even at their most repressive, the military's attempts to intimidate the political class had limitations. Although few politicians were principled opponents of military rule, they all subtly pushed back in search of opportunities to improve their lot. This is far from the armed resistance of the revolutionary Left or the courageous opposition of the progressive Catholic Church that has captured scholars' imaginations. Yet although politicians' apparent acquiescence was a key factor in the generals' decision to loosen their repressive grip in 1974, their submission was a farce. Most were biding their time, positioning themselves for a hoped-for return to political normality. Despite Médici's assurances that he required the collaboration of the political class, fear paralyzed most politicians. Few powers remained to legislators beyond offering timid criticisms, which would seldom appear in the censored press. As the British ambassador explained, "With the privileges and perquisites of their individual members so limited and with their collective powers so curtailed ... elections to the [Senate and Chamber] no longer offered its former attractions and their deliberations exercised small influence on the conduct of affairs."[4] Scholars described "a compliant façade of a Congress, shorn of any independent powers,"[5] and highlighted the "institutionally democratic façade and the domesticated semi-opposition."[6]

The generals' confidence was enhanced by the 1970 legislative elections, which brought a resounding victory for ARENA and the near-undoing of the MDB. In the climate of intimidation, in most states the MDB recruited fewer candidates than the number of seats open.[7] Most voters opposed to the regime simply spoiled their ballots or left them blank; nationwide such ballots outnumbered the votes for the MDB, which won only 90 of 310 seats in the Chamber and 6 of 44 Senate races, leaving it with only 7 of 66 senators.[8] Finally, ARENA still controlled all state legislative assemblies, with the exception of Guanabara (comprising the city of Rio de Janeiro). Only less disastrous vote totals in cities of the Southeast and South gave the MDB any hope for the future.[9] Nevertheless, this did nothing to help the party in the municipal elections of 1972, when ARENA won 90 percent of the mayorships.

"IT IS NOT NECESSARY TO LIVE": THE AUTÊNTICOS AND THE ANTI-CANDIDACY

Of the 90 MDB federal deputies elected in 1970, 20 to 30, most serving their first term, would soon distinguish themselves by the "virility" of their opposition, as one later described it.[10] Mostly in their thirties or early forties, they ranged from social democrats to socialists. Several were elected with the discreet support of the banned Brazilian Communist Party, which, unlike other leftist groups, rejected armed resistance.[11] In Brasília, often living in hotels without their families, they were drawn together by disgust with the cautious MDB leadership.[12] In conversations over coffee or meals in hotel restaurants, or as they wrote speeches in Congress's typing room (most deputies lacked offices in still-unfinished Brasília), they met colleagues who shared their convictions.[13] Collectively they were dubbed the autênticos, in contrast to so-called *moderados* (moderates) like Guimarães, who, in the autênticos' view, were too timid. They reserved the most indignation for so-called *adesistas*[14] like Guanabara governor, Antônio Chagas Freitas, a newspaper magnate and supporter of the 1964 coup who after AI-5 had built an MDB machine that collaborated with the regime.[15] Considering the regime's marginalization of the political class and disregard for civil liberties, what did these young deputies have to lose? In their minds, something, *anything*, had to be done to show the world that the Brazilian dictatorship did not enjoy unanimous support. Although they knew that they would probably end up being removed from Congress, still they attacked the regime.

The conflict between autênticos and moderados, with adesistas sometimes thwarting both, became the key conflict within the MDB. The moderados were annoyed; AI-5 had rid them of the headaches created by the "immature" deputies, but now they were confronted with another group whose careless, confrontational attitude the military might use to justify more repression. To them, the autênticos jeopardized all the party's work to ensure its members' survival. "We were seen as nutjobs," José Alencar Furtado recalled. "We dealt with the opposition of both the MDB and the dictatorship itself."[16] Strategy was not the only source of conflict. The upstart deputies were also eager to supplant their elders and ascend to key party leadership posts, a situation that reminded Guimarães of PSD conflicts when he was young and eager to challenge authority. Indeed, he always resented autênticos' labeling him a "moderate."[17] "If anyone were to compare the ideas of a 28- or 30-year-old autêntico with my ideas at the same time . . . ," Guimarães recalled, "they would see that many times I said more authentic things than the autênticos did. . . . In spite of all my moderation, I made frontal, substantial attacks on the military regime."[18]

The MDB found common ground in the anti-candidacy of 1973, an event that the autênticos would remember as the high point of their careers and the one that transformed Guimarães into a nationally known figure. The MDB had abstained from the 1966 and 1969 presidential "elections," and with barely a fifth of the votes in the electoral college, there was no point nominating a candidate in 1974.[19] Yet after Médici announced Geisel as his successor, the autênticos proposed that the MDB nominate its own candidate so as to use the free television time provided candidates to publicize the party's criticisms of the regime.[20] The autênticos first sought to recruit a nationalist general disenchanted with the regime's friendliness to foreign investment. When that bore no fruit, they courted the venerable lawyer and former governor of Pernambuco, Alexandre Barbosa Lima Sobrinho.[21] They envisioned a candidacy that would conduct a national campaign to denounce indirect elections; but if the courts did not allow TV access, they urged the party to abandon the candidacy.[22] Party leadership was sympathetic to their idea, as it offered an opportunity to oppose the regime within its own rules.

Ultimately the candidate chosen was Guimarães, who by September had warmed to the idea. During a night drinking whiskey with friends, an idea came to him: he would run as an "anti-candidate" to denounce the rigged election.[23] The September MDB convention ratified the anti-candidacy, with Lima as the running mate. At the insistence of the autênticos, the party agreed to hold another convention to reevaluate the anti-candidacy if needed. At the convention, Guimarães thrilled the autênticos by endorsing their desire for a more vigorous opposition: "It is not a candidate who will travel across the country. It is an anti-candidate, to denounce an anti-election, imposed by an anti-constitution."[24] Years later, Pinto recalled, "On the day of the convention, yes, Ulysses appears as a true oppositionist. He gave an excellent speech. . . . And we applauded! It was the first time I applauded Ulysses."[25]

The anti-candidacy launched the thin, bald, ascetic-looking, fifty-seven-year-old Guimarães to national prominence. A graduate of the São Paulo Law School, he had been a deputy since 1950. As a longtime member of the centrist PSD, he shared the party's penchant for taking both sides of an issue.[26] Although he had been a minister in Goulart's cabinet, in 1964 he joined the pro-coup forces in Congress in electing Castelo Branco and authored a proposal that would have allowed suspensions of political rights to last fifteen years instead of ten.[27] Despite joining the MDB, by 1968 he was rumored to be considering a switch to ARENA in exchange for a cabinet position in São Paulo.[28] In the Moreira Alves affair, he served on the Constitution and Justice Committee and gave a measured defense of constitutional immunity but did not play a conspicuous role.[29] As the former deputy Sabiá summarized his relevance in the late 1960s, "Ulysses didn't exist."[30] He was more interested in congressional maneuverings than contact with voters and had limited involvement in local paulista politics. In the evaluation of a British diplomat who spoke with him in mid-1973, "The democracy to which Guimarães wishes to return is very much qualified by being a democracy adapted to the stage of development of the Brazilian people; . . . meaning no democracy at all, but Government in the hands of 'those best fitted to exercise it.'"[31] Yet when the MDB president, Oscar Passos, was voted out in 1970, Guimarães, the party's highest-ranking vice president, was thrust into the presidency. Beginning with the anti-candidacy, Guimarães was transformed. Orestes Quércia, who worked closely with him for two decades, recalled, "Until then he was considered an appeaser, . . . someone who says 'yes' to everyone."[32] Francisco Pinto remembered, "That was when a new Ulysses was born, affirmative and incisive."[33] Or in the words of Gaspari, "That paulista who had barely gotten any votes and presided over a party without a past or a present ended up discovering the future."[34]

Yet the anti-candidacy's full potential to influence public opinion was thwarted —first, because it never reached a broad audience; second, because the press coverage it brought was of dubious significance; and third, because Guimarães refused to exit the race as the autênticos expected. Although Guimarães held rallies in fourteen of Brazil's twenty-two states, they were seldom held in public but rather indoors for invitees.[35] For the closing rally in Guanabara, the state party president, an ally of adesista governor Chagas Freitas, ignored the party's attempts to reserve the Tiradentes Palace, seat of the legislative assembly. When he arrived anyway, Guimarães found military police on the palace's steps.[36] Then, on November 20, the Supreme Electoral Court (TSE) ruled that free TV time applied only to direct elections, although the law made no such distinction.[37] Clearly the court had succumbed to pressure from the regime, which had no interest in allowing the MDB to disseminate its message to the masses.

Although the campaign increased newspaper coverage of the MDB by as much as 3,500 percent, the practical effects were limited.[38] The media were still under censorship.[39] And newspaper readership in Brazil had always been low; in 1972, Brazilian papers printed only 37 copies per 1,000 people, whereas US papers published 297 per 1,000.[40] A 1970 poll revealed that 45 percent of people in the D class (the lowest income group) in São Paulo's capital reported reading no newspaper; in the state's interior the number rose to 84 percent.[41] Rallies had failed to attract popular attention, the party was unable to preach its message through modern mass media, and newspaper coverage was of dubious utility. As the British ambassador explained, "Ulysses Guimarães . . . never succeeded in establishing his credibility as the representative of an effective Opposition. . . . They failed effectively to put their policies before the people."[42]

In the wake of the TSE decision, the party called a new convention, for November 28, to decide whether to continue. The autênticos suggested withdrawing from the race, but with only a third of the party's federal deputies in their camp, they lacked the votes needed to pass their proposal. They thus agreed to maintain the anti-candidacy, but Guimarães quietly assured them that he would quit the race just before the election.[43] To hold Guimarães to his promise, the autênticos resorted to blackmail, threatening to embarrass the party by boycotting the election if he dared present his candidacy at the electoral college.[44] But from Guimarães's likely perspective, the anti-candidacy was going well. He and Lima were receiving enthusiastic receptions from local MDB leaders (even if ordinary people never saw the rallies); moreover, the nearly forgotten party was attracting unprecedented press attention (even if few people were reading the reports). Who knew what positive electoral ramifications this might yield? Furthermore, Guimarães, president of a moribund opposition and never popular electorally, probably enjoyed being welcomed by local party militants, speaking to packed auditoriums, and being hounded for interviews. It was a level of attention he had never before received.[45] A US diplomat who had spoken with a reporter close to Lima wrote that the vice presidential candidate "is immensely flattered by the attention he draws when he appears in public, is enjoying himself hugely, and will campaign under any circumstance."[46]

As the vote approached, the autênticos expected Guimarães to exit the campaign in protest—"denounce and renounce," as one put it—perhaps even as he gave his speech as president of the party in Congress the day of the vote.[47] Yet a few days before the election, Guimarães double-crossed them. In a closed-door meeting with the autênticos, he informed them that he would not withdraw.[48] "I cannot follow through with what I told you I would do," he stated.[49] In justification, Guimarães and the party leadership argued that the military would never tolerate the insolence of a last-minute withdrawal. As he recalled years later, "All the possible weight of protest and denunciation was eloquently expressed in the anti-candidacy. I wasn't going to induce the party into and much less lend myself to infantile, sterile gestures."[50]

The autênticos were infuriated. From the beginning Guimarães had failed to give them credit for the idea of the anti-candidacy, and after they were not invited to many campaign events, the group was forced to announce its intent to hold a parallel campaign on Guimarães's behalf.[51] Now, in addition to keeping them out of the public eye, Guimarães was going to participate in the sham election instead of denouncing the regime's mockery of democracy. Two decades later, Furtado still remembered the episode with bitterness: "[Ulysses] could have arrived in that chamber like a giant, but he arrived like a dwarf. The anti-candidate turned into a candidate, betraying himself, providing a service to the dictatorship in an election with predetermined results."[52] Senator Petrônio Portella, ARENA president, fed this impression by praising the MDB for "giving a valid contribution to the strengthening of democracy in Brazil." Like the MDB leadership, he worried that a "confrontational posture" from the opposition might "damage the effort that is being made on behalf of political-institutional normality."[53]

On the morning of January 15, the electoral college gathered. The autênticos, still fuming, planned a dramatic act of defiance. Although only party presidents were allowed to give speeches, the autênticos voiced their objections via a procedural question. Furtado was chosen in a random drawing to speak for them.[54] Under the pretext of arguing that the rules of the Chamber of Deputies, not the Senate, should apply to the electoral college, he insisted:

In this country, the right to a free press is usurped by prior censorship. The right of minorities to be represented in this electoral college is usurped, thus banishing the principle of proportional representation. In this country . . . even individual [legal] guarantees are usurped by the laws of exception. . . . In this country, even the right of access to radio and television is usurped by a tie-breaking vote.[55]

Although procedural questions were not to be used to make a political speech, Senate president Torres made no serious attempt to interrupt; it was clear to the British ambassador that there had been a deal in place to keep the autênticos from making a scene during the "election."[56]

Guimarães read his half-hour speech in his methodical yet majestic style. Though his sonorous delivery, his voice rising to crescendos and falling to dramatic pauses, sounds almost pompous to the modern ear, for its listeners, it surely meant something else. For Guimarães, schooled in oratory during his years in law school, with a quarter century of experience giving congressional speeches, this was how one should deliver a historically important speech, with a style that reinforced the gravity of the moment, both in the present and for posterity, and that impressed listeners and readers alike with its erudition and poise.

Like the far-walking and mestizo boots of the guerrillas who expelled [the Dutch] from the Pernambucan recôncavo; the leather hats, and, although destitute of swords and blunderbusses, the hands of the Acreans and the Northerners; the Farroupilhan ideals hued by the ponchos and lent voice by the gallop of the horses, the vote is the weapon of this same people to guarantee its destiny as end, and not means, of the State; as sharer in the dividends of development, not its disinherited creator; as [an act of] self-defense as well, raising on our borders the barrier of impenetrability against capital that has no Pátria, which criminally persists in colonizing a Pátria that has no capital.[57]

MEDIA FILE 7. Clip of Ulysses Guimarães Speech before the electoral college, January 15, 1974.
SOURCE: Câmara dos Deputados, COAUD, Arquivo Sonoro, http://imagem.camara.gov.br/internet/audio/default.asp.

The focus of his speech was the regime's abandonment of liberal democracy. He intoned, "When the vote is taken away from the people, the people are expelled from the center to the periphery of history. . . . The [only ways to] protest become agitation and strikes labeled as subversion." He noted the absence of purged politicians with "profound bitterness." He called for the reestablishment of immunity, the revocation of AI-5, the elimination of torture, the end of censorship, and the repeal of decrees limiting student political mobilization. As an afterthought, he lamented government manipulation of inflation data, "which nourishes the divinization of the government in direct proportion to its starving of workers, civil servants, retirees, and pensioners."[58]

Next, ARENA president, Petrônio Portella, turned the tables by arguing that ARENA, not the MDB, was defending democracy. After all, his party held a majority in the electoral college because it had won elections. It was the MDB that was attacking democracy by being sore losers. "In the minority," Portella insisted, "with the pretension of being the holders of truth, they place themselves in opposition to the weight of our numbers, electing themselves tutelary guides of the Nation, the exclusive defenders of democratic principles." In a final jab, he mocked Guimarães's speech at the MDB convention in September, where he called on the party to navigate with purpose.

> We watch with admiration the great adventures of the old sailors. Without a compass ..., they faced the formidable sea.... "It is necessary to navigate. It is not necessary to live." We, however, prefer to remain faithful to our duty. It demands from us intelligence, foresight, courage. There is no place in it for adventure. Glory lies in formulating, conceiving, creating.... "It is not necessary to live. It is necessary to create."[59]

Next came the state-by-state roll call vote. As each elector was called, he shouted his vote from the Chamber floor. Yet when the turn came for the first autêntico, Domingo de Freitas Diniz, he stepped up to a microphone, where he could be sure he would be heard and recorded, and announced, "I refuse to vote, according to the terms of the declaration I signed that was delivered to the board." When Torres announced his vote as an abstention, Freitas Diniz protested that rather than abstaining, he was refusing to participate. "I refuse to vote." As each autêntico voted, he made a similar statement, omitted from the minutes but preserved in the recording: "I refuse to vote in an anti-election"; "I refuse to vote, and I return my vote to the Brazilian people, the ones glaringly absent from this spurious process"; "I refuse to vote, in accordance with my party platform."[60] It was the most dramatic moment of congressional defiance since the Moreira Alves vote.

MEDIA FILE 8. Clip of individual autêntico vote declarations, January 15, 1974.
SOURCE: Câmara dos Deputados, COAUD, Arquivo Sonoro, http://imagem.camara.gov.br/internet/audio/default.asp.

Geisel won 400–76. In a final gesture, twenty-three autênticos submitted a statement for publication in the *Diário do Congresso Nacional*. They explained that since the MDB platform was opposed to indirect elections, they had never had any intention of continuing until the election. Now that the MDB had betrayed itself, they were the only ones left to protest, even if it cost their careers. They concluded by dramatically reaffirming their perceived right to speak for a silenced nation.

> Public men do not become great by the number of times they are simply present, but rather by their capacity to reflect the anguish and hopes of the people, in every age. .

.. [T]he Pátria of tomorrow will be able to do justice to the few who assumed the risk of combining their gesture of inconformity with the protest of their voice.⁶¹

The 1969 constitution required that delegates vote for their party's candidate or risk expulsion from their party. Yet the MDB leadership, unwilling to lose a quarter of their representation in the Chamber, instead simply stripped the autênticos of party leadership posts.⁶² And even when the MDB failed to expel the autênticos, Geisel declined to use AI-5 to remove them. It had been four and a half years since the last cassação; how would it look if a quarter of the opposition was removed for boycotting a sham election? While subsequent years would show that Geisel was not averse to purging opponents, today tolerance ruled.

What, in the final analysis, was the significance of the anti-candidacy? Since television and newspaper coverage had been non-factors, it could not have altered popular perceptions of the MDB. And other than the poorly attended state rallies, the drama unfolded in distant Brasília, where a powerless Congress debated issues of passing local interest. Yet for the MDB politicians who lived it, the anti-candidacy was deeply meaningful. Guimarães discovered the allure of becoming a hero and the excitement of the spotlight. The anti-candidacy ultimately set him on a path to confrontation with the regime that would cement him as an autêntico himself. As for the autênticos, they had finally made the defiant gesture of which they dreamed. Considering the dire straits in which the opposition had found itself a year before, after another dismantling at the polls, even the quixotic anti-candidacy could be enormously encouraging.

BUILDING A PARTY FROM THE BOTTOM UP:
THE RISE OF ORESTES QUÉRCIA IN SÃO PAULO

While autênticos and moderados bickered in Brasília, other young MDB politicians eschewed frontal opposition. Resistance for the sake of conscience had its attractions to some, but it was too risky to appeal to most. Instead, led by Orestes Quércia, the energetic mayor of Campinas, another new generation would build the MDB from the bottom up. For better or worse, the "Revolution" had happened, and no anti-candidacy would change that. Instead, the way forward was to use grassroots organization to win elections. At the state and local levels, for ARENA and the MDB alike, politics were (and still are) ruled by mundane struggles for power and resources. Elections—the route to local power—were also the only way remaining to challenge the regime. Of course, if elections were the key, why would anyone join the MDB? Since all the governors except one belonged to ARENA and since they controlled the disbursement of funds to municipalities, an MDB mayor would be left on the outside looking in. Moreover, the regime had created mechanisms to accommodate local rivalries within ARENA. Under the *sublegenda* system instituted in 1968, each party could run up to three candidates in mayoral elections. Whichever party received the most total votes would win the election, with the mayoralty going to that party's top vote getter.[63] Since local rivalries were one of the few things that could drive a politician away from ARENA, creating space for those rivalries in ARENA was a brilliant approach. São Paulo showed how the system could pay off; in 1972 the MDB won the mayorships of only 58 out of 571 municipalities, along with only 80 municipal council seats across the state, compared to an astounding 4,930 for ARENA.[64]

Yet where most saw insurmountable obstacles, Quércia, the thirty-five-year-old former mayor of Campinas (Brazil's largest city where the mayor was still directly elected) saw opportunity. Born to an Italian immigrant grocer in the hamlet of Pedregulho in São Paulo's northeastern corner, Quércia began working in his father's shop at the age of ten.[65] At seventeen he moved to Campinas, where he studied law and became a reporter. By his eighteenth birthday, he was planning a run for municipal councilor in 1959.[66] He was defeated, but in 1963 he ran successfully on the ticket of the Partido Libertador (PL), the only party that would let him run.[67] He was simultaneously councilman, lawyer, and businessman, selling cornmeal, Volkswagens, and, later, real estate.[68] In 1966 he joined the MDB, mainly because most local factions had already joined ARENA. That year he was elected state deputy, and in 1968 he accepted an invitation to run for mayor of Campinas. Quércia suspected that the MDB had only invited him hoping to increase its vote total enough to elect one of its other two candidates.[69] Still he threw himself into campaigning. He was far from what the elites of this city built with coffee money thought a mayor should be, and he was endorsed by none of the local political factions. Quércia related that the current mayor visited local taverns and demurred that his candidate, the head of the local Jockey Club, wasn't the sort to campaign in bars. Quércia proudly visited the same bars, proclaiming himself a "bar candidate," unashamed to mingle with voters.[70] When he was not traveling from bar to bar, he was going house to house; he claimed to have personally visited five thousand families in their homes.

While the two other MDB candidates, campaigning during the Moreira Alves crisis, emphasized the struggle against "militarism," Quércia focused on education, public transportation, housing, and the cost of living, alongside the party's usual themes of indirect elections, attacks on civil liberties, and the increasing power of foreign corporations.[71] When the votes were counted, he had won more votes than the other candidates combined.[72] His victory was built on votes in working-class neighborhoods where his "man of the people" aura and focus on infrastructure and public health had resonated. "The people were tired of having the [same] old alternatives before them to choose between, alternatives that were nothing more than the city's old political forces that kept alternating in power," he said after the election.[73]

Quércia was ambitious, energetic, and a natural at using the tools of populist electoral politics that had developed in São Paulo between 1945 and 1964, through politicians such as Adhemar de Barros and Jânio Quadros. As mayor of Campinas, he emphasized efficient administration and public works. Since he "did not have an ideological conception of politics, but rather a strictly electoral one," Quércia avoided involving himself in MDB disputes. Instead, he exhibited an extraordinary ability to conciliate between party factions. He nurtured good relations with the PCB, which earned him a degree of trust from the MDB Left; in exchange, communists gained a patron in an opposition party dominated by traditional politicians. He also built relationships with intellectuals at the recently created State University of Campinas.[74]

Quércia's pragmatism hardly set him apart; indeed, the ability to navigate between factions is practically a requirement for politicians anywhere. Yet the waves of cassações had opened space for a new generation. And Quércia was a remarkably skilled negotiator and alliance builder. While not an adesista, his nonconfrontational approach toward the regime could anger autênticos and moderates alike. In 1968 he argued that his goal was "not to overthrow the government or conduct extremist agitation" but rather "create conditions for a [political] opening . . . through the party struggle, . . . even with help from the military."[75] Instead of focusing on attacks on civil liberties, Quércia emphasized that there were national problems beyond "direct elections and democratic freedom" and that "our task is to listen to the people's aspirations."[76] Two years later he held a convention for MDB mayors elected in 1972. The meeting produced the "Campinas Letter," which argued that the party should focus its energy on the everyday issues important to local politics.[77] Its tone was so conciliatory that even one of the most moderate MDB national leaders, Secretary General Thales Ramalho, fumed, "It clashes with . . . the MDB's platform, . . . its code of ethics, and its very principles."[78]

After his term ended in 1973, Quércia (whose anointed successor was elected with over 80 percent of the vote) set his sights on the MDB's Senate nomination in 1974. Yet as a journalist turned politician with few ties to the state's political elite (the reason he had entered the MDB to begin with), Quércia could expect no support from party leadership. Instead, he set about founding MDB directorates in municipalities where the party was not yet organized; as he built the party, he would also build a network of clients to support his own aspirations.[79] His message could be summarized as, "I'm going to the top, and I'll take you with me." He called on his allies in Campinas to organize directorates statewide. In larger cities, their task was easy, but in São Paulo's hundreds of small municipalities, they faced significant difficulties. As Quércia recalled, "Back then the campaign carried out against the MDB was to say that there was no use voting for the party, because [MDB] mayors wouldn't get anything from the government."[80] When the organizers arrived, they would first alert the ARENA mayor of their presence. They then searched for radio or press outlets known to be sympathetic to the MDB, or perhaps the local Catholic priest, and asked if they knew of anyone with a "spirit of opposition." The going was tough, since many people worried that the MDB was "a party full of subversives, full of communists." Sometimes, armed with only a name and address, they would ring a doorbell and ask whoever answered if they would like to join the MDB; often the resident "would run back inside . . . and talk to us through the little window in the door."[81]

Within a year, Quércia's team had expanded the number of MDB directorates in São Paulo from under two hundred to nearly five hundred. Not only would these directorates provide delegates to the 1974 convention that would select the party's Senate candidate, but they would also serve as a critical base of support for Quércia and other MDB candidates. Campaign events would finally be able to count on local members for on-the-ground planning, which might include services like notifying the ARENA mayor and police of a rally, procuring permits, arranging food and lodging for visiting bigwigs, and turning out a crowd. As Melhem puts it, "The party grew in the interior, but it was tangled up with local issues, with no ideological rigidity; its key point of reference was the dispute for the municipal administration."[82] And indeed, it appears that a "spirit of opposition" usually meant opposition to the ARENA faction in power locally, not the regime.[83] Quércia and his team quickly learned to start by reaching out to the ARENA candidate who had lost the 1972 mayoral election to another ARENA faction. Even if he did not join the MDB himself, he was often willing to provide names of people who might be interested.

Quércia's tireless work exemplified the bread and butter (or beans and rice) of Brazilian politics. While it was far from the lofty rhetoric and intraelite negotiation of someone like Guimarães, this was something local politicians could relate to. Even more important, it took advantage of the political space available during the most repressive years of military rule. Due to the military's dogged insistence on preserving parties and elections, this was a low-risk way to "oppose" the regime while advancing one's career. And this was something that the regime could do little about, because it was an "opposition" that challenged carefully if at all and focused on gaining electoral support through socioeconomic arguments and public works. Even if it could somehow cast such behavior as "subversive," the regime's repressive apparatus lacked the will or manpower to investigate so many local politicians. As the future would show, of the three opposition strategies, Quércia's would prove most effective.

"OUR PEOPLE ARE STILL AT A VERY LOW LEVEL": DÉTENTE AND "RELATIVE DEMOCRACY"

Thanks to Quércia and others like him, the MDB made significant strides; between 1971 and 1974 the party grew from 1,180 municipal directorates to more than 3,000 nationwide.[84] But how much good would this growth do if the regime remained as repressive as ever? Médici's term was set to expire in March 1974. After his unfulfilled promises to allow broadened participation for politicians, would his successor change anything? This question concerned both parties; after all, no matter how much arenistas enjoyed control of Congress and the governorships, they were no more satisfied than the MDB with military tutelage. Might Médici pick a successor who took more seriously politicians' desire to be entrusted with more influence? This was not just idle speculation, as it appeared that an eventual military retreat from direct political power might be on the table. In December 1971, General Alfredo Souto Malan stated at a ceremony promoting new generals, "The moment is in sight when the existence of sufficiently broad, diverse, and capable civilian groups will permit the military . . . to consider the prospect of . . . controlled disengagement."[85] However, although Army Minister Orlando Geisel was present at the speech, military contacts informed the US embassy that Médici was "incensed" and had "called [Geisel] on the carpet" for allowing it.[86] And even if the military were to withdraw from its decisive role in politics, what sort of system might replace it? No one knew.

In 1973 Médici's civilian chief of civilian staff, João Leitão de Abreu, asked the political scientist Samuel Huntington to offer an analysis of the Brazilian political situation. Although Médici did not implement any of Huntington's recommendations, the American scholar's confidential twelve-page report eventually served as a blueprint for his successor's "slow, gradual, and secure" liberalization.[87] Arguing that the current system was neither desirable nor sustainable, Huntington suggested three steps toward "decompression." First, he urged the institutionalization of a means of determining successions for executive offices, especially president. For Huntington, Mexico under the Revolutionary Institutional Party (PRI), where the president selected his successor (the *dedazo*) with input from an array of social groups (the military, labor unions, etc.), offered an example of this approach. Second, he suggested expanding the range of groups who had input on policy. Third, he advocated for "the liberalization of current restrictions on individual political and civil rights." The goal of these measures was not democracy but rather "assuring the stability of the government and preventing a possible return to the irresponsible and inefficient political conditions that prevailed before 1964." In other words, for Huntington and the generals who followed his advice, democracy and participation were not a goal but rather a means to consolidating the "Revolution."

But how to accomplish this? If the regime could not indefinitely impose its will through force, it would have to do it through party politics, specifically, through a regime-allied party. Mexico had done this through the PRI. However, ARENA lacked the internal coherence ascribed to Mexico's ruling party. "Brazilian political parties have always been weak," Huntington argued. "And the two parties today continue to be weak, because . . . they have been conceived of as simply electoral organizations intended to serve a populist project." What Brazil needed was parties that sought "to integrate, within the very party structure, organized social, economic, professional, and bureaucratic groups." The problem was that Brazil did not possess any such tradition. The solution was to create a new tradition: "a working political party that is tied to and bases itself on organized socioeconomic groups." This would require building on the corporatist tradition of the Vargas regime, in which businessmen, labor unions, farmers, the military, and other groups all felt they had a collective voice in policy making.[88] Prophetically, Huntington warned, "This may be the key for Brazil's political stability, because if the government does not do this in the coming years, the opposition certainly will."

Huntington's analysis demonstrated a remarkable grasp of the Brazilian political system for a novice. The problem lay with his solution of a coherent political party responsive to civil society. Huntington recognized that this was inconsistent with Brazilian political culture, but in keeping with his discipline's long-standing dismissive attitude toward culture, his answer was simply to turn ARENA into such a party. This solution was what the generals had dreamed of since party reorganization in 1965, a vision refined amid the repression of 1969. The problem was that neither Huntington nor the generals had any idea how to convince the political class to set aside its self-interest and rivalries and work together to represent society.

Since the regime currently lacked the kind of party foreign scholars thought it needed, for now it would have to make do with something well established in Brazilian tradition: Médici would select his own successor. In June 1973 Médici informed General Ernesto Geisel that he had chosen him.[89] The son of a German immigrant, Geisel had served as chief of military staff under Castelo Branco, but he was not close to Costa e Silva and spent his term as a justice of the Supreme Military Court. When Médici took office, Geisel received the important but politically isolated directorship of Petrobras, the state oil company. Along with his friend, the erudite, astute general Golbery do Couto e Silva, Geisel was known for his unyielding respect for the chain of command. Politicians had high hopes that Geisel might be a "liberal" who could offer an enhanced role for the political class. While his "liberalism" was far from a repudiation of the military tutelage that rankled politicians, perhaps he would deliver the limited return to "democracy" that Médici had promised. Though politicians could not have known it, in his initial meeting with Médici in Rio, Geisel allegedly refused to promise that he would not repeal AI-5, which, combined with his appointment of Golbery, an enemy of Médici, to the post of chief of civilian staff in his new administration, decisively demonstrated his independence.[90]

In his first cabinet meeting, Geisel promised a "sincere effort toward a gradual, but secure, perfection of democracy" based on "mutually respectful dialogue" that would foster "a healthy climate of basic consensus." In other words, the military would define "respectful dialogue" and "basic consensus" while allowing no substantive challenges to the "Revolution." With politicians now behaving better, this could involve the "greater participation from the responsible elites and the people." He hoped he would not have to use "exceptional instruments" like AI-5, but its repeal would be conditioned on "a creative political imagination, capable of instituting, at the opportune time, efficacious safeguards and prompt and truly efficient resources within the constitutional context."⁹¹ While the possibility of increased participation and the end of AI-5 was encouraging to politicians, it would require their continued good behavior.

No one, perhaps not even Geisel or Golbery, knew what this process would look like. Looking back, Geisel recalled, "We thought that when we left the government, the country would be more or less normalized. We didn't dare say, 'On such and such date, at such and such time, we're going to do this or that.'"⁹² They certainly did not have in mind a participatory democracy in any sense. Nor would the military tolerate a return to pre-1964 populist politics. Rather Geisel wanted what he later called a "relative democracy." Two decades later, he still insisted that European-style democracy could not work in Brazil, considering the "educational level, the mental level, the level of discernment, the economic level of the Brazilian people."⁹³ "I don't disagree that it's important to listen to the people," he stated, "but I believe that our people are still at a very low level. . . . Full, absolute democracy for Brazil is fiction. We must have democracy, we have to evolve toward a full democracy, but the stage we are at imposes certain limitations."⁹⁴ Under the system he envisioned, ordinary (literate) Brazilians could vote for municipal councils, state legislatures, Congress, and possibly also mayors. Yet the system would protect against their incompetence by preserving a powerful role for the military and controlling the selection of the president and governors. There was a place for a "responsible" opposition to offer "constructive" criticism but not unproductive and possibly subversive "contestation." Under no circumstances could the opposition come to power.⁹⁵ He wanted the "collaboration" of the political class and voters only if they never challenged him on anything he considered important and offered cautious criticism on specific policies without questioning the regime's legitimacy.

Private correspondence leaves little doubt that the new president and his advisers would have liked to keep the regime going indefinitely. In July 1974 Geisel's secretary, Heitor Ferreira, proposed changes to the terms of federal deputies in order to institute an electoral calendar favorable to the regime winning future elections. If his suggestions were adopted, he projected, the regime could continue through 2004 and beyond, with indirect elections for president and governors. "*If* it occurs like this, there will be no critical moments in sight. . . . The system can last." While the plan was never seriously considered, it demonstrates that indefinite indirect elections were anticipated, that it was considered feasible for Geisel to unilaterally amend the constitution, and that the regime would always be military dominated, since Ferreira mentioned problems posed by "factions formed by generals" attempting to influence indirect elections.⁹⁶ Whatever reforms Geisel had in mind, they fell far short of politicians' hopes.

Publicly, Geisel aroused further hopes in an August speech, when he referred to a "slow, gradual, and secure détente [*distensão*]" of the political system with "a maximum of possible economic, social, and political development and a minimum of indispensable security."[97] Distensão, with its fitful starts and the threat of "hardline" military backlash, is the key to understanding the remaining decade of the military regime. While sparking politicians' enthusiasm, Geisel's promises were tempered by warnings to "those who think to speed up this process by ... manipulating public opinion and, in doing so, [act] against the government."[98] The brilliance of Geisel's speeches was that one could read anything into them; officers distrustful of the political class were reassured that détente would not get out of control, and politicians could see the possibility of increased power. As an SNI report wryly noted, politicians were excited about a "perfection of democracy" but "abstained from commenting on the passages that allude to the responsibility that falls on the political class."[99]

Although Geisel's détente fell short of politicians' hopes, it was better than nothing. Golbery was so impressed with Huntington's report that he invited him to Brazil twice in 1974, where he queried him about the ideas contained in his paper.[100] In August Golbery met with São Paulo bishop Paulo Evaristo Arns, a persistent advocate for political prisoners.[101] In a meeting with Guimarães and Ramalho in early 1975, Golbery assured them that Geisel wanted to repeal AI-5, abolish the two-party system, and offer amnesty to those affected by the institutional acts. Golbery swore Guimarães and Ramalho to secrecy; as Guimarães would recall, "We left that meeting like the apostles after seeing the Transfiguration on Mount Tabor. Absolutely dazzled, holders of information as extraordinary as it was enrapturing, with the same recommendation as in the gospel: 'Tell no one what ye have seen.'"[102]

The strategy Geisel and Golbery followed sought to normalize the regime's relationship with corporatist groups, including the political class. Détente would reward politicians for their progress but without offering significant independence. As Santa Catarina ARENA deputy Aroldo Carvalho understood it, "Decompression is among the strategic objectives of the Brazilian Revolution. The behavior of politicians ... can offer evidence to the President of the Republic not only of the maturation of the political class, but above all of its qualification to lend its effective collaboration to those who direct the nation."[103] However, as Huntington's paper prefigured, under no circumstances should détente lead to a challenge to the "Revolution," and its triple pillars: development, security, and political reform. Any military "disengagement" was contingent on the political class accepting this model.

CONCLUSIONS

Between 1969 and 1974 the military implemented almost unopposed its plan to transform Brazil, and by 1974 it appeared it had been successful. Breathtaking economic growth, the defeat of "subversion," and meek politicians convinced many in the military that the "Revolution" was succeeding. A few noisy autênticos and some opportunists building directorates in the interior were hardly cause for concern. Yet all was not as it appeared. If the political class bowed to military tutelage, it was because they saw it not as proper but as necessary, and they pushed back to the extent they could. A few, like the autênticos, chose to courageously remind the generals of the illegitimacy of their rule. Others, like Quércia, opted to work behind the scenes to build up their personal following, aggressively pursuing their own advancement. Most, including most of ARENA's membership, resisted by doing as they always had: refusing to bury their rivalries and quietly hoping that they might one day again enjoy their old privileges. As ARENA senator Clodomir Millet put it in a meeting of ARENA legislators in the early 1970s, "We are politicians. We know what we want, and we know how far we can go under the circumstances. . . . Let's be coherent, and, at the same time, show that we are enlightened."[104] Or as ARENA's Filinto Müller told another meeting of legislators in 1972, their "common objective" was to "consolidate and enlarge our parliamentary prerogatives."[105]

But neither Médici nor Geisel appears to have fully appreciated just how strategic most politicians' acceptance of military tutelage was. Certainly some arenistas were enthusiastic about military rule, either because they genuinely believed in the military's ostensibly reformist project or because they enjoyed their proximity to power. And Quércia's strategy to accept the "Revolution" as a fait accompli fulfilled the generals' wish for an opposition that avoided "contestation" in favor of constructive criticism. Surrounded as they were by some who flattered them, others who opposed them within the rules, and a majority that appeared to have accepted military tutelage, it is little wonder that Geisel and Golbery judged it safe to relax authoritarian rule. This was not a concession from above, for at the height of the regime's power, no concessions were necessary. Rather it was an expression of both the regime's confidence in the success of its political model and its unease with an illiberal political system that placed heavy constraints on politics. Had the regime not proved itself worthy of politicians' support and the people's vote? But the generals would soon discover just how badly they had miscalculated.

5

"We Aren't a Flock of Little Sheep"

The Political Class and the Limits of Liberalization

As he left a dinner with Ulysses Guimarães, the sociologist Fernando Henrique Cardoso was uneasy. Cardoso, who came from a military family, had been forcibly retired from his post at the University of São Paulo by AI-5 in 1969.[1] After returning from exile, the co-formulator of dependency theory had helped found the Brazilian Center for Analysis and Planning (CEBRAP). At their early 1974 private dinner, Guimarães asked Cardoso to help develop a campaign strategy for that year's legislative elections. Speaking as one of the intellectuals who had opposed the regime in the 1960s, Cardoso recalled later, "We didn't trust the MDB, or parties in general. . . . We thought they were just a tool for the dictatorship to legitimate itself."[2] Guimarães shared Cardoso's unease, and afterward he asked a friend, "Look, all this about sociology, sociologists, socialism . . . these people aren't communists, are they?"[3]

Despite the reservations of Cardoso and Guimarães, the MDB's openness to new collaborators and strategies would constitute a turning point in the military regime. Starting with the 1974 elections, the MDB complemented its "monophonic plainsong" criticizing the regime's assault on liberal democracy with a focus on the socioeconomic issues that mattered most to voters—and it paid off.[4] Characteristically, the military responded with repression, not by annulling the elections, but by persecuting the leftists the generals believed had shaped the MDB's campaign. Yet this repression only further alienated already disillusioned politicians. Fearing that its project could be unraveling, the military resorted to extralegal measures to stack the deck for ARENA. But this too could backfire, as it did in 1978 when arenista Paulo Maluf defied the generals by running for governor of São Paulo against their anointed candidate. Faced with a resurgent opposition and restless allies, along with a declining economy, a regime that had looked unassailable in 1974 suddenly looked vulnerable.

"BRAZIL IS DOING WELL. ARE YOU?" 1974 AND THE REBIRTH OF THE MDB

Held eight months after Geisel took office, the November 1974 elections would select one-third of the Senate, the entire Chamber of Deputies, and all state deputies. As the only races pitting one ARENA candidate against one emedebista, those for the Senate assumed importance as a reflection of voters' attitudes toward the regime.[5] This time, in contrast to 1970, when harassment of its candidates had likely contributed to the MDB's atrocious showing, Geisel wanted the MDB to perform better, thereby strengthening Brazil's democratic credentials. As he told his secretary, "The victory over the MDB has to happen in such a way that it doesn't liquidate the party."[6] Many in the military and security apparatus supported this approach. An SNI report predicted that the elections would bring about "the desired valorization of the parties and politicians," enabling them to "contribute to the perfecting of the regime" while "demonstrat[ing] . . . creativity, not contestation, much less subversion."[7]

A free election was feasible precisely because the MDB's prospects were so poor. In August the magazine *Visão* predicted, "Even if [ARENA] loses two or three seats in the Senate and another ten in the Chamber of Deputies (which would be a surprise), this would not affect its formal dominion and the . . . impotence of the opposition."[8] The regime had presided over half a decade of double-digit economic growth, and inflation had (at least officially) fallen to historically low levels. If the military had resorted to torture and disappearances to eliminate the armed Left, for most Brazilians this only meant that they no longer had to worry about "terrorist" acts. As São Paulo's vice governor-elect put it, "A protest vote is inadmissible because . . . we are doing fine. You don't protest against what is good."[9] In September ARENA's national president, Piauí senator Petrônio Portella, predicted that his party would win the Senate races in every state except Guanabara.[10] More cautious members of party leadership admitted that of the twenty-two states, five presented serious difficulties for their candidates.[11]

But the party remained riven by personal rivalries, exacerbated by the gubernatorial selection process earlier that year. Geisel had sent Portella to each state to ascertain the political class's preference for their next governor, who would be "elected" by the ARENA-dominated state legislatures.[12] Yet consensus proved elusive. In Pernambuco, after four former governors were unable to agree on a name, Portella was met at the airport by fourteen prospective candidates sprinting across the runway to try for the first handshake.[13] In the end, he chose the one who appeared to have the broadest support, but Senator Etelvino Lins was so upset with the selection that he refused to run for reelection.[14] In São Paulo, after Portella met with the current governor, Laudo Natel, state deputies, and business leaders, the consensus choice was Delfim Neto, Médici's renowned finance minister. Instead Portella announced that Geisel had chosen the little-known Paulo Egydio Martins,

Castelo Branco's minister of industry and commerce.[15] As one senator remarked, "Consensus is what they call it when Petrônio Portella brings us a name, and no one's stupid enough to say they're against it."[16] Still, to placate ARENA factions whose candidates were not chosen for governor, Portella and Geisel often agreed to give them the Senate candidacy as a consolation prize. While this may have soothed ARENA egos, it meant that faction was prioritized over electability. And with their own positions secure, incoming governors might avoid supporting the Senate candidate, preferring the MDB to a rival arenista.[17] But at the time, none of these problems seemed significant.

Meanwhile, the MDB's outlook was bleak. In September Guimarães proclaimed, "What the MDB aims for isn't electoral success but, above all, that of the ideas and theses we defend."[18] Given regime intimidation, voter apathy, and candidate recruitment difficulties, his attitude was understandable. Though repression was reduced compared to 1970, it did not disappear. In July Justice Minister Armando Falcão asked the attorney general to instruct regional electoral prosecutors to challenge the candidacies of politicians "compromised by corruption or subversion."[19] In October Bahia autêntico deputy Francisco Pinto was expelled from Congress and imprisoned for six months after a March congressional speech in which he called General Augusto Pinochet, head of the Chilean junta, a fascist and "the cruelest of the characters who have tyrannized Latin America over the past few decades."[20] Candidate recruitment presented another difficulty. Few established politicians wanted to join a party that by design could never come to power and had been embarrassed in the past two elections. Things looked no better in 1974; in São Paulo, while Quércia sought to become the Senate nominee, April opinion polls gave his ARENA opponent, incumbent senator Carlos de Carvalho Pinto, a 75 to 7 percent advantage.[21] By September São Paulo senator André Franco Montoro, the MDB's campaign coordinator, guaranteed victory in only four Senate races and ventured that the party had a good chance in four more.[22] To achieve even these modest goals, the MDB would have to convince skeptical voters that it was not just "a tool for the dictatorship to legitimate itself." In 1970 blank and spoiled ballots nationwide had outnumbered the MDB's votes; that is, voters opposed to the regime would rather vote for no one than for the MDB.

Party leaders thus began to craft a nationally coordinated campaign message. Criticism of "political" issues like indirect elections, AI-5, and even torture had not resonated in 1970, and this time they faded into the background. Instead the MDB opted to expand its appeal to working-class voters. MDB leadership thus initiated contact with CEBRAP. Despite initial misgivings, for intellectuals who had been summarily dismissed from their university positions, it must have been exhilarating to be invited to influence public discourse. Besides, many at CEBRAP had been impressed by the anti-candidacy, and when they met Guimarães, they discovered that they had more in common than they expected. Ultimately, they wrote a campaign manual linking political issues with socioeconomic ones such as "the high cost of living, the disparities in income distribution, the tight wage policy . . . , the increasing incursions of foreign capital into the Brazilian industrial sector, and excessive centralization."[23] This approach ought not upset the military; after all, wasn't the stated purpose of the MDB to identify policies that needed improvement? As Montoro explained, the MDB simply "disagrees with the government every time it sees the people's interests harmed."[24] He repeated, "We are not putting the Revolution on trial. . . . Our enemy is not the government . . . but ARENA."[25]

Yet candidates remained hard to come by. In São Paulo, the ideal Senate candidate would be Guimarães, who had the name recognition to challenge Carvalho Pinto. But Guimarães refused. His reelection to the Chamber was certain; why would he serve as a sacrificial lamb in an unwinnable race? When Montoro reminded him of his words, "It is necessary to navigate, it is not necessary to live," Guimarães retorted, "At least a cautious man dies of old age."[26] In Rio Grande do Norte, "for absolute lack of anyone else who dared perform the role," the candidacy went to Agenor Maria, a former sailor, street vendor, and one-term ARENA federal deputy who was currently working as a truck driver.[27] His opponent, federal deputy Djalma Marinho, dismissed Maria out of hand. "I could never debate that boy. I have nothing to learn from him, and I'm too old to teach him anything."[28] In Paraná, Furtado also turned down the Senate candidacy; forty-one years later he admitted that he saw no reason to give up sure reelection to the Chamber to lose a Senate race.[29] The MDB also struggled to find candidates for deputy. In São Paulo, the party managed to recruit only forty-six candidates for federal deputy—barely half the eighty-six permitted by law.[30] In only two states did the opposition manage as many federal candidates as ARENA; in only one did the MDB run an equal number of state candidates.[31]

Candidate registration data at the São Paulo Regional Electoral Court (TRE-SP) reflect these difficulties, showing that the MDB fielded a slate of relative outsiders. For example, the MDB had a higher percentage of candidates under forty: 28.3 percent of federal deputy candidates versus 23.2 percent for ARENA; for state deputy, it was 39.1 percent versus 27.5 percent.[32] In addition, MDB candidates' occupations were less prestigious. While liberal professions (lawyers, doctors, engineers, economists, and teachers) were the largest occupational group in both parties, ARENA had many more such candidates.[33] The MDB slate included travel agents, carpet makers, elevator operators, drivers, electricians, filmmakers, and designers, careers seldom associated with political aspirations in Brazil.[34] MDB candidates were also less wealthy. Candidates were required to submit a declaration of assets listing the values of their land, houses, businesses, cars, jewelry, telephone lines, bank accounts, stocks, livestock, and so on. While 46.5 percent of ARENA federal candidates and 40.2 percent of state candidates claimed fewer than ten assets, 62.2 percent of MDB federal candidates and 74.6 percent of state candidates claimed fewer than ten.[35] These differences did not mean that the MDB was more open to nontraditional candidates but rather how limited its pool of potential candidates was. The party's discomfort with outsiders was thrown into vivid relief by its reaction to Quércia's Senate candidacy. Despite adopting his electoral strategy, party leadership attempted to block him from securing the nomination by launching a (failed) rival candidacy at the August São Paulo convention. While Quércia tactfully attributed their resistance to fear that an unknown politician could not beat Carvalho Pinto, the real issue was that he was an outsider from humble origins.[36]

Low expectations notwithstanding, Quércia and the MDB campaign would distinguish themselves with something uncommon in a country where personality tends to trump party: a unified message. In São Paulo, on September 12, the MDB gathered ten of its Senate candidates, a collection of state and federal deputies, and over a dozen presidents of state directorates. The attendees approved a statement endorsing "the struggle of the Brazilian people for development with democracy" and promised to work for "a better distribution of income, wage policy appropriate for the pace of Brazilian development, and the direction . . . of greater resources toward the education, health, and housing sectors."[37] Candidates received a CEBRAP-authored booklet filled with slogans, advice on how to use free television time, and statistics on the cost of living.[38] In response to government claims that per capita income was rising, candidates were instructed to highlight the unequal distribution of wealth: "What does per capita income mean? It's the average between someone who makes a million, and someone who makes 200. The average is good, but one is dying of hunger, while the other has everything"; or, "If I eat one chicken and you don't eat a chicken, on average we're each eating half a chicken."[39] When the party opened its São Paulo campaign headquarters, an overflow crowd listened to Guimãraes, Montoro, Quércia, and others decry the cost of living.[40] This focus was repeated by candidates across the state and probably the entire country. MDB campaign materials collected by air force intelligence in the city of São José dos Campos, for example, repeated the same themes.[41] To keep the campaign coordinated, party leadership agreed to meet weekly at Montoro's home to evaluate the previous week's developments.[42]

To introduce himself to the electorate, Quércia traveled across the state. At every stop, he emphasized face-to-face contact with voters. On a typical day, he traveled to Santos, where he met with coffee brokers, mingled with the populace as he walked to the municipal market, opened two campaign offices, greeted workers at the offices of the Santos Docks Company, visited working-class neighborhoods, met a commuter train to greet steelworkers, inaugurated another campaign office in nearby Cubatão, and concluded with visits to Praia Grande and Cidade Ocian.[43] At each stop, he reiterated the MDB's message. In the Paraíba Valley, he criticized "the ever higher concentration of wealth in the hands of an ever smaller minority."[44] In São Bernardo, he promised workers, "The fight against the current wage policy, the lack of assistance through social security, and the many other catastrophes that afflict the Brazilian worker cause constant concern in our struggle."[45] At the same time, he emphasized these issues alongside the party's usual themes; on a trip to Americana, "he brought up the principal themes of the MDB campaign, like development with social justice, the cost of living, the participation of students in national politics, and direct elections."[46] It was a brilliant strategy that appealed both to principled opponents of the military's assault on civil liberties and voters concerned with their day-to-day struggles without arousing the direct ire of the repressive apparatus.

ARENA's campaign could hardly have been more different. The opening of its São Paulo campaign office attracted a smaller than expected crowd that had to be entertained by a professional "crowd exciter" while awaiting tardy politicians.[47] ARENA's statewide campaign launch in Bauru fell similarly flat, perhaps because the party scheduled it at the same time as a television *novela*.[48] These hiccups set the tone for a campaign beset by difficulties accidental, idiosyncratic, and petty. The problems began with the Senate candidate himself. Carvalho Pinto came from one of the state's most venerable families; his father had been a state deputy; his grandfather, a senator; and his great-uncle Francisco Rodrigues Alves, president of Brazil from 1906 to 1912. And he himself had served as governor from 1958 to 1962. In 1963 he was invited to be Goulart's finance minister, but during the coup he sided with the military. Yet he always numbered among the regime's conditional "liberal" supporters; he nearly joined the MDB in 1966, and after AI-5, he had signed Krieger's telegram decrying the act.[49]

Whatever his feelings toward the regime, Carvalho Pinto was an elitist liberal to his core. Whereas Quércia spoke of empowering ordinary people to participate in politics, Carvalho Pinto spoke of teaching an ill-prepared electorate to accept limited democracy. "Democracy ... belongs to adults," he intoned, "and its authenticity depends on a permanent educative effort." While Quércia decried the effects of inflation on salaries, Carvalho Pinto pompously spoke of "the definitive institutionalization of the principles of the Revolution of 1964," now that the "stages of political-administrative cleansing and socioeconomic propulsion ... have come to a victorious conclusion."[50] Humble origins and years of door-to-door campaigning had endowed Quércia with the same language as voters; Carvalho Pinto struggled to shed his aristocratic image. Worse, he and his party ran a tone-deaf campaign that underestimated voters' capacity to make an informed decision. Geisel, ARENA, and Carvalho Pinto may have thought that working-class voters could not be trusted to vote "responsibly," but they forgot to ask the most important question: Did voters believe themselves incompetent?

Things soon went from bad to worse. In mid-September, not even a week into the official campaign, ARENA leadership decided that the Carvalho Pinto campaign needed "dynamism" and resolved to revamp his campaign strategy, a move repeated a month later. The initial reset kept Carvalho Pinto in his office, where he would receive visits from politicians from across the state; the second isolated him from voters and politicians alike in favor of a focus on recording TV ads.[51] The second reset was due in part to an inopportune illness that led the candidate to pull back from active campaigning. "The campaign is going well, it will be victorious, and there's no need for me to appear at rallies," he explained.[52]

In Carvalho Pinto's absence, the coordination of ARENA's São Paulo campaign fell to Paulo Egydio Martins, Geisel's designated governor. The forty-six-year-old Martins had gotten his start in politics as a university student; he had subsequently managed various mining firms, his business aspirations aided by his marriage into a family of industrialists. He had participated actively in plotting the coup, and after an unsuccessful run for mayor of São Paulo with the UDN in 1965, he was named industry and commerce minister for the remaining year of the Castelo Branco government. As minister, he became friends with Geisel, then chief of military staff, and the two remained in touch over the coming years.[53] While Martins was competent, committed, and well connected, he was a relative novice to campaigning, and he displayed an alarming propensity to make ill-advised off-the-cuff comments.

Martins criticized fellow arenistas, particularly businessmen, for blaming the regime for slowing economic growth instead of the global downturn resulting from the oil shock. "Until now," he claimed, "this class has . . . benefited from the economic stability the government achieved, and now, suddenly, just because they can't make as much money as they used to, they want to protest."[54] He compared a vote for Quércia to a vote for Cacareco, the zoo rhinoceros who had received over a hundred thousand protest votes in São Paulo's 1958 municipal elections.[55] "The vote isn't a weapon of protest," he argued. "It will not be possible to form a political consciousness in this country if the voters act like children."[56] Détente presumed that voters had matured sufficiently to realize that ARENA was the right choice. As for the MDB, he interpreted their focus on socioeconomic issues as a throwback to Brazil's populist past, perpetrated by "weak men who use the language of the past to . . . turn the people aside from the right path."[57]

Other prominent arenistas did little to help Carvalho Pinto. After belatedly endorsing Carvalho Pinto, federal deputy Adhemar de Barros Filho, son of the former governor, stated that his priority was "electing the greatest number of colleagues from the same political origin," that is, his old party. Supporting ARENA meant helping one's own allies and no one else.[58] The current governor, Laudo Natel, was similarly tepid, probably because as an *adhemarista* (Adhemar de Barros supporter) he was loath to support Carvalho Pinto, a disciple of Jânio Quadros. By late October, *Veja* reported as common knowledge that Carvalho Pinto's candidacy was in trouble because of the "indifference of various sectors of the party, and above all of the current governor."[59] At the same time that the generals promised an increased role for ARENA, détente showed its fundamental contradiction, for it demanded a sense of loyalty and self-sacrifice uncommon among many arenistas.

Nationally, ARENA was beset by these same problems. Some, like tense coexistence with former enemies, had been problems in past elections. Others took on heightened significance amid détente and a nascent economic downturn. ARENA had grown complacent, confident that the military would ensure its victories. More seriously, by persecuting the most principled opponents of their rule, the generals had attracted precisely the politicians they claimed to wish to eliminate: opportunists whose most notable quality was their boundless ability to say yes. Yet as the economic "miracle" began to fade and the opposition highlighted the uneven distribution of its benefits, ARENA politicians faced an unresolvable quandary. To which of their constituencies should they cater, the military or voters? When some government allies opted to court their voters, with a message suspiciously like the opposition's, Guimarães scoffed, "They all remained in Congress . . . these last few years without taking any measures to correct what they now consider a mistake. When they come out in favor of changes, they are either betraying the government to which they owe loyalty, or the electorate."[60] Deputy Aldo Fagundes smirked, "I'm sure it isn't easy to defend the refusal to keep wages even with inflation, exchange rate indexation, the uncontrolled increase in the cost of living, housing policy, the foreign debt, and the progressive transfer of our national riches to multinational corporations."[61] Even Portella, ARENA's president, grumbled that it was "inadmissible [to] publicly defend the opposition's position . . . with the aim of gaining electoral profits."[62]

By the eve of the election, there were abundant signs of concern for ARENA and optimism for the MDB. While the opposition had run a unified campaign focused on the day-to-day issues that affected voters, ARENA had been hampered by its rivalries and the contradiction between supporting the government and attracting voters. But how much difference would any of these factors make? Most voters did not attend rallies or read newspapers; what difference would it make to them if the old governor was helping the new one or if Carvalho Pinto could campaign in person? As the campaign neared a close, however, the effects of a new variable were only beginning to become clear: television.

The electoral code (as amended in 1966) required stations to set aside one hour of electoral programming per party during the afternoon and another in prime time.[63] The parties could use their hours as they wished—short films, Q&A sessions with voters, debates, or segments for individual candidates. While in 1966 there had been only 2,334,000 television sets in Brazil, by 1974 the number had risen to 8,781,000.[64] Although this represented fewer than one set for every ten Brazilians, the new medium provoked excitement among politicians comparable to that generated by social media a generation later. With a few minutes on television, a candidate could reach more voters than in months of grueling campaigning. With every point it climbed in the ratings, a party in São Paulo city gained thirty thousand viewers, a nearly unachievable number for rallies.[65] While radio projected a disembodied voice, television allowed candidates to create a visual persona. Still, politicians had little experience with this relatively new technology. A US political scientist who sat in on a television planning session noted that parties formulated strategy without viewer data or feedback.[66] Performing on camera also presented difficulties. Quércia admitted, "I really did have problems with television at the start of the campaign. . . . It was hard to work with all those people standing there, looking. I always felt better at rallies, being able to feel the reaction of the people I was speaking to."[67]

If the advantage from television belonged to either party, it was not the MDB. In São Paulo, the MDB recorded a film of Quércia walking and driving through downtown São Paulo, buying newspapers and being mobbed by adoring children—an attempt to present him as a man of the people.[68] The party also designed a cartoon with a talking sun telling candidates to vote for the MDB.[69] The talking sun was of poor quality, however, and since the cash-strapped party had spent less than a fifth as much as ARENA, the MDB could not afford to make more films.[70] Instead, they played the Quércia film so much that arenistas snickered that their message was, "Vote for Quércia. If you don't, he'll never stop riding around in a van and buying newspapers."[71] The ads did at least make Quércia into a star; when he arrived in Votuporanga, five hundred kilometers from the capital, fans surrounded his car requesting not speeches but autographs.[72]

Meanwhile, ARENA, with the help of an advertising firm headed by a former ARENA municipal councilor, recorded a greater variety of ads in São Paulo, including a series of images of the public works of the "Revolution" followed by an image of Carvalho Pinto. Another featured a boy explaining why his father was voting for Carvalho Pinto.[73] ARENA also collected documentaries about grinding poverty in the rest of the world, thinking to highlight the government's success at keeping Brazil immune from the global economic crisis—a strategy of dubious wisdom since working-class Brazilians who could ill afford rice and beans were unlikely to believe that the regime had defeated poverty at home.[74]

Had the election been carried out as a traditional campaign, ARENA, with its superior organization and funds, would have held an overwhelming edge. Television diminished that disadvantage. In Rio de Janeiro, the MDB's Roberto Saturnino Braga, a former one-term federal deputy, was facing Senator Paulo Torres, president of Congress. "I, who never knew how to build a political machine, . . . was greatly benefited by TV," Braga claimed. "One week after my candidacy was launched, the entire state of Rio had heard my name."[75] Only a year before, Quércia had observed an association between the MDB and subversion. Yet now, even if the MDB's message or technical quality was no more convincing, the fact that they were allowed to campaign on equal terms was a victory.[76] Ultimately television leveled the playing field.

By November it was clear that the MDB stood a better chance than expected. Representatives of the US consulate in São Paulo visited the state's largest cities and reported that a Quércia victory was likely, due to "a growing protest vote against the government's failure to come to grips with the deteriorating economic situation." Local ARENA leaders confided to the consulate that all was lost; one predicted a 3:1 margin for Quércia.[77] A poll the day before the election gave Quércia a 61 to 33 percent advantage.⁷⁸ Meanwhile, ARENA representatives from several states informed Portella that strong MDB candidacies had been contained, and Portella assured Geisel that the party feared no "compromising" defeats. Still, as the vice governor–elect of Minas sagely noted, nothing was certain: "The mind of a judge, the womb of a woman, and the ballot box—you don't know anything until they're opened."⁷⁹

There was nothing to distinguish election day under a military dictatorship from the 1945–64 "Populist Republic." *Cabos eleitorais* (allies of candidates who do the legwork of attracting voters) hovered outside polling places, passing out flyers and shouting the virtues of their candidates. At times they were joined by candidates seeking to eke out votes at the "mouth of the ballot box" (*boca de urna*).⁸⁰ Long lines greeted voters early in the morning; middle-class voters wanted to vote early so they could leave the city for a long weekend, and working-class voters, as one bar employee put it, "are already used to waking up early and getting in line."⁸¹

The next morning, with the tally barely begun, exit polls showed Quércia winning by 66 to 29 percent in the capital, with similar margins in other key cities. Even more shocking, the polls showed almost identical margins in the races for federal and state deputy.⁸² Partial results from Brazil's largest polling firm predicted that Quércia would carry the state by a 60–31 margin.⁸³ Nationwide, the MDB won sixteen of the twenty-two open Senate seats. In Santa Catarina, polls had predicted a twenty-point victory for ARENA, but when the votes were counted, the MDB had won by five. A late October poll in Paraná had shown a six-point advantage for ARENA; the MDB won by three.⁸⁴ The MDB also seized an outright majority in six state legislatures and Chamber of Deputies delegations, which meant that even if the next gubernatorial elections were indirect, the party would elect several governors, including in São Paulo, Rio de Janeiro, and Rio Grande do Sul. The opposition nearly doubled its representation in the Chamber, to 160 of 364 seats (44 percent), ending ARENA's supermajority. While ARENA still controlled the governorships, sixteen state legislatures, and Congress, its confidence was severely shaken.

How had this happened? With leftist "subversion" defeated and the economy on solid footing, voters were expected to continue to support the regime. Instead, ARENA had lost the national Senate vote by 4.5 million votes and only outpolled the MDB by one million in the Chamber. The MDB had nearly tripled its Senate representation and fell fewer than twenty-five seats short of a majority in the Chamber. SNI director, General João Batista Figueiredo, undoubtedly spoke for many when he fumed, "These shitty people don't know how to vote."⁸⁵ Geisel's secretary sneered, "What can you expect from an electorate like this, from little people like these?"⁸⁶

Two days later an SNI report grumbled, "In order for the vote to achieve its true role, it would be necessary for it to be free, but also, and above all, that it be enlightened." Of the report's thirteen suggested causes of the disaster, eight blamed the political class, including its "discontent with the secondary role to which it was relegated under the previous government." The parties shared the blame: the MDB for its subversion, ARENA for its lack of unity. "In the quest for the vote, on one side were those who could give a complete outlet for their demagogic impulses; on the other, those who had their demagoguery barely contained by constantly disrespected party commitments." The MDB's focus on socioeconomic inequality was really a "broad movement of contestation [and a] fruitful campaign of disinformation." As for ARENA, "no one imagined that that the party would be reduced to such a low level through the behavior of incapable and neglectful leaders and the lack of party unity." Significantly, the regime itself did not escape blame, as it had not done enough to replace "discredited names" with new leaders.[87] And in response to Geisel's secretary's snide question about what else one could expect from "little people," Golbery responded, "That by practicing, they'll get better at it."[88] Significantly, after a dramatic electoral defeat, an SNI report and a general in the regime's highest echelon still held to the military dream of reforming politics, if only everyone implicated with the past could be removed or reformed and voters could learn to vote "correctly."

Arenista explanations for the bloodbath naturally emphasized factors beyond the party's control. Carvalho Pinto blamed voters for lacking "a rational and broad view of the country's interests."[89] Others, who had future elections to run in and could ill afford to blame voter stupidity, cited other reasons beyond their control, especially a wave of global protest votes in 1974 in places such as the United States, France, and West Germany.[90] Privately, Chamber president, Flávio Marcílio, told his US embassy contacts that the defeat should be interpreted in light of the overthrow of authoritarian regimes in Greece and Portugal.[91] A few, including São Paulo senator Orlando Zancaner, insisted that the MDB had won because crafty leftists, adept at manipulating voters with socioeconomic arguments, had infiltrated it.[92]

These explanations all located the cause in the political context of 1974 rather than flaws in the regime's political model. Some arenistas were more honest. Several admitted that the opposition's focus on socioeconomic issues had been wise and that the MDB had presented its case in accessible language while ARENA addressed the middle and upper classes.[93] Many also cited divisions that had led some arenistas to fight each other more than the MDB.[94] Members of the old PSD grumbled that the UDN had been too dominant in ARENA, and their intransigence had led them to dismiss the MDB's message. If ARENA's leaders had demonstrated the flexibility of the former *pessedista* (PSD member) Guimarães, for example, the disaster might have been averted.[95] Or perhaps the fault belonged to party leadership (and the regime) for imposing candidates based on personal considerations rather than the will of the majority.[96]

A few ARENA leaders dared fault major regime figures. Senator Helvídio Nunes of Piauí blamed their privileging of technocrats at the expense of proven vote getters.[97] In the same vein, Maranhão senator José Sarney argued, "You can't practice politics without politicians. The Revolution in all its greatness will also have to recognize that a structure from a period of compression doesn't work during one of decompression."[98] That is, even if ARENA needed to change, the regime must also rethink its relationship with the political class. And while ARENA had proven its loyalty time and again, instead of reciprocating with trust of its own, the regime had imposed inviable candidates to placate political rivals. The only way to avoid this in the future would be to stop simply being the "government's party."[99]

MDB politicians like Guimarães, whose anti-candidacy had energized the opposition; Quércia, who had built the party in the country's largest state; and Montoro, the 1974 campaign coordinator, were eager to claim credit publicly and privately.[100] And the results that for ARENA were a sign of the Brazilian people's lack of political consciousness were for the MDB a sign of maturity: not demagoguery, but rather rational people voting in accordance with their interests. As Montoro explained, "More than the victory of parties or candidates, the elections ... represent a vigorous affirmation of the Brazilian consciousness and the maturity of the Brazilian people."[101] The results constituted "a revolution through the vote."[102]

Yet even as they reveled in their victory, MDB politicians struck a conciliatory tone. In a meeting with US diplomats, Montoro emphasized (in their paraphrase), "Now that the MDB campaign had been so successful, it would be foolish to adopt a vindictive tone, thus giving the military the opportunity to annul the election results and to thwart the prospects for a strengthened democracy."[103] Tancredo Neves reiterated that the MDB had always aimed for "responsible and constructive opposition" and that it would continue to reject "revenge and a yearning for bygone days."[104] Guimarães stated, "We do not intend to create obstacles or wage war between branches of government; besides, that would be unpatriotic." He believed that the military would not annul the elections on these grounds: "We never made slanderous or defamatory attacks. We never created tumult in parliamentary work.... What we want is dialogue."[105]

The willingness of some ARENA leaders to blame the government and the MDB's insistence that it would not rock the boat show that the two parties were not so far apart. While many arenistas may indeed have been less uncomfortable with indirect elections or human rights violations and while many emedebistas may have had a sincere desire to address social inequality, the political class was united in its desire to convince the military that its members had learned their lesson and could be allowed to reestablish their prerogatives.

The "maturity" displayed by both parties bore almost immediate fruit. In a late November speech, Brigadier Osvaldo Terra de Faria praised the elections for "fulfill[ing] the civic calendar of political renovation" and facilitating the "emergence of new leaders," something made possible by politicians' having changed their ways:[106] "If in the beginning the followers of unconditional liberalism ...

did not submit themselves to the . . . pedagogical-corrective process, today they have grasped the . . . rise of pragmatic Brazilian liberalism, which harmonizes . . . development and security, freedom and responsibility . . . in unwavering pursuit of a greater objective."[107]

Geisel's televised end-of-year address offered more evidence that the military did not see the elections as a repudiation. Indeed, they had proven the regime's commitment to democracy. He praised the MDB for its "moderation and self-discipline and abandonment of a "posture of contestation" while chastising ARENA for "benefitting—or perhaps we should say wearing itself out—from a long period of comfortable but softening majority status." Still, he warned the MDB that he would not tolerate "irresponsible attitudes of pure contestation."[108] Elections and politicians were important, but the game would be played on the military's terms.

Geisel's warning was a harbinger of things to come. In the face of this defeat, the regime resorted to increasingly desperate means to retain power. Not everyone in the military supported détente, and they would stop at nothing—even murder— to neutralize their foes. And even Geisel, who at least outwardly was more concerned than Médici with gaining the collaboration of the political class, was happy to remove his harshest critics from Congress and rewrite electoral law to obtain desired results. Two events, in 1975 and 1977, made it clear just how far the regime would go in its attempt to save its "Revolution" from collapse. As the former federal deputy Marco Antônio Tavares Coelho put it years later, "Political victories have a flip-side: . . . a wounded enemy is more dangerous."[109]

THE LIMITS OF DÉTENTE: THE MILITARY OVERREACTS TO THE 1974 ELECTIONS

While politicians tended to interpret the elections as a sign that their prerogatives might someday be restored, some in the military saw sinister forces at work: communists. While communists have long been a scapegoat on whom the Brazilian military and middle and upper classes have cast blame for everything from changing sexual mores to economic troubles, supposed communist plots have nearly always been exaggerated or invented.[110] The rare cases of actual subversion, such as the armed struggle of 1968–74, never threatened the regime. Yet this time the generals were partially right: members of the Soviet-aligned PCB assisted the MDB campaign, and a few were elected. Alberto Marcelo Gato, former president of the Santos metallurgical workers' union, was elected federal deputy from São Paulo; his fellow PCB militant Alberto Goldman had already been elected state deputy in 1970. The PCB's strategy of participating in elections differed markedly from their Chinese-aligned rivals in the Communist Party of Brazil (PCdoB), whose armed struggle the regime had liquidated mercilessly.

But why would the MDB, made up of ideologically flexible adesistas, liberal moderados, and principled social democratic autênticos, align with communists?

The answer did not lie in ideological affinity. Guimarães or Quércia would have made no better communists than Martins or Carvalho Pinto. The answer, rather, lay in the fact that in Brazil power was and is sustained by having a network of clients who owe loyalty to their patrons. But there were precious few clients to go around for MDB politicians. So just as they had welcomed candidates from the middle and working classes in 1974, the MDB welcomed communists. It is thus unsurprising that the emedebista who most assiduously courted communists was Quércia. As a longtime ally put it years later, Quércia "doesn't have many prejudices because he does not have a political background, he did not have a class position to defend, he came from Pedregulho [in the interior], he took night classes. . . . He does not have the ideological training to discriminate against someone who has a different point of view." Thus Quércia and Goldman were closely allied for nearly two decades. The same man who embraced dissident arenistas in the interior cultivated the friendship of communists because few others would; both offered low-hanging fruit to someone building a network of clients.

Suspicious of PCB involvement in the campaign, the regime's security services for months produced reports documenting communist "infiltration" in the MDB. While the PCB's support is indisputable, the often-fantastical reports attributed the MDB's victory almost entirely to communist machinations. Without offering evidence, the SNI argued that "secret agreements" between the PCB and the MDB had established that once in office PCB-supported candidates would carry out "subliminal actions" to "attack and criticize the accomplishments of the government." Worse still, they were supported by a communist-infiltrated press: "Even without offering solutions, these candidates, accustomed to demagogic attacks, enjoy the strong support of the Left that is active in the spoken and written press." The SNI suspected (correctly) that Marcelo Gato owed his election to PCB support; the banned party had raised funds by selling cat-shaped keychains (*gato* means "cat") near his hometown of Santos. More implausibly, federal deputy José de Camargo and state deputy Manoel Sala had supposedly received financial support from an unnamed Eastern Bloc country. Not even arenistas escaped suspicion; federal deputy Rafael Baldacci was accused of using communist money to support leftist candidates. As proof of this infiltration, the security services apprehended "highly subversive" campaign material, including a flyer that criticized the cost of living, "deficient" public transportation, and the "forsaken" health care system.[111] The paranoia ran so deep that when Tavares Coelho, former Minas Gerais federal deputy and PCB central committee member, was arrested, his interrogators tried to get him to confess that the PCB's "subversive" activities had been facilitated by none other than Golbery, Geisel's military chief of staff.[112]

The reports on communist support for the MDB total over two hundred pages. Dozens of candidates were accused of receiving PCB support. Much of the information was obtained through the torture of Tavares Coelho. If his words were recorded accurately, he was either a skilled dissembler or the PCB was heavily involved in the MDB victory. While information gained under torture is suspect, it is possible that Tavares Coelho offered the names of MDB congressmen with some protection from arrest instead of exposing his PCB comrades.

Where the security apparatus erred was not in the extent of PCB support for the opposition but rather in its conviction that this support had led to ARENA's electoral defeat. Left unexplained was how a small organization that had been banned for over two decades and had made practically no impact in 1970 or 1972 suddenly had the power to convince millions of voters to support the liberal, tepidly oppositionist MDB. Communists were a convenient scapegoat for an electoral defeat that owed far more to flaws in the regime's model of development and the skill of politicians such as Montoro and Quércia in exploiting them.

Suddenly the PCB, which had for years looked less menacing than the PCdoB and other revolutionary groups, seemed like the most dangerous communists of all. Armed resistance had never threatened the generals' hold. But in a dictatorship that portrayed itself as democratic, elections did. The regime's repressive gaze thus shifted from the already defeated armed resistance to the PCB and, by extension, the MDB. While it would have looked untoward to target the only legal opposition party, it was possible to do so by tying it to communists.[113] The year 1975 thus witnessed the most intense repression leftist parties in Brazil have ever faced, as two thousand actual or suspected communists were arrested nationwide. In São Paulo, eighty-eight suspected communists were arrested merely in the month of October. The detainees were kidnapped without warning and taken to state DOI-CODI headquarters, where they were subjected to torture before being turned over for prosecution.[114] At least three prisoners died in DOI-CODI custody in São Paulo between May 1975 and January 1976. Unlike the ordinary functioning of the justice system in Brazil, which disproportionately targets the poor and Black and Brown people, DOI-CODI cared little for social class. Those arrested included not only union leaders such as José "Frei Chico" Ferreira de Melo, vice president–elect of the São Caetano metalworkers' union and brother of future president Lula, but also military policemen with suspected PCB sympathies, as well as highly placed journalists such as São Paulo's TV Cultura director, Vladimir Herzog.[115]

The culmination of the military's overreaction to the 1974 elections came in October. On October 25, Herzog, head of São Paulo's state-owned station, TV Cultura, and a member of the PCB, voluntarily went to the São Paulo DOI-CODI for questioning. Later that day, he was dead. While the death certificate called it suicide and claimed he had left a note in his own hand, the photograph of his "hanged" body showed his feet dragging on the floor. Clearly Herzog had been murdered, probably during an interrogation gone wrong. While many communists had been killed before Herzog, under the repressive gaze of the Médici government reaction had been muted. Besides, every year Brazilian police executed thousands of working-class suspects with little outcry.[116] But now Herzog's death generated vast publicity and a strong MDB reaction. Herzog was one of them, or close to it—a member of the learned upper middle classes, sympathetic to the opposition. People like him were not supposed to become victims of police repression. And even if they had in the past, things were supposed to be different under détente.

Although Geisel had AI-5 at his disposal and could cassar anyone whose response was too heated, many MDB politicians were furious, and although they avoided accusing the military directly, they left little doubt as to their true feelings. J. G. de Araújo Jorge (MDB-RJ) pointed out that the military's explanation contained "a series of absolutely illogical conjectures."[117] Gamaliel Galvão (MDB-PR) went further: "I want to register here not words of sorrow . . . but rather words of protest and revulsion against the lack of security and tranquility imposed upon this country . . . by a confused and ill-defined system that [is] arbitrary, incapable of solving the people's problems, and allows things like this to happen."[118] The party's official response was given by José de Freitas Nobre, an autêntico and three-time president of the São Paulo state journalists' union. By choosing the former head of the union that represented Herzog to deliver its response, the MDB sent a none-too-subtle message. Freitas Nobre argued, "Even if we accept that it was a suicide, what kinds of pressure, of intimidation, of poor treatment are being inflicted upon prisoners to make them prefer death?" Suspected communists could be investigated, but "they should not suffer mistreatment, torture, and death, directly or indirectly." No doubt he spoke not only for journalists, but for many opposition politicians, when he said, "What happens to one could happen to another."[119]

At the same time discretion was still needed, and opposition leaders insisted that they would not create a climate of "agitation." After an ecumenical service in Herzog's honor, attended by eight thousand, was held in São Paulo's Sé Cathedral, the MDB's leader in the Chamber, Laerte Vieira, simply expressed relief that it had transpired peacefully.[120] Guimarães, the party's national president, limited himself to protesting that it should be the police, not the army, that investigated "subversive organizations."[121] After he—among many others—was kept from arriving at the memorial service on time due to military and police checkpoints, he protested that this violated freedom of assembly. A few days later, MDB Chamber vice-leader, Israel Dias Novaes, urged the party to take a "moderate" posture that avoided "provocations."[122]

With Herzog's death, Geisel's promises must have appeared hollow. While détente had brought freer elections and Geisel was relatively receptive to the input of his civilian allies, the regime had also unleashed unprecedented repression against the PCB, a leftist party that had rejected armed struggle in favor of discreet electoral mobilization. Former federal deputies such as Tavares Coelho had been imprisoned, and the director of São Paulo's public television had died in military custody. Although Geisel eventually sacked the head of the II Army, General Ednardo d'Avila Melo, who was responsible for DOI-CODI operations in São Paulo, this was small comfort for politicians. In 1975 and 1976 Geisel used AI-5 to purge ten politicians, mostly autênticos, including Marcelo Gato and Furtado.[123] Why play by the rules if the regime would not respect them? And although they defended the generals publicly, arenistas were certainly wondering: If the regime punished the opposition even when they followed its rules, how far could the generals be trusted to deal fairly with ARENA? For their part, the generals were concerned by the MDB's popularity in urban areas and the wealthiest states. In 1976 a new law banned most campaign television advertising.[124] With this new measure and its traditional dominance in rural Brazil, ARENA handily won the 1976 municipal elections.

With direct legislative and gubernatorial elections looming in 1978, Geisel feared that ARENA could lose Congress and governorships in key states such as São Paulo. He thus launched the regime's greatest assault on Brazilian institutions since the three military ministers had blocked Pedro Aleixo from assuming the presidency in 1969. In April 1977 the MDB, now with over a third of the seats in Congress, blocked a judicial reform proposal because it did not restore habeas corpus or judicial independence. In response, Geisel placed Congress in recess and decreed a constitutional amendment dubbed the "April package." Among other reforms, it maintained indirect gubernatorial elections and instituted them for one-third of senators. Conventions would select candidates for governor and senator, and electoral colleges, in which rural municipalities (usually controlled by ARENA) would enjoy disproportionate representation, would formally elect them in September.[125] The April package thus guaranteed ARENA a third of the Senate and nearly all the governorships.[126] It was the culmination of the military's repressive overreaction to its 1974 defeat. And it generated an unexpected reaction.

THE AUDACITY TO STRONG-ARM THE GENERALS: PAULO MALUF RUNS FOR GOVERNOR OF SÃO PAULO[127]

In contrast to the 1968 crisis that culminated in AI-5, the April package had not arisen from friction between the regime and the political class. Instead, it was a naked power grab that sought to keep ARENA dependent and the MDB in perpetual opposition. Golbery explained to the British ambassador that this had been necessary "because the opposition were effectively seeking to change the regime from that established in 1964." The MDB could win power but only "at an appropriate moment so long as they played the game."[128] As British diplomats put it, "President Geisel's policy of distensão is dead and there can be little hope of any further liberalising measures during the final two years of his presidency. . . . Those who felt that Brazil was set inexorably on the path to democracy will have to think again."[129]

An infuriated MDB briefly considered disbanding itself in protest of this latest assault. And ARENA, instead of appreciating Geisel's help, was also displeased. Though the party expressed little discontent publicly, a foreign diplomat noted:

ARENA are shamefaced and demoralised. They find it difficult to defend measures in which they had little hand themselves. They are dismayed that President Geisel has apparently thought it necessary to fix the MDB because he had no confidence that ARENA ... could do it for him. There is general dissatisfaction in their ranks.[130]

Here were proud homens públicos with decades of experience winning elections, but instead of trusting them to do their jobs, the generals thought they needed help. In São Paulo, the 1978 gubernatorial contest provided an unexpected opportunity for ARENA to finally rebel.

As 1978 began, the expectation was that the generals would select the new governors and the ARENA conventions would ratify their choices. Presumably, party factions in each state would agree on a candidate and relay their preference to Geisel and João Batista Figueiredo (anointed Geisel's successor in December 1977), who (provided the choice was acceptable) would endorse him before the state convention. Aspiring governors, in an attempt to curry favor with the generals, thus sought to demonstrate that they could lead the political class. In São Paulo, the state's political and economic importance made it vital that the generals approve a candidate who could unite ARENA and stave off surprises at the party's convention.[131] By this criterion, two-time former governor Laudo Natel had the best prospects. Since the end of his last term in 1975, when he was replaced by Martins, he claimed to have made 1,730 trips to the state's interior to cultivate contacts with local political elites.[132] More important, he had twice demonstrated his unswerving loyalty and was close friends with Figueiredo.[133] Despite Laudo Natel's perceived advantage, at least six other arenistas, including Delfim Neto, architect of the "economic miracle," and Olavo Setúbal, current mayor of São Paulo city, were also seeking the nomination. The press engaged in frenzied speculation as the candidates formed competing alliances, traded thinly veiled insults, traveled to Brasília to meet with regime figures, and showcased their real or invented support among politicians and voters.

One candidate, Paulo Maluf, employed a very different strategy. Appointed mayor of São Paulo from 1969 to 1971, this son of Lebanese immigrants harbored higher aspirations. Yet Costa e Silva, his political patron and a personal friend of his wife, had died in 1969, and he was now a peripheral player in state politics, though he had managed to get himself elected president of the São Paulo Trade Association. But when Geisel decreed the April package, Maluf saw his opening.[134] In April 1977 he invited Geisel to a meeting on foreign trade he was hosting in São Paulo. He pulled the president aside and asked, "You have delegated to the convention the choice of gubernatorial candidate. Can anyone who wants participate in the convention?" "Yes," Geisel responded. Years later Maluf recalled, "I took him at his word."[135]

Instead of courting the generals, he chose to focus on the approximately 1,260 delegates (chosen from the ranks of local ARENA party members) who would participate in the convention. He spent the next year making weekly visits to the interior, using his position as president of the São Paulo Trade Association to gain access to delegates. While vacationing in Paris, he spent his time writing postcards, as he ascertained the delegates would be flattered to receive mail from France.[136] Maluf reasoned that if one of the criteria for a candidate was the ability to unite ARENA, what better way to do so than by winning the convention?[137] Every Wednesday in São Paulo, Maluf hosted a lunch for prominent arenistas. Then after every lunch, even during the Carnaval holiday, he departed for a whirlwind tour of the interior, visiting delegates in as many as forty-two municipalities and staying in their homes to maximize time spent with them.[138] Maluf claimed that in 1977 he had made 625 such visits, and he produced a map showing where he had been, with colored pins representing his support in each of the state's municipalities.[139] Most striking about Maluf's campaign was how he took advantage of the generals' arbitrary measures to justify his candidacy. Everyone else knew that the convention would do no more than endorse Geisel and Figueiredo's candidate. Yet Maluf argued that if Geisel had created a law to govern the elections, "this law ... exists to be obeyed."[140] He insisted that by acting in accordance with the April package, he was collaborating with, not opposing, Geisel, adding, "They will thank me in the future."[141]

On April 24 Geisel and Figueiredo announced that the new governor would be Laudo Natel.[142] Perhaps in a nod to the oppositionist mood in his state, Natel proclaimed his support for amnesty for the regime's purged and exiled opponents, the revocation of AI-5, students' right to protest, and a multiparty system. While he wished that the election had been direct, the indirect contest, with its numerous unofficial candidates, had "resembled direct elections."[143] However, the press gave no credibility to Natel's pledges. A *Folha* editorial criticized the "monarchical" selection process and proposed that ARENA abolish its "useless and redundant" convention, which would merely bestow its "submissive and affirmative" vote on Natel.[144] Much of the paulista political class was similarly indignant, either because they disagreed with the top-down process or because the generals had passed over their candidate. Other arenistas, reluctant to anger the future president and governor, offered polite congratulations and calls for unity.[145] Yet their conciliatory tone barely masked major discontent. In the state legislature, only a few ARENA deputies bothered defending the generals' choice. Most remained silent as their MDB colleagues denounced the entire process. One brave arenista asked, "Will the country have to continue watching as Brazil is divided into pieces to be distributed according to personal preferences? Do you call this a revolution? ... If this was the intent of 1964, then I must say ... that I was duped. ... Enough! Enough! It's time for democracy!"[146]

Most arenistas did no more than grumble; Maluf acted. He had remained mired in obscurity since the end of his stint as state secretary of transportation in 1975 (a position Natel had appointed him to). He was irrelevant enough by 1978 that

Delfim Neto referred to him as "a burnt-out match who doesn't interest anyone."[147] Yet Maluf stubbornly refused to withdraw, even as ARENA's national president, Francelino Pereira, urged dissident candidates to "understand perfectly the reach of a revolutionary decision and place this decision above their personal convictions."[148] Maluf later claimed that he had received phone calls and visits from a series of prominent figures. Television executive Roberto Marinho warned him that defying the generals could carry heavy repercussions, and Air Force Minister Délio Jardim de Mattos hinted at a cabinet position if he withdrew.[149] An ARENA source told *Veja*, "No one believes that Maluf will go until the end. He'll agree to any accord and accept any position to save his career."[150]

Yet in response to one politician who questioned his resolve, Maluf offered to renounce politics forever if he failed to present his candidacy at the convention.[151] He reiterated, "The convention . . . will not ratify—it will decide. . . . Those who say that the convention will ratify are toadies, not democrats."[152] Maluf never challenged the regime on ideological grounds. Rather, he was likely motivated by self-interest. In an indirect election in the easily controlled state legislature, Maluf's outsider status would have doomed him, while in a direct one, he would have lost to the MDB. Given that the regime might well allow direct elections in 1982, a convention with a set of delegates Maluf could form relationships with, followed by an indirect election, was the best chance he would ever have. Thus he continued his campaigning, even spending the Corpus Christi holiday calling delegates from the six phones cluttering his desk.[153] His staff sent weekly letters and newspaper clippings about his candidacy to the delegates, and he continued to host delegates and ARENA leaders every Wednesday for lunch.[154]

Meanwhile, Natel began to outline plans for his next administration and recruit ARENA candidates for the November elections. Martins tried to warn him that his position was precarious and that he ought to campaign more aggressively, but he responded, "Paulo, I have been governor of São Paulo twice. I will be for a third time. Do you think that you still need to tell me anything?"[155] Similarly, he warned prospective challengers: "No one ignores that my selection was revolutionary . . . so why don't we quit playing games?"[156] The convention would be "just the legal ratification of a choice that . . . was accepted by the leaders of the party."[157] But in the days before the convention, with Maluf's campaign gaining steam, Natel launched a belated push for support. In addition to submitting a petition for candidacy with the signatures of 879 delegates (more than Maluf's petition),[158] he began to actively campaign among them for the first time, reminding undecided delegates that he enjoyed the approval of the future president.[159] To drive this point home, Figueiredo sent a telegram urging the delegates to vote for Natel, reminding them of the "national importance of the São Paulo convention for party cohesion."[160] Would this be enough to put Natel over the top?

As the day of the convention dawned, each candidate mobilized an army of supporters to appear at the seat of the state legislature, where the convention would be held. Supporters of both men filled the area in front of the palace, spilling into the street and the adjacent Ibirapuera Park.[161] Natel's supporters carried banners, balloons, and signs emblazoned with the slogan, "Laudo is a person like us," and a hired publicity firm sent a dozen vans fitted with loudspeakers and posters.[162] Maluf's partisans carried their own signs and passed out flyers proclaiming Maluf "the delegates' candidate, with Geisel and Figueiredo."[163] They were led by attractive, young, women supporters (dubbed "malufettes" by the press), who had been bused in by a *malufista* former mayor.[164] Natel boasted a band, but whenever it started a song, Maluf's supporters moved in, dancing, waving banners, and cheering, prompting *laudistas* to comment, "Laudo brings the band, and Maluf has the party."[165] Former governor Sodré, who had at times run afoul of the regime during his 1967–71 administration, compared the civic spirit to the state's 1932 armed rebellion against Getúlio Vargas, an event whose memory lived on in paulista lore as a symbol of the state's courage in defying centralizing regimes. "The people reveal in their hearts the democratic sensitivity that motivated the Constitutionalist Revolution. We aren't a flock of little sheep who accept top-down impositions," Sodré said.[166]

At 9:00 a.m., state ARENA president Cláudio Lembo formally opened the proceedings.[167] Maluf, himself a delegate, was among the first to vote. He then joined Natel to greet the delegates, full of energy as he flew from one to another; in five minutes, reporters counted thirty-one hugs and sixty expressions of thanks or greeting.[168] "Every delegate was greeted.... He knew by heart the names, the cities, and even the personal details of every delegate," wrote one reporter.[169] He asked one delegate about the chicken that had been sick when he visited and complimented another on the *kibbeh* (a Middle Eastern appetizer) his wife had served.[170] When one delegate asked how he could remember so many names, Maluf responded, "But how could I forget you? You're all my friends. We are going to govern together for four years."[171] Meanwhile, Natel greeted each delegate with a smile and a piece of candy, and delegates paid his photographers to take their picture with him. Yet few delegates sought out Natel, unless brought by his allies.[172] After all, with his demands that politicians meekly accept his nomination, he had demonstrated a marked disdain for delegates' opinions, whereas Maluf had spent a year cultivating their friendship.

Yet despite the animated atmosphere outside and the personal attention of the candidates inside, some delegates were unimpressed by the "democracy" on display. One remarked that it would have been a shame to stay home watching *Os Trapalhões* (a popular comedy program) when the best comedians were right there in the Legislative Assembly.[173] And São Paulo municipal councilor, Carlos Sampaio Dória (who shortly thereafter would leave ARENA and join the MDB), issued a statement that was remarkable for having come from a regime ally.

> This convention has been an uncommon, almost forgotten, event of a type to which São Paulo arenistas and the country were no longer accustomed: a contest. Cold due

to the absence of the people, stripped of any real democratic meaning, but a contest all the same. If it had not been for . . . the determination to challenge, to assume risks, to not surrender to intimidation, today we would be watching . . . a subservient, cowardly, and despicable convention. . . . Whatever the outcome of this convention, it will not lessen—indeed, it will highlight—the paulistas' yearning to see restored, in their fullness, their basic rights as citizens. . . . Give back to the people, without further delay[,] . . . the freedoms and prerogatives inherent to a democratic state.[174]

Around 4:00 p.m., as the voting was winding down, an exhausted Natel withdrew to an allied state deputy's office to await the results.[175] Shortly after 5:00, the tally began. The gallery, designed to accommodate a few hundred people, was soon packed with 3,500 chain-smoking spectators. By 7:20, with one box partially counted, Maluf led by fifteen votes.[176] Amid the haze of cigarette smoke, the smell of something burning filled the chamber, and someone shouted that there was a fire. Lembo assured the crowd that it was only a problem with the ventilation system, but as the smell grew stronger and the smoke thicker, it became clear there was a fire. Lembo's advice to evacuate calmly went unheeded as the chamber fell into a panic.[177]

Maluf and his supporters' worst fears seemed to be coming true. Earlier, a malufista had handed a lantern to state deputy Antônio Salim Curiati, a close Maluf confidant, saying, "If the lights go out, illuminate the ballot boxes. You know how conventions are. Laudo's people are capable of anything."[178] This was not mere paranoia: politicians had noted that the Nove de Julho Palace's electricity often went out during important votes.[179] An SNI report pointedly noted that although Lembo insisted that the laudistas were not responsible for the fire, "the area was full of military police and DOPS agents tied to Natel, many of whom were aware of the problem with the ventilation system."[180] For his part, Maluf remained convinced nearly four decades later that the fire had been set intentionally.[181] As they fled, some malufistas could be heard cursing ARENA, while others called for Maluf's observers to stand ready with their lanterns: "Illuminate the ballot boxes! If you don't, they'll disappear!"[182] Maluf frantically approached the dais as Lembo, the ARENA executive committee, and Olavo Drummond (an observer sent by the Regional Electoral Court, or TRE) debated what to do. Panting and wide-eyed, Maluf climbed the wall separating the floor from the dais, shouting, "It's sabotage! They put this smoke in here on purpose! The count has to happen here!," as he clutched the ballot boxes.[183] Lembo attempted to separate Maluf from the boxes, and he and Drummond agreed, over Maluf's protests, that the counting could continue at the TRE's headquarters.[184]

Lembo, Maluf, Drummond, and the boxes hastily exited the palace.[185] Outside they met a crowd of delegates and spectators. Politicians and delegates from both camps, in a moment of solidarity, held hands to create a wall around Lembo, the state ARENA executive committee, and the boxes. Sure enough, the electricity went out, but the malufistas immediately lit their lanterns. With no power and smoke pouring from the building, a police van was commandeered to transfer the ballots to TRE headquarters. Maluf attempted to jump into the van but was forcibly removed, and it pulled out, forcing its way through a crowd of booing politicians.[186]

Maluf, hair disheveled and glasses missing, rushed to TRE headquarters. Natel, who had retired to await the results by telephone, was conspicuously absent. However, the TRE president informed Lembo that since the court's role was that of observer, it would be inappropriate for convention proceedings to take place there.[187] Around 9:30, it was decided that the tally would continue at the spacious Anhembi Convention Center, but when the ballot boxes and the accompanying caravan arrived, it turned out that the Japanese Brazilian community had reserved the hall for a "Miss Nissei" pageant. The organizer refused to suspend the pageant, arguing that it was more important to the Japanese Brazilians than choosing a governor. So the executive committee met hastily and voted to continue the count in a tiny room next to the convention hall, with space for only the committee, the candidates' observers, and a few reporters. Perhaps because of Maluf's vocal protestations, candidates were specifically excluded.[188]

As the count recommenced, unofficial updates from the room made it clear that Maluf's lead would hold. Boisterous supporters began to chant, "One, two, three, four, São Paulo's given an example once more!" When the final announcement came near 2:00 a.m.—that Maluf had won by a count of 617 to 589—the malufistas erupted in cheers and carried Maluf on their shoulders to the convention hall, by now vacated by the pageant. Maluf dedicated his victory to the person whose will he had flouted: "I offer this victory to President Geisel . . . who, through his steadfastness, maintained the April reform, which permitted the delegates to choose their candidates in a free and democratic election."[189] The malufistas applauded wildly, and one shouted, "Next, the Presidency of the Republic!"[190]

The convention illustrates the tense relationship between the regime and its civilian allies. In 1978 the government faced foes not only among the MDB and communists but also among students, progressive Catholic bishops, and labor unions. The generals needed loyalty from their civilian allies more than ever, but Maluf and a majority of ARENA's delegates betrayed them. A municipal councilman had criticized the regime in language befitting the opposition, a former governor had favorably compared it to an armed revolt against another despotic central government, delegates had mocked the proceedings, and the fire had provoked speculation that the regime would resort to sabotage to defeat dissidence. Worst of all, Maluf had ignored the will of Geisel and Figueiredo, even as he justified his candidacy with their own rules, and a sizable bloc of ARENA politicians had joined in his insubordination. As the SNI report put it, "Maluf's victory in the convention was ARENA politicians' first gesture of rebellion, albeit within the laws issued by the Revolution, against the federal government."[191]

How much of a rebellion did the convention represent? Some delegates voted for Maluf because they resented federal meddling; delegates from the city of Guarulhos commented, "São Paulo said no. It said 'Enough!' to the system, and Maluf deserves our support for having the courage to believe in the sovereignty of the convention." Others used their vote to express their dissatisfaction with the regime's economic policy. One delegate from the interior remarked, "I haven't been able to sell my oranges or my sugarcane. The only way I found to voice my discontent with the government's agricultural policy was to vote for Maluf."[192] Others may have voted for Maluf because they were offered incentives or because their local faction saw support for Maluf as its ticket to political power. Whatever their individual motivations, the delegates knew that their vote represented a gesture of insubordination. Geisel and Figueiredo had endorsed Natel, and Figueiredo had sent a telegram demanding the delegates' compliance. The last time ARENA had so openly defied the generals it had received AI-5 in answer, and many of those who had rebelled were cassado in the following months. Yet despite the risks, they voted for Maluf, illustrating the depth of their dissatisfaction with their marginalization.[193]

The next day, a stunned Legislative Assembly met in the slightly damaged Nove de Julho Palace. Malufista Curiati called the "very democratic" convention "a historic moment" that had "offered an example to Brazil."[194] For ARENA state deputy Paulo Kobayashi, the convention proved that "the Revolution, and its measures in São Paulo, has entirely exhausted itself," since it could not "manage to make its party[,] . . . which for 12 years never contested revolutionary measures, swallow preprepared meals."[195] Opposition deputies were similarly pleased. According to Horácio Ortiz, "The victory of the ARENA opposition was a demonstration that no one else in the government's own party will allow impositions."[196]

Meanwhile, the press was rife with speculation that Geisel and Figueiredo, offended by Maluf's insolence, might be seeking a means of preventing his election.[197] Publicly, Geisel's spokesman insisted, "The only role for the government is to accept the result in accordance with the political and democratic process that has been consistently developed . . . over the last several months."[198] A Figueiredo confidant revealed that the next president was urging ARENA to support Maluf, "as long as everything is in order with him."[199] Still, if they changed their minds, two options were available to remove Maluf legally. The first was through a pending investigation of Maluf's in-laws' Lutfalla Textile and Weaving Company for allegedly pocketing a federal bailout intended to prevent the corporation's collapse. Although Maluf had not been directly implicated, his wife was a shareholder, and if the government froze or confiscated her holdings, Maluf could be ruled ineligible to hold public office. On June 5, only hours after the convention, a congressional investigatory committee recommended the confiscation of Lutfalla's assets.[200] On August 6, Geisel did so. Yet a presidential spokesman insisted that the case would not affect Maluf's candidacy.[201] This was likely because if Maluf were declared ineligible, the timing, so soon after the convention, would be suspicious.[202] And if the Lutfallas had so easily pocketed their bailout, what did this say about the regime's ability to combat corruption? The scandal was embarrassing, and the inclination was to ignore it.

A less far-fetched possibility was a legal challenge to the convention, which Natel filed on June 13. His lawyers pointed out that in the minutes, the number of votes for governor did not match the number of votes for senator or the number of delegates. The most likely culprit, they argued, was the chaos surrounding the fire, when votes could have been lost. They also claimed inconsistencies on the convention sign-in sheet, including missing and duplicated pages, double signatures, and blank lines. With so many problems in an election decided by a twenty-eight-vote margin, Natel argued, the only fair course of action was to annul the convention.[203] The party executive committee offered a refutation accounting for most of the inconsistencies, and Maluf's lawyers pointed out that Natel had made none of these complaints during the convention.[204] Although Natel's case was weak, under a regime that shamelessly manipulated the judicial system, the outcome was far from certain.[205] This was the perfect chance for the generals to eliminate Maluf without getting their hands dirty. Would they apply pressure on the court to rule in Natel's favor? Although the TRE was made up of career judges who had spent years in the judicial system, judges drawn from upper-middle-class and elite families were hardly impervious to political influences. But on June 29, by a 5–1 vote, the TRE dismissed Natel's challenge, ruling that Maluf and the executive committee had sufficiently accounted for the discrepancies and that the party had taken adequate precautions to protect the ballots.[206]

Natel immediately appealed to the TSE in Brasília to overturn the regional court's decision. Since the TRE had rejected all Natel's arguments, in his appeal he was left to argue that minor clerical errors in the vote totals in the handwritten minutes should invalidate the convention.[207] When questioned, Maluf repeated the same mantra, "I have faith in the justice system."[208] Nevertheless, as he was undoubtedly aware, in a nation long governed by "revolutionary decisions" and "laws of exception," such faith could be misplaced. Sure enough, on July 13 Brazil's chief prosecutor, Henrique Fonseca de Araújo, submitted a brief endorsing Natel's appeal, arguing that even if the tabulated results from the convention could explain the discrepancies, supplemental documents lacked the same validity as the minutes. The minutes showed a discrepancy of 30 votes between the totals for indirectly elected senator and governor, a margin greater than that separating Maluf and Natel.[209] Araújo's brief was without merit. The total of 1,194 votes for senator was a simple clerical error, and it could be easily proven that 1,224 delegates had cast ballots in that race, the same number as voted for governor. Why should a minor miscalculation on handwritten sheets of paper, hastily scrawled at 2:00 a.m., invalidate the entire convention?

The explanation for Araújo's opinion lay in the fact that if the convention were invalidated, the state ARENA directorate would have to nominate a new candidate. And allies of Natel appeared to hold an advantage in the directorate.[210] Although Araújo claimed that Geisel and Figueiredo had no role in his brief, there were reports that Figueiredo was showing it off in his office the afternoon before its release.[211] The brief looked like—and indeed probably was—a thinly veiled effort to salvage Natel's candidacy. But the TSE decision stunned everyone. On July 17, by a 4–2 vote, the court ruled in Maluf's favor.[212] The chief federal prosecutor, likely at the behest of the generals, had publicly pressured the judges, and they ignored him. At the suggestion of "influential people," Natel chose not to appeal to the STF.[213]

Did Geisel and Figueiredo really want to eliminate Maluf? It is difficult to be certain as the only hints are press speculation and the regime's history of ridding itself of troublesome politicians. Maluf pointed out in our interview later that it was only natural that the future president wanted his friend as governor, but he also insisted that Figueiredo did nothing to block his candidacy either.[214] Regardless, the most striking aspect of the legal challenges is that, whatever they wished, the generals found themselves effectively barred from removing Maluf. The Lutfalla case raised questions about the regime's handling of corruption, and the electoral justice system could not be relied on to annul the convention. Besides, Maluf's candidacy had followed the letter of the April package perfectly. How could Geisel simply ignore his own law?[215] To make matters more complicated, such blatant federal meddling in state affairs might upset ARENA politicians nationally, and they could refuse to support Figueiredo in the indirect presidential election and vote for an MDB candidate.[216] The convention's aftermath illustrates the constraints the regime faced in its attempts to legitimize authoritarian rule with the trappings of liberal democracy. Open rebellion from ARENA, even if based more on self-interest than disagreement with military rule, represented a serious threat to that project.

CONCLUSIONS

The years 1974–78 marked an irrevocable turning point for Brazil's military regime. In early 1974 the generals were presiding over a roaring economy, and the radical Left had been practically eliminated through violence, imprisonment, or exile. However reluctantly, politicians appeared to have accepted military tutelage, and the regime-allied party enjoyed a supermajority in both houses of Congress. But only four years later, the MDB had scored a stunning electoral victory, and Geisel was forced to resort to extralegal measures to keep them from taking control of Congress and key governorships. Most significantly, the generals' faithful allies in ARENA had turned on them in Brazil's most important state, offering a clear sign that the political class had not learned its lesson as well as the generals thought.

What happened in these four years? Certainly the failure to significantly reduce inequality played a role in the MDB's 1974 electoral victory. But the generals' failure was not economic. Indeed, until the early 1980s the regime's management of the economy, with its focus on state-directed development and regulated access for foreign corporations, brought the greatest economic stability Brazil had seen in decades. Rather, the failure was political. As Huntington had argued, a cooperative political class was essential to the institutionalization of the regime. But greater responsibility for the political class and the strengthening of the regime for the long term were predicated on politicians learning to behave correctly. By 1974 the generals perhaps believed their own rhetoric about a Brazil freed of economic crisis, leftist subversion, and a corrupt, rivalry-riven political class. They miscalculated badly.

The MDB's victory in 1974 showed that by following Quércia's model, the opposition could play by the rules of the game and win elections. The persecution of the PCB, the death of Herzog in 1975, and the use of AI-5 to decree electoral reforms to benefit ARENA demonstrated that even if politicians followed the rules to the letter, the regime would either reinvent the rules or employ blatant repression to neutralize its foes. The political class's faith in détente was deeply shaken. The greatest proof of this came in São Paulo, as Maluf's victory, validated by the legal system, showed that even the military's allies were fed up. The regime was in crisis.

Still, the student movement, labor unions, and other groups that would soon be collectively referred to as "civil society" remained relatively quiet if agitated. But on the eve of Maluf's victory, strikes in São Paulo would demonstrate that it was not only the military's grip on politicians that was tenuous, but its very grip on the Brazilian people. As strikes proliferated over the next two years, led by a dynamic union leader who would one day become Brazil's first working-class president, the regime was forced to contend with an ever-expanding cast of foes. And the MDB, in a move away from the elitism of many of its members, would embrace the workers' struggle because they recognized that only with mass support could they gain power. It is to these strikes and the political class's response that the next chapter turns.

6

"We Cannot Think about Democracy the Way We Used To"

The ABC Strikes and the Challenge of Popular Mobilization

On May Day 1979, up to 130,000 workers packed a stadium in the São Paulo suburb of São Bernardo do Campo to hear their leader, Luiz Inácio da Silva (commonly known as "Lula"), speak. Only a few weeks before, Lula had led metallurgical workers in the cities of Santo André, São Bernardo, and São Caetano (known colloquially as ABC) in a strike that had shaken Brazil. In a stunning statement in a country where working-class political participation had long been limited to casting votes, Lula insisted, "It's up to us, the workers, to change the rules of the game, and instead of being ordered around like we are today, to start giving the orders around here."[1] Such a scene must have been disconcerting to many Brazilian politicians, business leaders, and intellectuals. The thousands of workers were not simply asking for higher salaries or a greater role in the political system. Rather, they were calling for a fundamental reshaping of long-standing social relations, in which the working majority would seize the political initiative from the "directing classes."

In 1964, the majority of Brazil's politicians, along with practically the entire business elite, had supported a coup to drive away the specter of popular mobilization. Yet now workers mobilized not at the urging of a reformist politician like Goulart, a member of the landowning elite, but on their own initiative, unwilling to accept that the powerful should get a free pass as ever rising inflation ate away at workers' salaries. How would the politicians, military officers, business leaders, and intellectuals who saw policy making as their exclusive domain react? By resorting to repression, as Brazil's elites had done for centuries? By seeking to appropriate the workers' struggle for their own ends? Or by joining the workers in demanding a new Brazil?

It is almost universally acknowledged that the ABC strikes and the wave of worker mobilization they unleashed were a pivotal moment in Brazilian history that shaped a generation of workers and set the stage for the massive expansion of social rights that accompanied the country's democratization in the 1980s. They have also attracted interest because of their central importance in the political trajectory of a future president, Lula.[2] The important role that politicians played in the strikes, particularly in 1980, has gone completely unacknowledged, along with the shifts they provoked in the way many Brazilian politicians responded to the very sort of working-class mobilization that the country's elites have feared for centuries. Opposition politicians, along with a few brave government allies, finally overcame their fear of the regime as they supported the workers' struggle, not only by giving congressional speeches, but also by risking their own safety to protect union leaders and striking workers from repression. Joining the workers in the streets were not only the autênticos but also leftist revolutionaries and intellectuals who were entering politics for the first time, as well as moderate oppositionists. Just as politicians in 1968 had rushed to UnB to protect students, in 1979 and 1980 they rushed to São Bernardo, this time to defend not the children of the elite but working-class trade unionists.

1978: "THE MOST PEACEFUL STRIKE EVER SEEN IN SÃO PAULO"

In early 1978 worker unrest was far from the minds of Brazil's politicians. Geisel had named his successor, but Minas Gerais senator José de Magalhães Pinto had also sought the ARENA nomination, and he began to issue increasingly severe criticisms of the regime. The MDB was considering running a candidate against Figueiredo in the October electoral college vote. They would soon select General Euler Bentes Monteiro, a leading representative of factions of the military convinced that Geisel and the generals surrounding him had betrayed the "Revolution" by concentrating power in their own hands and failing to formulate a sufficiently nationalist economic policy.[3] And on the horizon were the November elections, which would elect a third of the Senate, the entire Chamber of Deputies, and all state legislatures.

Yet as the political class and the military debated the country's future, other groups began to demand a voice. The student movement, cautious since 1968, returned to the streets, not only to demand educational reforms, but also to protest the regime's authoritarianism as embodied in the April package.[4] In February the Brazilian Committee for Amnesty (Comitê Brasileiro Pela Anistia) was founded, demanding a "broad, general, and unrestricted amnesty" for exiled foes of the regime, political prisoners, and those affected by institutional acts.[5] In July the Unified Black Movement would be formed in São Paulo, calling attention to the unequal treatment of Afro-Brazilians.[6] The country's first gay rights organization was founded in 1978, and the women's movement was growing rapidly.[7] These movements brought together intellectuals, activists, and members of the middle class inspired by discourses of human rights, economic justice, and identity politics. As the economist Luiz Carlos Bresser Pereira put it, it appeared that "the process of the disintegration of the authoritarian political model being applied in Brazil is accelerating day by day."[8]

Of all these social movements the most organized was labor, above all, in São Paulo, whose heavy industries formed the backbone of the Brazilian economy.[9] Since the mid-1970s, a new generation of dynamic leaders such as Lula had encouraged greater contact between union leaders and workers and sought the end of state tutelage of unions. In 1977, a study revealed that since 1973 the regime had been underreporting annual inflation rates, which were used as the basis for wage adjustments; as a result, in the years since metalworkers had lost 34.1 percent of the value of their wages. Led by Lula, the São Bernardo metalworkers' union launched a campaign to pressure the government to restore their lost salary via a mandated raise.[10]

By 1978, Lula had become recognized as a spokesperson for workers. When he spoke at the National Encounter for Democracy in Rio de Janeiro, the British embassy noted that his speech "articulat[ed] dissatisfaction with the present regime, but without any clear ideological content."[11] Still, independent union leaders were cause for unease. The security services had been keeping an eye on Lula as early as 1976, when a report from naval intelligence to the Justice Ministry highlighted a "highly subversive speech," in which he allegedly claimed, "All the revolutionary governments have been of poor character," and called for unity among workers, "*so that we can go back to the way things were before 1964.*"[12] In Lula, the intelligence services saw the specter of a return of the "agitation" of the Goulart years; the fact that the brother who had recruited him for the union was a communist did not help matters. Similarly, in a June 1978 meeting of the CSN, Planning Minister João Paulo Reis Velloso commented, "The unions are apparently conducting themselves with a degree of independence. . . . Obviously we need to keep an eye on [their] behavior. . . . If they are acting to defend the legitimate economic interests of the workers, or if other influences exist."[13]

On the other hand, many opposition politicians and intellectuals were encouraged by this more combative unionism, which repeated much of what the MDB had preached since 1974. In May 1978, Cardoso argued, "I don't believe that we can think about democracy, now, the way we used to. . . . The number of workers in Brazil has doubled. A substantive democracy will depend on articulations between the diverse social classes."[14] And Senators Montoro and Quércia attended 1978 May Day festivities in Santo André, where Montoro blasted the government's wage policy, called for direct negotiations between unions and employers, and affirmed that Brazilian history was not one of wars or generals but was a "history of the workers' struggle."[15] Even a few regime supporters spoke positively about the workers' movement. The legal scholar Miguel Reale had supported the coup and helped Costa e Silva write his proposed amendments to the constitution in 1969. Yet now he wrote that in contrast to old conceptions of liberalism, which focused on individual and electoral rights, a new "liberalism with participation" should recognize that "the right to participate socially and culturally in the wealth of the community, both in the realm of making decisions and in access to better forms of distribution of wealth, is inherent to every citizen."[16]

Yet many unionists were unimpressed with the politicians embracing their cause. As Arnaldo Gonçalves, president of the Santos metalworkers' union, explained, "If a bill favorable to workers arrives in Congress but will harm the class of politicians, they'll vote in favor of their class. Most politicians are businessmen, landowners, bankers." As for intellectuals: "If they want to help the worker, great. What is not possible is for them to want to command the working class."[17] Pedro Gomes Sampaio, president of the Santos oil workers' union, pointedly explained, "The opposition should take note that the working class is changing and could join together to itself become the opposition. . . . If the MDB does not take note, it is going to be left on the outside."[18] For both, the argument was the same: workers could unite with other social groups to oppose the regime, but workers must represent their own interests.

May Day brought this latent discontent with politicians to the fore. When Montoro and Quércia arrived in Santo André, they received boos from the assembled workers, who cheered as one shouted, "We don't need well-dressed and well-fed deputies and senators going to Congress to pretend like they are defending our interests."[19] Zé Maria de Almeida, a metalworker who was imprisoned for thirty days in 1977 for passing out pamphlets for the Trotskyist student group Liga Operária, called on workers not to support the MDB but to form their own political party: "The bosses have organizations, they have legislation that protects them. . . . And the workers—how will they defend themselves? . . . Let's organize ourselves and form a party that will construct a more just society—a socialist party."[20] Quércia agreed that workers might need their own party, but he argued that it should be more a labor (*trabalhista*) party than a socialist one, in order to "avoid deformations."[21]

In the São Paulo suburb of Osasco, 2,500 workers and students gathered at a rally "without rulers, bosses, politicians, or *pelegos*," in protest of their unions' excessively conciliatory leadership. Special scorn was reserved for union leaders attending a banquet at the governor's mansion. "The minimum wage we receive won't even buy a bottle of wine at the dinner they're going to hold today," one protester said.[22] Even some of the most conciliatory union leaders sounded combative notes. São Paulo state metalworkers' union president, Joaquim dos Santos Andrade, demanded "union freedom, . . . the return of the rule of law, and

... full democracy." "Brazilian unionism has been distorted," he lamented, "just like the political parties, ... which are submitted to the same situation that has obliged the unions to be what they are today: entities under the total tutelage of the government."[23]

The MDB was surprised to discover the disregard in which unionists held them. Quércia and Montoro claimed that the jeers in Santo André had originated from leftist students mixed among the workers.[24] The boos must have particularly stung Montoro, who thought of himself as highly engaged with labor issues.[25] Three days later, he gave a Senate speech decrying falling real wages and proposing direct negotiations between unions and employers, a 20 percent raise for salaried workers, and the establishment of a "democratic political model and the participation of the sectors of the community in decisions that have to do with them."[26] Still, a *Folha* editorialist, Samuel Wainer, pointed out that the boos were a response to the party "instinctively orienting its political behavior toward liberal sectors, intellectuals, and ... the urban middle class."[27]

On May 12, 1,600 metalworkers at the Saab-Scania automobile factory in São Bernardo concluded that they could not count on politicians' promises or the labor court system, and they launched Brazil's first strike in a decade, demanding a raise on top of the inflation-based adjustment they had received for 1978.[28] By May 16, the strikes had grown to 20,000 participants in some of the main plants in suburban São Paulo.[29] Rather than make their demands through the union to the labor courts, as the law required, workers negotiated directly with their employers. Even when the Regional Labor Court (TRT) ruled by a 15–1 vote that the strikes were illegal, the number of strikers grew, and they were joined by 15,000 workers in Santo André.[30] Despite thinly veiled threats from state and federal authoritites to send in police to break up the strikes, Egydio insisted that he would order police intervention only if he received a written request from the federal government, which never came.[31] Geisel spokesman Colonel Rubem Ludwig sanguinely observed that the strike was "a sign of the times we live in" and that labor legislation "recognizes all these rights."[32]

For the military and its civilian allies, although the labor mobilization of the early 1960s had been a sign that Brazil was sliding toward social disaggregation and communism, Lula's dynamic leadership and the workers' peaceful approach to making their demands rendered these strikes less threatening. A few went so far as to endorse them. Cláudio Lembo, state ARENA president, admitted, "The workers may indeed be breaking the law," but added, "The truth is that the current labor arrangement is obsolete, the government's wage policy does not satisfy, and all of this will necessarily have to be replaced by something new."[33] For the Labor Ministry and ARENA politicians, amid the deteriorating economic context it was reasonable to expect workers, whose decline in real wages was beyond dispute, to be discontented.

For the MDB, after the events of May Day, the strikes represented a fortuitous opportunity to demonstrate their solidarity. Quércia insisted that what mattered was not whether the strikes were legal but whether they were just: "[This] is a legitimate strike, because it originates with human beings who . . . have the right to demand better days, better salaries. . . . This strike . . . is a demonstration that popular longing . . . cannot remain subordinated, limited by the rigid structure imposed by our legal organization."[34] Montoro insisted that the strikes' "illegality" did not change three facts: the cost of living was rising, real wages were falling, and the government had based salary adjustments on falsified statistics.[35]

The workers found other allies among clerics, civil society movements, and intellectuals. Cardinal Paulo Evaristo Arns, archbishop of São Paulo, stated, "We cannot restrict ourselves to the law when Justice demands more."[36] The economist Eduardo Suplicy criticized the government for forbidding radio and television to report on the strikes, hesitating to meet with union leaders, and refusing to provide the formula it used for calculating salary adjustments.[37] One of the most eloquent defenses came from Cardoso, who was just launching a Senate candidacy.

> It is democratization on the march, . . . from the feet of the people, from each one of us, from all those who are neither callous right-wingers nor ignoble exploiters. The union movement is reborn. Hope for better days is reborn. Eagerness to organize, speak, propose alternatives, negotiate is reborn. Now we can begin to speak of democracy without adjectives. It comes from below. . . . Everyone . . . who does not limit himself or herself to thinking of democracy as a crystal birdcage to make the interests of oligarchies and elites glitter, salutes the movement of the paulista workers as the sign of a more promising tomorrow. May it arrive soon, for we all want democracy—now.[38]

Despite Cardoso's praise, what was most striking was the projection onto workers of his position. The workers he imagined were centrists engaged not in a fight to transform long-standing social relations but in a benign struggle for just wages and political democracy. Although unionists had demonstrated little interest in party politics, he insisted, "[Workers] know that . . . there is a moment for politics. Without it, the poorest workers . . . end up being highly exploited when there are not strong unions and national political parties that support them."[39] Even a renowned progressive academic was unable to imagine a world in which workers did not rely on a "national party" dominated, in all likelihood, by career politicians.

Despite the attempts of politicians, students, and intellectuals to render aid, they found that unions were hesitant to accept anything beyond moral support. When politicians called Lula asking how they could help, he refused to take their calls, stating that they should simply give legislative speeches—speeches that he knew no one paid attention to.[40] As for students, who had participated in the May Day rally in Osasco and were known to have "infiltrated" factories to instruct workers about class struggle, Lula said, "I think that the students, if they really want to help workers, should stay in the universities."⁴¹ For Lula, independence for labor should not only be from state intervention but also from anyone who presumed to speak for them.

By May 30, the metalworkers had successfully negotiated raises and returned to work.⁴² For the first time since 1968, workers had defied the regime's laws restricting strikes, and they had won. Although union leaders such as Lula had assisted with mediation, the strikes had arisen without direct union involvement, and victory had been easy, with no significant opposition from the government. The regime was likely hesitant because the generals realized that as annual raises were quickly lost to inflation, the workers' demands were not unreasonable. Why couldn't the "Revolution" accommodate a labor movement that accepted the rules of a capitalist economy while avoiding leftist subversion? Arenistas were similarly wary; with elections six months away, it would be unwise to attack working-class demands. After all, ARENA's failure to connect with the working class had led to the fiasco of 1974.

For their part, MDB politicians were unprepared for politically articulate unions and perplexed by workers' ambivalence to them. But this did not stop them from seeing the electoral potential of a mobilized working class, and party leaders eventually invited Lula to a meeting at Cardoso's apartment in the hope of convincing him to join the MDB.⁴³ Quércia argued that the workers' struggle could be incorporated into the MDB: "Everything [union leaders] hope for . . . can be found within the MDB. . . . We think it's important for the union leaders to participate in the MDB, where they can apply pressure for the realization of the projects that interest them."⁴⁴ And when General Monteiro, the MDB's presidential candidate, met privately with Lula and autênticos union leaders, he begged them, "Don't let your organization be characterized by political behavior, don't let any type of outside forces distort your principle objectives, but continue being a instrument of struggle specifically for labor problems."⁴⁵ In the view of opposition leaders, the workers' struggle for fairer wages and labor laws should be incorporated into the struggle against the regime. Lula and his allied unionists, however, were formulating a vision of working-class politics that challenged an entire centuries-old socioeconomic system.

Nevertheless, with only two parties, the MDB was the only route to political office for these union leaders and their sympathizers among intellectuals. The 1978 elections saw several unionists and leftist allies on the MDB ticket. Benedito Marcílio, president of the Santo André metalworkers' union, was elected federal deputy. Aurélio Peres, a São Paulo metallurgical unionist, militant in the PCdoB, and activist against the rising cost of living, had run with no hope of winning but merely to gain attention for communists; he was elected with nearly fifty thousand votes.⁴⁶ The twenty-eight-year-old Geraldo Siqueira Filho was a former Trotskyist student activist who had been arrested in 1970 for passing out pamphlets to workers; one of his comrades was tortured and killed in DOPS custody. In 1978, he was elected state deputy for São Paulo.⁴⁷ His colleague in the legislative assembly, Irma Passoni, was a former nun and an organizer of ecclesiastical base communities; when she joined the state legislature, conservative politicians grumbled that she welcomed "tie-less ragamuffins" to her office.⁴⁸ Eduardo Suplicy, the economist who had defended the strikes in the press, was also elected state deputy. These new deputies would play a key role in supporting workers' mobilization in 1979.

1979: "IT IS UP TO THE WORKERS TO CHANGE THE RULES OF THE GAME"

On March 15, 1979, Figueiredo, chief of military staff under Médici and head of the SNI under Geisel, was inaugurated as Brazil's fifth consecutive general-president. His father had commanded troops for the paulista rebels in the Constitutionalist Revolution and after the fall of the Estado Novo was elected federal deputy from the UDN; two of his brothers also became generals. As early as 1976, a foreign diplomat noted that he was Geisel's most likely choice as his successor.⁴⁹ When Geisel designated him in 1977, despite a thwarted plot by General Sylvio Frota to pressure Geisel into naming him instead, there had been little consultation of the Armed Forces and virtually none of civilian politicians; Figueiredo was Geisel's personal choice. Not only would he maintain détente, but he also expanded it to *abertura*—political opening. In the evaluation of the British embassy, Figueiredo believed in "less repression, some more liberty, and, indeed, more democracy within the limits set by the revolutionary framework, the concept of 'relative democracy,' and the accepted need for the State to maintain protective mechanisms in its own defence."⁵⁰ While professing devotion to democracy, he warned that "intransigence," signified by the MDB "attempting to impose the victory of its ideas," could delay abertura.⁵¹ Whatever authoritarian measures they relaxed, the generals refused to lose control. But Figueiredo's ability to impose his will on politicians would face limitations due to Geisel's most significant reform: the repeal of AI-5. On September 21, 1978, Congress approved a constitutional amendment replacing it with "safeguards" designed to "defend" the regime against subversion. Although the revocation of AI-5 received the enthusiastic support of ARENA, it garnered only one MDB vote, as the party protested that the "safeguards" were as authoritarian as the act. Although the amendment restored parliamentary immunity (with limited exceptions) and habeas corpus, it also created a "state of emergency" that could suspend civil liberties for up to 180 days without congressional approval.⁵² For the MDB, the reforms constituted the institutionalization of a decade-old state of exception.

Still, change was in the air. Although politicians speculated about what other reforms Figueiredo might permit, such as amnesty, a multiparty system, or direct gubernatorial elections, these changes would have limited immediate relevance for workers, who faced the same declining real wages as a year earlier. For 1979,

São Paulo's metallurgical unions demanded a 29 percent raise above the inflation rate.⁵³ While most unions accepted a compromise offered by their bosses, united in the Federation of Industries of the State of São Paulo (FIESP), the ABC unions rejected the offer, and on March 12, three days before Figueiredo's inauguration, over 150,000 metalworkers went on strike.⁵⁴ Two days later, workers in several unions in the interior held assemblies in which they forced their union leadership to withdraw their acceptance of the FIESP proposal.⁵⁵

Maluf, sworn in the same day as Figueiredo, reacted sanguinely, affirming, "Strikes are a right in democracies."⁵⁶ Labor Minister Murilo Macedo, a career banker who had just served as São Paulo business and finance secretary, promised that he would only take a hard line if all other solutions failed: "[I will] maintain dialogue until it breaks down. I will continue until every option has been exhausted."⁵⁷ ARENA president, José Sarney, senator from Maranhão, admitted, "All classes have the right to manifest their demands," but he added that it was important to remain attentive, in order to make sure that "people who wish to exploit [the workers] politically" did not take control of the labor movement.⁵⁸ Indeed, this would remain the great fear of government officials and ARENA politicians alike—that undereducated workers might allow students or communist agitators to co-opt what should be an apolitical movement.

Yet this tolerance evaporated as it became clear that unlike 1978, this new strike was not a spontaneous occurrence; rather, the three local ABC metalworkers' unions voted to strike, and their leaders entered direct negotiations with FIESP, authorized by the businesses to negotiate on their behalf. This time, striking workers, instead of sitting at their stations without working, went to the streets and organized picket lines.⁵⁹ In São Bernardo, the union organized daily assemblies in the Costa e Silva Municipal Stadium; up to 80,000 workers came to hear Lula and other union leaders report on negotiations and vote whether to continue the strike as FIESP rejected their demands.⁶⁰ And this time, the workers, who usually lived paycheck to paycheck, were able to avail themselves of food banks organized by their wives, charity organizations, and, above all, the Catholic Church, led by Cláudio Hummes, bishop of ABC.⁶¹ MDB federal deputies launched a relief fund; within a week, 120 of 189 deputies had donated a total of 150,000 cruzeiros ($6,643 at the time).⁶² As the strike entered its second week, the São Bernardo union issued a note soliciting support, arguing that theirs was "a struggle of all Brazilians and democrats, of those who, in the most diverse areas, struggle for [civil] liberties, amnesty, a constitutional assembly, for the establishment of . . . the true rule of law."⁶³

Within three days of the start of the strike, the TRT ruled that it was illegal; Lula commented that while the labor courts could take two years to resolve a worker's complaint against a business, the TRT had ruled for the bosses within hours.⁶⁴ As in 1978, the unions ignored the ruling. Regime officials and ARENA politicians now criticized the strike as an assault on law and order. Senator Antônio Lomanto Júnior of Bahia argued, "[The strike] is considered illegal by the justice system, . . .

which has conducted itself with complete . . . impartiality."[65] Similarly, Jarbas Passarinho, the Pará senator who had served as labor minister under Costa e Silva, asserted, "At this moment of democratic opening, when all of us are struggling for the implantation . . . of the rule of law, you cannot . . . just completely ignore a law."[66] Maluf bluntly cited the infamous quotation attributed to First Republic president Washington Luis: "It's no longer an economic matter—it's become a police matter."[67]

Montoro retorted, "The strike . . . is not a police matter; it's a question of justice."[68] Quércia, in a speech that used the word *just* or *justice* sixteen times, argued that the law arenistas defended was "an arbitrary law, a law of force, a law of violence. The workers stripped this law of its power last year, just as they are doing in the current strike, because what motivates the spirit of this strike is justice, and this law is not just." If the strike was illegal, the law should be brought into line with justice.[69] Senator Marcos Freire commented that ARENA did not have the moral standing to demand respect for the law: "In this country, laws have been systematically disrespected, violated, beaten down, without these voices who want to speak up now . . . ever having defended the highest law, the Constitution." Labor laws, particularly the Vargas-era, corporatist Consolidation of Labor Laws (CLT), "which imposes an odious tutelage on unions," were the problem, not strikes.[70]

Yet for the regime and its ARENA allies, the problem was not simply that the strikes were illegal; they might also have been subversive. Otávio Gonzaga Júnior, the new state secretary of public safety, claimed that the workers had been infiltrated by the Trotskyist student-worker group Convergência Socialista and remarked that the pickets reminded him of "an old communist tactic."[71] DOPS director, Romeu Tuma, added that his officers had caught Convergência members distributing to workers a newsletter dedicated to the strike.[72] When a socialist organization passed out propaganda and participated in pickets, what could it be other than a subversive plot? Senator Aloysio Chaves leapt on the claim of leftist infiltration, which proved, he argued, that the strike was not simply an attempt to gain better salaries for workers.[73]

Some MDB politicians responded by denying the possibility of infiltration. Rio de Janeiro's Roberto Saturnino Braga insisted, "There is nothing political about the movement, nothing of ideology, nothing of infiltration. It is a legitimate movement, sprung spontaneously from the breast of the working class."[74] Quércia, however, argued that if there was a leftist faction in the strike, it was surely made up of workers, who had a right to hold any political philosophy.[75] Strike leaders in ABC, cognizant that "infiltration" would serve to justify repression, also dismissed these claims. At a rally, Lula denied "any influence of any group foreign to our class."[76] Almir Pazzianoto, an MDB state deputy and the lawyer for the São Bernardo union, told workers that if they were "radical," it was radicalism in defense of a better life: "Yes, we are radicalizing. We are radicalizing so that we can bring food to the worker's table, so that he can give the minimum condition of survival to his wife and children."[77]

Despite these defenses, repression came quickly. The São Paulo military police sent its riot force, with two thousand officers, forty bulletproof cars, and weapons ranging from electric truncheons to AR-15 rifles.[78] Repression was widespread, with daily reports of violence. On the first day of the strike, even before the TRT ruled it illegal, military police appeared at a picket line outside a São Bernardo factory. They cursed the unionists, beat them with clubs, and pulled guns on them.[79] Over the coming days, riot police were housed inside the Volkswagen factory, from which they made periodic sorties to harass workers.[80] By the third day, armed police stood guard outside some of the factories to prevent lines from forming.[81] In Santo André, police threatened picketing workers with arrest and beating.[82] The situation became so tense that the government, only a week into Figueiredo's term, considered declaring a state of emergency.[83] As violence escalated, Lula protested, "Just to defend the boss's sidewalk, the police beat up workers, the main ones responsible for the greatness of the country."[84]

Police violence helped produce a shift in opposition politicians' involvement, as members of the MDB began to intervene to protect workers. Those who took to the streets in 1979 had few ties to the traditional political class. Instead, they were former student activists, Catholic organizers, and communist sympathizers who had entered politics the year before. New state deputies like Siqueira Filho, Suplicy, and the nine-month pregnant Passoni drove to São Bernardo almost daily in their official vehicles, attempting to deter violence against workers. They were joined by federal deputies such as Alberto Goldman (who had just moved from the state legislature to Congress), the journalist Audálio Dantas, and the autêntico Airton Soares, a second-term deputy who previously served as a lawyer for political prisoners.[85] With Lula's blessing, they joined picket lines as early as 4:00 a.m. to report incidents of police violence to state officials.[86] Strikers waiting at bus stops to convince their fellows to skip work were only saved from violence when deputies, journalists, and Bishop Hummes joined them.[87]

On March 21, Macedo flew to São Paulo to broker an agreement.[88] Yet the next day, the unions rejected FIESP's counterproposal because it failed to budge on the amount of the salary adjustment. Lula scoffed that the proposal did not deserve "even 50 votes" from the workers in the stadium.[89] Hours later, Macedo, with the authority granted by the CLT, decreed intervention in the ABC unions. Lula, Marcílio, and the São Caetano union president were removed from their posts. The intervention order parroted the government's law and order argument. It read in part, "The defense of professional interests by resorting to a strike is only justified inasmuch as said right places itself within the framework of legality.... The tolerance of disobedience to what has been judged... is incompatible with social peace and citizens' rights."[90]

For workers, intervention demonstrated how hollow a promise abertura was.[91] As a Minas Gerais union president bitterly noted, "We have witnessed a demonstration of the promised abertura. . . . There is no way to deny that we live in a military dictatorship."[92] Indeed, the intervention looked like nothing less than an invasion. Police secured the streets around the unions' headquarters early on the morning of March 23, arresting workers who got in their way and throwing them, battered and bleeding, into police vans. Workers fought back with kicks, rocks, and sticks, and several police officers were taken to the hospital.[93] When the MDB state deputy Geraldo Siqueira tried to stop an arrest, a punch in the face from a DOPS agent knocked him to the ground—an act of disrespect remarkably similar to the beating São Paulo deputy Santilli Sobrinho had taken at UnB a decade before.[94] The police moved into the unions' buildings, holding hundreds of workers inside for hours; those inside the São Bernardo union were only freed when state deputy Wanderlei Macris made a phone call to Maluf to intervene.[95]

São Bernardo was in an uproar. Up to 20,000 infuriated workers gathered in the plaza around the city hall, since the police had blocked off their usual meeting place in the municipal stadium a block away. One thousand riot police arrived and used tear gas to try to break up the demonstration, but the workers threw the canisters back and refused to leave. Fearing an imminent battle, Tito Costa, the MDB mayor, came down from his office and gave a speech asking the workers to return home. The police commander joined Costa, taking the microphone to say that he too was the son of a worker but begging them to leave before he had to resort to force. The workers responded by singing the national anthem, and the teary-eyed commander withdrew to call his superiors; with their permission, the riot police withdrew. Bishop Hummes then led the workers in the Lord's Prayer before they left.

The next day, 25,000 workers filled the plaza. Cardoso and several MDB deputies stood watch, not only to express solidarity, but also to make sure that a restless crowd did not get out of control. "Where is the mayor?" Cardoso asked. "If he doesn't arrive soon, someone's going to have to take charge and calm this crowd down." He pulled aside the union treasurer, Djalma Bom, the highest-ranking union official around, and asked him to "talk to the people, in order to avoid provocations." Bom then gave a speech reminding the workers that their battle was with the bosses and asked them to go home.[96] The following day, Sunday, Hummes held a "metalworkers' Mass," attended by 4,000 workers in a church designed for 1,500. In the first row sat Lula, Marcílio, and MDB deputies. An additional 15,000 workers stood outside, listening via loudspeakers.[97] After the Mass, Hummes invited Lula and Marcílio to speak. The intervention notwithstanding, they retook command of the strike, urging the workers to stand firm but to avoid confrontations with police.[98] On Monday, however, the strike was smaller. Though the workers in front of the city hall may have been disposed to maintain the strike, two weeks of repression had taken their toll, and for many, bills and rent would be due April 1.⁹⁹ The unions and FIESP thus reached an agreement on March 27. The strike would end immediately; a commission of union leaders, businessmen, and labor ministry officials would negotiate a salary adjustment within forty-five days, and Lula and the other deposed leaders would be restored to their positions. In a new stadium assembly, 70,000 workers approved the agreement.¹⁰⁰

One month passed, and no deal had been reached on the wage adjustment. By May Day, the possibility of a new strike loomed. One year earlier, May Day had demonstrated workers' restlessness. This year it showcased a mobilized working class in open rebellion against recalcitrant employers and government tutelage. Fifty thousand workers attended an open-air Mass in front of the São Bernardo city hall, where a choir sang a Portuguese rendition of "We Shall Not Be Moved." In place of the usual penitential rite, they prayed, "Christ, the workers were forced to go on strike, to seek a small pay raise, while the multinationals have enormous profits. Christ, help us to correct injustice."¹⁰¹ Meanwhile, the state government held its May Day festivities in Pacaembu Stadium. Perhaps 5,000 workers milled about the stadium, surrounded by banners reading, "Workers, the Labor Ministry is always on your side."¹⁰²

That afternoon, an astounding 130,000 workers packed the São Bernardo municipal stadium and the surrounding streets for an unprecedented "United May Day" rally that brought together workers, politicians, and a cross section of civil society. Tito Costa proclaimed ABC "the social capital of Brazil" and read a message from Guimarães: "Only your organization and struggle will enable the workers to have an effective participation in the fruits of the nation's economic development, opposing themselves to an authoritarian and unjust regime that enables the scandalous enrichment of few to the detriment of the whole of the Brazilian nation."¹⁰³ The workers listened to representatives of the Brazilian Amnesty Committee, UNE, and the women's movement, as well as federal deputy, Aurélio Peres, speaking on behalf of the Movement against the Cost of Living. A worker read a "Manifesto to the Nation" signed by unions and civil society groups. "Because workers have acquired consciousness," it read, "this May Day is a historic moment. It proves that the workers have begun to recover their own voice, to incorporate themselves into the national political scene, and to demand their effective participation in the economic, social, and political development of the country." Finally, Lula spoke. To thunderous applause, he said, "Today workers . . . understand that only uniting around their common cause will allow the entire class to achieve its political emancipation. . . . It's up to us, the workers, to change the rules of the game, and instead of being ordered around like we are today, to start giving the orders around here."¹⁰⁴

Here was a speech that challenged the status quo, nearly a call for (peaceful) revolution. The *Folha* called Lula's speech "as hard as granite and as incompetent as a high school student writing a paper about a topic he or she doesn't understand." The worst part was the call for workers to "give the orders," which was "excessively fervent and sullied with a strong dose of romanticism."[105] *O Estado* directed an editorial to Lula, who they accused of "growing Manichaeism." "ABC is not the Sierra Maestra, Brazil is not Cuba, capitalism has 300 years of experience, and the Brazilian people do not want some other system."[106] The press could accept workers mobilizing for better salaries, but mobilization to transform social relations was more than the papers' owners, themselves practically a part of the political class, could accept.

On May 11, the ABC unions and FIESP finally reached an agreement, which the workers ratified in an assembly.[107] Four days later, Macedo revoked the intervention in the ABC unions and authorized the return of their presidents.[108] After a two-and-a-half-week strike and two months of mobilization, the unions ended up with exactly the salary adjustment FIESP had offered to begin with. The strike was a failure, and it had aroused the ire of the military, the police, and ARENA politicians. As Macedo put it, "Strikes for the sake of strikes are inconceivable in modern unionism, [which] must be apolitical.... There is no place among us for class struggle.... Thus [the government] will act against movements that are offensive to the law, peace, and the national common good."[109] When a bus strike shut down public transportation in the state capital in May, Maluf commented that "liberty is being used as an excuse for licentiousness," and "many people are confusing democracy with anarchy."[110] The vision that ARENA politicians, and certainly the generals as well, had for workers was not so different from the one the generals had for the political class: limited freedom to criticize and offer "constructive" suggestions while always letting others have the final word.

Yet some of the strike's effects on labor were positive. In contrast to the year before, when Lula rejected overtures from politicians and social movements, this year he acknowledged that the workers fought in the context of a broader struggle against authoritarianism. As a result, the strike received the solidarity not only of leftist students but also the amnesty and cost of living movements and the Catholic Church. For the first time since defending students in 1968, politicians rushed to the streets to protect demonstrators from repression. At the same time, the politicians supporting the workers in the streets were usually civil society activists or communists. Meanwhile, politicians like Ulysses, Montoro, and Quércia refrained from joining their leftist colleagues at the factory gates, instead remaining in Brasília or São Paulo, where they gave speeches and proposed changes to labor law. Beneath all this was a latent tension between MDB politicians and workers fed up not only with military authoritarianism and government tutelage but also with a system of social relations in which the political class was profoundly implicated. Opposition politicians sympathized with the workers' struggle to cast off government supervision, and some of them were eager to protect the workers from violence, but how would they react if workers attempted to "start giving the orders around here"?

Over the next year, the political situation would change more dramatically than at any time in a decade. It had been ten years since over three hundred politicians had been removed from office in the wake of AI-5, and men like Mário Covas were eager to reenter politics. In late August, Congress approved an amnesty law that pardoned everyone who since 1961 had committed "political crimes," had their political rights suspended, or been purged from the civil service, judicial system, military, or unions. However, the amnesty excluded those convicted of "terrorism, assault, kidnapping, and personal attacks." Moreover, by offering amnesty to anyone who committed "crimes of any nature related to political crimes," the law pardoned military or police personnel who had tortured political prisoners. The MDB strenuously opposed both these latter measures, but ultimately the government's bill passed, excluding the guerrillas who had suffered the worst of the regime's violence but pardoning those who had tortured them.

The next step in abertura came in October: party reform. While politicians abhorred the ARENA/MDB binary, the MDB was incensed by a key provision in the bill: it would abolish the existing parties as a precondition to forming new ones. The party argued that the measure constituted a naked attempt to divide and conquer the opposition, since it was taken for granted that ARENA legislators would join the government party while the MDB's moderate/autêntico divide and the return of amnestied politicians would cause it to splinter. Despite spirited MDB opposition, the ARENA majority approved the bill, and Figueiredo signed it. Over the following months, politicians scrambled to form and join new parties. ARENA was reconstituted as the Party of Social Democracy (PDS). ARENA liberals such as former São Paulo mayor Olavo Setúbal and state party president Cláudio Lembo joined MDB "moderates" like Tancredo Neves to form the Popular Party (PP). The majority of MDB politicians joined the Party of the Brazilian Democratic Movement (PMDB), which, like its predecessor, billed itself as a broad front for the restoration of democracy. Former Rio Grande do Sul governor, Leonel Brizola, and Ivette Vargas, niece of Getúlio, were locked in a bitter dispute to found a Brazilian Labor Party (PTB) with the same name as the Vargas-founded labor party dissolved in 1965.

1980: THE REPUBLIC OF SÃO BERNARDO

The smallest new party was the Workers' Party (PT), formed by Lula, members of the labor movement, and a coalition of progressive politicians, Catholic activists, and leftist intellectuals. The party's program crystallized the consciousness that had developed among unionists through the strikes: "The great majorities who construct the wealth of the nation want to speak for themselves. They no longer expect that the conquest of their . . . interests will come from the dominant elites." The party was "born from the will for political independence of workers," who must participate in "all of society's decisions," not simply labor. "[The workers] know that the country will only be truly independent when the State is directed by the working masses."[111] While the other parties had arisen through negotiations between factions of the political class, the PT proposed something unprecedented in Brazil. Whereas the PMDB proposed incorporating workers into a struggle against authoritarianism, and labor parties claimed to speak on their behalf, the PT asserted that the masses should speak for themselves.

Intellectuals like the political scientists Francisco Weffort and José Álvaro Moisés, the economist Paul Singer of CEBRAP, and the historian Sérgio Buarque de Holanda were founding members of the new party. They were joined by politicians, among them, federal deputy Airton Soares, former deputy Plínio Sampaio, and São Paulo state deputies Suplicy, Siqueira, and Passoni, all of whom followed up on their solidarity with workers the year before. Yet the majority of opposition politicians joined the PMDB, while many longtime labor allies, including the Santo André union president Marcílio, joined one of the labor parties. Certainly they had legitimate electoral reasons to spurn a small regional workers' party. Yet the rejection of the PT by figures such as Montoro, a former labor minister and longtime workers' advocate in Congress, or Cardoso, who had long argued for the integration of workers into national politics, strongly indicates that many politicians and intellectuals were uneasy with the sociopolitical changes that the PT envisioned.

Cardoso's failure to join was especially striking. In 1978, when he ran for the Senate, he received the unconditional support of Lula, who he said told him, in a jab at Montoro, "You don't do what those others do, who spend their time giving lessons to workers, telling them what to do, and you don't call yourself the workers' senator."[112] Yet when Lula founded the PT, Cardoso was absent. In part, this was due to ambition. Cardoso had finished second to Montoro in the 1978 Senate race, and if Montoro won the governorship in 1982 and left the Senate, Cardoso would serve the remaining four years of his term—but only if he remained in Montoro's party. Yet more fundamentally, Cardoso's decision stemmed from an abiding suspicion of mass mobilization. In a 1972 article for the *New Left Review*, he argued that "progressive social integration" could not originate from "the State or bourgeois groups," but neither could the "marginalized sector" (i.e., the working class) be "the strategic (or revolutionary) side of dependent industrialized societies." To create a more just society, what was needed was "denunciation of marginalization as a consequence of capitalist growth and the organization of unstructured masses—indispensable tasks of analysis and practical politics."[113] Of course, if the state, bourgeois industrialist and business classes, and "unstructured masses" were all untrustworthy, that left only analysts and "practical" politicians like Cardoso. When Cardoso worried in front of São Bernardo's city hall that workers would get out of control without guidance, this merely repeated views he had espoused since at least 1972. Despite his progressive politics, he remained doubtful that the working class could direct its own destiny.

The PT, then, would have to be built without the support of some of its most natural allies. Moreover, Lula placed himself in the precarious position of having two roles; in addition to leading a new party, he remained head of the country's most militant union. As the annual salary negotiations approached, Lula's dual roles would add a new dynamic to the labor movement. For 1980 the unions demanded a reduction from a 48- to a 40-hour workweek, union representatives in factories, and a "productivity raise" of 15 percent. FIESP flatly rejected the first two proposals and offered only a 5 percent raise above inflation.[114] On March 30–31, the ABC metalworkers again voted to strike.[115] Several unions in the interior voted to join.[116] The opposition parties in the legislative assembly immediately announced that they would keep a team of deputies waiting by telephones twenty-four hours a day, ready to assist workers.[117]

On April 1, the TRT met for the formality of declaring the strikes illegal. Yet in an astounding decision, the labor court ruled 13–11 that it was legally unqualified to rule on the strike's legality and set the productivity wage adjustment at 6 to 7 percent, depending on salary.[118] The next day, Lula presented the decision to the stadium assembly and asked the union lawyer, state deputy Pazzianoto, to explain the ruling. Yet as Pazzianoto spoke, military helicopters began making passes overhead. The rotors blew a gale over the stadium, the noise was deafening, and soldiers aboard pointed their machine guns at the throng below. Cardoso had accompanied Pazzianoto and recalled years later, "When the helicopter accelerates like that, it's terrible. You don't know what will happen."[119] It was a naked attempt at intimidation. As the helicopters roared overhead, Lula put the continuation of the strike to a vote, and despite their court victory, the workers raised their hands to vote to continue the strike until they received a concession on the question of the union representative and a moratorium on layoffs.[120] Pazzianoto warned Lula that he should quit while he was ahead, but the strike continued all the same.[121]

After a week without progress, despite Macedo's constant presence in São Paulo pressuring for a solution, the government, arguing that the TRT ruling was flawed, appealed to the Supreme Labor Court.[122] Before the court could rule, Macedo was called to Brasília, where Golbery allegedly instructed him to end the strike any way he could.[123] The same day, the presidents of the opposition parties issued a joint statement: "The impasse . . . owes itself to the intransigence of the regime, the accomplice of large economic interests and the wealthy classes," whose "true objective [is] the perpetuation of an unjust and iniquitous social order through the maintenance of power in the hands of a privileged minority."[124] The opposition was correct in its accusation of regime complicity with employers, as Golbery and Macedo instructed FIESP, which had been inclined to accept the TRT ruling, to ask the court to reconsider.[125] On April 14, by a 14–12 vote, the court reversed its own ruling; several judges issued opinions directly contradicting opinions of two weeks before.[126]

Labor Minister Macedo made halfhearted attempts to mend fences with workers. He claimed that no intervention was coming yet and that he was only concerned with getting the workers back to work as quickly as possible in order to minimize the wages they lost from the strike. Trying to improve his public image, he agreed to an interview with a television reporter who brought questions from metalworkers. "Minister, you say that the strike is illegal. Is it also illegal for the worker to go hungry?" "If you had a daughter my age, making the salary that I make working 11 hours a day, . . . would you be in favor of or opposed to the strike?" "You said that the workers of São Bernardo make good money. Would you like to trade salaries with me?" Such aggressive questions violated nearly five centuries of Brazilian social norms governing how slaves should address their masters and workers speak to their employers. Upon discovering what the questions were, Macedo canceled the interview.[127]

Lula and the unions defied the new decision, vowing that the strike would continue.[128] The stage was set for a showdown. Two days later, military police in São Bernardo arrested twenty-nine strikers for attempting to block nonstriking workers from going to work. Shots were fired, and workers were beaten, reported PT federal deputy Airton Soares.[129] As the unrest escalated, on the evening of April 17 Macedo again declared government intervention in the São Bernardo and Santo André unions (the São Caetano and interior unions had gone back to work).[130] Once again Lula and Marcílio were removed, but this time they would never return. Sources told the press that the order had come from Figueiredo himself, against Macedo's wishes.[131]

In São Bernardo, Lula gave a short speech to a crowd of workers: "The union is not this building; the union is each of you, wherever you are. If I go to prison and hear that the strike has ended without our victory, I'm going to be pissed off." He then led the workers in a rendition of Geraldo Vandré's song "Pra não dizer que não falei das flores": "Come on, let's go / Those who wait will never know anything / Those who know choose the time / They don't wait for things to happen." Back inside, Lula, his directorate, and politicians stayed awake all night, waiting for government interventors to arrive. While Lula sat on a sofa, politicians, journalists, and academics speculated about Lula as a leader, Lula as future president of Brazil.[132]

The next morning, the interventor arrived and police descended on the building while three hundred workers outside remained determined to resist. Pazzianoto and PMDB state deputy Flávio Bierrenbach attempted to persuade the police to withdraw, but Bierrenbach was knocked to the ground by the butt of a riot shield, and Pazzianoto was nearly trampled. Workers threw rocks and pieces of pavement, and the police responded with tear gas. The battle continued for hours, as more workers arrived and rained rocks on the police.[133] In São Paulo, Maluf remarked that Lula was finished; in six months the workers would forget him.[134]

The following morning, DOPS agents arrived at Lula's house and arrested him for "violating the national security law." PT state deputy Siqueira, who had been sleeping at Lula's house to ensure his safety after DOPS director Tuma had surreptitiously warned him that an arrest was imminent, attempted to accompany Lula but was forbidden by the arresting officers.[135] Nearly simultaneously, nine other union leaders, two "political militants," a journalist, and other civil society activists were arrested.[136] PT deputy Soares and São Paulo federal deputy João Cunha rushed to DOPS headquarters, where they managed to see Lula and the other prisoners.[137] The next evening, twenty-five opposition deputies and senators from across Brazil, including paulista autêntico Freitas Nobre and Robson Marinho, PMDB president of the São Paulo legislative assembly, went to DOPS to see the prisoners, but Romeu Tuma advised the legislators that they were being held incommunicado.[138]

The arrests dominated congressional debate for weeks. Members of the opposition parties were unequivocal in taking the side of the workers. PMDB senator Pedro Simon argued that the workers' militancy was part of a broad mobilization of society that could have only positive connotations. "A society that is agitated, debating, arguing . . . contributes to the future of this country and is not, as some imagine, something that creates crises and problems," Simon insisted.[139] Other opposition senators highlighted the regime's disingenuousness in promising political opening. Evandro Carreira (PMDB-AM) was perhaps the most impassioned: "On the part of the government, there is not really a desire for abertura, but the exclusive intention of directing the nation as though we were a cowardly herd, a nation of slaves with necks bowed before the scourge of the foreman."[140] Speaking for Brizola's labor party, Paraná's Francisco Leite Chaves asked why the regime cast strikes as a security threat: "They want free initiative for economic organizations to rake in profits . . . , but as soon as pertinent and just manifestations come from workers who are exploited like wild animals, the masters of power and privilege become afraid and indignant and loose the police to take charge of the repression."[141] Even PDS politicians quietly advocated for the workers. PDS members of the Chamber's Labor and Social Relations Committee sent Macedo a proposal for reforms to the CLT, including "the strengthening of collective bargaining," a new law regulating strikes, and new restrictions on mass layoffs.[142]

Certainly opposition politicians saw part of their role as holding the regime accountable for its inconsistencies from the rostrum. Above all, however, they promoted dialogue in the face of government heavy-handedness. And who more natural to facilitate negotiation than the elected representatives of the people? Even before the intervention, Marcos Freire begged the Senate to send a commission to São Paulo to help mediate. He told his colleagues, "This Senate should not just wait as a mere spectator."[143] PT senator Henrique Santillo insisted, "We have the duty—not just as men of the opposition, but also . . . the party that supports the government— . . . to exhaust every possibility to solve this impasse."[144] As Senator Teotônio Vilela explained, the situation was rapidly heading toward a crisis, and "if we are not able to do anything, tomorrow we will be held responsible, because . . . the appeal of the workers . . . was directed at all of us."[145]

Before the arrests, the only politicians directly involved had been PT deputies and a few leftist PMDB politicians. Yet after the arrests, possessed by a belief that it was their duty to take up negotiations, opposition legislators made the one-and-a-half-hour flight from Brasília to São Paulo to meet with FIESP representatives, the police, state officials, local politicians, and unionists in an attempt to broker a solution. Perhaps without Lula to keep the workers in check, politicians feared they might respond to police provocations with violence. Perhaps they sensed an opportunity to earn workers' loyalty and enhance their credibility with a vibrant social movement. Or perhaps authoritarian military rule had caused these members of the political class to shift their attitude toward popular mobilization. After living under military tutelage for sixteen years, they may have had a new appreciation for workers' experience under the tutelage of the Labor Ministry—or even under that of the elite of which they were themselves a part.

Of all the politicians who supported the strikes, none was more active than the Alagoas PMDB senator Teotônio Vilela. A former member of the UDN, he had supported the coup in 1964. He was elected to the Senate for ARENA in 1966, and he had signed the telegram pledging support for Costa e Silva in the wake of AI-5. Yet by the time Geisel took office, Vilela had become disillusioned, and he became an even fiercer critic than most of the MDB. In 1978, he was the only member of ARENA to vote against the replacement of AI-5 with authoritarian "safeguards," and in 1979, he finally joinned the MDB.[146] The morning that Lula was imprisoned, Severo Gomes, former minister of industry and commerce under Geisel whose increasing discontent had led to his dismissal in 1977, searched desperately for a politician to help him jumpstart negotiations between the unions and FIESP. The first to agree was Vilela, who took the next plane to São Paulo and commenced a dizzying succession of meetings.[147]

Vilela would remain in the area for the next three weeks, only flying back to Brasília to give the Senate updates on his efforts. In the first three days, he met with federal and state deputies; Cardinal Arns; the Commission of Justice and Peace; state security secretary Gonzaga Júnior; and Theobaldo de Nigris, president of FIESP, who promised to reopen negotiations. He also spoke with Justice Minister Ibrahim Abi-Ackel.[148] And he met clandestinely in prison with Lula after Gonzaga Júnior convinced Maluf to authorize the visit.[149] In the end, however, his efforts came to naught. By April 30, Vilela was fuming: "When we searched for those who hold power, the ones who are responsible for it disappeared, and we remained without interlocutors, the opposition and that immense mass of . . . striking workers. . . . The military operation launched in São Bernardo is simply a strategy to revalidate power."[150]

Many other politicians, including Montoro, Quércia, Guimarães, and Freitas Nobre, abandoned Brasília, making São Paulo and the ABC region their base of operations and returning only briefly to the federal capital to offer updates via speeches. On Tuesday, April 22, Guimarães, Cardoso, Covas (now serving as state president of the PMDB), Vilela, and others attended an assembly at the principal church in São Bernardo. They did not speak to the crowd; instead, they met with union leaders after the assembly ended. Vilela informed them that de Nigris had advised him that he had received a call from Brasília advising him not to restart negotiations and raged, "You don't play around with something important like this. I'm not a child. You don't make a commitment only to break it without giving any satisfaction."[151]

The situation was rapidly deteriorating. Though violence against workers, who had heeded appeals not to form picket lines, was sporadic, strong police presence outside church assemblies and inconsistent permission to use plazas to accommodate the overflow kept workers off balance. On Saturday, April 26, one week after Lula's arrest, the tense situation exploded into crisis. After an assembly at a church, deputies and senators were giving rides to city hall to three union leaders in official legislative assembly cars. Suddenly, the car carrying Quércia, PMDB state deputy Fernando Morais, and union member Enilson Simões de Moura (called "o Alemão," the German) was surrounded by four police cars and forced to stop. About twenty agents jumped out and rushed the car, machine guns pointed, and demanded that the legislators hand over Alemão. Quércia and Morais demanded that the officers identify themselves and produce a warrant, which they refused to do. When Quércia rolled down a window slightly to continue to argue, an agent threw a canister of tear gas into the car.[152]

While Quércia and Morais were arguing over Alemão's arrest, a car carrying Freitas Nobre (PMDB leader in the Chamber), Siqueira, and two unionists was also stopped. As Freitas Nobre and Siqueira hurried to lock the doors, shouting officers with machine guns stormed the car, opened the doors, removed the unionists, and sped off. Meanwhile, Montoro had arrived in yet another car and when he saw what was happening stopped and shouted, in the middle of the avenue, "Identify yourselves and leave, because the person talking to you is a Senator of the Republic!" When they refused, Montoro excoriated them for ignoring parliamentary immunity and told them that without a warrant no one was going anywhere. Just then, another officer arrived and identified himself as a DOPS agent but insisted that DOPS had nothing to do with the arrests. He attempted to take control of the situation by getting into Quércia's car and ordering the driver to take them to DOPS headquarters. Quércia, however, instructed the driver to take them to city hall. The car proceeded to city hall, already surrounded by cavalry, soldiers, firemen, and riot police with German shepherds.[153]

At city hall, the crowd of politicians and Alemão, accompanied by a dozen plainclothes officers, took the elevator to the mayor's office.[154] Vilela had arrived too and promptly called DOPS chief Tuma to demand an explanation. Tuma insisted that this was not a DOPS operation. At the same time, Montoro was arguing with the DOPS agent that he could not arrest Alemão without a warrant; even after a call to Raymundo Faoro, head of the Order of Brazilian Lawyers (OAB) confirmed that warrantless arrests were illegal, the agent insisted that "in special cases like this" warrants were not necessary.[155] Finally, a call to Gonzaga Júnior revealed that the warrant was en route.[156]

While politicians argued with the officers, Alemão was locked in Costa's office. Vilela was on the phone again, this time with Abi-Ackel, who already knew what was happening and was only surprised that a fourth union leader, Osmar Mendonça, had not been arrested too. "He wanted to know where [Osmar] was, but I wasn't going to tell him," Vilela said after he hung up. Vilela then called the president of the national vehicle manufacturers' association. Though his exaggerated description of the situation received laughs from some of the reporters and politicians, it vividly illustrates how invested Vilela was.

> They can take even the last worker in ABC, but you will be responsible for this national catastrophe. I also am a businessman. . . . Nothing justifies what is happening here; it is like a military operation of extermination. When they finish with the workers, next it will be us politicians. Then they'll finish off the students, the Church, the middle class—then what will be left of this country? You will be responsible for this.[157]

Costa was overheard commenting, "The republic of São Bernardo has been overthrown, but it is still a republic." Finally, another officer arrived, warrant in hand. Alemão was arrested and hauled out through a crowd of dozens of politicians.[158]

In response to this latest authoritarian measure, federal deputy João Cunha gave a speech so aggressive that even in this era of abertura it was withheld from publication in the *Diário da Câmara dos Deputados* (but preserved in a recording). He claimed that the events in São Bernardo "once again unmasked . . . the democratic cynicism of Mr. João Figueiredo, sung in prose and verse by the shameless and corrupt strategy of the regime." He blasted the regime for "oppressing, offending, marginalizing, alienating, and compromising the rights of our people" and promised that one day they would have to answer to "the people, whose harm against traitors is implacable." "Yoked to corruption, strangled by hidden ties, controlled by the powerful, they have no explanations beyond lies, violence, and explosions of authoritarianism and the clownish spectacle of the half-dozen generals who sustain them."[159]

MEDIA FILE 9. Clip of João Cunha speech criticizing attacks on legislators, April 28, 1980.
SOURCE: Câmara dos Deputados, COAUD, Arquivo Sonoro, http://imagem.camara.gov.br/internet/audio/default.asp.

Despite the arrests, the strike continued. "For every leader that is imprisoned, five more climb up here to speak," proclaimed the leader of the April 28 assembly.[160] Three days later, May Day arrived. While the workers prepared to hold a mass, the police prepared to repress any demonstrations. When workers in the plaza outside the church unfurled banners, the police chief ordered them removed; when the workers refused, the first canisters of tear gas were thrown. State deputy Irma Passoni called for calm to no avail, as workers grabbed the canisters and tossed them back. Yet just as the situation was spinning out of control, after a conversation with Vilela the police commander decided to withdraw.[161] One hundred thousand ebullient workers marched from the church to city hall, followed by a boisterous rally in the stadium.[162] It was the strike's final moment of glory. Hungry and running out of money, fearful that their employers would fire them after a month of absences, and worn out by police violence, workers drifted back to work. On May 11, they voted to end the strike.[163] A week and a half later, Lula and his fellow union leaders were released but faced a charge of "violating national security" for inciting an illegal strike. Despite providing some of the most emotionally gripping moments Brazil had ever seen, the final ABC metalworkers' strike had ended in total defeat.

CONCLUSIONS

As the final strike ended, José Álvaro Moisés, a political scientist and PT founding member, speculated, "Perhaps the ABC metalworkers' strike of 1980 will be recognized in Brazilian history as the episode that opened the process of the conquest of the fundamental rights of citizenship."[164] He was right. Despite the defeat of this strike, the metalworkers' movement was the catalyst for changes in Brazilian social relations that have endured for a generation. A mobilized working class demanded not simply better wages, but the right to enjoy and even define citizenship, "to start giving the orders around here." Although over the next few years the generals kept trying to salvage their "Revolution," one of its fundamental premises—a demobilized populace that passively accepted military fiat—had been dealt a punishing blow. And four and a half years later, as the next chapter shows, a vibrant civil society, acting in concert with the political class, would play a key role in finally forcing the regime from power.

The Populist Republic (1945-64) had witnessed a similar expansion in workers' political consciousness. As a host of labor histories have shown, the end of World War II and the fall of Vargas brought new opportunities for workers, above all, in industrializing São Paulo.[165] As a worker at a factory in São Miguel Paulista recalled, back in Bahia his political involvement had been limited to voting, but in São Paulo he was able to join a party and be heard: "[Here in São Paulo] we were part of it, and there [in Bahia], they gave us only the vote, just the vote, and we were gone."[166] For most workers before 1964, political participation meant the opportunity to pursue their interests within the system.[167] At times this might mean using Vargas's corporatist labor law and the labor court system to their advantage.[168] It could also mean joining a party that offered to advocate for their interests, most frequently the laborist PTB. Even the PCB (which, although officially banned, remained a significant force) largely chose to work within the system, allying itself and the workers it organized with populist politicians like Vargas or Adhemar de Barros in an effort to wrest at least some gains for the working class.[169] And when the Left did flex its muscle in the immediate postwar years and then again under Goulart, reaction was swift and decisive, with the PCB banned in 1947 and Goulart deposed in 1964.

Scholars have rightly challenged the assumption that the "new unionism" of 1978–80 was a reaction against the supposedly "sell-out" unions of the three preceding decades.[170] But an overemphasis on continuities obscures very real differences. In fact, the 1978–80 strikes went much further than any of the worker mobilizations of the Populist Republic, for instead of joining a laborist party such as Brizola's Democratic Labor Party (PDT), Lula and the metalworkers joined with intellectuals and civil society activists to form their own party, the PT. Moreover, they demanded fundamental changes to a centuries-old system of social relations that kept "peons" subservient to their bosses and the rest of their "betters" in the socioeconomic elite, including the political class. The last two times the political class had felt their class privileges threatened by popular demands, in 1947 and 1964, the vast majority of politicians had supported or accepted the banning of the PCB and the military coup. This time, even most regime allies were reluctant to criticize the strikes, and oppositionists, leftists and liberals alike, risked their physical integrity to defend the metalworkers from police repression. Certainly this support had limits. And decades later, in 2016, a majority of the political class leapt at the opportunity to carry out a parliamentary coup to stifle popular demands again. But in 1980 cracks were appearing in politicians' conviction that the power to determine Brazil's social, political, and economic course could continue to reside exclusively with people like them. By 1985, when the regime finally fell, these cracks would become too wide to seal.

7

"I Want to Vote for President"

Diretas Já, the Political Class, and the Demise of the Military Dictatorship

As the sun set on April 16, 1984, a multitude the likes of which Brazil had never seen marched through São Paulo, demanding the approval of a constitutional amendment establishing *diretas já*—direct presidential elections now. Clad in yellow shirts emblazoned with the slogan, "I want to vote for president," undeterred by sporadic showers falling from a cloudy sky, 1.5 million Brazilians of every age, color, and class chanted, "Cry Figueiredo, Figueiredo cry! Cry Figueiredo, your hour has arrived," as they converged on Anhangabaú Valley, which separated the two halves of the city's center. From a massive stage, politicians and pop culture icons demanded direct elections to replace the stacked electoral college that was to select Figueiredo's successor in January 1985. Two decades' worth of opponents of the regime were there—from old leftists such as Brizola and Arraes to veterans of the struggle against the dictatorship like Guimarães, Montoro, Quércia, and Covas to new leaders such as Cardoso and Lula, as well as former student leaders, some of whom were now politicians after once having hated them. As the rally ended, the multitude, arms held high, sang the national anthem as yellow confetti fell. That night, in the words of the journalist Ricardo Kotscho, "democracy was within the reach of the hands of everyone, in the fluttering of the green and yellow flags, in the heartfelt sincerity of the singing, in the joy of a people reencountering their destiny."[1]

The Diretas Já campaign of 1984 provided some of the iconic images of Brazilian history. It appeared that the regime's demise was nigh, that the generals would finally have to accede to popular demand. A poll showed that 83 percent of Brazilians, including 75 percent of those who identified with the government-allied party, the Party of Social Democracy (PDS), which replaced ARENA after the 1980 reform, supported direct elections.[2] After two decades of the regime's attempts to deny, demonize, or deflect discontent, the message was unmistakable: Brazilians had rejected military rule. As the twentieth anniversary of the "Revolution" passed on March 31, it appeared more like a funeral to most.

Like the strikes in São Bernardo, the denouement of the regime in 1984–85 featured the enthusiastic support of opposition politicians—and greater tolerance among many members of the PDS—for the sort of popular mobilization that Brazilian elites had always seen as a threat. Yet after the amendment failed to pass, PDS delegates dissatisfied with their eventual candidate abandoned the regime and engineered a deal to support the PMDB's Tancredo Neves. Ultimately popular mobilization was not sufficient to topple the regime; it only fell when the heartfelt cry of the streets was complemented by the discontent of the political class. It is in Diretas Já and the electoral college negotiations that we see the culmination of politicians' dissatisfaction, which manifested itself most powerfully when it was the product of factionalism and self-interest. The problems with building a democracy in which the political class was never forced to confront its penchant for authoritarianism and residual unease with the expansion of citizenship would become clear only gradually over the next three decades.

HANGING ON BY THEIR FINGERNAILS: THE MILITARY ATTEMPTS TO RETAIN POWER

Between 1980 and 1984, Figueiredo and his military collaborators stubbornly attempted to maintain control. Having failed to win politicians' enthusiastic collaboration and no longer able to threaten them with cassação, Figueiredo nonetheless hoped to perpetuate military influence to keep the Left, politicians, and the masses under control. The government thus utilized a host of electoral manipulations to keep its dubiously reliable PDS allies in power. As the Portuguese embassy telegrammed home, "It has become definitively evident [that the] regime only plans [to use the] liberalizing process to recycle its internal and external image, attempting to make any eventual alternation in power as difficult as possible."[3] In 1981, a new law instituted mandatory straight party voting for the 1982 municipal, state, and congressional elections, with the expectation that local votes for the government-allied party would carry PDS gubernatorial candidates to victory and preserve the party's congressional majority.[4] The next year, a constitutional amendment changed the means of determining the composition of the electoral college that would elect the next president so as to guarantee a PDS majority. The same amendment also changed the quorum for approving future amendments back to two-thirds; even if the opposition took control of Congress, they would be unable to change the rules.[5]

These efforts were challenged by the deteriorating economic situation, as the 1980s witnessed Brazil's most dire recession in half a century. In the wake of the Iranian Revolution, the second oil shock again drove up the price of petroleum.

A simultaneous rise in world interest rates raised the cost of servicing the foreign debt, which had risen tenfold from 1970 to 1980. To stimulate an increase in exports, the government devalued the currency; inflation rose accordingly, from 55.8 percent in 1979 to 223 percent in 1984. Inconsistent wage policy and inflation caused a precipitous decline in real wages as the "lost decade" wore on. After averaging 8.9 percent growth between 1968 and 1980, GDP fell by an average of 0.6 percent between 1981 and 1984.[6] The regime's chief source of legitimacy had always been its economic record. Yet now, with the economy in freefall, the generals stubbornly held on.

In 1982, the opposition won a collective five-seat majority in the Chamber of Deputies, though the PDS retained a comfortable majority in the Senate.[7] The PDS also secured a thirty-vote advantage in the 686-seat electoral college. At the state level, the opposition won ten governorships, including Rio de Janeiro, where Brizola was elected. In São Paulo, Montoro achieved his dream of becoming governor, frustrated in 1978 by the April package, with Quércia as his running mate; together, the four opposition candidates won 77 percent of the vote.[8] Cardoso, as the MDB's runner-up in the 1978 Senate race, assumed Montoro's seat. After debate about whether the PMDB could in good conscience nominate a mayor for the city of São Paulo (mayors of state capitals were still appointed by the governors), Montoro chose Covas, who was promptly approved by the opposition-dominated state legislature.[9] Paradoxically, it was the PDS that protested that the mayor should be chosen by direct election or, failing that, by a "broad popular consultation."[10] Montoro refused the latter option, fearing that a poll of the populace might express a preference for a non-PMDB politician.[11] Even for the most committed oppositionists, democracy was suspect if it might produce an undesired outcome.

Though straight party voting was supposed to help the PDS, it had the opposite effect in São Paulo, as Montoro's voters also voted for PMDB mayors; as a result, the party increased its control of municipal governments from 41 to over 300. The number rose as new PDS mayors began switching to the PMDB, fearful that if they remained in what was now the opposition, their municipalities would lose benefits from the state government.[12] As for Maluf, he was elected federal deputy with the highest vote total in Brazilian history.[13] Maluf had no interest in a legislative career; he was going to Brasília to build ties with the senators and deputies who would select Figueiredo's successor. When he took his first postelection trip to Brasília, he told Nelson Marchezan, PDS leader in the Chamber, "I've arrived for my internship."[14]

The military claimed that the "Revolution" had been necessary to neutralize a communist threat, repair the economy, and reform the political class under military tutelage. Yet by the end of 1983, no one besides the most paranoid members of the intelligence services feared a communist revolution. The economy was in collapse, and Figueiredo had submitted to an International Monetary Fund (IMF) austerity plan. Finally, most of the regime's remaining politician supporters were sycophants who could abandon the party as soon as it lost an election—precisely the kind of politician the generals had claimed to revile in 1964 and 1968. And all the while, Figueiredo and his cronies continued to manipulate the rules to perpetuate what remained of a "Revolution" in crisis. It was at this moment that some in the opposition saw an opportunity to end the generals' project. It was time for direct presidential elections.

"DEMOCRACY WITHIN REACH": THE POLITICAL CLASS AND MASS MOBILIZATION IN DIRETAS JÁ

A month after arriving in Congress in February 1983, first-term PMDB deputy, Dante de Oliveira, proposed a constitutional amendment instituting direct elections for Figueiredo's successor.[15] The amendment's passage would be an uphill battle in light of the two-thirds requirement for passing constitutional amendments in a Chamber of Deputies where the PDS controlled 235 of 479 seats, not to mention a Senate that included the indirectly elected PDS senators of 1978. Traditional political bargaining would not convince PDS politicians to vote against a system that guaranteed their party the presidency and the purse strings it controlled. But what if they were pressured by a populace that could vote them out?

Starting in November 1983, the three largest opposition parties—PMDB, PDT, and PT—developed a plan to apply that pressure. Together with the country's labor and student unions and the progressive Catholic Church, they organized a rally outside São Paulo's Pacaembu Stadium. There was no hint that history would remember this as the beginning of the greatest mass mobilization Brazil had ever seen. Although the organizers invited opposition governors and passed out nearly a million flyers, only fifteen thousand people gathered in the Charles Miller Plaza on November 27. It was not even clear what the purpose of the rally was: in addition to direct presidential elections, the flyer cited rising unemployment, declining real wages, IMF austerity measures, and US interventions in Grenada and Nicaragua.[16] Most striking was the near-total absence of politicians, other than Cardoso and Lula, even though six opposition governors had arrived in São Paulo the day before to join Montoro to sign an open letter demanding direct presidential elections.[17] Politicians' spirited defense of striking workers three and a half years before notwithstanding, men like Montoro, Tancredo Neves, Paraná governor José Richa, and Pará governor Jader Barbalho still prioritized political manifestos over popular mobilization.[18]

Meanwhile, PDS presidential hopefuls began to prepare for indirect elections. In three of the previous four successions, the president had designated a general as his successor, and the military and ARENA had fallen in line. Figueiredo, however, was determined to hand power to a civilian, and aspirants began jockeying for his favor, just as gubernatorial hopefuls had for fifteen years. As early as January 1983, the divergences ran so deep that Army Minister Walter Pires privately confided to a friend that he could foresee the military possibly supporting Tancredo Neves as a "name of consensus."[19] Things only grew more muddled in December, when Figueiredo announced that he would allow the PDS to select a candidate on its own.[20] Successfully selecting one's successor is the ultimate mark of prestige in Brazilian politics, and Figueiredo's lack of interest was the most dramatic example of his exhaustion in the wake of serious heart problems.[21] Yet it is also likely his decision was due to the difficulties of keeping his allies in line. Far from becoming the selfless ruling class the generals envisioned, the PDS was showing that when the opportunity arose, they would fall back into the same self-interested bickering that had led the military to distrust them all along. As Tancredo Neves presciently observed, "The PDS succession is going to be like a fight with sickles in a dark room."[22]

By this point, three leading PDS candidates had emerged. For Maluf, Figueiredo's withdrawal was the best possible scenario, since, notwithstanding his best efforts to ingratiate himself, the president still saw him as a shamelessly corrupt self-promoter—the very type of politician the "Revolution" was to have reformed.[23] On one occasion, Figueiredo's sons had approached Maluf to request public financing for a business venture. Maluf scoffed at their plan to build a *drive-in* (a parking lot with individual cubicles to provide privacy to amorous couples): "This is ridiculous. You are General Figureiredo's sons; you have to think bigger than that."[24] Figueiredo, incensed, fumed to PDS president José Sarney, "I am going to kill Maluf, with a dagger in his belly, if it's necessary. He tried to corrupt me through my sons."[25] A secret report from the National Security Council (CSN) shared some of Figueiredo's concerns, for although Maluf was "a successful businessman, intelligent, ambitious, and courageous," he was believed to seek "personal projection," and although he was "a legislator from the party, he is not part the government."[26] Although Maluf denied it in our interview, it seems probable that part of the resistance to him was based on his Syrian Lebanese ethnicity. The Brazilian popular imagination has long cast Arab Brazilians (together with Jews) as grasping, conniving, and indiscreetly dishonest.[27] Regardless of his actions, his ethnicity rendered him inherently corrupt in the eyes of the press, ARENA leadership, and the generals.[28]

The second candidate, Vice President Aureliano Chaves, had as federal deputy voted against the 1968 request to prosecute Moreira Alves. After escaping the 1969 purges, he worked his way into the military's good graces by being exactly the sort of politician they professed to want: honest, hardworking, and obedient. Geisel selected him to govern his native Minas Gerais beginning in 1975, and in 1978 he was named Figueiredo's running mate.[29] When Figueiredo twice went to the United States for heart surgery, Chaves assumed the presidency on an interim basis, winning universal praise for his work ethic, equanimity, and leadership. The sense that Chaves was taking advantage of his illness to audition for the presidency infuriated Figueiredo. Unlike Maluf, his campaign was based on pronouncements to the press and meetings with politicians and businessmen. Polls indicated that the hardworking administrator would stand an excellent chance in direct elections; not coincidentally, Chaves affirmed his support for Diretas Já in early February.[30] The only military candidate was Mario Andreazza, an army colonel who had spent much of the prevous two decades in political posts, first as minister of transportation under Costa e Silva and then as minister of the interior under Figueiredo. Although he demonstrated neither Maluf's gusto for campaigning nor Chaves's political skill, there were rumors that Figueiredo might support him given his aversion to the other two.

As 1984 began, the opposition parties found themselves shut out, except for the occasional obvervation that if Maluf or Andreazza were the nominee, an opposition candidate would need only twenty-nine defections in the electoral college to win an indirect election.[31] But no one knew for certain who the PDS candidate would be. If it were the popular Chaves, would it be possible to peel twenty-nine electors away from him? And if it were Maluf, might he buy off the electors as he was rumored to have done in São Paulo in 1978? As a result, the PMDB and PDT made the strategic decision to join the PT in building a mass movement to obtain approval for the Dante de Oliveira amendment reinstituting direct elections immediately.

The first rally held with the support of an opposition governor was in Curitiba, on January 12. It was an unqualified success, with a crowd of over fifty thousand, though the SNI reported only fifteen thousand.[32] The master of ceremonies, at this demonstration and subsequent ones, was Osmar Santos, perhaps the greatest play-by-play commentator in Brazilian soccer history. Singers such as the samba composer Martinho da Vila entertained the crowd between speeches by film and TV actors and leading opposition politicians. Argentine president Raúl Alfonsín, whose own election two months before had ended his country's violent 1976–83 military dictatorship, sent an emissary to communicate his support. Paraná senator Álvaro Dias exclaimed, "This demonstration of ours is going to drown out the whisper of that spurious electoral college." To thunderous applause, Guimarães shouted, "We are going to take this disgusting and repugnant Bastille that is the electoral college. . . . The outstretched hand of President Figueiredo has not touched the desperate hand of unemployed Brazilians."[33]

Bolstered by Curitiba, the parties ramped up their planning for a "monster rally" in São Paulo. Pamphlets were passed out across the city and at mini-rallies held in neighborhoods, with residents invited to participate in mock elections. The women's movement, civil servant organizations, and a host of other groups organized their own events.[34] The movement gained an influential ally in the *Folha de S. Paulo*, which began to run almost daily editorials demanding direct elections.[35] Leading opposition figures went on radio or television to encourage people to attend.[36] Organizers chose a local holiday, the anniversary of the founding of the city, to maximize attendance, and Montoro announced that public transportation would be free.

By late afternoon on January 25, at least 300,000 people had arrived for what became a four-hour rally. Osmar Santos led the crowd in a chant, "*Um, dois, três, quatro, cinco mil!* We want to elect the president of Brazil!" The actor Carlos Vereza quoted a Charlie Chaplin line from *The Great Dictator*: "Dictators die. And the power they took from the people will return to the people."[37] Guimarães called the electoral college "a pestilent cellar where the dictatorship has imprisoned 60 million voter registrations."[38] Even a PDS state deputy spoke, though he was nearly drowned out by boos. Montoro told the crowd, "I was asked if there are 300,000 or 400,000 people here. But the answer is different: the hopes of 130 million Brazilians are here." Agents of federal and state security agencies sent to monitor the event could not help but marvel. An observer from the Department of Social Communication (the security agency that replaced DOPS—with many of the same officers—when Montoro abolished it in 1983) captured how this protest differed from any Brazil had ever seen: "In contrast with what used to happen, when the multitude was carried along by the speakers, today what one could see was the multitude running the show—clapping, singing, waving banners and flags."[39]

For three months the demonstrations continued: 60,000 in Belém; 300,000 in Belo Horizonte; 250,000 in Goiânia; 200,000 in Porto Alegre. Some politicians feared this unprecedented mobilization. "What are we going to with all these people?," Neves asked Lula and Brizola in Belo Horizonte. Yet other politicians—patriarchs like Guimarães and Montoro and upstarts like Lula alike—were moved, even energized. Montoro mused, "The people have wisdom. They know what they need, and this is the foundation of democracy."[40] As Lula remarked years later, "All we want is the people in the street, damnit! You don't have to be afraid, do you? Put them in the street and see what happens."[41] At every step, through speeches, media appearances, interviews, and newspaper columns, opposition politicians were at the center of the organizing. Guimarães became a national superstar; there was little doubt that the once timid people pleaser would be elected president if the amendment passed.

Yet it was not only the rallies that made Diretas Já remarkable but also the intensity of organizing at the neighborhood level. The Cultural and Recreational Association of the São Paulo neighborhood of Vila Prudente held a simulated election, won by Guimarães.[42] A "diretas" versus "indiretas" soccer match organized in São Paulo's Aclimação Park by student and neighborhood organizations featured a *pró-indiretas* team made up of players representing Figueiredo, Maluf, and other regime figures, with the IMF as referee. The Maluf player carried the ball in his arms, Figueiredo nearly collapsed from a "heart attack," and the IMF referee allowed all the indiretas players to act as goalkeepers. In the end, rule-breaking notwithstanding, the "diretas" side, comprising players representing women, students, workers, and the press, won 4 to 3.[43] In Bela Vista, Carnaval festivities were transformed into impromptu diretas demonstrations.[44] These local protests were often organized in concert with the official organizing committees for the rallies, as a way to encourage greater attendance.[45]

What made the demonstrations so successful? The support of leading media outlets may have contributed, although the Globo television network's position was ambivalent. Certainly Brazil's economic crisis played a leading role. And the presence of actors, singers, and athletes, along with opposition governors purchasing publicity and waiving public transportation fares on rally days, could not have hurt. Yet, above all, Diretas Já showcased the democratic potential of an alliance between a vibrant, mobilized civil society and the political class. As *Veja* put it, "Never before have so many people wanted the same thing at the same time."[46]

As momentum built, PDS politicians began to join the cause. Before the first rally in São Paulo, 75 percent of the 247 PDS mayors in the state signed a manifesto in support of direct elections.[47] A *pró-diretas* group of PDS politicians actively participated in organizing rallies.[48] Even the PDS's national president, José Sarney, announced that he would not enforce party fidelity when the amendment came to a vote.[49] With such staggering numbers in the streets, with opinion polls showing such support, many PDS politicians were unwilling to risk their careers over this. Motivated by expedience above all else, they knew a sinking ship when they saw it.

As the congressional vote on the amendment drew near, the opposition parties planned two massive final demonstrations—one in Rio de Janeiro, Brazil's cultural soul, and another in São Paulo, its economic heart. At the Rio rally on April 10, a million people gathered behind the city's Candelaria cathedral on the avenue named for Getúlio Vargas, filling the 12-lane, 72-meter-wide avenue for an entire kilometer.[50] The rally was not without minor incidents; the tensest moment came when a PT faction called the Foundation of Socialist Youth unfurled a huge red banner near the stage calling for a general strike. Brizola asked them to take it down, saying, "This is going to ruin the rally." When they refused, he urged the crowd around the students, "Pull that banner down! This isn't the place to create disorder."[51]

But the enduring memory of that day was its intense emotion. The press called it a combination of the World Cup and Carnaval—the two events that give Brazilians joy like no other.[52] The only word *Jornal da Tarde* could find to describe politicians' feelings was *perplexidade*—astonishment. "I've never seen anything like this," said Lula, the man who had once spoken to a stadium of 200,000 striking workers. Neves turned to Guimarães and told him, "Congress cannot remain indifferent to a demonstration like this." Guimarães nodded: "We are going to have diretas." The ninety-year-old lawyer and legal scholar Sobral Pinto, veteran of the resistance against Vargas, gazed over the crowd and pronounced, "The people want to get their citizenship back."[53] Or as the journalist Ricardo Kotscho put it, poetically as always:

The artist, the factory worker, the teacher, the liberal professional, the unemployed, the businessman, the white-collar worker, the laborer, the student, the journalist, the poet, everyone, of every color and size, with every fear and dream, yesterday let out their holy wrath and their beautiful certainty that... being Brazilian is something to be proud of.[54]

But the denouement of Diretas Já would happen in São Paulo. Indeed, for a century, Brazilian democracy has lived or died with São Paulo. Amid Vargas's assault on state autonomy, paulistas rebelled in the Constitutionalist Revolution of 1932. Three decades later, São Paulo's March of the Family with God for Liberty tolled the death knell for the Goulart presidency. And in 2016, even larger demonstrations on Avenida Paulista would help legitimize the political class and judiciary's congressional coup against President Dilma Rousseff and the PT. But on this night, 1.4 million paulistas stood together against authoritarianism and for democracy. As Lula pointed out in his speech, "Twenty years after [the March of the Family], I think that 80 percent of the people [who were there] have realized their mistake."[55]

Practically all the politicians who had led the opposition were there, along with several who had supported it. Neves came down from Minas Gerais, and Brizola flew in from Rio. Francisco Pinto, who had been imprisoned a decade before for criticizing Pinochet, was there, as was Miguel Arraes, former governor of Pernambuco who had been purged in the first days after the coup. Severo Gomes, former Geisel cabinet member, now a PMDB senator, attended with fellow senator Cardoso. Quércia was there. New politicians like Lula and his former union colleagues attended.[56] Even Teotônio Vilela, who had died in November, was present, represented by a four-meter puppet made of steel, styrofoam, paper, and paint.[57]

Nearly one and a half million people filled the center of São Paulo for a march from the Praça da Sé to Anhangabaú Valley. Covas commented on its historical significance: "I think that today will be the day that the people will demonstrate this new posture: they are no longer a passive actor, an amorphous mass who don't know what they want and need tutelage from immobilizing forces that maintain them captive and submissive."[58] Speaking with a reporter, Brizola recalled that the military had justified its coup by claiming that popular mobilization had demanded an intervention. "Now on the same streets," he said, "multitudes many times larger are marching and gathering, also requesting the end of the present regime, through direct elections. If they were so in touch [with popular demands] in 1964, why aren't they now?"[59]

When the rally departed the Praça da Sé, politicians experienced a moment of panic as their security team was unable to keep control of the half-kilometer march to Anhangabaú. Eventually, they had to give up on their plan to reach the valley and simply let the crowd sweep them along, as they locked arms and clutched a long banner like a shield. Montoro was sweating heavily, Guimarães looked pale, and Cardoso desperately tried to keep order; the only politician who looked at ease was Lula.[60] It was Diretas Já in microcosm. What had begun as an attempt by opposition politicians to use the people to achieve their goals was now on the verge of escaping their control. Their only choices were to be swept along or trampled.

After the rally had ended, as the crowd was dispersing, Brizola, hair wet, dripping sweat, shirt unbuttoned to his chest, stood for a moment on the edge of the stage, gazing out over the multitude. He turned to former federal deputy Adhemar de Barros Filho, a regime supporter from the beginning, and said, "Brazil has changed with this magnificent demonstration." He was right. The rally in São Paulo was the moment when the potential of an alliance between liberal politicians and the masses was on display. It was a moment when radical change appeared possible, not just a change of government, but a fundamental reordering of one of the world's most unequal, unjust countries. It was exhilarating undoubtedly for leftist militants, social movement leaders, and even a few politicians; it was certainly cause for concern for others who wished only to seize the reins of power for themselves. But on the night of April 16, 1984, for one brief moment—perhaps the only such moment Brazil has seen before or since—what the political class and the military alike wanted did not seem to matter.

"I SAW THE PEOPLE BORN OF THE MASSES": THE PROMISE AND LIMITS OF POPULAR MOBILIZATION

This unprecedented challenge to the military's project forced Figueiredo to make concessions. In February, he called prospective PDS candidates to Brasília for a meeting whose sole objective was to convince Chaves to cease his support for direct elections.[61] The next month, he explained that he supported direct elections but not right away: "I know that many people are in favor of direct elections. I am too, but all things in due time, . . . for the next presidential election."[62] After the April 10 rally in Rio, Figueiredo, who was on a trip abroad at the time, commented that if he had been in Brazil, "I would have been the million-and-first person at the rally."[63] On April 17, Figueiredo proposed his own amendment, which would maintain the indirect election for 1985, followed by direct elections in 1988.[64] While Figueiredo could sense the regime's impending demise, he and the generals who supported him were still hopeful that they could salvage something of their project. A regime that had resorted to extralegal measures for two decades may have dreamed that by 1988 it could engineer another solution. Or perhaps the generals and their civilian allies could find a popular candidate by 1988 who could win a direct election and help the military's project survive just a little longer.[65]

Yet when none of this was enough to stem the tide, the military resorted to its time-honored tactic of repression. Hoping to impede demonstrators from converging on Brasília, Figueiredo imposed a state of emergency in the Federal

District. Checkpoints along highways and at airports, manned by eight thousand soldiers, kept out anyone without official business in the capital.[66] Even politicians arriving by plane to vote were subjected to questioning by military police as they disembarked at the airport.[67] Television coverage was tightly controlled.

But Figueiredo's greatest weapon was still regime-allied politicians. To achieve a two-thirds majority, 76 PDS deputies would have to vote for the amendment.[68] Tacitly acknowledging the unpopularity of voting against direct elections, Figueiredo encouraged PDS governors to pressure deputies from their states to skip the vote if they could not bring themselves to vote no.[69] He also summoned PDS deputies in favor of diretas já to the presidential palace to lobby them directly.[70] And the day before the vote, the military announced that the restrictions on TV and radio broadcasts would be expanded to include a prohibition on reporting the names of deputies who voted for or against the amendment—a clear attempt to make PDS deputies feel less concerned about voting no.[71] Would Figueiredo's actions be enough? Would PDS politicians be willing to break with the regime so dramatically? After all, the times when they had done so had been few and far between.

The day before the vote, Guimarães gave one of the greatest speeches in Brazil's history, one that revealed how far he had come since his quixotic anti-candidacy offered paeans to democracy while almost ignoring the plight of ordinary people. The recording reveals Guimarães at his best. Echoing through a nearly silent chamber, his sentences begin with the high pitch of a prophet proclaiming a redemption that draws nigh; they end lower, shifting the emphasis to the weight of the responsibility that has fallen on the deputies as they make this historic decision.

> The streets and plazas of Brazil were filled with the colossal and sonorous assemblies of protest and repudiation of the government. . . . I saw millions of unemployed . . . demand the right to help construct the prosperity of the Nation. I saw the workers rejecting the inhuman . . . deterioration of their earnings. . . . I saw also the strength of the Brazilian woman—citizen, worker, and housewife, demanding equality. . . . I saw the students . . . crying out for new jobs and access to education in an economy gnawed away by the cancer of 5 million unemployed, 12 million underemployed, 40 million souls in absolute misery. . . . I saw the artists, the churches, the journalists, the writers, the professors . . . standing on the platforms of the people. I saw minorities determined to break the handcuffs of discrimination, Blacks forcing open the doors of equal opportunity, Indians, the original owners of the land who are today without land. . . .
>
> I saw yellow clothe Brazil in hope. I saw history gush forth on the streets and from the throats of the people. I saw through the omnipotence of the direct vote the resurrection of political participation and the legitimate pressures on behalf of those who have been left out and treated unjustly. I saw the largest movement of men, women, youths, and institutions in our nearly 500 years of history. I saw legions of democrats pitch the tents of struggle, not to support charismatic leaders or political parties, but rather to achieve a government that would be their allied brother, not their hangman. I saw the people be born of the masses. I saw the rainbow radiating the alliance

between the workers and democracy, I saw the disgraced, the dispossessed, and the unemployed convince themselves that there are no rights or well-being without citizenship, and that if bad politics destroy them, only good politics can save them.[72]

Gone were the focus on liberal institutions as a means unto themselves and the abstract appeals to a faceless Brazilian people that had dominated the Moreira Alves debate sixteen years before. Now Guimarães cited the people he had encountered in the streets—workers, women, Afro-Brazilians, students, professionals, Indigenous people—conscious of their rights as citizens and determined to work to build a more just, democratic Brazil. Guimarães illustrates the transformations taking place among some in the political class at the twilight of military rule. Although they were still wealthy white men whose commitment to respecting popular demands varied, the strikes and Diretas Já had forced them to realize that the country could not continue to be engineered to benefit the few at the expense of the many. Brazil would never be the same.

MEDIA FILE 10. Clip of Ulysses Guimarães speech before the vote on the Dante de Oliveira Amendment, April 24, 1984.
SOURCE: Câmara dos Deputados, COAUD, Arquivo Sonoro, http://imagem.camara.gov.br/internet/audio/default.asp.

Regardless of their commitment to liberal or participatory democracy, all the politicians present could agree that they were making history. That sense that no matter the result, this moment would reverberate through the ages to come, had perhaps not pervaded Congress so strongly since December 12, 1968, the day of the vote on Moreira Alves's immunity. The parallels with 1968 were on vivid display after Guimarães finished his speech, to thunderous applause. Students in the gallery began chanting, "Um, dois, três, quatro, cinco mil / We want to elect the president of Brazil." Joined by the politicians on the floor below, they sang the national anthem. A *Folha* reporter turned to his old friend, São Paulo mayor Mário Covas, and asked, "Doesn't this party remind you of another one, oh, about fifteen years ago?" Another politician who had been purged from Congress after the Moreira Alves vote commented uneasily, "I don't think the national anthem should be sung at times like this. It never ends well."[73]

Sure enough, a scant two hours after Guimarães's speech, hundreds of military police surrounded Congress to prevent any more protesters from joining the eight hundred students already inside. When a reporter tried to film the human wall around Congress, he was detained; when PMDB deputy João Herman Neto jumped in to defend the journalist, an officer arrested him, until his commanding officer reminded him that legislators could not be arrested while carrying out their duties. After three hours, the three military ministers called off the troops, but huddled in their offices, grabbing dinner in one of Congress's buffets, or wandering the halls, politicians worried into the night whether the same thing might happen the next day.[74] If the troops did return, perhaps that would be the final push the amendment needed, as this assault on their dignity might affect PDS politicians in a way that millions in the streets had not.[75]

Finally, the morning of April 25 dawned. After over a decade of playing by the military's rules, painstakingly building support at the local and state levels, promising a better life for ordinary Brazilians, and finally standing shoulder to shoulder with the working class, the opposition had its best chance to undo the military's project, using against it the very institutions it had manipulated for two decades. Although only the Chamber of Deputies would vote, Congress would meet in a joint session; if the amendment passed, the senators would hold their own vote. At last the time came for the vote, late in the evening of April 25—a strategic decision by party leaders, who allowed debate to drag late into the night in the hopes that if the amendment were defeated restless crowds gathered in the streets to await the results would have dispersed.[76] One by one, the deputies voted. It did not take long for the PDS's strategy to be revealed. As the president of the Senate, Moacyr Dalla, called on the PDS deputies by name, more often than not he received silence in response; they had decided to skip the session. Since constitutional amendments required a two-thirds majority of the entire Congress, not simply a two-thirds majority of those present, it soon became clear that Diretas Já would fail. A more cynical reading might point out that this was simply the latest act in a two-decade drama in which government-allied politicians put the will of the generals before their constituents. But there is another way to see the PDS's absence: not even the generals' most stalwart allies were willing to take a public stand in favor of the regime by voting no. They might not be ready to rebel, they might hope the regime endured, but now they were hedging their bets. As Neves presciently put it, when a close journalist friend called with the words, "It's all over," to tell him that the amendment would not pass, "Of course it isn't over. It's only just begun."[77]

"ONLY GOOD POLITICS CAN SAVE THEM": THE POLITICAL CLASS AND THE 1985 ELECTION

In the weeks following the defeat of the amendment, the opposition debated its next move. Despite this setback, there were still other options for achieving immediate direct elections, such as an amendment to Figueiredo's proposed constitutional amendment. Of course, any legislative solution would require a two-thirds majority, which would only be achieved through more popular mobilization. But there were risks to holding new rallies; if they were smaller than the recent ones, they could doom a new amendment. Worse yet, the popular disgust with the defeat of Diretas Já could lead to unruly demonstrations that might escape the control of opposition leadership.[78] Whatever had changed since 1964 in the political class's attitudes to popular mobilization, crowds were still sometimes as threatening as they were inspiring.

Another possibility was compromise, perhaps via a shortened term for the president chosen by the electoral college, with direct elections to follow in one to three years. However, as Guimarães pointed out, the regime had failed to deliver democracy in two decades; there was no reason to think it would do so in one or two more years.[79] Brizola proffered another solution—that the PMDB compete in the electoral college but that the president chosen have but a two-year term—an idea that would conveniently allow him to serve out his gubernatorial term before running.[80] Two months later, Montoro offered the same idea, certainly for the same reason.[81] Despite their admirable willingness to endorse popular mobilization, Brizola and Montoro were happy to accept indirect elections, provided it served their ambitions. These discussions were also occurring internally among the military, and a late April or early May analysis by the CSN's general secretariat identified nine possible solutions.[82]

The third option was to play by the rules of the game whose legitimacy Diretas Já had challenged: to participate in the electoral college and try to flip sixteen PDS deputies. This had been discussed as early as the day Diretas Já failed, when the PMDB's governors met in Brasília and concluded that the fight for direct elections was lost.[83] The problem was that this option had several possible results. What if some PDS politicians voted for an opposition candidate but more opposition electors boycotted the indirect election? How would the still-unresolved contest for the PDS nomination factor in? Were some candidates (i.e., Maluf) more likely to provoke defections, and were some (i.e., Chaves) more likely to unify? For his part, Neves continued to insist that he remained committed to direct elections: "I eat direct elections, drink direct elections, sleep direct elections. Good thing 'elections' is a feminine noun."[84]

Keep fighting, negotiate, or change tactics? There were no easy answers. The strategy chosen—competing in the electoral college—not only had a clear path to success but was also the one with which most politicians were most comfortable.[85] Montoro, Brizola, and Neves may have been uneasy being swept away by protesters, but they were in their element when it came to backroom deals with men like themselves. Forced to choose between following up on their protestations of democratic commitment and doing politics as usual, the opposition chose the latter. This was an open secret, as a CSN report to Figueiredo made clear:

> If the direct election of the President of the Republic is not desired at this time by the government, there are signs that it is also not [desired] by the main opposition leaders, above all from the PMDB. After all, the difficulty of finding a candidate capable of bringing together popular preferences, at a national level, combined with the perception that the electoral college offers conditions for an opposition candidate to be chosen, leads those leaders to prefer indirect elections.[86]

Or as Maluf recalled, "When Tancredo saw that he could win through an indirect election, he became the biggest defender of indirect elections." Diretas Já had been "just marketing."[87]

If Guimarães had been the face of Diretas Já, Neves became the face of *Indiretas* Já. Just as Guimarães, reviled by the military, would never have been a viable candidate in indirect elections, the conciliatory longtime federal deputy and current governor of Minas would never have won direct elections. In 1980, Neves had left the MDB to help found the short-lived Popular Party, which combined the most moderate elements of the old MDB with arenista liberals weary of military tutelage. He was someone who "had never revealed the slightest enthusiasm for popular pressure, instead preferring backroom deals."[88] Now, however, Neves was the candidate most likely to siphon off PDS votes in the electoral college; his much-reviled moderation was what made him acceptable to PDS liberals and the military.

Thus to win Neves had to appeal more to the military and PDS than to the Left. Less than a week after the amendment failed, Neves briefly met with Figueiredo during a presidential visit to Minas. In a speech, he highlighted his state's gratitude for what Figueiredo had done "to improve our institutions. And for what you will still do, in the attainment of your patriotic goals, Brazil and its people will grant you the recognition of history."[89] By early July, he had also met with Chaves and PDS president José Sarney.[90] Neves's appetite for a dialogue—in which he would become the consensus candidate—was clear. His very definition of politics illustrated his moderation. As he put it in an op-ed, he saw politics as "a discussion that leads to agreement, and as an agreement that leads to the realization of the common good, within the limits imposed by . . . our disagreements."[91] Left unstated was who would participate in this discussion, but it is easy to guess: the political class. Privately, Neves hedged his bets. His victory hinged on Maluf winning the PDS nomination; what if Figueiredo decided to endorse Andreazza at the convention to prevent this? As he explained to Andreazza in a private meeting, "I'm too old to chase after adventures. [If you are Figueiredo's candidate], I'm not going to give up my position as governor of Minas. On top of that, I'll personally guarantee you seventy votes [in the electoral college]."[92] Neves's commitment to democracy, while undoubtedly sincere, carried less weight with him than his own interests, and he had no problem supporting a sixth military president if the exigencies of the moment dictated it.

Meanwhile the PDS searched for a consensus candidate who could stave off defections to Neves. However, neither Maluf nor Andreazza nor Chaves appeared inclined to compromise. After twenty years of trying to reform the political class, the regime faced the same old contradiction: to achieve its goals, the military was forced to rely on the self-interested, "physiological" politicians who they had hated all along. And through mid-1984, it became clear that reforming politics and preserving whatever legitimacy remained to the "Revolution" were the last things on *pedessistas*' minds. It never had been their priority; why would it become one now? Just as in 1964, what they cared most about was supporting the winning side. Attempting to break the impasse, Sarney proposed a party primary. With little time to organize, it would not include all party members but rather assorted elected and appointed PDS politicians, for a total of 80,000 to 100,000 voters.[93] The candidate chosen would likely have been Chaves.[94] Maluf announced that he wouldn't allow his name to be included, arguing, "The big primary, the constitutional one, is the PDS convention."[95] He recognized that a primary would have shut him out by taking the nomination out of the hands of the convention delegates whose loyalty he had cultivated.

On June 11, the PDS national executive committee met to debate Sarney's proposal. The 4-by-10-meter room was packed with malufistas, who arrived an hour early to ensure their entry. The night before, Figueiredo had asked Sarney not to push for the primary, since one of the candidates was not in agreement. Seeking to buy time, Sarney suggested that the party postpone the decision. The malufistas, however, were adamant: the primary could not happen. Tempers flared. Former Rio Grande do Sul governor José Amaral de Sousa protested that opponents of the primary were afraid of the people. The malufistas interrupted, "So why don't you support diretas já?," and started sardonically chanting, "Diretas Já!" The meeting was falling into chaos. At this point, Sarney—who had come to the meeting armed[96]—made a shocking announcement: he was resigning as PDS president on the spot. Amid pleas to reconsider, he walked out.[97] Within two weeks, his replacement, Santa Catarina senator Jorge Bornhausen, resigned in turn, in protest of further malufista tactics to defeat the primary. He was replaced by Rio de Janeiro senator Ernâni do Amaral Peixoto, son-in-law of the late Getúlio Vargas, a longtime member of the MDB, and a Maluf ally.[98] Maluf's takeover of the PDS was complete—but at what cost?

The slow-motion implosion of the PDS created a new opportunity for direct elections. Figueiredo's proposed constitutional amendment instituted direct elections in 1988; an amendment to that amendment could change the date to 1985. Yet PMDB support was tepid. The party held a few rallies to demonstrate popular support for diretas já, but in São Paulo, despite projections of a crowd of 300,000, perhaps 100,000 showed up.[99] And as rumors grew that Figueiredo would withdraw his amendment rather than risk direct elections, PMDB leadership agreed to postpone the vote in Congress—giving Figueiredo more time to withdraw it.[100] This certainly had something to do with the fact that only a week before the ten opposition governors had met in São Paulo and announced their endorsement of a Neves candidacy in the electoral college, after Sarney's resignation had strengthened the opposition's hope that it could win over PDS defectors.[101] Why bother with the uncertainty of a direct election if the PMDB could win in the electoral college? Allowing ordinary people to decide the fate of the nation was a solution best avoided—so long as one's own side could win by more failsafe means anyway.

Thus the PMDB continued to give lip service to diretas já while preparing to compete in the electoral college with Neves. On June 28, Figueiredo, unwilling to trust the PDS to pass it without alterations, announced that he was withdrawing his amendment.[102] This was the death knell for Diretas Já. The election would be indirect.

An opposition victory in the electoral college, however, would be predicated on PDS defections, more likely if Maluf won the party's nomination. This possibility had been raised as early as mid-1983, in a confidential CSN report: "Maluf winning the party's convention . . . is a highly likely possibility. . . . The PDS could reach an agreement to defeat him through abstaining . . ., leading to the election of a united opposition candidate."[103] By January 1984, the opposition had come to the same conclusion, as Neves confided to a reporter that he thought he could defeat Maluf in the electoral college.[104] Such speculation now became reality. Shortly after his resignation, Sarney told Fernando Henrique Cardoso, "The PDS dissidence had no leaders. Now it does. I am willing to march with Tancredo."[105] By the first week of July, the press was rife with reports of a "liberal front" of Maluf foes within the PDS willing to support Neves, and on July 5 the Frente Liberal (FL) released its manifesto. "A government of national reconciliation is the path we identify to [bring] change and transformation," it stated in part.[106] Chaves, however, conditioned his support on the PMDB giving the FL the right to select Neves's running mate, and after Pernambuco senator Marco Maciel turned him down, he approached Sarney. According to Sarney's biographer, when he protested that his recent position as PDS president should disqualify him, Chaves countered that that was exactly why he should be the vice presidential candidate: PDS dissidents would support their former leader who had stood up to Maluf.[107] On July 19, the deal was sealed: the FL would support Neves.[108] Quickly, Sarney agreed to be vice president. The regime's most erstwhile ally, who had stood with the generals through two decades of repressive and manipulative attempts to reform politics, abandoned it, in part, perhaps, due to principle but certainly also because it suited his personal aspirations.

The alliance between the FL and the PMDB should have ensured Neves's victory. But the opposition's advantage could be offset if its more "radical" elements, incensed with the selection of Sarney, failed to support him. This possibility was plausible enough that a CSN report proposed no fewer than eight potential permutations, of which only three favored Neves.[109] In late July, Federal Deputy Flávio Bierrenbach argued, "Any PMDB candidate who eventually manages to achieve power through the electoral college will have no authority or legitimacy to face the challenges that lie ahead."[110] In retrospect, Neves realized these concerns were unfounded: "When they realized that without this alliance, we would continue with at least twenty more years of . . . this regime that suppresses liberty, they fell into line."

At any rate, PMDB opposition was more often personal than ideological. Minas Gerais senator Itamar Franco was one of the most forceful dissidents. "We are stoned because we defend our principles and don't jump over to the other side. And these people [the FL] leave the side they were on, because the ship is sinking," he stated. However, Franco's displeasure probably had more to do with his rivalry with Neves in Minas; after Neves's PP had merged with the PMDB, the party replaced Franco with Neves as its 1982 gubernatorial candidate.[111] Similarly, some of the greatest opposition came from Sarney's own state. The Maranhão presidents of the PMDB, PDT, and PT lambasted him as "a delegate of the 1964 coup" who had used his posts to promote "oligarchical nepotism" and "the greatest administrative corruption in the history of Maranhão."[112] To complicate matters, the other opposition parties had little to gain from a PMDB-FL deal. The PDT argued, "The people did not go to the streets to ask for a president who would remain for four or six years. . . . Only the lust for power . . . would lead the opposition to the imprudent idea of believing it had a right to a full term through this mechanism that was built with the goal of keeping the people from making decisions."[113] The PT was also intransigent. To those who argued that it was possible to participate in the electoral college while working toward direct elections, Francisco Weffort scoffed, "There is no way to reconcile the irreconcilable. It's like trying to suck on sugarcane and whistle at the same time."[114] Or as PT vice president Jacob Bittar put it, "The people want to vote, and the PT prefers to err with the people than make a deal against them through backroom conclaves."[115]

If the number of oppositionists who refused to support the PMDB candidates counterbalanced the number of pedessistas who defected, the PDS could still win the election. PMDB leadership thus rebuffed accusations that they had abandoned their principles. In mid-July, as rumors of an accord between the PMDB and the FL grew, Guimarães, once the most forceful advocate for diretas já, insisted (with evident discomfort), "We are going to use the snake's venom to fight the snake. Use the tools of the System itself to enter the enemy fortress and defeat it"—a mishmash of metaphors that ignored the fact that snakes are immune to their own venom.[116] As for Sarney, what could be done? "It was necessary to remind experienced comrades that politics is reality. . . . 'Mathematically speaking, we can't elect Tancredo without the Frente Liberal's votes. . . . Or do you think we should let Maluf be elected?'"[117]

Meanwhile the PDS held its convention. It was eerily similar to the 1978 paulista ARENA convention, where Natel had basked in the generals' support while Maluf courted the delegates. This time the person filling Natel's role was Andreazza, who, despite his limited appetite for campaigning, could count on Figueiredo's (rumored) endorsement. As late as the day the convention began, the outcome remained in doubt; a rumored SNI forecast even gave Andreazza a razor-thin advantage.[118] Also just as in 1978, "malufettes" (attractive young women hired to chant Maluf's praises before the overwhelmingly male delegates) appeared, though they had to compete for space with the *andreazzettes*, women of all ages who looked suspiciously like employees of the Ministry of Transportation.[119] Maluf spent the first day circulating among the delegates, hugging them and greeting them by name; when Andreazza briefly appeared, Maluf enveloped him in a hug as though Andreazza were his guest. Maluf correctly recognized that only a fraction of the delegates would be power brokers at the state or national level. If he bypassed state bosses and took his case directly to what Cardoso reportedly referred to as the "lumpen-bourgeoisie," he would win.[120] It was almost democratic. And it worked. Maluf won by a count of 493–350. Just as in 1978, when he dedicated his victory over Natel to Geisel, this time he credited his win to Figueiredo, gushing, "The political class has emerged victorious. It can take pride in having chosen the future President. Without pressure or backroom deals." "The PDS is the only party that gave this example," he continued, in a biting but reasonably accurate comparison of his campaign to that of Neves and Sarney.[121]

One day later, the PMDB held its convention. Since Neves and Sarney had no competitors, the only question was how many delegates would refuse to vote for Sarney. After the ballots for both offices were counted, Sarney had 113 fewer votes than Neves; about a sixth of the delegates were still unwilling to accept him.[122] In his victory speech, Neves did his best to balance faithfulness to his party's platform with the need to reassure the military. While he called for a new constitution, the renegotiation of Brazil's foreign debt, and land reform, he also praised the military for "sustaining our free institutions, projecting our national pride, and [serving as] an instrument for the consolidation of our democracy."[123] Meanwhile, the delegates taunted Maluf, chanting, "Salim, Salim, Salim, your joy is at an end!"[124]

The best chance the PDS always had was to find a consensus candidate, and Maluf was anything but. Although Andreazza announced that he would support Maluf in the electoral college, he added that his support was "merely personal" and that he would not campaign for the PDS nominee.[125] To drive the emptiness of that endorsement home, Andreazza's vice presidential candidate announced that he would support Neves.[126] Meanwhile, Figueiredo warned his cabinet that he would dismiss them if they refused to support Maluf.[127] But the very day he endorsed Maluf, Figueiredo met with PDS governors and told them that they should only decide whether to support Maluf after consulting their constituents.[128] One can nearly feel sympathy for Figueiredo's quandary. As he allegedly put it to two cabinet ministers in a private meeting before the convention, "We should not support Andreazza because he's from the military, and we shouldn't support Maluf because he's a thief."[129] Party leadership was similarly disinclined. Nelson Marchezan, leader of the PDS in the Câmara, told Figueiredo, "I will only vote for that son of a bitch . . . if it comes down to my vote, and only out of solidarity with you!"[130] It was clear that Andreazza, Figueiredo, and party leadership would do the bare minimum—or nothing at all—to help Maluf. Even before the convention, it seemed likely that enough regime allies had defected to the FL to decide the election. Over the coming months it became a certainty, as a stream of pedessistas announced their support for Neves.

Only one possible barrier remained to Neves's election, but it was formidable: the military. Since the decree of AI-2 in 1965, every time the political class challenged their "Revolution," the generals had resorted to extralegal measures or electoral manipulations. Might the military step in again? Most of the military was not enamored with Maluf, but they were also enraged at the betrayal of their civilian allies. Some also feared that the opposition might punish them if it came to power; hadn't Argentina's civilian government recently put generals—including former presidents—on trial? Might Neves attempt this? These generals and officers thus attempted to stoke mistrust of Neves. On more than one occasion, "students" caught spray painting communist slogans or wielding communist banners at rallies turned out to be undercover members of the military.[131] Could another coup be on the agenda?

Perhaps. On August 24, Army Minister Walter Pires released a statement lamenting the existence of "those who abandoned their commitment to a past so present that it appears recent . . . as though it were ethical to forget, to satisfy personal interests, attitudes and positions freely adopted." "The Army will be vigilant and will not fail the nation," he warned.[132] Less than two weeks later, Air Force Minister Délio Jardim de Matos railed, "History does not speak kindly of cowards, and even less so of traitors. It is necessary to distinguish between the moral courage of those who change their points of view and the audacity of those who seek only to preserve their own interests."[133] Then, on September 21, for the first time since 1969, the high commands of all three military branches met to discuss politics. Afterward, the army and air force released statements bemoaning "the increasing and worrisome radicalization" and "the campaign to discredit civil and military authorities." They warned of "the risks that radicalization can represent for the stability of the succession."[134] There was indeed legitimate cause for alarm. In a September 19 emergency meeting that included Figueiredo, the ministers of the army, navy, and air force, the military chief of staff, the head of the SNI, and the chief of the joint military staff, one of the attendees stated, "If anything goes wrong, we can turn the tables."[135] As the *Folha* put it, "Something is in the air, . . . but no one knows what it is."[136]

But every time a threat appeared, something else happened to reassure politicians that a coup was unlikely. As Senator Afonso Camargo noted, "In every [military] statement, there was something positive we could take advantage of. And we did."[137] After the meeting of the military high commands, the aggressive statements of the army and the air force were counterbalanced by the navy: "The Navy . . . reaffirm[s] before public opinion its position of faithfully fulfilling its constitutional duties, . . . maintaining itself, as always, removed from political-party activities."[138] Without the support of the navy, it was doubtful that the army or air force would act. Internal discussions reflected this. A report of the general secretariat of the CSN, likely from late July or early August, stated, "The Armed Forces have disengaged themselves from politics."[139] And although politicians could not have known it, Figueiredo was privately proclaiming his openness to an opposition victory. As early as the eve of the rejection of the Dante de Oliveira amendment in April, he had confided to a PDS politician, "Tancredo Neves is a trustworthy name for national conciliation. He is moderate and acceptable."[140] The president is reported to have responded to the private suggestion that the military might turn the tables, "You'll have to overthrow me or kill me to turn those tables."[141]

To be on the safe side, Neves continued to meet with top military brass. Between August and December, he met with all three military ministers—with Pires of the army thrice and with de Matos of the air force and Alfredo Karam of the navy once each—and assured them that his government would have no hint of *revanchismo*, or revenge. He hinted to de Matos that he would not pry too deeply into possible corruption by one of Figueiredo's sons and assured Pires and Karam that he would listen to them as he chose their successors.[142] So blatant were Neves's attempts to reassure the military that Maluf would later claim, "Tancredo baptized me as the military regime's candidate, when he was actually [their] candidate."[143] At any rate, by November it was clear that the military would not step in to save what remained of its "Revolution." When the Supreme Electoral Court twice ruled against Maluf when he attempted to invoke party fidelity requirements to force the PDS to vote for him, there was no doubt about the outcome: Neves would become president. The military regime was over.[144]

On January 15, 1985, the electoral college met for Brazil's last indirect election. Before the vote, Maluf gave a speech. At first glance, it was largely self-promotion. The man who had resisted direct elections every step of the way now took credit for Brazil's democratization: "My candidacy guaranteed the political process. Civilian. Free. Democratic. . . . The firmness of my decision [to participate in the election] made possible and sustained the candidacy of my illustrious opponent." But it would be a mistake to see this speech as simple self-flattery. For much of Maluf's speech focused not on his own role in Brazil's democratization but rather on the problems the next president would face. The solutions he identified were a testament to how far the political class had come. He called for a constitutional assembly to write a replacement for the military's 1969 document. He advocated raising taxes on the rich and lowering them for the middle and working classes, using "fiscal justice to end unjust and excessive income inequality." He suggested a significant increase to the minimum wage. "I became a brother to the dreams of the emergent classes, to build the foundation of the just and modern society we wish for."[145] When even the politicians who remained faithful to the regime to the bitter end accepted, even if only discursively, that Brazil belonged to all Brazilians, not simply the elite, it showed how much the political class had changed under the military regime.

The time came for the final roll call vote. One by one, senators, deputies, and representatives of the state legislatures voted. Although the written record did not transcribe their statements, the audio recording reveals that many politicians did not simply vote but also sought to justify their vote. "For changes to the economic model and the tax model, Tancredo Neves." "Out of respect for the institutions of our political parties, I vote for Paulo Salim Maluf." "In the name of Rubens Paiva and all those the dictatorship killed or disappeared, Tancredo Neves."[146] Fittingly, the deciding vote that toppled the regime was cast by PMDB deputy João Cunha, probably the most fearless politician of all in his uncompromising opposition, who hailed from São Paulo, the state that led the resistance to the regime. Cunha's unrehearsed words captured perfectly the significance of that day: "Twenty-one years ago I thought that the dream of [becoming] a great nation had ended. God has granted me the honor to today, with my vote, strike the final blow against the fascist, sell-out dictatorship that made my Pátria unhappy. I vote for Tancredo Neves and for victory!"[147] The military regime had begun in the Chamber of Deputies on April 1, 1964, when Congress declared the presidency vacant in the wake of the coup. It was fitting that it ended in the same room.

MEDIA FILE 11. João Cunha electoral college vote, January 15, 1985.
SOURCE: Câmara dos Deputados, COAUD, Arquivo Sonoro, http://imagem.camara.gov.br/internet/audio/default.asp.

CONCLUSIONS

The military regime finally came to an ignominious end in the wake of the two things the officers of 1964 most loathed: popular mobilization and self-serving politicking. With Diretas Já defeated, the military could have kept a vestige of its project under Maluf. Yet it was their disgust with Maluf, the unprincipled, self-interested type of politician they had spent two decades relying on while unsuccessfully seeking to reform, that led the Armed Forces to accept Neves. As Andreazza confided to a friend, "The ones who made the Revolution of 1964 were us, the colonels, Figueiredo and me. We took to the streets, and we exposed ourselves to [possible] defeat.... Now, it's all being thrown away. It was all for nothing. Corruption is running rampant, and it will only get much worse."[148] Like Emperor Pedro II and Getúlio Vargas before them, and like the PT governments (2003–2016) after them, the generals' national project was stymied first and foremost by the political class.

In many respects, the political class that toppled the regime in 1985 was the same as that of 1964: self-interested, rich white men motivated by the desire to keep their privileges, more comfortable making backroom deals than coexisting with popular mobilization. The eagerness of the PMDB to embrace a negotiated solution after Diretas Já failed is illustrative. Similarly, the PDS dissidents betrayed the regime not out of principles—for they had few to begin with—but rather because they refused to go down with a sinking ship. And the aristocratic, conciliatory Neves was closer to the values of the political class than the brash Maluf, who bypassed the national political elite and took his case directly to his party's rank and file, the *baixo clero* (lit., "low clergy") of the political class. Maluf's efforts to cultivate about 1,000 convention delegates and 670 or so electoral college members were too crass, too democratic, for PDS politicians to stomach.[149] PDS dissidents' support for Neves was significant for many reasons, but it did not signify an awakening democratic consciousness. But this is only half the story. In the face of a mobilized civil society that expanded their conceptions of democracy, they realized they could no longer rule Brazil alone, and over the coming three decades they would be forced to accept a greatly expanded political role for the popular classes. Unlike the generals, politicians were beholden to an electorate whose desires they could not entirely ignore. Yes, they were always self-interested and often corrupt. But since the regime ended, they have been responsive to popular demands like never before.

The year 1984 offered a clear contrast to 1964, when a faction of conservative officers infatuated with modernization, national security ideology, and morality had inaugurated an audacious authoritarian project that would attempt to demobilize the Left, engineer lasting economic development, and impose military tutelage on politicians and the nation. Although the first decade of military rule had witnessed resounding success on all three fronts, by the end of the second decade, the project lay in tatters. The Left, after the failure of its armed struggle, had come to embrace the sole channel of resistance that the regime was unwilling to close—parties and elections—creating a generation of student leaders, guerrillas, and returning exiles who were becoming a force in electoral politics. On the economic front, the Brazilian "miracle" had shattered under blows from rising oil prices, foreign debt, and inflation. Even amid these failures, the regime might have endured if its leaders had been able to convince the political class of the wisdom of a tutelage that impinged on their honor and privileges. Like Vargas before them, the generals who led the regime dreamed of reshaping the political class to fit their vision for Brazil. In their attempts to accomplish this, they employed both sticks (the usurpation of the political class's presumed prerogatives) and carrots (the promise to return some of what had been taken). Yet the failure of politicians to accept their permanent subordination meant that the military's political project remained fundamentally unstable. Politicians were transformed under military rule but not in the way the military had hoped. And even as they became more willing to accept a more participatory democracy, they preserved the group consciousness that had inspired much of their resistance all along.

Whether intentional or inadvertent, the resistance of politicians took many forms: the principled stance of the autênticos, the ambition-driven electioneering of Quércia and Maluf, or the stubborn refusal of untold thousands of others to give up their plotting and bickering as they waited for the storm to pass. In so doing, they made the storm pass. The dilemma only gradually became clear to the military, steeped in 150 years of Brazilian liberalism. From the outset they had been unwilling to do away with legislatures or elections. Yet by maintaining these institutions, by admitting that they needed the political class, the military laid the groundwork for its "Revolution's" undoing. By the time they realized what was happening, it was too late.

. . .

On January 15, 1985, moments after the electoral college chose him as Brazil's first civilian president since 1964 and brought the regime to a close, Neves gave a speech:

> It was not easy to get here. Not even the anticipation of the certainty of victory these last months erases the scars and sacrifices of the history of struggle that now comes to a close. . . . There were many moments of discouragement and tiredness, when we asked ourselves if it was worth it to fight. But every time this temptation assailed us, the moving sight of the people resisting and hoping re-created within us all the energy that we thought lost, and we began anew, the next day, as if nothing had been lost. . . .
>
> Never in our history have we had so many people in the streets demanding the recovery of the rights of citizenship and demonstrating their support for a candidate. . . . We will not disperse. We will continue gathered, like in the public plazas, with the same emotion, the same dignity, and the same resolve.
>
> Nearly two hundred years ago, Tiradentes, that hero driven crazy by hope, told us, "If we all want to, we can make this country into a great nation."
>
> Let's do it.[150]

MEDIA FILE 12. Clip of Tancredo Neves speech before the electoral college, January 15, 1985.
SOURCE: Câmara dos Deputados, COAUD, Arquivo Sonoro, http://imagem.camara.gov.br/internet/audio/default.asp.

Conclusion

Freedom, Justice, and Solidarity for Brazil? The Political Class under Dictatorship and Democracy

In 1941, the Austrian writer Stefan Zweig coined the term "land of the future" to describe Brazil.[1] And as Brazilians often add wryly, "And it always will be." After a "lost decade" of debt and hyperinflation, in the mid-1990s that future finally began to arrive. Paradoxically, it was under the New Republic (1985–present), particularly after 2002, that a democratic Brazil achieved two of the generals' three goals: economic stability and reduced social unrest (what the military called "subversion"). No one could have imagined in 1985 that in three decades Brazil would reduce the number of people living in poverty by the tens of millions, emerge as a global economic and diplomatic power, and even host the World Cup and Olympic Games. At the same time, a chastened military accepted a reduced political role, a development that, together with the massive increase in popular mobilization, offered hope that Brazil could achieve its new constitution's goal to create a society that was *livre, justa, e solidária*. Freedom, justice, and solidarity for a country that had known too little of all three. As always, however, the success or failure of this project would hinge on the collaboration of the political class.

Tragically, Neves fell ill on the eve of his inauguration and died without taking office. In one of history's crueler ironies, he was replaced by Sarney, one of the last politicians to abandon the generals. Yet Sarney, always a pragmatic Brazilian liberal, could read the tea leaves as well as anyone, and he recognized the depth of Brazilians' yearning for change. The generals' most faithful ally presided over the restoration of direct presidential elections, the granting of the vote to illiterates, the legalization of the PCB and PCdoB, and the promulgation of a new constitution in 1988 that, despite flaws, reflected the political class's expanded conception of citizenship. When Sarney handed the presidential sash to his successor, Fernando Collor de Mello, in 1990, it was the first time since 1960 that one civilian president had peacefully relinquished power to another, the first of five such transfers over the next three decades. Although Collor resigned in 1992 after he was impeached on corruption charges, his vice president, Itamar Franco, together with Fernando Henrique Cardoso, his minister of finance, implemented the famed "real plan," which ended hyperinflation that had reached 2,477 percent in 1993.

The success of the real plan propelled Cardoso and his party, the Party of Brazilian Social Democracy, to the presidency.[2] Considering his past as a Marxist sociologist, one might have expected Cardoso to turn Brazil sharply to the left. Once in office, however, Cardoso embraced neoliberal economic prescriptions, particularly the privatization of state-owned industries.[3] But Cardoso also implemented policies that reduced illiteracy, expanded access to education, improved health care, and combated racism. Between 1990 and 2000, quality of life (as measured by the Human Development Index) had risen in 99.9 percent of municipalities.[4] Brazil became a global model for its HIV prevention and treatment programs, with universal free condom distribution and free antiretrovirals for anyone living with the virus.[5]

Yet it was under the governments of the PT's Lula (2003–10) and Dilma Rousseff (2011–16) that the promise of Brazil's democratization was most fully realized. After losing three consecutive times, in 2002 Lula and the PT scaled back their socialist rhetoric in favor of a more attainable social democracy that preserved orthodox macroeconomic policy. In part this constituted an acknowledgment that Cardoso's stabilization plan had worked, but it was also a concession to reality in a fragmented party system in which the PT never controlled more than 17.5 percent of the seats in the Chamber of Deputies. While compromises like these earned the party the condemnation of some on the Brazilian and international radical Left, the thirteen years of PT rule produced the greatest reductions in equality and advances toward inclusion in Brazil's history.[6] The minimum wage was increased by nearly 80 percent. Unemployment fell from 13 to 7 percent. GDP rose from $1.3 trillion to $1.8 trillion, and by 2012, Brazil's economy had become the seventh largest in the world. Extreme poverty fell from 11 to 4 percent. The Gini measure of inequality fell from 0.58 to 0.52. The percentage of eighteen- to twenty-four-year-olds going to college rose from 11 to 18 percent.[7] Brazil became recognized as a global model for reducing inequality.

These accomplishments stemmed from the lessons the political class learned during the military dictatorship, particularly the realization that if Brazil were to enjoy long-term democratic stability, its political elite would have to accept expanded participation and reduced socioeconomic exclusion. For twenty-one years, politicians had been subjected to a form of authoritarian tutelage not so different from the paternalism they had attempted to exercise over the popular classes for five centuries. Undoubtedly some still yearned for the days when they could stifle popular aspirations, but the growth of civil society meant those days were gone. Like Guimarães, Montoro, and the rest at the final Diretas Já protest, politicians could let themselves be swept along by the crowd or be trampled. The popular forces they had helped unleash could not be easily stopped.

While it is often said that history is the study of change over time, it would be more accurate (not to mention Hegelian) to say that it is the study of the tensions between continuity and change as they interact amid present contingencies. How can the changes and continuities among the political class under the military regime explain the contradictions of Brazil's democratization when politicians combined their openness to increased popular participation with a determination to salvage what they could of the power, wealth, and impunity that people like them had enjoyed since time immemorial? The continuities, amply noted by scholars of democratic consolidation, help explain the parliamentary coup that toppled the left-wing government of Dilma Rousseff in 2016 and the political class's collaboration with the racist, sexist, homophobic Bolsonaro since 2018.[8] The changes, while more subtle, give hope that this conservative reaction against the advances of the past three and a half decades will founder.

This tension appears in nearly every chapter.[9] Chapter 1 emphasized the familial, racial, and class affinities that bound liberal politicians to leftist university students, the presumed leaders of Brazil by merit or birth. Today Brazilian politics (along with the judiciary and many civil service positions) remains a largely hereditary affair in which the youths of today are anointed the leaders of tomorrow.[10] Even when someone new climbs into the political elite, they usually adopt this value as their own; indeed, one need look no further than Bolsonaro, an army captain from a hamlet in the interior of São Paulo whose three oldest sons are now all elected politicians whom he protects as assiduously as politicians defended students in 1968.

Another persistent tendency among the Brazilian political class is the desire to restore, preserve, or enhance its members' prerogatives. As discussed in chapter 2, when the Chamber of Deputies took a stand on parliamentary immunity, they showed that they believed something vital—their right to lead Brazil and express themselves as they saw fit—had been taken away. In a democratic Brazil, the political class restored many of these privileges. Despite its progressive mechanisms to facilitate popular participation, the 1988 constitution also maintained the political class's prerogatives largely intact. The constitution reversed many of the military's centralizing measures and devolved power to states and municipalities, as was in vogue throughout Latin America in the era of neoliberalism, thus returning significant local power to the very political class that the military had (justifiably, some might argue) mistrusted.[11]

It was not just prerogatives that the political class wanted back; it was their de facto impunity as members of Brazil's socioeconomic elite (the *classes dirigentes* in Brazilian parlance). Chapter 3 emphasized the resentment politicians felt as the dictatorship mistreated them in the wake of AI-5. However, their indignation did not arise solely from their respect for liberal institutions but also from the belief that their wealth, power, and status should exempt them from repression.[12] Even the autênticos were more concerned with the violence perpetrated on university-educated "subversives" than with the nearly genocidal violence the Brazilian state has always visited on those seen as socially and racially inferior. Today university students are seldom taken to interrogation centers to be tortured, but young Black men returning home from a night on the town can still be stopped by the police and summarily executed under the flimsiest of pretenses.[13] Despite widespread outrage among social movements, the political class has shown little interest in restraining the police forces that keep the masses at bay. If anything, the role of repressive institutions has grown, with a dramatic increase in the number of former military and police elected to Congress, culminating in the election of the soldier Bolsonaro, who openly advocates that police kill more *bandidos* (criminals).[14]

Chapters 4 and 5 illustrated another enduring characteristic of the political class: the primacy of the local pursuit of power over ideology or party. While a few courageous autênticos opted for frontal opposition based on the dictatorship's gross violations of democratic norms, most members of the political class collaborated with the military or simply kept their heads down, hoping to wait out the storm under the tree. When opposition did emerge, it was not because the autênticos convinced the rank and file of politicians that their cause was just but because pragmatists like Quércia and Maluf promised them a chance at seizing local- and state-level power from their rivals. This disregard for party and ideology endures. Today, an astounding twenty-four parties are represented in the Chamber of Deputies, which makes Brazil the foremost country in the world for "party fragmentation." The result is a politics of coalition building that uses patronage (particularly cabinet appointments) to secure the conditional collaboration of ideologically bankrupt parties. This was precisely the tendency the military sought to resolve with the two-party system, but as their own concessions like sublegendas showed, combating fisiologismo was and remains an uphill, perhaps unwinnable, battle.

Chapters 6 and 7 demonstrated the promises and limits of the political class's embrace of popular mobilization, even as they harnessed it to topple the regime that had so vexed them. Although politicians risked their physical integrity to protect workers in 1980, men like Cardoso and Montoro balked at Lula's call for a nation directed by workers instead of elites who acted on their behalf. Similarly, in the 1984 succession crisis, although the democratic opposition was willing to use mass mobilization to topple the regime, they were more comfortable with backroom deals like the one that elected Neves and Sarney, icons of the chameleon-like traditional elite. This instrumental use of popular mobilization endures. *O povo na rua* (the people in the streets) sounds laudable, until one analyzes which povo is in the street and whose ends they serve. This attitude, dormant since the 1992 impeachment of Collor, came to the fore again in 2015–16, as the political class embraced the media-fueled "mass mobilization" of the middle and upper classes to overthrow Rousseff.[15] The political class remains willing to endorse popular mobilization but only when it serves their ends.

It is indisputable that the military regime failed in its attempts to transform the political class into a pliant, patriotic elite that governed for the common good. None of this is particularly surprising. Ultimately, we humans are animals like any other. Like our chimpanzee cousins, we endlessly jockey for status, using others as tools to achieve our personal ends. Why is it surprising that the Brazilian political class would seek to transfer power to their children, assiduously defend their own prerogatives and impunity, elevate personal advancement over principles, and use the masses only when convenient? Are they any different from North American and European politicians, status-obsessed primates like themselves? These do not make Brazilian politicians deficient compared to a Global North ideal: they make them human.

It is more fruitful, as well as politically useful, to examine the changes. Brazilian elites have always sought to preserve their prerogatives to benefit themselves and their children, but they have not always countenanced the level of popular mobilization seen since the late 1970s. Continuities are to be expected. It is in the changes among the political class under military rule that we can best ascertain the prospects for a reversal of the politically and socially regressive agenda that has dominated Brazil since 2016. Chapters 1 and 2 showed that a decisive portion of the Chamber of Deputies chose to collectively rebel when they saw their children and prerogatives threatened by an encroaching military. But is that all that was happening? As the final debate around the Moreira Alves case demonstrated, the political class was motivated not only by their prerogatives, but by a reverence for what they understood as democracy. Elitist and liberal though these values might have been, they also showed that the political class cared deeply about being faithful representatives of the people as they understood them. Unlike the military (and today the judiciary, federal prosecutors, and other civil servants), politicians recognize that they are beholden to the will of their voters. If public opinion turns against Bolsonaro as it turned against Dilma and the PT, the military and civil service will have the luxury of remaining silent, but the political class will have to pick a side.

Chapters 3 and 4 analyzed the shock and frustration felt by politicians as the military trampled on their dignity and privileges. Most of the political class had accepted a military coup in 1964, which they thought would be merely the latest in a long line of brief military interventions that had upended Brazilian politics since the fall of the Empire in 1889. After twenty-one years of traumatic and humiliating military tutelage, politicians were determined not to allow such a disaster to befall them again. To be sure, the military's relative withdrawal from politics, particularly since the election of Collor in 1992, owes much to a consensus among the Armed Forces that another direct political intervention would be ill advised. But the fact remains that every previous military intervention was legitimized by the acquiescence of a decisive majority of the political class—something unlikely to happen again any time soon.[16]

Whereas in 1968 the political class defended a narrowly defined liberal democracy, by 1974 the opposition had begun to realize that their only path to power lay in expanding their appeal to the working class by emphasizing the bread-and-butter issues that mattered to them. Chapter 5 showed how this change in strategy was implemented above all in São Paulo, via an alliance between the liberal Montoro, the pragmatic upstart Quércia, and the ambitious intellectual Fernando Henrique Cardoso. The most immediate effect of this approach was an MDB landslide in that year's Senate elections, but the long-term consequences would be even more important. Although development had long been a sacred value for the Brazilian upper classes and intelligentsia, 1974 was when the terms of the debate began to shift to emphasize development in the pursuit of reducing inequality.[17] This was perhaps the most enduring legacy of the military regime and the transformations it wrought on the political class. The advances that began under Cardoso and intensified under the PT signified a profound change in the material conditions and social relations of one of the world's most unequal countries.

The final two chapters used the 1978–80 São Paulo metalworker strikes and the 1984 Diretas Já demonstrations to illustrate how many in the political class embraced mass mobilization to help rid themselves of military tutelage. The hundreds of thousands of striking paulista workers and the millions of protesters demanding direct elections were a nearly unprecedented sight in Brazil. To be sure, the acceptance of mass mobilization was often instrumental and always conditional, and politicians still preferred, when they could, to resolve impasses with backroom deals (what political scientists call "elite pacts"), but once the genie of popular mobilization had been let out of the bottle, it was impossible to put it back in. Mass protests played a decisive role in convincing the political class to support the impeachments of Collor (1992) and Rousseff (2016) alike. Strikes also remained a universally accepted strategy for the working class to negotiate for better living and working conditions.[18] In a country whose elites had long lived by the mantra, "The social question is a police question," this newfound tolerance for mass participation in politics was vastly significant.

Thus did the political class's attitudes concerning democracy, the military's role in politics, and mass mobilization shift under military rule. These changes were the product of thousands upon thousands of individual choices based not simply on principle, but more commonly the exigencies of the moment. When a politician saw police harass a student daughter, a friend cassado by the military, a hated rival join their party, an opportunity for self-advancement via a new electoral strategy, the military ignoring the rules of the game, workers needing protection, or the masses demanding direct elections, they made decisions that collectively altered the course of Brazilian history and began to transform the way the political class understood its relationship with the Brazilian people. Though their wealth, education, socialization, and the other factors producing their dispositions did not change, some of those fundamental ways of seeing the world did shift, and the political class's habitus changed accordingly. Habitus shaped the decisions politicians made, and the decisions in turn reshaped the habitus.[19] Moreover, since 1985 the political class has begun to undergo a metamorphosis to become more reflective of Brazilian society. In 1978, only 4 of 420 federal deputies were women; four decades later, 77 women were elected to a Chamber of 513 seats.[20] In 1982, only 4 federal deputies identified as Black or Brown;[21] by 2018, this number had risen to 125.[22] Significantly, however, this diversification of the political class has been largely limited to race and gender. When it comes to social class, Congress remains nearly as elitist as ever. Although the proportion of lawyers in the Chamber fell from 56 to 19.1 percent between 1978 and 2018, that of businesspeople and industrialists rose from 11.4 to 26.3 percent.[23] Rich lawyers have been replaced by rich businesspeople. While working-class people have made some inroads, the two largest nontraditional professions represented in Congress today are military or police and evangelical pastors, both groups that tend to promote submission to authority and resist broad social transformation. While today's political class is no longer made up exclusively of wealthy, conservative, white men, it is still largely made up of wealthy, conservative people who, when push comes to shove, will side against popular aspirations to protect the interests of their social class—as the past decade of Brazilian politics has shown in lurid detail.

When I completed the first iteration of this project in 2013, the argument seemed straightforward: two decades of forced submission to military tutelage had created a genuine democratic and participatory consciousness among the political class, paving the way for the New Republic's unprecedented expansion of democracy and opportunity. But progress is never linear; it is contested, contingent, and subject to innumerable setbacks as it threatens entrenched power and wealth. No one in early 2013 could have foreseen the mass protests that rocked Brazil that June, the media-driven demonstrations against Rousseff, the farcical impeachment trial, the return to neoliberalism by Rousseff's vice president, Michel Temer, or the imprisonment of Lula on trumped up corruption charges, which enabled the election of the most right-wing politician in Brazil to the presidency. How deep could the changes wrought by the regime really have been if the bulk of the political class could so easily be persuaded to endorse all this? Doesn't this prove that Brazilian elites are just as deficient as democratization literature posited?

The problem with this line of reasoning is not so much that it is invalid but rather that it ascribes the greatest significance to the least surprising characteristics of the political class. Why would we expect politicians anywhere to put ideology, the common good, and party identification before an opportunity to enjoy political power and personal gain? After all, the four years of the Trump presidency demonstrated just how unbeholden the Republican Party is to democratic norms. And even as the Democratic Party cast itself as the party of norms, institutions, and social justice, Joe Biden was reminding wealthy donors that "nothing would fundamentally change" if he was elected. Can we truly claim that the United States is an "advanced democracy" anymore (if it ever was one to begin with)? Of course Brazilian politicians abandoned Rousseff and Lula when the winds changed. They had done exactly the same in 1985, when they fled the military's sinking ship, and in 1964, when they helped overthrow Goulart because of the threat he was thought to represent to entrenched social relations.

These continuities only serve to highlight the significant transformations that did occur among the political class. The definitive rejection of direct military interventions in politics, the recognition that the goal of development should be the reduction of inequality, and the acceptance of strikes and mass mobilization as a fact of life were all major changes for a political elite that has always been defined by the use of force to keep popular aspirations at bay. These shifts helped create unprecedented opportunities for workers, Afro-Brazilians, Indigenous people, LGBTQ+ people, landless and homeless workers, and many others to advocate for their rights as Brazilian citizens, to challenge old hierarchies, and to realize a new sense of dignity, empowerment, and self-respect. Today Bolsonaro might wish he had the opportunity to rule in such an authoritarian manner as the generals of a generation ago, but over forty years of expanded participation and reduced inequality have left their mark, and it is doubtful that he could suppress popular longings for long if he ever tried in earnest to do so.

Today, amid Bolsonaro's assault on the working class and marginalized groups, Tancredo Neves's words ring as true as they did in 1985: "We will not disperse. We will continue gathered . . . with the same emotion, the same dignity, and the same resolve. Nearly two hundred years ago, Tiradentes, that hero driven crazy by hope, told us, 'If we all want to, we can make this country into a great nation.' Let's do it." Aided by the changes that occurred in the political class between 1964 and 1985, the Brazilian people have spent the past three decades fulfilling this admonition. Those of us who have been moved and inspired by their struggle know that neither a coup nor unjust imprisonments nor even a Far Right demagogue will hold them back for long.

NOTES

INTRODUCTION: A NATION FOR ALL OR A FEW? THE POLITICAL CLASS, THE PEOPLE, AND THE RISE AND FALL OF BRAZIL'S MILITARY DICTATORSHIP

1. "Pronunciamento do Presidente da República, Luiz Inácio Lula da Silva, na sessão solene de posse no Congresso Nacional," Presidência da República, Secretaria de Imprensa e Divulgação, 1 Jan. 2003, http://www.biblioteca.presidencia.gov.br/presidencia/ex-presidentes/luiz-inacio-lula-da-silva/discursos/discursos-de-posse/discurso-de-posse-10-mandato.

2. "Leia a íntegra do discurso de Bolsonaro na cerimônia de posse no Congresso," *Folha de S. Paulo* (henceforth *Folha*), 1 Jan. 2019, https://www1.folha.uol.com.br/poder/2019/01/leia-a-integra-do-discurso-de-bolsonaro-na-cerimonia-de-posse-no-congresso.shtml.

3. Brazilian scholars have engaged in a spirited debate over the proper term for the government that ruled Brazil from 1964 to 1985. Was the regime military in character, or did the collaboration of civilian politicians and technocrats render the regime "civil-military"? For a detailed discussion of this debate, see André Pagliarini, "'De onde? Para onde?' The Continuity Question and the Debate over Brazil's 'Civil'-Military Dictatorship," *Latin American Research Review* 52:5 (2016); 760–74, https://dx.doi.org/10.25222/larr.216. See also Carlos Fico, "Ditadura militar brasileira: Aproximações teóricas e historiográficas," *Tempo e Argumento* 9:20 (2017): 5–24, https://dx.doi.org/10.5965/2175180309202017005. Although this book is about the central role of civilian politicians, the role of the military was much more extensive than at any other time in Brazil's history. I thus have chosen to use "military" instead of "civil-military." There has also been some debate as to whether "regime" or "dictatorship" is more appropriate. On the regime vs. dictatorship question, in general I refer to the regime as it existed in 1964–68 and 1978–85 as a "regime," reserving "dictatorship" for the years when the military was able to govern nearly absolutely under Institutional Act No. 5 (AI-5). For a dissenting view for 1964–68, see Marcos Silva, ed., *Brasil 1964/1968: A ditadura já era ditadura* (São Paulo: LCTE Editora, 2006).

4. Frances Hagopian, *Traditional Politics and Regime Change in Brazil* (Cambridge: Cambridge University Press, 1996), 17.

5. Andrew J. Kirkendall, *Class Mates: Male Student Culture and and the Making of a Political Class in Nineteenth-Century Brazil* (Lincoln: University of Nebraska Press, 2002), 1. After World War II, having a military father and attending a military school became increasingly correlated with reaching the officer corps. See Alfred Stepan, *The Military in Politics: Changing Patterns in Brazil* (Princeton, NJ: Princeton University Press, 1971), 40.

6. A variety of reformist projects throughout the twentieth century sought to loosen the stranglehold of the political class on state power, but *tenentismo* and the Revolution of 1930, the Estado Novo of Vargas, the military dictatorship, and the constitutional convention of 1987–88 all failed to mount a lasting challenge to its rule.

7. Throughout this book, mention of ideas held by "the military" does not imply a lack of ideological diversity in the Armed Forces before 1964. The military had been instrumental in the transition from empire to republic in 1889, as well as the failed 1922 *tenentista* uprising and the 1930 overthrow of the First Republic. Between 1930 and 1964, the military contained significant leftist factions; indeed, the longtime leader of the Brazilian Communist Party (PCB), Luis Carlos Prestes, had been a tenentista. After the coup, the social group most targeted by the regime was not civilian politicians but leftist members of the military. According to the 2014 National Truth Commission (CNV), 6,591 members of the Armed Forces were forced into early retirement, arrested, or otherwise persecuted by the victors of 1964 (Leticia Mori, "A história dos 6,5 mil membros das Forças Armadas perseguidos pela ditadura militar, *BBC Brasil*, 13 Dec. 2018, https://www.bbc.com/portuguese/brasil-46532955). See also João Quartim de Moraes, *A esquerda militar no Brasil: Da conspiração republicana à guerrilha dos tenentes* (São Paulo: Editora Siciliano, 1991); João Quartim de Moraes, *A esquerda militar no Brasil: Da coluna a comuna* (São Paulo: Editora Siciliano, 1994); and Carlos Henrique Lopes Pimentel, "O anticomunismo e a esquerda militar no Brasil: uma análise historiográfica," *História em Reflexão* 5:10 (2011): 1–12.

8. On the widespread belief within the military that civilian politicians were largely corrupt, see Diego Knack, "O combate à corrupção durante a Ditadura Militar por meio da Comissão Geral de Investigações (1968–1978)" (Thesis, Universidade Federal do Rio de Janeiro, 2014), 3–4.

9. After fifteen years in power, in 1945 the populist dictator Getúlio Vargas was forced to resign under military pressure. In 1954, this time as democratically elected president, he faced an identical situation, but rather than resign he shot himself in the heart. In both cases, the military allowed free elections to take place shortly thereafter.

10. One group that did not fit into either the categories of political class or social movement during this period was Brazil's business elites (*empresariado*). Although they were closely tied to the political class, particularly in industrialized São Paulo, the business class was distinguished in the sources I consulted by its nearly unconditional support for the regime until the eve of its fall. Indeed, the military's grandiose infrastructure projects created close ties to the business class in the construction sector. For a remarkable study of the latter's relationship with the regime, see Pedro Henrique Pedreira Campos, *"Estranhas catedrais": As empreiteiras brasileiras e a ditadura civil-militar, 1964–1988* (Niterói: EdUFF, 2014). When the business class did oppose the dictatorship, it was as a result of discontent with the more nationalist and state-centered aspects of the generals' economic policy, which, in contrast to both the Argentine and Chilean regimes, was too "statist" to suit them.

11. In many respects the Brazilian regime most closely resembled Greece's "Regime of the Colonels" (1967–74) and South Korea's military-dominated "Fifth Republic" (1979–87). Like Brazil's generals, the Greek junta called their coup a "Revolution" that had saved democracy from communism. Also similarly to Brazil, the Greek junta was less violently repressive than many other Cold War military dictatorships. However, in Greece the Hellenic Parliament was dissolved for the duration of the junta. See Theodore A. Couloumbis, "The Greek Junta Phenomenon," *Polity* 6 (1974): 345–74; George Doukas, "Party Elites and Democratization in Greece," *Parliamentary Affairs* 46 (1993): 506–16; and Ioannis Tzortzis, *Greek Democracy and the Junta: Regime Crisis and the Failed Transition of 1973* (London: Bloomsbury, 2020). Like Brazil, South Korea's "Fifth Republic" was a military-dominated regime that employed indirect elections for president and kept the country's National Assembly mostly open. Also like Brazil, despite initial economic success, military authoritarianism and increased social inequality led to pressure from students and workers, eventually precipitating a return to democracy and elite acceptance of mass political participation. See James Cotton, "From Authoritarianism to Democracy in South Korea," *Political Studies* 37:2 (1989): 244–59, https://dx.doi.org/10.1111/j.1467-9248.1989.tb01481.x; Byong-Man Ahn, *Elites and Political Power in South Korea* (Cheltenham: Edward Elgar, 2003); Sŏn-hyŏk Kim, *The Politics of Democratization in Korea: The Role of Civil Society* (Pittsburgh, PA: University of Pittsburgh Press, 2000).

12. For comparisons between the Brazilian, Argentine, Chilean, and Uruguayan dictatorships, see Rodrigo Patto Sá Motta, ed., *Ditaduras militares: Brasil, Argentina, Chile e Uruguai* (Belo Horizonte: Editora UFMG, 2015); and Anthony W. Pereira, *Political (In)justice: Authoritarianism and the Rule of Law in Brazil, Chile, and Argentina*, Pitt Latin American Series (Pittsburgh, PA: University of Pittsburgh Press, 2005). In emphasizing the differences between the Brazilian and Southern Cone regions, I do not intend to minimize the undemocratic nature of the Brazilian regime. I thus explicitly reject the trend on the Brazilian Right to praise the regime's accomplishments and deemphasize its authoritarianism. For a representative example, see Marco Antônio Villa, *Ditadura à brasileira: A democracia golpeada à esquerda e à direita* (São Paulo: Leya, 2014).

13. Stepan, *The Military in Politics*, 30–71, 172–203.

14. Robert Michels, *Political Parties: A Sociological Study of the Oligarchical Tendencies of Modern Democracy* (Glencoe, IL: Free Press, [1911] 1958); Gaetano Mosca, *The Ruling Class (Elementi di scienza politica)* (New York: McGraw-Hill, [1896] 1939); Vilfredo Pareto, *The Mind and Society*, (New York: Dover, [1916] 1935).

15. Tom Bottomore, *Élites and Society*, 2nd ed. (New York: Routledge, 1993).

16. Ibid., 10.

17. John Higley and Michael G. Burton, *Elite Foundations of Liberal Democracy* (Lanham, MD: Rowman & Littlefield, 2006), 4.

18. Michels, *Political Parties*, 408.

19. Michael Hartmann, *The Sociology of Elites* (London: Routledge, 2012), 22.

20. See, e.g., Bottomore, *Élites and Society*; Robert A. Dahl, *Who Governs? Democracy and Power in an American City* (New Haven, CT: Yale University Press, 1961); Harold D. Lasswell and Abraham Kaplan, *Power and Society: A Framework for Political Inquiry* (New Haven, CT: Yale University Press, 1950); C. Wright Mills, *The Power Elite* (New York: Oxford University Press, 1956). Still, postwar elite theorists were unable to come to any agreement on who belongs to the political class or even what it should be called. See Alan Zuckerman,

"The Concept 'Political Elite': Lessons from Mosca and Pareto," *Journal of Politics* 39:2 (1977): 324–44.

21. For Brazil, see Fernando Henrique Cardoso, "Partidos e deputados em São Paulo: passado e presente," in *Os partidos e as eleições no Brasil*, ed. Bolivar Lamounier and Fernando Henrique Cardoso (Rio de Janeiro: Paz e Terra, 1975): 45–75; Joel G. Verner, "The Structure of the Public Careers of Brazilian Legislators, 1963–1970," *International Journal of Comparative Sociology* 16:1–2 (1975): 64–80; Alessandra Carvalho, "Elites políticas durante o regime militar: um estudo sobre os parlamentares da ARENA e do MDB" (PhD dissertation, Universidade Federal do Rio de Janeiro, 2008); David V. Fleischer, *Thirty Years of Legislative Recruitment in Brazil* (Washington, DC: Center of Brazilian Studies, 1976); Leôncio Martins Rodrigues, *Partidos, ideologia e composição social: Um estudo das bancadas partidárias na Câmara dos Deputados* (São Paulo: Edusp, 2002).

22. Pierre Bourdieu, *Outline of a Theory of Practice* (Cambridge: Cambridge University Press, 1977), 72.

23. Hartmann, *Sociology of Elites*, 48.

24. Pierre Bourdieu, *Distinction: A Social Critique of the Judgment of Taste* (Cambridge, MA: Harvard University Press, [1979] 2004), 330; cited in Hartmann, *Sociology of Elites*, 49.

25. David Samuels, *Ambassadors of the State: Federalism, Ambition, and Congressional Politics in Brazil* (New York: Cambridge University Press, 2002).

26. Among federal deputies elected in 1978, the single most common profession was lawyer (56.2%), followed by professor (21.4%) and people engaged in agriculture and animal husbandry (i.e., landowners) (12.6%). See *Deputados brasileiros Repertório biográfico dos membros da Câmara dos Deputados, Nona Legislatura (1979–1983)* (Brasília: Câmara dos Deputados, Centro de Documentação e Informação, Coordenação de Publicações, 1979). Alfred Stepan discovered that among fathers of cadets, the three most common professions were military (37.6%), civil servant (13.9%), and merchant (12.8%). See Stepan, *The Military in Politics*, 33. To generalize, the political class was drawn from the upper and upper-middle classes, while military officers came from military or solidly middle-class backgrounds.

27. For more on the military's identity and political role, see Edmundo Campos Coelho, *Em busca de identidade: O Exército e a política na sociedade brasileira*, 2nd ed. (Rio de Janeiro: Editora Record, 2000); Frank Daniel McCann, *Soldiers of the Pátria: A History of the Brazilian Army, 1889–1937* (Stanford, CA: Stanford University Press, 2004).

28. On São Paulo's midcentury industrialization and urbanization, see John D. French, *Lula and His Politics of Cunning: From Metalworker to President of Brazil* (Chapel Hill: University of North Carolina Press, 2020).

29. Thomas E. Skidmore, *The Politics of Military Rule in Brazil, 1964–85* (New York: Oxford University Press, 1988), 138.

30. Stepan, *The Military in Politics*; Alfred Stepan, ed., *Authoritarian Brazil: Origins, Policies, and Future* (New Haven, CT: Yale University Press, 1973); Philippe C. Schmitter, "The 'Portugalization' of Brazil?," in Stepan, *Authoritarian Brazil*, 179–232, Juan J. Linz, "The Future of an Authoritarian Situation or the Institutionalization of a Military Regime: The Case of Brazil," in Stepan, *Authoritarian Brazil*, 233–54. For representative examples of the latter, see Schmitter, "The 'Portugalization' of Brazil?"; and Linz, "The Future of an Authoritarian Situation."

31. Thomas E. Skidmore, "Brazil's Slow Road to Democratization: 1974–1985," in *Democratizing Brazil: Problems of Transition and Consolidation*, ed. Alfred Stepan (New York: Oxford University Press, 1989), 5–42; Leslie Bethell and Celso Castro, "Politics in Brazil under Military Rule, 1964–1985," in *Brazil since 1930*, ed. Leslie Bethell, Cambridge History of Latin America (Cambridge: Cambridge University Press, 2008), 165–230.

32. Elio Gaspari, *A ditadura escancarada: As Ilusões Armadas* (São Paulo: Companhia das Letras, 2002); Elio Gaspari, *A ditadura derrotada: O Sacerdote e o Feiticeiro* (São Paulo: Companhia das Letras, 2003), Elio Gaspari, *A ditadura encurralada* (São Paulo: Companhia de Letras, 2004); Elio Gaspari, *A ditadura acabada* (São Paulo: Companhia das Letras, 2016).

33. For 1974, see Fernando Henrique Cardoso and Bolivar Lamounier, eds., *Os partidos e as eleições no Brasil* (Rio de Janeiro: Paz e Terra, 1975). For similar studies of the 1976 and 1978 elections, see Fábio Wanderley Reis, ed., *Os partidos e o regime: A lógica do processo eleitoral brasileiro* (São Paulo: Edições Símbolo, 1978); Bolivar Lamounier, ed., *Voto de desconfiança: Eleições e mudança política no Brasil: 1970–1979* (Petrópolis: Editora Vozes, 1980).

34. For representative examples, see Maria Helena Moreira Alves, *State and Opposition in Military Brazil* (Austin: University of Texas Press, 1985); Scott Mainwaring, *The Catholic Church and Politics in Brazil, 1916–1985* (Stanford, CA: Stanford University Press, 1986); Rachel Meneguello, *PT: A formação de um partido, 1979–1982* (São Paulo: Paz e Terra, 1989); Sonia E. Alvarez, *Engendering Democracy in Brazil: Women's Movements in Transition Politics* (Princeton, NJ: Princeton University Press, 1990); Margaret E. Keck, *The Workers' Party and Democratization in Brazil* (New Haven, CT: Yale University Press, 1992); Leigh A. Payne, *Brazilian Industrialists and Democratic Change* (Baltimore: Johns Hopkins University Press, 1994); Sebastião C. Velasco e Cruz, *Empresariado e estado na transição brasileira: Um estudo sobre a economia política do autoritarismo (1974–1977)* (Campinas: Editora da UNICAMP, 1995); Stepan, *Democratizing Brazil*.

35. Jean Rossiaud and Ilse Scherer-Warren, *A democracia inacabável: Memórias do futuro* (Florianópolis: Universidade Federal de Santa Catarina, 2000), 7.

36. Alves, *State and Opposition in Military Brazil*, 9.

37. Carlos Fico, "Versões e controvérsias sobre 1964 e a ditadura militar," *Revista Brasileira de História* 24:47 (2004): 29–60; Pagliarini, "'De onde? Para onde?'" For an early study that emphasized the role of the regime's allies among the business class, see René Armand Dreifuss, *1964, a conquista do estado: Ação política, poder e golpe de classe* (Petrópolis: Editora Vozes, 1981).

38. Lucia Grinberg, *Partido político ou bode expiatório: Um estudo sobre a Aliança Renovadora Nacional, ARENA (1965–1979)* (Rio de Janeiro: Mauad X, 2009). See also Margaret Sarles Jenks, "Political Parties in Authoritarian Brazil" (PhD dissertation, Duke University, 1979).

39. Célia Soibelmann Melhem, *Política de botinas amarelas: O MDB-PMDB paulista de 1965 a 1988* (São Paulo: Editora Hucitec, 1998). See also Maria D'Alva Gil Kinzo, *Legal Opposition Politics under Authoritarian Rule in Brazil: The Case of the MDB, 1966 79* (New York: St. Martin's Press, 1988).

40. Hagopian, *Traditional Politics and Regime Change in Brazil*. See also Alessandra Carvalho, "Elites políticas durante o regime militar: Um estudo sobre os parlamentares da ARENA e do MDB" (PhD dissertation, Universidade Federal do Rio de Janeiro, 2008).

41. Bolivar Lamounier, "*Authoritarian Brazil* Revisited: The Impact of Elections on the *Abertura*," in Stepan, *Democratizing Brazil*, 52; emphasis in original.

42. Hagopian, *Traditional Politics and Regime Change in Brazil*, 6.

43. John D. French, *Drowning in Laws: Labor Law and Brazilian Political Culture* (Chapel Hill: University of North Carolina Press, 2004), xi.

44. Marcio Goldman and Moacir Palmeira, *Antropologia, voto e representação política* (Rio de Janeiro: Contra Capa, 1996); Irlys Barreira, *Chuva de papeis: Ritos e símbolos de campanhas eleitorais no Brasil* (Rio de Janeiro: Relume Dumará; Núcleo de Antropologia da Política, 1998); Judy Bieber, *Power, Patronage, and Political Violence: State Building on a Brazilian Frontier, 1822–1889* (Lincoln: University of Nebraska Press, 1999); French, *Drowning in Laws*; James Holston, *Insurgent Citizenship: Disjunctions of Democracy and Modernity in Brazil* (Princeton, NJ: Princeton University Press, 2008); James P. Woodard, *A Place in Politics: São Paulo, Brazil, from Seigneurial Republicanism to Regionalist Revolt* (Durham, NC: Duke University Press, 2009).

45. Emilia Viotti da Costa, *The Brazilian Empire: Myths and Histories*, rev. ed. (Chapel Hill: University of North Carolina Press, 2000), xix.

46. Maud Chirio, *A política nos quartéis: Revoltas e protestos de oficiais na ditadura militar brasileira*, trans. André Telles (Rio de Janeiro: Zahar, 2012).

47. Anne-Marie Smith, *A Forced Agreement: Press Acquiescence to Censorship in Brazil* (Pittsburgh, PA: University of Pittsburgh Press, 1997), 40–41. For studies of the Brazilian press during this period, see Maria Aparecida de Aquino, *Censura, imprensa, estado autoritário (1968—1978): O exercício cotidiano da dominação e da resistência, o estado de São Paulo e movimento* (Bauru: Editora da Universidade do Sagrado Coração, 1999); Juliana Gazzotti, "Jornal da Tarde (1966–75): Ideologia liberal e ditadura militar" (PhD dissertation, Universidade Federal de São Carlos, 2004); Beatriz Kushnir, *Cães de guarda: Jornalistas e censores, do AI-5 à constituição de 1988* (São Paulo: FAPESP and Boitempo Editorial, 2004).

48. For a more detailed discussion of this remarkable collection, see Bryan Pitts, Yahn Wagner, and Madeleine Roberts, "Sound and Politics: The Audio Archive of Brazil's Chamber of Deputies," *Latin American Research Review* 55:1 (2020): 135–47.

49. The documents generated by the regime's intelligence services must be used with caution, as they constitute less a historical record of the actions of those the regime targeted as "subversive" than a record of the intelligence services' often-contrived justifications for persecuting perceived enemies. As a result, when I use these sources, I am careful to indicate either the alleged nature of the crimes or, in a few cases, to withhold the name of the politician accused. For an outstanding critical treatment of these archives, see Pedro Ivo Carneiro Teixeirense, "Reinventando o inimigo: História, política e memória na montagem dos dossiês e contra-dossiês da ditadura militar brasileira (1964–2001)" (PhD dissertation, Universidade Federal do Rio de Janeiro, 2017).

1. "THE BLOOD OF THE YOUTH IS FLOWING": THE POLITICAL CLASS AND ITS CHILDREN TAKE ON THE MILITARY IN 1968

An earlier version of this chapter was published as Bryan Pitts, "'O sangue da mocidade está correndo': a classe política e seus filhos enfrentam os militares em 1968," *Revista Brasileira de História* 34:67 (2014): 39–65, https://doi.org/10.1590/S0102-01882014000100003. Reprinted with permission.

1. "O significado maior de uma vitória," *O Estado de S. Paulo* (henceforth *O Estado*), 2 Apr. 1964.
2. The unlikelihood that an aspiring populist dictator in the mold of the semifascist Vargas was preparing to turn Brazil over to Soviet-style Communists remained unnoted.
3. "São Paulo repete 32," *O Estado*, 1 Apr. 1964.
4. Herbert Levy (UDN-SP), *Diário da Câmara dos Deputados (DCD)*, 2 Apr. 1964, 1959.
5. "Empolgou São Paulo a vitória das armas libertadoras," *O Estado*, 2 Apr. 1964.
6. Paulo Egydio Martins et al., *Paulo Egydio conta: Depoimento ao CPDOC-FGV* (São Paulo: Imprensa Oficial do Estado, 2007), 188.
7. *Cassar* (part. *cassado*, n.s. *cassação*, n.p. *cassações*) means "to annul, cancel, repeal, revoke, or abrogate." It most commonly refers to the act of removing someone from a position in a government institution, whether obtained by election, appointment, or civil service exam. This usage does not have an equivalent in English, and I have thus left it untranslated.
8. André Franco Montoro and Pedro Rodrigues de Albuquerque Cavalcanti, *Memórias em linha reta* (São Paulo: Editora SENAC, 2000), 140.
9. There is a rich literature on the main political parties between 1945 and 1965. For the UDN, see Maria Victoria de Mesquita Benevides, *A UDN e o udenismo: Ambiguïdades do liberalismo brasileiro (1945-1965)* (Rio de Janeiro: Paz e Terra, 1981). For the Social Democratic Party (PSD), see Lucia Hippolito, *De raposas e reformistas: O PSD e a experiência democrática brasileira (1945-1964)* (Rio de Janeiro: Paz e Terra, 1985). For the Brazilian Labor Party (PTB), see Maria Celina Soares d'Araújo, *O Partido Trabalhista Brasileiro e os dilemas dos partidos classistas* (Rio de Janeiro: Fundação Getúlio Vargas, Centro de Pesquisa e Documentação de História Contemporânea do Brasil, 1991). The establishment of indirect elections and the abolition of the old parties were only the two most dramatic of a host of changes to electoral law that the regime engineered. Leonardo Augusto de Andrade Barbosa, "The Ballot under the Bayonet: Election Law in the First Years of the Brazilian Civil-Military Regime (1964-1967)," *Revista Direito GV* 13 (2017), https://dx.doi.org/10.1590/2317-6172201707.
10. Montoro and Cavalcanti, *Memórias em linha reta*, 143.
11. Martins et al., *Paulo Egydio conta*, 202-3.
12. "Silencia o governador; reina ordem no Estado," *O Estado*, 28 Oct. 1965.
13. "Nota da UDN de São Paulo," *O Estado*, 28 Oct. 1965.
14. "Nota oficial do PSD," *O Estado*, 28 Oct. 1965.
15. "Falcão: Govêrno não vai pedir o recesso," *O Estado*, 28 Oct. 1965.
16. A one-party system was rejected, as it would have been incompatible with the generals' concern with maintaining the appearance of liberal democracy; an opposition was needed, if only for show.
17. Skidmore, *The Politics of Military Rule*, 48. Federal deputy Ulysses Guimarães received credit for selecting the name. At first, the new party was leaning toward calling itself the Brazilian Democratic Alliance (ADB) to differentiate itself from ARENA. But Ulysses argued that it was necessary to select a name with masculine gender, as opposed to the feminine *aliança*. He remembered that jokes and political cartoons had frequently portrayed the UDN (a feminine *união*) as a woman, while the PSD (a masculine *partido*) had appeared as a man. He hoped to encourage the same representation of ARENA and the MDB, with the *movimento* portrayed as a man and the aliança as a woman. See Luiz Gutemberg, *Moisés, codinome Ulysses Guimarães: Uma biografia* (São Paulo: Companhia das Letras, 1994), 99.

As Lucia Grinberg has demonstrated in her analysis of regime-era political cartoons, this gendered representation did indeed come to fruition; Grinberg, *Partido político ou bode expiatório*, 233–85.

18. José de Lurtz Sabiá, interview with the author, São Paulo, 8 June 2015.
19. Kinzo, *Legal Opposition Politics*, 18, 240 n. 40.
20. Interview with Edgard and Rosa Turisco, Goiânia, 2 May 2015. Rosa and Edgard are two of the children of federal deputy Almir Turisco d'Araújo (MDB-GO). Although poor health and failing memory prevented their 98-year-old father from giving a full interview, Rosa and Edgard generously offered me their memories of his career.
21. In our interview, Sabiá referred to the new constitution as "disgusting." It is likely that many politicians shared his sentiment. Sabiá, interview with author.
22. Tel. Brasília 430, 25 Jan. 1967, National Archives and Records Administration, College Park (NARA), RG 59, Box 1906, Pol BRAZ 15-2.
23. Airgram 175, 16 Jan. 1968, NARA, RG 59, Box 1901, Pol 2 BRAZ.
24. Airgram 132, 5 Jan. 1968, NARA, RG 59, Box 1901, Pol 2 BRAZ.
25. Victoria Langland, *Speaking of Flowers: Student Movements and the Making and Remembering of 1968 in Military Brazil* (Durham, NC: Duke University Press, 2013), 107–8.
26. Sadi Bogado (MDB-RJ), *DCD*, 26 June 1968, 3675.
27. Breno da Silveira (MDB-GB), *DCD*, 3 Apr. 1968, 1062–63.
28. Interview with Edgard and Rosa Araújo.
29. Paulo Nunes Leal (ARENA-RO), *DCD*, 30 Mar. 1968, 937.
30. Mário Piva (MDB-BA), *DCD*, 30 Mar. 1968, 951.
31. Paulo Campos (MDB-GO), *DCD*, 29 June 1968, 3794.
32. Paulo Macarini (MDB-SC), *DCD*, 3 Sept. 1968, 5754; Márcio Moreira Alves, *A velha classe* (Rio de Janeiro: Editora Arte Nova, 1964), 15. For the percentage who were university graduates, see Carvalho, "Elites políticas durante o regime militar," 86.
33. José Mandelli (MDB-RS), *DCD*, 26 June 1968, 3671.
34. Lila Covas and Luci Molina, *Lila Covas: Histórias e receitas de uma vida* (São Paulo: Global Editora, 2007), 89.
35. "Prontuário Del. 24.280: Júlio de Mesquita Neto," Departamento de Ordem e Política Social (DOPS), Arquivo Público do Estado de São Paulo (APESP); "Prontuário Del. 6.699: Roberto de Abreu Sodré," DOPS, APESP; Roberto de Abreu Sodré, *No espelho do tempo: Meio século de política* (São Paulo: Best Seller, 1995), 34.
36. Miguel Feu Rosa (ARENA-ES), *DCD*, 30 Mar. 1968, 937.
37. Léo de Almeida Neves, interview with the author, São Paulo, 2 June 2015.
38. José Mandelli (MDB-RS), *DCD*, 26 June 1968, 3671.
39. Otávio Caruso da Rocha (MDB-RS), *DCD*, 3 Apr. 1968, 1077.
40. Data on the racial composition the student body were seldom collected by Brazilian universities in the 1960s, but a few scholars attempted to quantify class composition. Given the close correlation between race and class in Brazil to this day, a predominantly middle-class student body would certainly be predominantly white.
41. João Roberto Martins Filho, *Movimento estudantil e ditadura militar: 1964–1968* (São Paulo: Papirus, 1987), 36; Langland, *Speaking of Flowers*, 72. Despite such strong growth, by 1968 university students made up only 0.2% of Brazil's population. Artur José Poerner, *O poder jovem: História da participação política dos estudantes brasileiros*, 4th ed. (Rio de Janeiro: Fundação Biblioteca Nacional, 1995), 43.

NOTES   189

42. Vilma Pereira, interview with the author, Brasília, 10 April 2015.
43. For a study that emphasizes the middle-class (and thus, implicitly, white) status of university students, see Martins Filho, *Movimento estudantil e ditadura militar*.
44. Márcio Moreira Alves (MDB-GB), *DCD*, 30 Mar. 1968, 950.
45. Antônio Cunha Bueno (ARENA-SP), *DCD*, 24 Oct. 1968, Suplemento, 10. For Cunha Bueno's participation in student politics during the Estado Novo, see Glauco Carneiro, *Cunha Bueno: História de um político* (São Paulo: Livraria Pioneira Editora, 1982), 45–61.
46. Oceano Carleial (ARENA-AL), *DCD*, 2 Apr. 1968, 997.
47. Nazir Miguel (ARENA-SP), *DCD*, 3 Apr. 1968, 1067.
48. For a defense of the police, see Antônio de Lisboa Machado (ARENA-GO), *DCD*, 3 Apr. 1968, 1062. For an attack on student violence, see Paulo d'Araújo Freire (ARENA-MG), *DCD*, 3 Apr. 1968, 1067.
49. Haroldo Leon Peres (ARENA-PR), *DCD*, 30 Mar. 1968, 953.
50. Jayme Portella de Mello, *A Revolução e o Governo Costa e Silva* (Rio de Janeiro: Guavira Editores, 1979), 560, 564–65. Portella's argument, sustained throughout his 150-page discussion of the events of 1968, was that politicians—both "subversive" MDB leftists and counterrevolutionary arenistas—were solely responsible for that year's political crisis.
51. Ministério do Exército, I Exército, IIa Região Militar, "Termo de perguntas feitas ao deputado Mário Covas," 23 Dec. 1968, Fundação Mário Covas (FMC), Box 138.
52. Márcio Moreira Alves, *68 mudou o mundo* (Rio de Janeiro: Editora Nova Fronteira, 1993), 143–44.
53. "Informe no. 212/QG4," Arquivo Nacional—Rio de Janeiro (AN-RJ), Centro de Informações de Segurança da Aeronáutica (CISA), BR_AN_BSB_VAZ_036_0115, 18 June 1968.
54. Franklin Martins, Preface to Antonio de Padua Gurgel, *A rebelião dos estudantes: Brasília, 1968* (Brasília: Editora UnB, 2002), 19–20.
55. Gurgel, *A rebelião dos estudantes*, 19–20.
56. "Assim o 10 de maio," *Folha da Tarde*, 2 May 1968. The nail-studded potato comes from Sodré, *No espelho do tempo*, 157.
57. "Aconteceu no palanque tomado," *Folha da Tarde*, 2 May 1968.
58. "Governador diz que pagou preço pela liberdade," *Folha da Tarde*, 2 May 1968.
59. Despite their isolation in Brasília, federal politicians were still interested in following events in their home states; to monitor the student movement at home, they instructed state deputies to attend rallies. "Informação no. 227/EMAER," AN-RJ, SNI, BR_AN_BSB_N8_0_PSN_EST_101, 29 July 1968.
60. João Alves de Macedo (ARENA-BA), *DCD, Suplemento*, 31 Oct. 1968, 19.
61. Martins, in Gurgel, *A rebelião dos estudantes*, 31.
62. In the 1960s (and today), federal politicians nearly invariably fled Brasília at the close of the Thursday session to spend a long weekend in their home state (or Rio), returning late Monday.
63. Gurgel, *A rebelião dos estudantes*, 123, 131, 134–35.
64. Interview with Mario Covas, in *AI-5: O dia que não existiu* (2001).
65. Osvaldo Martins, "Surge um líder," in *Mario Covas, democracia: Defender, conquistar, praticar*, ed. Osvaldo Martins (São Paulo: Fundação Mario Covas, 2011), 48–49.
66. "DOPS e PM invadem a Universidade de Brasília," *Jornal do Brasil* (henceforth *JB*), 30 Aug. 1968; Carlos Castello Branco, "De onde parte o terror em Brasília," *JB*, 30 Aug. 1968.

67. For interviews with students, along with footage of the invasion, see *Barra 68: Sem perder a ternura*, (Europa Filmes, 2002).

68. The number was reached by comparing a newspaper report and several congressional speeches. See "DOPS e PM invadem a Universidade de Brasília"; Márcio Moreira Alves (MDB-GB), Fernando Gama (MDB-PR), Hermano Alves (MDB-GB), and Elias Carmo (ARENA-MG), *DCD*, Suplemento, 30 Aug. 1968, 16, 23, 25; Vianna (MDB-PB), *Diário do Senado Federal* (henceforth *DSF*), 30 Aug. 1968, 2503, 2505; Covas (MDB-SP), *DCD*, 24 Oct. 1968, 7532.

69. Castello Branco, "De onde parte o terror em Brasília"; "DOPS e PM invadem a Universidade de Brasília," *JB*, 30 Aug. 1968.

70. Aurélio Vianna (MDB-PB), *DSF*, 30 Aug. 1968, 2503.

71. Aurélio Vianna (MDB-PB), *DSF*, 30 Aug. 1968, 2504.

72. "Flashes," *JB*, 30 Aug. 1968.

73. "DOPS e PM invadem a Universidade de Brasília."

74. "Flashes."

75. Carlos Castello Branco, "Quem tem responsabilidade e quem é irresponsável no Govêrno," *JB*, 31 Aug. 1968.

76. Castello Branco, "De onde parte o terror em Brasília."

77. Eugênio Doin Vieira (MDB-SC) and Antônio Carlos Pereira Pinto (MDB-RJ), *DCD*, 30 Aug. 1968, 5661, 5665–56.

78. Getúlio Moura (MDB-RJ), *DCD*, 30 Aug. 1968, 5665.

79. José Martins Rodrigues (MDB-CE), 5661.

80. "Justificativa de Sátiro foi vaiada," *JB*, 30 Aug. 1968.

81. Wilson Martins (MDB-MG), *DCD*, Suplemento, 30 Aug. 1968, 11.

82. Márcio Moreira Alves (MDB-GB), *DCD*, Suplemento, 30 Aug. 1968, 16.

83. Gastone Righi Cuoghi (MDB-SP), *DCD*, Suplemento, 30 Aug. 1968, 16.

84. *DCD*, Suplemento, 30 Aug. 1968, 17; "Justificativa de Sátiro foi vaiada."

85. Harold Leon Peres (ARENA-PR), *DCD*, Suplemento, 30 Aug. 1968, 22.

86. Carlos de Brito Velho (ARENA-RS), *DCD*, Suplemento, 30 Aug. 1968, 22.

87. Haroldo Peres (ARENA-PR), *DCD*, Suplemento, 30 Aug. 1968, 22.

88. Unírio Machado (MDB-RS), *DCD*, Suplemento, 30 Aug. 1968, 22.

89. Eurípides Cardoso de Menezes (ARENA-GB), *DCD*, 30 Aug. 1968, 7532.

90. Mário Covas, *DCD*, 24 Oct. 1968, 7530–34.

91. Gurgel, *A rebelião dos estudantes*, 270. The saying, "Politics is the art of swallowing toads," attributed to First Republic senator José Gomes Pinheiro Machado, expresses the conviction that politics requires unpleasant compromises.

92. Eugênio Doin Vieira (MDB-SC), *DCD*, 3 Sept. 1968, 5753.

93. Hermano Alves (MDB-GB), *DCD*, 3 Sept. 1968, 5750–51.

94. José Martins Rodrigues (MDB-CE) and Hermano Alves (MDB-GB), *DCD*, 3 Sept. 1968, 5751–53. Luiz Alves de Lima e Silva, Duke of Caxias (1803–80), one of the foremost military commanders and politicians of the Empire, is universally acclaimed as the father of the Brazilian Armed Forces.

95. Francisco da Chagas Rodrigues (MDB-GB), *DCD*, 3 Sept. 1968, 5752.

96. Jairo Brum (MDB-RS), *DCD*, 3 Sept. 1968, 5752.

97. Paulo d'Araújo Freire (ARENA-MG), *DCD*, 3 Sept. 1968, 5751.

98. Márcio Moreira Alves (MDB-GB), *DCD*, 3 Sept. 1968, 5755; emphasis added.
99. Mariano Beck (MDB-RS), *DCD*, 3 Sept. 1968, 5755. To discover which signatories were married to politicians, I compared the list with the *Dicionário Histórico Biográfico Brasileiro* (*DHBB*), which usually notes the name of each entry's spouse.
100. Márcio Moreira Alves (MDB-GB), *DCD*, 4 Sept. 1968, Suplemento, 9. "Operation Lysistrata" refers to Aristophanes's play *Lysistrata*, in which Greek women withhold sex until their husbands agree to end the Peloponnesian War.
101. Márcio Moreira Alves, *A Grain of Mustard Seed: The Awakening of the Brazilian Revolution* (Garden City, NY: Anchor Books, 1973), 12–13.
102. Márcio Moreira Alves, interview with CPDOC-FGV, 8 Dec. 1997.
103. For more on the shootout in Alagoas, see Jorge Oliveira, *Curral da morte: O impeachment de sangue, poder e política no Nordeste* (Rio de Janeiro: Editora Record, 2010).
104. See Márcio Moreira Alves, *Torturas e torturados* (Rio de Janeiro: Empresa Jornalística, 1967).
105. Moreira Alves, *A Grain of Mustard Seed*, 15.
106. Ibid., 15–16.
107. José Penedo (ARENA-BA), *DCD*, 26 Nov. 1968, 8454.
108. Castello Branco, "Quem tem responsabilidade e quem é irresponsável no Govêrno."
109. For the typed notes, see Augusto Rademaker to Luis Antônio da Gama e Silva, 20 Sept. 1968, CD-CEDI, Dossiê Márcio Moreira Alves, 15–16. For the published version, see *DCD*, 4 Sept. 1968, Suplemento, 9.
110. Ernani Sátiro (ARENA-PB), *DCD*, 3 Sept. 1968, 5757.
111. It is not clear who distributed the speech in the barracks, as news reports at the time ventured no guesses. Twenty-five years later Moreira Alves claimed that it had been General Emílio Garrástazu Médici, head of the SNI. See Moreira Alves, *A Grain of Mustard Seed*, 151.
112. Moreira Alves had been in the military's sights for some time. After the publication of his 1967 book, *Torturas e torturados*, the Federal Police obtained a copy and wrote a scathing review. "'Torturas e torturados,'" AN-RJ, CISA, BR_AN_BSB_VAZ_040A_0003, 20 July 1967.
113. Martins, in Gurgel, *A rebelião dos estudantes*, 20.
114. See, e.g., Maria Paula Nascimento Araújo, *Memórias estudantis: da fundação da UNE aos nossos dias* (Rio de Janeiro: Relume Dumará, Ediouro, 2007), Jeffrey L. Gould, "Solidarity under Siege: The Latin American Left, 1968," *American Historical Review* 114, no. 2 (2009): 348–75, https://dx.doi.org/10.1086/ahr.114.2.348; Martins Filho, *Movimento estudantil e ditadura militar*.
115. For an analysis of the process by which some former revolutionaries became politicians, see Kenneth P. Serbin, *From Revolution to Power in Brazil: How Radical Leftists Embraced Capitalism and Struggled with Leadership* (South Bend, IN: University of Notre Dame Press, 2019).

2. "THE FUNERAL OF DEMOCRACY": THE SHOWDOWN WITH THE MILITARY AND INSTITUTIONAL ACT NO. 5

A previous version of the section "'To the King, I Give All, Except My Honor': The Congressional Debate" was published as Bryan Pitts, "'O funeral da democracia': o caso Moreira

Alves, a cultura política das elites e o estabelecimento de uma ditadura no Brasil," in *Paulistânia eleitoral: ensaios, imagens, dados*, ed. José D'Amico Bauab (São Paulo: TRE-SP, Imprensa Oficial, 2011). Reprinted with permission.

1. Márcio Moreira Alves (MDB-GB), *DCD*, 1 June 2000, Suplemento, "Documentos referentes à sessão matunina do dia 12-12-1968," 98.
2. "Cassações: Novos informes," *Folha*, 15 Oct. 1968; "Processo contra Márcio vai ao Supremo," *Folha*, 12 Oct. 1968. As Moreira Alves pointed out, although Tavares claimed to speak on behalf of the aggrieved rank and file, his complaint was sent only 24 hours after the second speech was printed—hardly enough time to poll soldiers. "Razões do Deputado Márcio Moreira Alves perante a Comissão de Constituição e Justiça," 18 Nov. 1968, CD-CEDI, "Dossiê Márcio Moreira Alves," 167–69.
3. Tavares to Costa e Silva, 5 Sept. 1968, CD-CEDI, "Dossiê Márcio Moreira Alves," 6–7.
4. "Gama e Silva," in *DHBB*, http://www.fgv.br/CPDOC/BUSCA/Busca/BuscaConsultar.aspx. Accessed 28 Sept. 2012.
5. Olympio Mourão Filho and Hélio Silva, *Memórias, a verdade de um revolucionário* (Porto Alegre: L&PM Editores, 1978), 448.
6. Souza e Mello to Gama e Silva, 19 Sept. 1968, CD-CEDI, "Dossiê Márcio Moreira Alves," 8.
7. Rademaker to Gama e Silva, 20 Sept. 1968, CD-CEDI, "Dossiê Márcio Moreira Alves," 9–10.
8. Gama e Silva to Décio Miranda, 2 Oct. 1968, CD-CEDI, "Dossiê Márcio Moreira Alves," 4; Gama e Silva to Costa e Silva, 26 Sept. 1968, CD-CEDI, "Dossiê Márcio Moreira Alves," 18–33.
9. Gama e Silva to Costa e Silva, 26 Sept. 1968, 19.
10. Ricardo A. Setti, "Esperança é a rejeição no Supremo," *Jornal da Tarde* [henceforth *JT*], 16 Oct. 1968.
11. "Costa quer respeito às regras do jogo," *Folha*, 23 Oct. 1968, 3; Ricardo A. Setti, "Assunto agora é aumento," *JT*, 8 Nov. 1968; Carlos Castello Branco, "Coluna de Castello," *JB*, 8 Nov. 1968.
12. Special session: "Arena quer elaborar estatuto de decoro," *JB*, 23 Oct. 1968. Censure and forfeiture: "Dnar Mendes quer suspender e cortar subsídios para disciplinar deputados," *JT*, 5 Nov. 1968. Amendment: "Agora, até a Constituição pode mudar," *JT*, 7 Nov. 1968.
13. Airgram Rio de Janeiro A-1150, 29 Oct. 1968, NARA, RG 59, Box 1901.
14. Intelligence Note 973, 17 Dec. 1968, NARA, RG 59, Box 1905.
15. Moreira Alves, *A Grain of Mustard Seed*, 18–19; Moreira Alves, *68 mudou o mundo*, 165.
16. Moreira Alves, *A Grain of Mustard Seed*, 19–21.
17. Aliomar Baleeiro, "Representação no. 786—Distrito Federal," 31 Oct. 1968, CD-CEDI, Dossiê Márcio Moreira Alves, 39–40.
18. Luiz Gallotti to Bonifácio, 6 Nov. 1968, CD-CEDI, "Dossiê Márcio Moreira Alves," 1.
19. Tel. Brasília 3196, 13 Nov. 1968, NARA, RG 59, Box 1905.
20. "Choques em Vila Isabel matam um estudante," *JB*, 23 Oct. 1968; "A Câmara dá sinais de que concederá licença para a cassação do deputado," *Folha*, 24 Oct. 1968; "A fala censurada," *JT*, 25 Oct. 1968.
21. "Inclina-se a Câmara para permitir a cassação," *JB*, 24 Oct. 1968.

22. "Evolução da crise leva pessimismo e desalento a políticos da ARENA," *JB*, 24 Oct. 1968.
23. Interview with Freire, in *AI-5: O dia que não existiu*.
24. Interview with Covas, in *AI-5: O dia que não existiu*.
25. "Cassações: Pronto o pedido de licença," *Folha*, 5 Nov. 1968.
26. Tel. Brasília 3173, 30 Oct. 1968, NARA, RG 59, Box 3061; "Pronto processo contra deputado de SP," *Folha, Edição da Tarde*, 31 Oct. 1968.
27. "Krieger prefere calar sobre a situação," *JB*, 23 Oct. 1968.
28. "Chegou à Câmara processo contra Hermano," *JT*, 13 Nov. 1968.
29. Daniel Krieger, *Desde as Missões . . . : Saudades, lutas, esperanças* (Rio de Janeiro: J. Olympio Editora, 1977), 179–189, 198–200.
30. "Daniel Krieger," in *DHBB*, http://www.fgv.br/CPDOC/BUSCA/Busca/BuscaConsultar.aspx. Accessed 28 Sept. 2012.
31. Krieger, *Desde as Missões*, 330–31.
32. "Krieger prefere calar sobre a situação."
33. Portella de Mello, *A Revolução e o governo Costa e Silva*, 586.
34. Krieger, *Desde as Missões*, 335.
35. Portella de Mello, *A Revolução e o governo Costa e Silva*, 611.
36. Interview with Freire, in *AI-5: O dia que não existiu*.
37. Carlos Castello Branco, "Coluna de Castello," *JB*, 23 Oct. 1968.
38. Tel. Rio 13116, 28 Oct. 1968, NARA, RG 59, Box 1905.
39. Tel. Rio 13997, 4 Dec. 1968, NARA, RG 59, Box 1905.
40. "Costa quer respeito às regras do jogo," *Folha*, 23 Oct. 1068; "Presidente é contra qualquer solução extra institucional," *JB*, 23 Oct. 1968.
41. "Estamos na trégua da rainha," *JT*, 5 Nov. 1968.
42. "Militares começam a reagir contra cassação de deputado," *Folha*, 14 Oct. 1968.
43. "Problema maior é a cassação de Márcio," *JB*, 23 Oct. 1968.
44. "Costa debaterá cassação com Alto Comando Militar, amanhã," *Folha*, 20 Oct. 1968.
45. "Albuquerque adverte: Forças Armadas repelirão provocações," *Folha*, 9 Nov. 1968.
46. Vandré's 1968 song "Pra não dizer que não falei das flores" accused the military of teaching soldiers to "die for the country and live without reason" and urged listeners, "Come on, let's go / If you wait you'll never know / The ones who know choose the time / They don't wait for it to happen."
47. "Razões do Deputado Márcio Moreira Alves perante a Comissão de Constituição e Justiça," 18 Nov. 1968, CD-CEDI, "Dossiê Márcio Moreira Alves," 157.
48. Ibid., 202.
49. Lauro Leitão, "Parecer," 21 Nov. 1968, CD-CEDI, "Dossiê Márcio Moreira Alves," 129–56.
50. Pedroso Horta to Comissão de Constituição e Justiça, 27 Nov. 1968, CD-CEDI, "Dossiê Márcio Moreira Alves," 198–233.
51. "Costa e Silva comanda as pressões," *JT*, 26 Nov. 1968.
52. "Governo já tem maioria contra Márcio na Comissão de Justiça," *Folha*, 26 Nov. 1968; "Só em janeiro a votação do caso Márcio," *Folha*, 27 Nov. 1968. For a slightly different version, see Krieger, *Desde as Missões*, 333–34.
53. "Cresce a pressão militar," *JT*, 23 Nov. 1968.

54. "Informe Especial no. 96/SG-1/68," AN-RJ, CISA, BR_AN_BSB_N8_0_PSN_EST_101, 12 Dec. 1968.
55. Interview with Covas, in *AI-5: O dia que não existiu.*
56. Martins, *Mario Covas, democracia: Defender, conquistar, praticar*, 51.
57. "Só em janeiro a votação do caso Marcio," *Folha*, 27 Nov. 1968.
58. "Márcio: Governo agora quer urgência," *Folha, Edição da Tarde*, 27 Nov. 1968.
59. Skidmore, *The Politics of Military Rule*, 80.
60. Djalma Marinho and Lauro Leitão, 12 Dec. 1968, CD-CEDI, "Dossiê Márcio Moreira Alves," 242–43.
61. For Marinho as unassuming, see "Ser um bom partido, eis a questão," *Veja*, 11 Dec. 1968. For the quotations from his speech, see "Ao rei tudo, menos a honra," *JB*, 21 Apr. 2004. The Calderón de la Barca quotation is from *El Alcalde de Zalamea*. Although the line has entered Brazilian political lore, it does not appear in press transcriptions or the version in Krieger's biography. See "Comissão aprova cassação de Márcio; Djalma Marinho renuncia," *Folha*, 11 Dec. 1968; "MDB quer aproveitar a hora," *JT*, 11 Dec. 1968; Krieger, *Desde as Missões*, 339–41.
62. "O Govêrno vai vencer assim," *JT*, 28 Nov. 1968.
63. Portella de Mello, *A Revolução e o governo Costa e Silva*, 625, 632.
64. "MDB suspende a obstrução," *JT*, 5 Dec. 1968.
65. "A nota do Exército," *JT*, 7 Dec. 1968.
66. "Governo pode recorrer a um novo Ato," *Folha*, 4 Dec. 1968.
67. "Covas: Cassação é problema da Câmara," *Folha*, 6 Nov. 1968.
68. "Esperada decisão do caso Márcio antes do recesso de dezembro," *Folha*, 1 Nov. 1968.
69. These speeches only came to light decades later when a former congressional employee came forward with the typed minutes; they were belatedly published in the *Diário da Câmara* on 1 June 2000. DCD, 1 June 2000, Suplemento, "Documentos referentes à sessão matunina do dia 12–12–1968."
70. For the percentage of deputies who had degrees in law, see Carvalho, *Forças armadas e política no Brasil*, 86.
71. Carlos de Brito Velho (ARENA-RS), *DCD*, 12 Dec. 1968, 9008.
72. Nísia Carone (MDB-MG), Câmara dos Deputados, Coordenação de Audiovisual (CD-COAUD), Arquivo Sonoro, 12 Dec. 1968.
73. Benedito Ferreira (ARENA-GO), *DCD*, 10 Dec. 1968, 8886. "Polish" referred to Vargas's 1937 constitution, modeled upon Poland's authoritarian, corporatist April Constitution of 1935.
74. "Declaração de voto," *DCD*, 12 Dec. 1968, 9004.
75. Nísia Carone, CD-COAUD, Arquivo Sonoro, 12 Dec. 1968.
76. Miguel Feu Rosa (ARENA-ES), *DCD*, 1 June 2000, Suplemento, 35.
77. Jonas Carlos da Silva (ARENA-CE), *DCD*, 30 Nov. 1968, 8603.
78. Jairo Brum (MDB-RS), *DCD*, 12 Dec. 1968, 9009.
79. Mário Covas (MDB-SP), *DCD*, 1 June 2000, Suplemento, 109.
80. Antônio Magalhães (MDB-GO), *DCD*, 12 Dec. 1968, 8978.
81. Alcides Flores Soares (ARENA-RS), *DCD*, 12 Dec. 1968, 9010.
82. Mário Gurgel (MDB-ES), *DCD*, 1 June 2000, Suplemento, 58; Jairo Brum (MDB-RS), *DCD*, 12 Dec. 1968, 9009.

83. Carlos de Brito Velho (ARENA-RS), *DCD*, 12 Dec. 1968.
84. *DCD*, 4 Dec. 1968, 8687; *DCD*, 12 Dec. 1968, 8984, 9002, 9007.
85. Eugênio Doin Vieira (MDB-RS), *DCD*, 1 June 2000, Suplemento, 67.
86. Moreira Alves, *A Grain of Mustard Seed*, 22.
87. Alfredo de Arruda Câmara (ARENA-PE), *DCD*, 12 Dec. 1968, 9003.
88. Joel Ferreira (MDB-AM), *DCD*, 1 June 2000, Suplemento, 56.
89. Paulo d'Araújo Freire (ARENA-MG), *DCD*, 12 Dec. 1968, 8979.
90. Getúlio Moura (MDB-RJ), *DCD*, 12 Dec. 1968, 8984.
91. Interview with Júlia Steinbruch (MDB-RJ), in *AI-5: O dia que não existiu*.
92. Mário Maia (MDB-AC), *DCD*, 10 Dec. 1968, 8885.
93. Feliciano Figueiredo (MDB-GO), *DCD*, 12 Dec. 1968, 9007. *Fisiológicos* (lit., "physiologues") is a derisive term for politicians devoid of principle. In contrast to ideologues, who defend ideas, "physiologues" base their actions on the physical world, that is, on reality and pragmatism. For a story about the origin of the term from MDB deputy Ulysses Guimarães, see Gutemberg, *Moisés, codinome Ulysses Guimarães*, 103.
94. Bernardo Cabral (MDB-AM), *DCD*, 12 Dec. 1968, 9002.
95. Alfredo de Arruda Câmara (ARENA-PE), *DCD*, 12 Dec. 1968, 903. Rommel's cup of poison refers to the forced suicide of Field Marshall Erwin Rommel, accused in the 1944 plot to assassinate Hitler. The Latin quote translates as, "Hail, Caesar, those who are about to die salute you." The scriptural allusion is from Matthew 23:27.
96. Nísia Carone, *DCD*, 1 June 2000, Suplemento, 51.
97. Yukishigue Tamura (ARENA-SP), *DCD*, 12 Dec. 1968, 9010.
98. Unírio Machado (MDB-RS), *DCD*, 1 June 2000, Suplemento, 65.
99. Márcio Moreira Alves (MDB-GB), *DCD*, 1 June 2000, Suplemento, 88.
100. Ibid., 98.
101. Mário Covas (MDB-SP), *DCD*, 1 June 2000, Suplemento, 99.
102. Ibid., 105, 100.
103. Ibid., 109.
104. For the comparison to religious creeds, see Elizabeth Paes dos Santos, "A palavra como arma: Análise do discurso do Deputado Mário Covas em defesa da imunidade parlamentar" (Monograph, Curso de Especialização em Processo Legislativo da Câmara dos Deputados, Cefor, 2007), 48, 55.
105. Mário Covas (MDB-SP), *DCD*, 1 June 2000, Suplemento, 110–111.
106. Geraldo Freire (ARENA-MG), *DCD*, 1 June 2000, Suplemento, 113, 109, 114.
107. Ibid., 117.
108. "Rejeição da licença surpreendeu os próprios emedebistas," *Folha*, 13 Dec. 1968.
109. *Turco* was a common term for Arab Brazilians, since their Syrian and Lebanese ancestors who immigrated to Brazil before World War I arrived with Ottoman passports.
110. Martins, *Mario Covas, democracia: Defender, conquistar, praticar*, 61–62.
111. *DCD*, 1 June 2000, Suplemento, 136.
112. "Alegria e tristeza na Camara após a decisão," *Folha*, 13 Dec. 1968; Interview with Covas, in *AI-5: O dia que não existiu*.
113. Moreira Alves, *A Grain of Mustard Seed*, 25.
114. "Comissão votará hoje a licença para processo," *JB*, 10 Dec. 1968.
115. Tel. Brasília 3245, 12 Dec. 1968, NARA, RG 59, Box 1906.

116. Ibid.
117. Tel. 600, 13 Dec. 1968, Arquivo Histórico-Diplomático do Ministério de Negócios Estrangeiros (MNE), Lisbon, Brazil 1968 Incoming Telegrams, Pasta 3.
118. Gaspari, *A ditadura envergonhada*, 331.
119. "Deputados acompanharam acontecimentos," *JB*, 14 Dec. 1968.
120. "Costa acha que o que falta é fé em Deus," *JT*, 13 Dec. 1968.
121. "Militares decidem caminhos da crise," *JT*, 13 Dec. 1961.
122. "Deputados acompanharam acontecimentos."
123. "Os últimos momentos do Congresso," *JT*, 14 Dec. 1968.
124. "Esperavam 'conduta de grandeza,'" *Correio da Manhã*, 14 Dec. 1968.
125. "Deputados não acreditavam em Ato," *Correio da Manhã*, 14 Dec. 1968.
126. "Deputados acompanharam acontecimentos." In the Gospel of John, the disciple Thomas doubts the Resurrection, saying, "Unless I see the mark of the nails in his hands, and put my finger in the mark of the nails and my hand in his side, I will not believe" (John 20:25).
127. Tel. Rio de Janeiro 14310, 14 Dec. 1968, NARA, RG 59, Box 1910.
128. "Parecia uma vitória, era o naufrágio," *Veja*, 18 Dec. 1968.
129. "Decorridos 14 minutos de sabado, o Congresso já estava vazio," *Folha*, 15 Dec. 1968.
130. See Alves, *State and Opposition in Military Brazil*, 94–95; Moreira Alves, *A Grain of Mustard Seed*, 1; Gaspari, *A ditadura envergonhada*, 339; among many others. Only a few scholars have acknowledged the importance of the decision to absolve Moreira Alves. See Carlos Fico, *Como eles agiam. Os subterrâneos da ditadura militar: Espionagem e polícia política* (Rio de Janeiro: Editora Record, 2001), 65; Skidmore, *The Politics of Military Rule*, 79–81; Bethell and Castro, "Politics in Brazil under Military Rule," 185. The scholar who argued most strongly for the central role of the political class in the crisis was Lucia Grinberg; see Grinberg, *Partido político ou bode expiatório*, 125–30.
131. Portella de Mello, *A Revolução e o governo Costa e Silva*, 633, 608.
132. "Gama anuncia normas para prisões," *JT*, 21 Dec. 1968.
133. Interview with Ernesto Geisel, in Maria Celina Soares d'Araújo and Celso Castro, *Ernesto Geisel* (Rio de Janeiro: Editora Fundação Getúlio Vargas, 1997), 203, 208.
134. "Revolução, ano zero," *Veja*, 18 Dec. 1968.

3. "THE POLITICAL CLASS HAS LEARNED NOTHING":
THE MILITARY PUNISHES THE POLITICAL CLASS

1. Untitled account of imprisonment by Mário Covas, 20–21 Dec. 1968, FMC, Box 138, Folder 18. Wesley Soares of the Fundação Mário Covas provided a typed transcription.
2. See Hélio Silva, *1933—A crise do tenentismo: O ciclo de Vargas* (Rio de Janeiro: Civilização Brasileira, 1968).
3. For a comparison of the Estado Novo and the military regime, see Thomas E. Skidmore, "Politics and Economic Policy Making in Authoritarian Brazil, 1937–71," in Stepan, *Authoritarian Brazil*, 7–46. For a study that emphasizes the differences, see Fernando Henrique Cardoso, "Associated-Dependent Development: Theoretical and Practical Implications," in Stepan, *Authoritarian Brazil*, 142–76.

4. Coelho, *Em busca de identidade*.
5. "Ata da 46a sessão do Conselho de Segurança Nacional," 7 Feb. 1969, ANB, 126. Available at http://www.an.gov.br/sian/inicial.asp.
6. Diego Knack has made a similar argument about the corruption investigations the regime carried out under the aegis of the General Investigations Commission (CGI). Knack, "O combate à corrupção durante a Ditadura Militar," 6. This instrumental use of corruption accusations to neutralize political foes has a long history in Brazilian democracy, from Carlos Lacerda's accusations against Vargas and Kubitschek in the 1950s to the corruption-driven impeachment of Fernando Collor de Mello amid unprecedented economic crisis in 1992 to Sérgio Moro's use of an "anticorruption" task force to imprison Lula shortly before the 2018 presidential election.
7. Spanish Ambassador to Chile Miguel de Lojendio to Ministro de Asuntos Exteriores, 3 Jan. 1969, Ministerio de Asuntos Exteriores, Madrid (MAE), 10.671/1; Ana Beatriz Nader, *Autênticos do MDB, semeadores da democracia: História oral de vida política* (São Paulo: Paz e Terra, 1998), 134–36.
8. James N. Green, *We Cannot Remain Silent: Opposition to the Brazilian Military Dictatorship in the United States*, Radical Perspectives (Durham, NC: Duke University Press, 2010), 179–82.
9. "Hermano Alves," in *DHBB*, FGV-CPDOC. Available at http://www.fgv.br/CPDOC/BUSCA/Busca/BuscaConsultar.aspx.
10. "Os boatos de prisões e as prisões de ontem," *JT*, 14 Dec. 1968.
11. "Prisões na Guanabara e em SP," *Folha*, 14 Dec. 1968.
12. Untitled account of imprisonment by Mário Covas.
13. "Morre em SP Hélio Navarro, deputado que se opôs ao regime militar," *Folha*, 18 Sept. 2002. Available at http://www1.folha.uol.com.br/folha/brasil/ult96u37986.shtml
14. "Os boatos de prisões e as prisões de ontem."
15. Tel. Rio de Janeiro 14379, 17 Dec. 1968, NARA, RG 59, Box 1901, Pol 2 BRAZ.
16. John W. F. Dulles, *Resisting Brazil's Military Regime: An Account of the Battles of Sobral Pinto* (Austin: University of Texas Press, 2007), 145–46.
17. "Sobral Pinto," in *DHBB*. Available at http://www.fgv.br/cpdoc/busca/Busca/BuscaConsultar.aspx. Accessed 14 Mar. 2013.
18. Untitled account of imprisonment by Mário Covas.
19. Ibid.
20. Ministério do Exército, I Exército, IIa Região Militar, "Termo de perguntas feitas ao deputado Mário Covas," 23 Dec. 1968, FMC, Box 138.
21. Ibid.
22. Ibid.
23. Untitled account of imprisonment by Mário Covas.
24. Lila Covas and Luci Molina, *Lila Covas: Histórias e receitas de uma vida* (São Paulo: Global Editora, 2007), 99.
25. "Recording of the 43rd Session of the CSN," 13 Dec. 1968, available at http://www1.folha.uol.com.br/folha/treinamento/hotsites/ai5/reuniao/audioReuniao/audioReuniao.mp3. See also "Ata da 43a sessão do Conselho de Segurança Nacional," 13 Dec. 1968, ANB, 1–3, available at http://www.an.gov.br/sian/inicial.asp. The audio was lost for fifteen years

before the former secretary of Ernesto Geisel, the fourth military president (1974–79), found a cassette in a box in the garage of General Golbery do Couto e Silva, Geisel's chief of civilian staff. He gave it to the *Folha* journalist Élio Gaspari, who shared copies with other researchers. Finally, in 2008, the *Folha* digitized the recording and placed it online. See Chico Felitti, "Fita com registro da reunião que editou o ato está envolvido em sumiços, rompimentos e morte," *Folha*, 12 Dec. 2008, http://www1.folha.uol.com.br/folha/treinamento/novoemfolha46/ult10100u478757.shtml

26. "Ata da 43a sessão do Conselho de Segurança Nacional," 3–4.
27. Ibid., 4–6.
28. Ibid., 6.
29. Ibid., 7.
30. Ibid., 9–10.
31. Antônio Delfim Neto, interview with author, São Paulo, 15 June 2015.
32. "Ata da 43a sessão do Conselho de Segurança Nacional," 8–9.
33. Tel. 614, Paulo Castilho to MNE, 19 Dec. 1968, MNE, Brazil 1968 Outgoing Telegrams, Pasta 3.
34. "Ata da 43a sessão do Conselho de Segurança Nacional," 13–14.
35. Portella de Mello, *A Revolução e o governo Costa e Silva*, 651.
36. Mourão Filho and Silva, *Mémorias*, 450.
37. "Ata da 43a sessão do Conselho de Segurança Nacional," 25.
38. Ibid., 25–27.
39. "Só alguns ministros esperaram o discurso de Gama e Silva," *JT*, 15 Dec. 1968.
40. Krieger, *Desde au Missões*, 342.
41. Ibid., 343.
42. "Costa explica o nôvo Ato," *JT*, 17 Dec. 1968.
43. "Gen. Assunção: 'Tantas revoluções quantas forem necessárias,'" *Folha*, 26 Jan. 1969.
44. São Paulo A-123, 1 Oct. 1969, NARA, RG 59, Box 1906.
45. Krieger, *Desde au Missões*, 347–48.
46. Tel. Rio de Janeiro 3086, 25 Apr. 1969, NARA, RG 59, Box 1907.
47. "O Ato, aqui e no exterior," *JT*, 16 Dec. 1968.
48. "Os últimos momentos do Congresso," *JT*, 14 Dec. 1968.
49. "Gama anuncia normas para prisões," *JT*, 21 Dec. 1968.
50. Tel. Brasília 3280, 21 Dec. 1968, NARA, RG 59, Box 1907.
51. Airgram São Paulo A-7, 10 Jan. 1969, NARA, RG 59, Box 1908.
52. "Presidente continua recebendo mensagens de solidariedade," *Folha*, 16 Dec. 1968.
53. Airgram Belo Horizonte 1, 2 Jan. 1969, NARA, RG 59, Box 1900.
54. Tel. São Paulo 2721, 17 Dec. 1968, NARA, RG 59, Box 1907.
55. Tel. State Dept. 15567, 31 Jan. 1969, NARA, RG 59, Box 1903.
56. "Deputado pede apoio à Revolução," *JB*, 20 Dec. 1968.
57. "Maioria da bancada da Arena no Senado presta solidariedade ao governo," *JB*, 27 Dec. 1968.
58. Airgram 1271, 31 Dec. 1968, NARA, RG 59, Box 1907.
59. Untitled account of imprisonment by Mário Covas. "Alípios" refers to the above-cited Alípio de Carvalho. "Bonifácios" refers to the president of the Chamber of Deputies, and "Geraldos" refers to the ARENA vice-leader who spearheaded the attempt to secure

the prosecution of Moreira Alves. "Camarilla" was used in the PRI's Mexico to refer to the legions of self-interested state and local politicians who hitched their wagons to national figures.

60. "Shock and depression" and "hopelessness": Tel. Brasília 3254, 14 Dec. 1968, NARA, RG 59, Box 1907. "Deep despair": Airgram Belo Horizonte 1, 2 Jan. 1969, NARA, RG 59, Box 1900. "Apprehension," "cynicism," and "uncertain and fearful": Airgram São Paulo 7, 10 Jan. 1969, NARA, RG 59. "Gloom and tension" and "that military men . . .": Airgram São Paulo 23, 14 Feb. 1969, NARA, RG 59, Box 1908. "Dismay and pessimism" and "self-preservation and financial self-interest": Tel. Brasília 3280, 21 Dec. 1968, NARA, RG 59, Box 1907.

61. Tel. Brasília 3254, 14 Dec. 1968, NARA, RG 59, Box 1907. Carvalho ultimately remained in the government-allied party until 1983.

62. Statistics on cassações are drawn from Paulo Adolfo Martins de Oliveira, *Atos Institucionais: Sanções políticas* (Brasília: Câmara dos Deputados, Centro de Documentação e Informação, 2000). Oliveira, secretary-general of the Chamber of Deputies during the regime, pored over the *Diário Oficial* daily, clipping the notice every time the regime removed politicians from office, suspended citizens' political rights, or fired public employees. By the time cassações ended in 1977, he had sent over 4,800 names to the library of the Chamber of Deputies. The Chamber published the list in 2000. Each entry includes name, profession, sanction applied, and date. Politicians are usually listed according to the office they held, though they are occasionally listed by profession—lawyer, engineer, etc. Here I have limited myself to those whose profession is listed as current or former president, governor, senator, federal deputy, state deputy, mayor, and city councilor, as well as *suplentes* (substitutes for political office) and a few politicians listed under other professions, for a total of 584 between 10 Apr. 1964 and 30 June 1977. For an earlier but no less thorough statistical analysis of the cassações, see Lucia Klein and Marcus Faria Figueiredo, *Legitimidade e coação no brasil pos-64* (Rio de Janeiro: Forense-Universitária, 1978).

63. Aviso G/999, 28 Dec. 1968, in "Proposta para cassação de mandato e suspensão de direitos políticos," AN-RJ, SNI, A0885472–1975, 29 Sept. 1975.

64. Gastone Righi Cuoghi and Luciene Prieto Cuoghi, interview with author, Santos, 5 June 2015.

65. Claudio Lacerda, *Carlos Lacerda e os anos sessenta: Oposição* (Rio de Janeiro: Editora Nova Fronteira, 1998).

66. "Ata da 44a sessão do Conselho de Segurança Nacional," 30 Dec. 1968, ANB, pp. 2–3. Available at http://www.an.gov.br/sian/inicial.asp.

67. Gláucio Ary Dillon Soares, "As políticas de cassações," *Dados* 21 (1977): 82. Soares did not have access to the still-classified CSN minutes. Instead, his creative analysis revealed statistical correlations between votes against the regime and removal from office. The minutes largely validate his argument, though they reveal a stronger role for personal vendettas than Soares expected.

68. Soares, "As políticas de cassações," 81.

69. "Ata da 45a sessão do Conselho de Segurança Nacional," 10 Jan. 1969, ANB, 113. Available at http://www.an.gov.br/sian/inicial.asp.

70. It appears that CSN members sometimes falsely told cassado politicians that they had defended them. For example, in João Herculino's (MDB-MG) memoirs, he claims that no fewer than five members of the council defended him to Costa e Silva, but the minutes

record no such thing. "Ata da 45a sessão do Conselho de Segurança Nacional," 64; João Herculino de Souza Lopes, *Minhas melhores lembranças* (Brasília: Dom Quixote Editora), 73.

71. "Ata da 44a sessão do Conselho de Segurança Nacional," 30 Dec. 1968, ANB, 27–28. Available at http://www.an.gov.br/sian/inicial.asp. There was indisputably no love lost between Gama e Silva and Sabiá; forty-seven years later, Sabiá missed no opportunities to speak poorly of his fellow paulista in our oral history interview.

72. Krieger, *Desde au Missões*, 327.

73. "Ata da 44a sessão do Conselho de Segurança Nacional," 29.

74. Ibid.

75. "Ata da 45a sessão do Conselho de Segurança Nacional," 16 Jan 1969, ANB, 50. Available at http://www.an.gov.br/sian/inicial.asp. Nearly half a century later, although he had never listened to the recording of the CSN meeting, Sabiá expressed certainty in our oral history interview that he had been the victim of grudges held by a "gang" of civilian CSN members from São Paulo. Sabiá, interview with author.

76. "Ata da 45a sessão do Conselho de Segurança Nacional," 16 Jan 1969, ANB, 2; "Hary Normanton," in *DHBB*, available at http://www.fgv.br/CPDOC/BUSCA/Busca/BuscaConsultar.aspx.

77. "Ata da 45a sessão do Conselho de Segurança Nacional," 16 Jan 1969, ANB, 31–33.

78. Ibid., 74–76.

79. Ibid., 125–32.

80. Ibid., 103.

81. Ibid., 103–4.

82. Ibid., 104. In our 2015 interview, Delfim Neto admitted that Covas's cassação had been unjust. He added that by the time a name got to the CSN, the decision had already been made, and it would be pointless to object; while this was undoubtedly true, it does not explain why he argued so strenuously against the proposed lighter punishment.

83. "Ata da 45a sessão do Conselho de Segurança Nacional," 16 Jan 1969, ANB, 104–5.

84. Ibid., 108.

85. Ibid., 108–9.

86. Ibid., 110–11.

87. Ibid., 111.

88. Ibid.

89. Martins et al., *Paulo Egydio conta*, 221.

90. "Ata da 48a sessão do Conselho de Segurança Nacional," 29 Apr. 1969, ANB, 47–48. Available at http://www.an.gov.br/sian/inicial.asp.

91. Ibid., 50–51.

92. Delfim Neto, interview with author.

93. Airgram Brasília A-10, 13 Mar. 1969, NARA, RG 59, Box 1907, Pol 15-2 BRAZ.

94. "Ata da 46a sessão do Conselho de Segurança Nacional," 134–35.

95. Ibid., 137, 134.

96. Intelligence Note 351, George C. Denney Jr. to the Secretary of State, 7 May 1969, NARA, RG 59, Box 1900.

97. Intelligence Note 381, Thomas L. Hughes to the Acting Secretary, 15 May 1969, NARA, RG 59, Box 1900.

98. Bolívar Poeta de Siqueira to ARENA national directorate, 14 August 1969, FGV-CPDOC, Arquivo ARENA, cg.1965.08.31, Rolo 1, Pasta 3.

99. Sabiá, interview with author.
100. Tel. Rio de Janeiro 1964, 14 March 1969, NARA, RG 59, Box 1907, Pol 15-4 BRAZ.
101. "Ata da 47a sessão do Conselho de Segurança Nacional," 13 March 1969, ANB, 136–138. Available at http://www.an.gov.br/sian/inicial.asp.
102. Ibid., 138.
103. Tel. Rio de Janeiro 1964.
104. Tel. São Paulo 376, 1 May 1969, NARA, RG 59, Box 1907, Pol 15-4 BRAZ.
105. Tel. São Paulo 398, 6 May 1969, NARA, RG 59, Box 1907, Pol 15-4 BRAZ. See also Sodré, *No espelho do tempo*, 181–82.
106. Neves, interview with author.
107. Righi, interview with author. Righi recalled during our interview that when he was held in Santos, the commander of the installation, General Oswaldo Muniz Oliva, once showed off his "subversive" prisoners to his teenage sons. One of the young men was named Aloízio Mercadante; he would later become a leading figure in the leftist Workers' Party (PT).
108. Covas and Molina, *Lila Covas*, 106.
109. Edgard and Rosa d'Araújo, interview with author.
110. Carneiro, *Cunha Bueno*, 165.
111. Covas and Molina, *Lila Covas*, 112.
112. Carneiro, *Cunha Bueno*, 169.
113. Ibid. A few years later, when the climate was less tense, it was not necessary to be so circumspect. In 1976, after his cassação was announced, José Alencar Furtado's Brasília apartment was packed with commiserating friends and colleagues; a major even dropped by to offer his solidarity on behalf of fellow officers. Furtado, interview with author, Brasília, 22 June 2015. Special thanks to Malena Rehbein Rodrigues for placing me in contact with Furtado's daughter Dione, who arranged the interview.
114. Sabiá, interview with author. And Azevedo was himself cassado in September.
115. Covas and Molina, *Lila Covas*, 106.
116. Interview with Covas, in Celia Soibelmann Melhem and Sonia Morgenstern Russo, *Dr. Ulysses, o homem que pensou o Brasil: 39 depoimentos sobre a trajetória do Sr. Diretas* (São Paulo: Artemeios, 2004), 277.
117. Covas and Molina, *Lila Covas*, 111.
118. Interview with Müller, in Nader, *Autênticos do MDB*, 74.
119. Carneiro, *Cunha Bueno*, 167.
120. Ibid., 165.
121. "Henrique Henkin," "Hélio Navarro," and "Gastone Righi Cuocci," in *DHBB*. Available at http://www.fgv.br/CPDOC/BUSCA/Busca/BuscaConsultar.aspx. They would not be the last politicians to advocate for political prisoners. By the early 1970s, the families of disappeared prisoners were writing or visiting Congress so often to plead for help locating their loved ones that federal deputy Laerte Vieira, one of the most strident members of the MDB, referred to it as "the last recourse of the desperate." Pereira, interview with author.
122. Righi, interview with author.
123. Airgram São Paulo A-98, 9 May 1969, NARA, RG 59, Box 1903, Pol 12 BRAZ.
124. Martins et al., *Paulo Egydio conta*, 375–76.
125. Covas and Molina, *Lila Covas*, 97, 101–3. Despite the difficult turn their lives took, Mário and Lila Covas took vacations to Europe and Argentina during the 1970s. In São

Paulo, they rented an apartment in the Jardins neighborhood, home to the city's moneyed elites, and eventually bought one in Pinheiros, within walking distance of the city's swankiest shopping mall (120–22).

126. "Ata da nona consulta ao Conselho de Segurança Nacional," 29 Sept. 1969, ANB, 8–14. Available at http://www.an.gov.br/sian/inicial.asp.

127. Nelson Jobim and Walter Costa Porto, eds., *Legislação eleitoral no Brasil: Do século XVI aos nossos dias*, vol. 3 (Brasília: Senado Federal, Secretaria de Documentação e Informação, Subsecretaria de Biblioteca, 1996), 208.

128. Antônio Carlos Pojo do Rego, *O congresso brasileiro e o regime militar (1964–1985)* (Rio de Janeiro: FGV Editora, 2008), 93.

129. Nota Informativa Circular 5, 22 Feb. 1969, MAE 10.671/1; "Governo quer Congresso funcionando," *Folha*, 7 Feb. 1969; Carlos Castello Branco, "Superada a idéia de fechar o Congresso," *JB*, 7 Feb. 1969.

130. Tel. Brasília 92, 26 Feb. 1969, NARA, RG 59, Box 1907, Pol 15-2 BRAZ.

131. "Ata da 47a sessão do Conselho de Segurança Nacional," 201.

132. Despacho 299, 22 Apr. 1969, MAE 11.178/111.

133. Tel. Brasília 256, 15 June 1969, NARA, RG 59, Box 1903, Pol 12 BRAZ.

134. Motion approved by the national directorate of ARENA, 11 June 1969, FGV-CP-DOC, Arquivo ARENA, cg.1965.08.31, Rolo 1, Pasta 3.

135. Tel. Brasília 284, 10 July 1969, NARA, RG 59, Box 1903, Pol 12 BRAZ.

136. Airgram Brasília A-32, 17 July 1969, NARA, RG 59, Box 1903, Pol 12 BRAZ.

137. María de los Angeles Yannuzzi, *Política y dictadura: Los partidos políticos y el "proceso de reorganización nacional" 1976–1982* (Rosario: Editorial Fundación Ross, 1996), 65–79.

138. Ricardo A. Yocelevzky R., *Chile: Partidos políticos, democracia y dictadura: 1970–1990* (Mexico City: Fondo de Cultura Económica, 2002). This corporatist approach was less attractive to the Argentine generals, no doubt due to its prior use by Perón to supposedly disastrous effect.

139. In Uruguay the military also banned parties and sought to institutionalize their rule through a plebiscite. However, after their proposed constitutional reforms were rejected in 1980, they permitted the refounding of the old Colorado and Blanco parties to help manage a gradual redemocratization. Juan Rial, *Partidos políticos, democracia y autoritarismo*, vol. 2 (Montevideo: Ediciones de la Banda Oriental, 1984).

140. Tel. Brasília 347, 20 Aug. 1969, NARA, RG 59, Box 1907, Pol. 15-4 BRAZ.

141. For exhaustive accounts of these tense weeks, see Carlos Chagas, *113 dias de angústia: Impedimento e morte de um presidente*, 2nd ed. (Porto Alegre: L&PM Editores, 1979); Portella de Mello, *A Revolução e o governo Costa e Silva*, 803–61.

142. "A revolução dentro da Revolução," *Veja*, 24 Sept. 1969, 17.

143. Nota Informativa no. 106, 8 Oct. 1969, MAE, 11.181/19.

144. The MDB attended the congressional session that "elected" Médici but abstained from voting. This decision was taken over the protests of several members of the national directorate, including São Paulo deputy Franco Montoro, who argued that the party should boycott the session altogether. Kinzo, *Legal Opposition Politics*, 123.

145. "Relatório Periódico de Informações no. 10/69," AN-RJ, CGI-PM, BR_DFANBSB_ AAJ_IPM_942, 11 Oct. 1969, 10–11.

146. "Médici promete apoio aos trabalhadores dos campos," *JB*, 31 Oct. 1969.

147. Tel. Brasília 515, 3 Dec. 1969, NARA, RG 59, Box 1906, Pol 15-1 BRAZ.

148. "Nunca houve democracia plena no país, diz Médici," *JB*, 28 Feb. 1970.
149. Ibid.
150. Roberto Nogueira Médici, Maria Celina Soares d'Araújo, and Gláucio Ary Dillon Soares, *Médici, o depoimento* (Rio de Janeiro: Mauad, 1995), 31.
151. "'Os politicos não entendem a Revolução,'" *Veja*, 24 Sept. 1969.
152. Milton Campos and Antônio Gontijo de Carvalho, *Testemunhos e ensinamentos* (Rio de Janeiro: Livraria José Olympio, 1972), 289–90.

4. "SHELTERED UNDER THE TREE": THE EVERYDAY PRACTICE OF POLITICS UNDER DICTATORIAL RULE

1. "O poder emana do povo: É o voto," *Folha*, 16 Jan. 1974.
2. Interview with Pinto, in Nader, *Autênticos do MDB*, 168.
3. For growth rate, see Skidmore, *The Politics of Military Rule*, 138. For approval rating, see "Pesquisa de opinião pública realizada no Estado de São Paulo por solicitação da empresa Folha da Manhã, S/A," Aug. 1982, Arquivo Edgard Leuenroth (AEL), IBOPE, Pesquisas Especiais, PE 125/01, 5.
4. Sir David Hunt to C. D. Wiggin, "Annual Report for 1970," 20 Jan. 1971, British National Archive (BNA), FCO 7/1888.
5. Skidmore, "Politics and Economic Policy Making in Authoritarian Brazil," 16.
6. Schmitter, "The 'Portugalization' of Brazil?," 211.
7. Kinzo, *Legal Opposition Politics*, 127–28, 251 n. 142.
8. One of the Senate victories was in São Paulo, where former Goulart labor minister André Franco Montoro won a seat. Montoro was elected with the support of ARENA factions that preferred him to their own candidate, an ally of Adhemar de Barros. See Melhem, *Política de botinas amarelas*, 114–15.
9. Skidmore, *The Politics of Military Rule*, 115–16.
10. Furtado, interview with author.
11. Interviews with Fernando Lyra and Francisco Pinto, in Nader, *Autênticos do MDB*, 114, 162.
12. On living in a hotel, see Neves, interview with author.
13. Interviews with Eloy Lenzi, Fernando Cunha, Francisco Amaral, Francisco Pinto, Lysâneas Maciel, and José Santilli Sobrinho, in Nader, *Autênticos do MDB*, 81, 101–2, 131, 167–68, 285, 357–58.
14. *Adesista* is derived from *aderir* (adhere) and was used pejoratively to describe politicians who adapted to any new situation, allying themselves with whomever was in power.
15. For discussions of Chagas Freitas and politics in Guanabara and Rio de Janeiro under the regime, see Eli Diniz, *Voto e máquina política: patronagem e clientelismo no Rio de Janeiro* (Rio de Janeiro: Paz e Terra, 1982); Carlos Eduardo Sarmento, *O espelho partido da metrópole: Chagas Freitas e o campo político carioca (1950–1983). Liderança, voto e estruturas clientelistas* (Rio de Janeiro: Folha Seca/FAPERJ, 2008).
16. Furtado, interview with author.
17. Kinzo, *Legal Opposition Politics*, 133–36.
18. Gutemberg, *Moisés, codinome Ulysses Guimarães*, 100–101.
19. The electoral college included the members of the Chamber of Deputies, the 66 senators, and 7 representatives of state legislatures from each state. The MDB had only 101 votes.

20. Kinzo, *Legal Opposition Politics*, 138.
21. Interviews with Lyra and Pinto, in Nader, *Autênticos do MDB*, 119–20, 175.
22. Interviews with Furtado, Lyra, Pinto, Domingos de Freitas Diniz, Maciel, Marcondes Gadelha, and Santilli Sobrinho, in Nader, *Autênticos do MDB*, 51–52, 120, 175, 202–3, 298, 310, 361.
23. Gutemberg, *Moisés, codinome Ulysses Guimarães*, 126.
24. Gaspari, *A ditadura derrotada*, 242; Gutemberg, *Moisés, codinome Ulysses Guimarães*, 122.
25. Nader, *Autênticos do MDB*, 51.
26. Gaspari, *A ditadura derrotada*, 241.
27. A. C. Scartezini, *Dr. Ulysses: uma biografia* (São Paulo: Marco Zero, 1993), 44.
28. Airgram Brasília A-281, 24 May 1968, NARA, RG 59, Box 1903, Pol. 12 BRAZ.
29. *Diário da Câmara dos Deputados*, 6 Dec. 1968, Suplemento, 14–16.
30. Sabiá, interview with author.
31. George Hall to Sir David Hunt, 12 June 1973, BNA, FCO 7/2407.
32. Interview with Quércia, in Melhem and Russo, *Dr. Ulysses, o homem que pensou o Brasil*, 326.
33. Interview with Pinto, in Nader, *Autênticos do MDB*, 175.
34. Gaspari, *A ditadura derrotada*, 241.
35. Gutemberg, *Moisés, codinome Ulysses Guimarães*, 133–34.
36. "A antiderrota," *Veja*, 16 Jan. 1974; Gutemberg, *Moisés, codinome Ulysses Guimarães*, 133–34.
37. "4 a 3: TSE entende que radio e TV só em diretas," *Folha*, 21 Nov. 1973.
38. Gutemberg, *Moisés, codinome Ulysses Guimarães,,* 133–34.
39. Interview with Barbosa Lima, in Melhem and Russo, *Dr. Ulysses, o homem que pensou o Brasil*, 50.
40. Smith, *A Forced Agreement*, 40–41.
41. "Pesquisa sobre leituras de jornais, Estado de São Paulo, outubro 1970," AEL, IBOPE, PE 116/08, 4.
42. Ambassador Derek Dodson to FCO, 21 Jan. 1974, BNA, FCO 7-2583.
43. Interviews with Furtado, Fernando Cunha, Pinto, Freitas Diniz, Maciel, Gadelha, Nadyr Rossetti, and Santilli Sobrinho, in Nader, *Autênticos do MDB*, 51–52, 98–99, 175–76, 203, 288–89, 310, 333, 361–62.
44. Tel. Brasília 8236, 4 Dec. 1973, NARA, RG 59 [retrieved from Access to Archival Databases, http://aad.archives.gov, 12 May 2010]. See also D. S. Cape to FCO, 12 Dec. 1973, BNA, FCO 7/2407.
45. Interview with Maciel, in Marieta de Moraes Ferreira, Dora Rocha, and Américo Freire, orgs., *Vozes da oposição* (Rio de Janeiro: Grafline Editora, 2001), 40.
46. Tel. Brasília 6380, 2 Oct. 1974, NARA, RG 59 [retrieved from Access to Archival Databases, http://aad.archives.gov, 15 Apr. 2013].
47. Interview with Maciel, in Nader, *Autênticos do MDB*, 288.
48. Interview with Furtado, in Nader, *Autênticos do MDB*, 51–52.
49. Furtado, interview with author.
50. Gutemberg, *Moisés, codinome Ulysses Guimarães*, 134.

51. "'Autenticos' farão campanha à parte," *Folha*, 21 Oct. 1973; Interview with Maciel, in Ferreira, Rocha, and Freire, *Vozes da oposição*, 40; Célia Costa and Juliana Gagliardi, "Lysâneas: Um autêntico do MDB," *Revista de Estudos Históricos* 37 (2006): 37.
52. Interview with Furtado, in Nader, *Autênticos do MDB*, 52.
53. "Única preocupação de Portela é o MDB," *Folha*, 15 Jan. 1974.
54. Furtado, interview with author.
55. José Alencar Furtado (MDB-PR), *Diário do Congresso Nacional* [hereafter *DCN*], Jan. 1974, 19–20.
56. Derek Dodson to Alec Douglas, 21 Jan. 1974, BNA, FCO 7/2583.
57. Ulysses Guimarães (MDB-SP), *DCN*, 16 Jan. 1974, 21–23. The guerrillas of Pernambuco were the residents of the colony's sugar-growing region who drove out the Dutch, who held parts of northeastern Brazil in 1630–54. The Acreans and Northerners were the late nineteenth-century settlers of the rubber-rich Bolivian region of Acre who seized the territory for Brazil. The "Farroupilhan" ideals refer to Rio Grande do Sul's unsuccessful 1835–45 republican war of independence against the Brazilian Empire.
58. Ulysses Guimarães (MDB-SP), *DCN*, 16 Jan. 1974, 21–23.
59. Petrônio Portella (ARENA-PI), *DCN*, 16 Jan. 1974, 23–25.
60. "Sessão do Colégio Eleitoral para eleição do Presidente e Vice-Presidente da República," CD-COAUD, Arquivo Sonoro, 15 Jan. 1974.
61. "Declaração de Voto," *DCN*, 16 Jan. 1974, 29–30.
62. "Valeu a pena lutar," *Folha*, 16 Jan. 1974; "Punição do MDB para os autênticos," *Folha*, 16 Jan. 1974.
63. See Lei no. 5.453, 14 June 1968, in Jobim and Porto, *Legislação eleitoral no Brasil*, 167–70.
64. David Capistrano Filho and Antonio Roque Citadini, *PMDB no poder* (São Paulo: CERIFA, Oboré Editorial, 1982), 20; cited in Melhem, *Política de botinas amarelas*, 113.
65. Sebastião Nery, *Grandes pecados da imprensa* (São Paulo: Geração Editorial, 2000), 189.
66. Sebastião Nery, *As 16 derrotas que abalaram o Brasil* (Rio de Janeiro: F. Alves Editora, 1975), 34.
67. Melhem, *Política de botinas amarelas*, 180.
68. Nery, *Grandes pecados da imprensa*, 190.
69. Melhem, *Política de botinas amarelas*, 180–81, 104–5.
70. Ibid., 105.
71. "Vitória do candidato do MDB em Campinas, é o ponto central das discussões sobre política," *Folha*, 20 Nov. 1968.
72. Nery, *As 16 derrotas que abalaram o Brasil*, 34.
73. "Vitória do candidato do MDB . . . "
74. Melhem, *Política de botinas amarelas*, 181–82.
75. "Vitória do candidato do MDB em Campinas, é o ponto central das discussões sobre política."
76. Quércia, in *O Estado*, 7 Feb. 1971; quoted in Kinzo, *Legal Opposition Politics*, 133.
77. Jenks, "Political Parties in Authoritarian Brazil," 235–36.
78. "MDB quer crescer sem concessão," *Folha*, 10 Jan. 1973.

79. "Quércia trabalha," *Folha*, 14 Apr. 1974.
80. Interview with Quércia in Sonia Morgenstern Russo and Celia Soibelmann Melhem, *PMDB, democracia sempre* (São Paulo: Global, 1987), 204.
81. Melhem, *Política de botinas amarelas*, 186.
82. Ibid., 187.
83. Brazilians express the fluidity of political affiliations with the paired terms *situação* and *oposição* (situation and opposition). Politicians allied with the ruling party at any level are referred to as being "in the situation," implying the transient nature of both political power and alliances. Its opposite, "in the opposition," indicates opposition to "the situation"; that is, opposition to the current status quo, which could change tomorrow, turning the opposition into the situation, in which case, many members of the new opposition would shift loyalties to the new situation.
84. "A oposição na hora de falar," *Veja*, 16 Oct. 1974.
85. "Malan vê os civis capazes de assumir o poder," *Jornal do Brasil*, 15 Dec. 1971.
86. Tel. Brasília 2026, 29 Dec. 1971, NARA, RG 59, Box 1691, DEF 9 BRAZ.
87. The original of Huntington's paper has never been located. However, a Portuguese translation was made and entrusted to Leitão de Abreu, who distributed it to some close friends. One copy went to the career diplomat Paulo Nogueira Batista, who later donated his papers to the Center for Research and Documentation of Brazil's Contemporary History (CPDOC). It was discovered by Rejane Hoeveler, who used it as a source for her perceptive 2012 undergraduate thesis on the 1972–73 move toward decompression. Thanks to Hoeveler for sharing her findings with me. See Rejane Carolina Hoeveler, "Ditadura e democracia restrita: A elaboração do projeto de descompressão controlada no Brasil, 1972–1973" (Thesis, Universidade Federal do Rio de Janeiro, 2012).
88. This was similar to the model later adopted in Chile, although Pinochet and the ideologically-aligned gremialistas preferred a direct relationship between the state and social groups, without a party as intermediary. See Yocelevzky R., *Partidos políticos*.
89. For a day-by-day account of Médici's selection of Geisel, see Gaspari, *A ditadura derrotada*, 215–28.
90. Ibid., 217–19, 224.
91. Ernesto Geisel, *Discursos*, vol. 1 (Brasília: Assessoria de Imprensa e Relações Públicas da Presidência da República, 1975), 38.
92. d'Araújo and Castro, *Ernesto Geisel*, 264.
93. Ibid., 444.
94. Ibid.
95. Skidmore, *The Politics of Military Rule*, 164.
96. Heitor Ferreira to Ernesto Geisel, "Um detalhe eleitoral para o modelo politico brasileiro," 28 July 1974, FGV-CPDOC, EG pr. 1974.07.10.
97. Geisel, *Discursos*, 122. The word *distensão* means "distension," which in English indicates stretching, expansion, or swelling. In this context, it has been variously glossed as "liberalization," "decompression," "opening," or "decompression." However, the best translation is "détente," used by Bolivar Lamounier, which carries its French meaning of relaxation and appears to be close to what Geisel had in mind. Moreover, the Brazilian press in the early 1970s frequently used the word *distensão* to refer to the less tense relationship developing between the United States and the Soviet Union—called détente in English. See

Jenks, "Political Parties in Authoritarian Brazil," 229; Skidmore, *The Politics of Military Rule*, 164–74; Bethell and Castro, "Politics in Brazil under Military Rule," 202; Kinzo, *Legal Opposition Politics*, 145; Lamounier, "*Authoritarian Brazil* Revisited," 56.

98. Geisel, *Discursos*, 122.
99. SNI report to Geisel, March 1974, FGV-CPDOC, EG pr. 1974.03.00/1.
100. Skidmore, *The Politics of Military Rule*, 165–67, 364 n.117.
101. Evanize Sydow and Marilda Ferri, *Dom Paulo Evaristo Arns: Um homem amado e perseguido* (Petrópolis: Editora Vozes, 1999), 171.
102. Gutemberg, *Moisés, codinome Ulysses Guimarães*, 145–51. In Matthew 17:1–9, Mark 9:2–9, and Luke 9:28–36, the disciples Peter, James, and John are sworn to secrecy after witnessing Jesus transfigured and conversing with Moses and Elijah on Mount Tabor.
103. "Deputado fala em descompressão," *Folha*, 19 Sept. 1974.
104. Grinberg, *Partido político ou bode expiatório*, 157–58.
105. Ibid., 161.

5. "WE AREN'T A FLOCK OF LITTLE SHEEP": THE POLITICAL CLASS AND THE LIMITS OF LIBERALIZATION

1. Cardoso's great-grandfather was a general, federal deputy, senator, and provincial president under the Empire, and his father, also a military officer, was involved in the tenentista movement of the 1920s and had served a term as a PTB federal deputy from São Paulo. "Fernando Henrique Cardoso," *DHBB*, http://www.fgv.br/cpdoc/busca/Busca/Busca Consultar.aspx.
2. Interview with Cardoso, in Russo and Melhem, *PMDB, democracia sempre*, 25.
3. Wellington Moreira Franco, Testimonial for the 80th birthday of Fernando Henrique Cardoso, *80 FHC*, 2011. Available at http://www.fhc80anos.com.br/depoimentos.php?id=50.
4. "A oposição na hora de falar."
5. The Senate elections were statewide; each party was permitted one candidate (with a designated alternate, or suplente). For the Chamber of Deputies and state legislatures, Brazil uses an open-list proportional system in which all candidates for an office run in one statewide election, and each voter selects one candidate (or simply a party). The seats are divided among the parties based (roughly) on the percentage of valid votes received by each. Candidates thus run not only against other parties but also against others in their own party. For a description of the system today, see Jairo Nicolau, "O sistema eleitoral de lista aberta no Brasil," *Dados* 49:4 (2006): 689–720, https://doi.org/10.1590/S0011-52582006000400002.
6. Gaspari, *A ditadura derrotada*, 454.
7. CPDOC, Arquivo Geisel, EG pr 1974.03.00/1, "Apreciação Sumária no. 11/74," 5 Sept. 1974, 1–2.
8. "Um acordo para o bem da nação," *Visão*, 5 Aug. 1974, cited in Sebastião Carlos Velasco e Cruz and Carlos Estevam Martins, "De Castello a Figueiredo: Uma incursão na pre-história da 'abertura,'" in *Sociedade e política no Brasil pós-64*, ed. Bernardo Sorj and Maria Hermínia Tavares de Almeida (São Paulo: Editora Brasiliense, 1984), 49.
9. "Ferreira Filho diz que voto de protesto é inadmissível," *Folha*, 2 Nov. 1974.
10. "Portela acha possível derrota só na Guanabara," *Folha*, 19 Sept. 1974.
11. "Arena analisa sua posição," *Folha*, 8 Sept. 1974.

12. Although AI-3 had established indirect gubernatorial elections in 1966, the 1967 constitution reinstituted direct elections. However, the regime would continue to impose indirect elections on an ad hoc basis via constitutional amendments that it either decreed or rammed through Congress. For an account of ARENA dissatisfaction with the 1972 amendment that restored indirect elections for 1974, see Grinberg, *Partido político ou bode expiatório*, 167.

13. "As longas listas," *Veja*, 15 May 1974.

14. "O fim da missão Portella," *Veja*, 19 June 1974.

15. Carlos Estevam Martins, "O balanço da campanha," in *Os partidos e as eleições no Brasil*, ed. Bolivar Lamounier and Fernando Henrique Cardoso (Rio de Janeiro: Paz e Terra, 1975), 80–82.

16. "As longas listas."

17. Jenks, "Political Parties in Authoritarian Brazil," 248–49.

18. "O bê-a-bá da campanha," *Veja*, 18 Sept. 1974, 25.

19. Armando Falcão to José Carlos Moreira Alves, 11 July 1974, AN-RJ, DSI-MJ, Caixa 3527/08194, SECOM 596/74. The electoral courts ignored Falcão's missive, at least in São Paulo. All candidates were required to submit a background check from their state's political-social police (DOPS). Although the DOPS files of paulista candidates were replete with accusations of corruption and subversion, this did not stop the TRE from approving a candidacy.

20. "Supremo condena à prisão deputado Francisco Pinto," *Folha*, 11 Oct. 1974. According to his father-in-law, federal deputy José Alencar Furtado, although Geisel offered to pardon him after less than three months, Pinto refused to leave, preferring to serve out his sentence. Furtado, interview with author.

21. Nery, *Grandes pecados da imprensa*, 194.

22. "Painel: O tema é nosso," *Folha*, 13 Sept. 1974.

23. Kinzo, *Legal Opposition Politics*, 148.

24. "Voto em branco preocupa o MDB."

25. "Montoro diz que MDB obtém na campanha um 'status' de partido," *JB*, 2 Nov. 1974.

26. Interview with Montoro in Melhem and Russo, *Dr. Ulysses, o homem que pensou o Brasil*, 40.

27. Nery, *As 16 derrotas que abalaram o Brasil*, 71–72. For "for absolute lack . . . ," see "Procuram-se eleitores, vivos," *Veja*, 28 Sept. 1974.

28. "Procuram-se eleitores, vivos"; "Agenor Nunes derrota Djalma Marinho, valendo-se da desunião da Arena," *Jornal do Brasil*, 17 Nov. 1974.

29. Furtado, interview with author.

30. "Candidato do MDB-SP ao Senado é Orestes Quércia," *Folha*, 12 Aug. 1974; Centro de Memória Eleitoral, Tribunal Regional Eleitoral—São Paulo (TRE-SP), Caixas 2750–59.

31. Jenks, "Political Parties in Authoritarian Brazil," 249–52.

32. Registros de Candidatura 1974, Caixas 2750–2759, TRE-SP; *DHBB*.

33. Since the Empire, the Brazilian political class had been dominated by members of the liberal professions, in particular, lawyers. See John W. F. Dulles, *The São Paulo Law School and the Anti-Vargas Resistance (1938–1945)* (Austin: University of Texas Press, 1986); Kirkendall, *Class Mates*.

34. Registros de Candidatura 1974, Caixas 2750–59, TRE-SP.

35. Registros de Candidatura 1974, Caixas 2750-2759, TRE-SP; *DHBB*.
36. Melhem and Russo, *Dr. Ulysses, o homem que pensou o Brasil*, 326.
37. "Voto em branco preocupa o MDB."
38. "O MDB já decidiu como será sua campanha em todo o país," *JT*, 13 Sept. 1974.
39. Interview with Montoro in Melhem and Russo, *Dr. Ulysses, o homem que pensou o Brasil*, 39-40.
40. "Oposição inaugura seu comitê central," *Folha*, 27 Sept. 1974.
41. "Discursos proferidos pelos candidatos do MDB no Cine São José no dia 15 de setembro de 1974," AN-RJ, CISA, BR_AN_BSB_VAZ_016_0036, 18 Sept. 1974.
42. "Quércia tem certeza de vitória," *Folha*, 8 Oct. 1974.
43. "Quércia inaugura comitês em Santos," *Folha*, 2 Oct. 1974.
44. "Quércia justifica campanha," *Folha*, 17 Sept. 1974.
45. "Quércia fala a trabalhadores em S. Bernardo," *Folha*, 14 Oct. 1974.
46. "CP e Quércia prosseguem campanhas pelo interior," *Folha*, 21 Sept. 1974.
47. "Comitê da Arena reune Laudo e Egídio," *Folha*, 12 Sept. 1974.
48. "O comício volta às ruas," *Folha*, 15 Sept. 1974.
49. Melhem, *Política de botinas amarelas*, 189.
50. "CP: participação para consolidar," *Folha*, 2 Aug. 1974.
51. "Arena vai dinamizar campanha ao Senado," *Folha*, 17 Sept. 1974; "Carolo justifica mudanças na campanha dos arenistas," *Folha*, 13 Oct. 1974.
52. "Campanha de Egídio terá uma pausa forçada," *Folha*, 1 Oct. 1974; "O senador faz uma reunião e diz que está bom," *JT*, 11 Oct. 1974.
53. Martins et al., *Paulo Egydio conta*, 367-69.
54. "Curso político de madureza," *Veja*, 23 Oct. 1974, 24.
55. "Paulo Egídio adverte as elites e o empresariado," *Folha*, 14 Oct. 1974.
56. "Egídio: o voto é forma de escolha, não de protesto," *Folha*, 17 Oct. 1974; "Egídio renova advertência de que é preciso maturidade," *Folha*, 1 Nov. 1974.
57. "Paulo Egídio: A Arena não atira pedras, constrói usinas com elas," *Folha*, 21 Oct. 1974.
58. "Ex-pessepistas decidem apoiar Carvalho Pinto," *Folha*, 27 Sept. 1974.
59. "Uma ciranda de boa vontade," *Veja*, 30 Oct. 1974, 25.
60. "Presidente do MDB confia em 'surpresas,'" *Folha*, 4 Sept. 1974.
61. "Deputado diz que a Arena usa as teses da oposição," *Folha*, 8 Sept. 1974.
62. "Portela: Arenista não usa tese de Oposição," *Folha*, 24 Sept. 1974.
63. Lei no. 4.737, 15 July 1965 and Lei no. 4.961, 4 May 1966 in Jobim and Porto, *Legislação eleitoral no Brasil*, 57, 114.
64. Sérgio Mattos, *História da televisão brasileira: Uma visão econômica, social e política* (Petrópolis: Editora Vozes, 2002), 83-84.
65. "A telecampanha," *Veja*, 16 Oct. 1974, 26.
66. Jenks, "Political Parties in Authoritarian Brazil," 244-45.
67. "O senador: Agora começam as preocupações de Quércia," *JT*, 18 Nov. 1974.
68. Interview with Montoro, in Russo and Melhem, *PMDB, democracia sempre*, 17.
69. "Os publicitários analisam seu trabalho," *JT*, 15 Nov. 1974.
70. "Resultados de um mês de campanha," *JT*, 17 Oct. 1974; "Os publicitários analisam seu trabalho."
71. "Resultados de um mês de campanha."

72. "A oposição na hora de falar."
73. "Os publicitários analisam seu trabalho."
74. "A oposição na hora de falar."
75. "MDB e Arena na hora de votar," *Veja*, 13 Nov. 1974.
76. Jenks, "Political Parties in Authoritarian Brazil," 243–46.
77. Tel. São Paulo 7892, 15 Oct. 1974, NARA, RG 59 [retrieved from Access to Archival Databases, http://aad.archives.gov, 4 May 2010].
78. "Quércia pode vencer por 1 milhão e 700 mil votos," *JB*, 16 Nov. 1974.
79. "Uma ciranda de boa vontade," 24–25.
80. "A cidade vive um dia de eleições," *Folha*, 16 Nov. 1974.
81. "Fila para votar: é a pressa," *JT*, 16 Nov. 1974.
82. "Previsão dá a vitória a Quércia," *Folha*, 16 Nov. 1974.
83. "O IBOPE dá a vitória ao MDB," *JT*, 16 Nov. 1974.
84. "Quércia pode vencer por 1 milhão e 700 mil votos."
85. Figueiredo to Ferreira, cited in Gaspari, *A ditadura derrotada*, 474.
86. Ferreira to Geisel, with an annotation by Golbery, cited in Gaspari, *A ditadura derrotada*, 474.
87. "Apreciação Sumária no. 15/74," 18 Nov. 1974, CPDOC, Arquivo Geisel, EG pr 1974.03.00/1.
88. Gaspari, *A ditadura derrotada*, 474.
89. "Carvalho Pinto diz que cumpriu sua missão," *Folha*, 20 Nov. 1974.
90. "Políticos comentam origens do malogro" *Folha*, 19 Nov. 1974; "Para Laudo, a situação do mundo afetou os resultados," *Folha*, 26 Nov. 1974; "Herbert explica derrota," *Folha*, 21 Nov. 1974.
91. Tel. Brasília 8923, 26 Nov. 1974, NARA, RG 59 [retrieved from Access to Archival Databases, http://aad.archives.gov, 4 May 2010].
92. "Zancaner vê infiltrações no MDB," 21 Nov. 1974.
93. "Brasília: A discreta ausência arenista," *Folha*, 17 Nov. 1974; "Para líder da Arena, é procurar as razões."
94. "Brasília: A discreta ausência arenista"; "Para os candidatos da Arena, a expectativa," *Folha*, 18 Nov. 1974.
95. "Querem estilo PSD na Arena," *Folha*, 24 Nov. 1974.
96. "Marcilio atribui a derrota à liderança," *Folha*, 19 Nov. 1974.
97. "Derrota é atribuída a mentalidade tecnocrata," *Folha*, 31 Dec. 1974.
98. "A Arena utilizou base política já ultrapassada, diz Sarney," *Folha*, 4 Dec. 1974.
99. "Virgílio Távora dá 'receita' para Arena," *Folha*, 21 Dec. 1974; "Gen. Golbery ouve apelo no Congresso," *Folha*, 4 Dec. 1974.
100. "Ulisses presta homenagem a Geisel," *Folha*, 17 Nov. 1974; "Povo mostrou que quer diálogo, diz Quércia"; Armando Rolemberg, "Entrevista: Franco Montoro," *Veja*, 27 Nov. 1974; Tel. Brasília 8740.
101. "Renovação e não revanchismo, diz Montoro," *Folha*, 17 Nov. 1974.
102. Tel. Brasília 8740, 20 Nov. 1974, NARA, RG 59 [retrieved from Access to Archival Databases, http://aad.archives.gov, 4 May 2010].
103. Ibid.
104. "A iniciativa não cabe ao MDB, diz Tancredo," *Folha*, 19 Nov. 1974.
105. "MDB não fará guerra de poderes, diz Ulisses," *Folha*, 20 Nov. 1974.

106. "Palavra das Forças Armadas," *Folha*, 28 Nov. 1974.
107. Ibid.
108. "Geisel afirma que instrumentos de exceção serão mantidos," *Folha*, 31 Dec. 1974.
109. Marco Antônio Tavares Coelho, *Herança de um sonho: As memórias de um comunista* (Rio de Janeiro: Editora Record, 2000), 360.
110. For an outstanding analysis of right-wing officers and their allies among the intelligentsia who blamed communism for a host of ills, particularly changing sexual mores, see Benjamin A. Cowan, *Securing Sex: Morality and Repression in the Making of Cold War Brazil* (Chapel Hill: University of North Carolina Press, 2016).
111. Collection of SNI reports on 1974 elections, AN-RJ, A0829201–1975, 15 Apr. 1975.
112. Coelho, *Em busca de identidade*, 361.
113. Ibid., 360.
114. The fact that there could even be a trial with the possibility of acquittal distinguished the Brazilian military regime from its Southern Cone counterparts, where trials were either nonexistent, as in Argentina, or a sham, as in Chile. See Pereira, *Political (In)justice*.
115. For this summary of the repression of the PCB, I rely heavily on French, *Lula and His Politics of Cunning*, chap. 10.
116. Ruy Lopes, "O espanto até a morte," *Folha*, 30 Oct. 1975.
117. J. G. de Araújo Jorge (MDB-RJ), *DCD*, 28 Oct. 1975, 9451.
118. Gamaliel Galvâo (MDB-PR), *DCD*, 28 Oct. 1975, 9457.
119. José de Freitas Nobre (MDB-SP), *DCD*, 28 Oct. 1975, 9472.
120. "Calma do culto tranquiliza os congressistas, *Folha*, 1 Nov. 1975.
121. "Ulisses: Tarefa da polícia," *Folha*, 29 Oct. 1975.
122. "O MDB pensa em moderar suas críticas," *JT*, 6 Nov. 1975.
123. The military had bigger fish in its sights; in June 1976 the SNI wrote encyclopedic reports on the "political antecedents" of Quércia (50 pp.) and Guimarães (32 pp.). It is possible that these were prepared in advance of potential cassações. "Orestes Quércia" and "Ulysses Silveira Guimarães," AN-RJ, SNI, A0937800–1976, June 1976, 1–50, 66–97. FHC was also being watched; the SNI claimed that his think tank, CEBRAP, had received donations from abroad and that Cardoso, a retired professor, owned no fewer than three homes. "Fernando Henrique Cardoso" and "CEBRAP," AN-RJ, SNI, A0975175–1976, 6 Sept. and 20 Sept. 1976.
124. Lei no. 6.339, 1 July 1976, in Jobim and Porto, *Legislação eleitoral no Brasil*, 290–91.
125. In previous indirect elections, the state legislatures had selected governors. Now, with the MDB in control of six state legislatures, the new formula added representatives of rural municipalities to the electors.
126. The sole exception was Rio de Janeiro, where the machine of Governor Chagas Freitas guaranteed the party enough votes to elect the governor, even with the addition of rural electors.
127. A previous version of this section was published as Bryan Pitts, "The Audacity to Strong-Arm the Generals: Paulo Maluf and the 1978 São Paulo Gubernatorial Contest," *Hispanic American Historical Review* 92:3 (2012): 471–505.
128. Norman Statham to FCO, 19 Apr. 1977, BNA, FCO, 7/3279.
129. Alan Munro to FCO, Tel. 34, 15 April 1977, BNA, FCO, 7/3279; Stanley Duncan to A. J. Collins, 15 Apr. 1977, BNA, FCO, 7/3279.

130. Norman Statham to FCO, "Brazil: Political Situation," 24 May 1977, BNA, FCO 7/3279.
131. "A equação ainda incompleta," *Veja*, 31 Aug. 1977, 21.
132. "Natel e Maluf em campanha: Até no Carnaval," *JT*, 8 Feb. 1978.
133. "Com Figueiredo, Laudo é certo, diz Adhemar Fº.," *Folha*, 14 July 1977.
134. Paulo Salim Maluf and Tão Gomes Pinto, *Ele: Paulo Maluf, trajetória da audácia* (São Paulo: Ediouro, 2008), 80–81.
135. Paulo Maluf, interview with author, Brasília, 15 Apr. 2015.
136. "E a política dos cartões postais funcionou," *JT*, 6 June 1978.
137. "Maluf se acha capaz de orientar a ARENA," *Folha*, 27 Jan. 1978.
138. "Natel e Maluf em campanha: Até no Carnaval"; Maluf, interview with author.
139. "Sou a segunda força política, diz Maluf," *Folha*, 18 Jan. 1978.
140. "Maluf registrará," *Folha*, 4 Apr. 1978.
141. "Maluf diz que no futuro ainda vão lhe agradecer," *Folha*, 9 May 1978.
142. "Moraes Rego em São Paulo, sucessão estava definida," *O Estado de S. Paulo*, 26 Apr. 1978.
143. "Natel defende abertura, anistia, fim do AI-5 . . . ," *O Estado de S. Paulo*, 26 Apr. 1978.
144. "Sucessão de erros," *Folha*, 26 Apr. 1978, 2. See also Alberto Dines, "As perigosas repetições," *Folha*, 26 Apr. 1978.
145. "Cunha critica o 'despudor servil' dos envolvidos," *Folha*, 27 Apr. 1978; "Próximo governo unirá a ARENA, diz Lehmann," *Folha*, 27 Apr. 1978.
146. Marco Antonio Castello Branco (ARENA), *Diário Oficial: Estado de São Paulo*, 5 May 1978, 77–78.
147. "Maluf é rejeitado pelos dois blocos."
148. "Levanta, sacode a poeira," *Veja*, 10 May 1978.
149. Maluf and Pinto, *Ele: Paulo Maluf*, 90–9190–9191.
150. "Levanta, sacode a poeira."
151. Ennio Pesco, "Momento político," *JT*, 18 May 1978.
152. "Maluf crê na autonomia da Convenção," *Folha*, 30 April 1978.
153. "A caça aos votos de 1260 paulistas," *Veja*, 31 May 1978; "Focos rebeldes," *Veja*, 31 May 1978.
154. "Em reunião de arenistas Maluf diz que continua," *Folha*, 25 May 1978.
155. Martins et al., *Paulo Egydio conta*, 509.
156. "Natel faz advertência, Dória deixa cargo," *O Estado de S. Paulo*, 17 May 1978.
157. "Natel diz que irá à convenção tranquilo," *Folha*, 29 May 1978.
158. "De um lado, 9 assinaturas; do outro, 678," *Folha*, 3 June 1978.
159. "Pelo voto, promessas e pressões," *O Estado*, 2 June 1978.
160. "Figueiredo quer apoio ao Laudo," *Folha*, 1 June 1978.
161. "Propaganda empata," *Folha*, 5 June 1978.
162. "Crônica do dia em que a ARENA escolheu Salim Maluf," *JT*, 6 June 1978; "Propaganda empata."
163. "Propaganda empata."
164. "De manhã a noite, Maluf trabalhou na boca da urna," *Folha*, 5 June 1978.
165. "Propaganda empata."

166. "Ambiente de festa e muita animação," *Tribuna de Santos*, 5 June 1978. The Constitutionalist Revolution was essential to the formation of paulista political culture. For the most complete analysis of the formation of paulista identity, see Barbara Weinstein, *The Color of Modernity: São Paulo and the Making of Race and Nation in Brazil* (Durham, NC: Duke University Press, 2015).

167. "Ata da reunião da Convenção Regional da Aliança Renovadora Nacional." CEMEL, *Impugnação 877*, Caixa 2755, 122.

168. "De manhã a noite Maluf trabalhou na boca da urna."

169. "Maluf," *JT*, 5 June 1978.

170. "De manhã a noite Maluf trabalhou na boca da urna."

171. "Maluf."

172. "Em nove horas, Natel só fez uma pausa, bastante tenso," *Folha*, 5 June 1978.

173. "Crônica do dia em que a ARENA escolheu Salim Maluf."

174. "Para Sampáio Dória a convenção da ARENA valeu pela disputa," *Diário Popular*, 5 June 1978.

175. "Laudo," *JT*, 5 June 1978.

176. "Incêndio e tumulto na convenção," *O Estado*, 6 June 1978.

177. "A apuração," *JT*, 5 June 1978.

178. "A votação," *JT*, 5 June 1978. Natel's biography insinuates that Maluf's allies brought lanterns because *they* intended to set the fire and steal the convention, an accusation never made at the time. Ricardo Viveiros, *Laudo Natel: Um bandeirante* (São Paulo: Imprensa Oficial do Estado de São Paulo, 2010), 209–10.

179. "Deputados estranham cortes de luz sempre nas eleições," *Folha*, 17 Mar. 1977.

180. "Convenção da ARENA à escolha do candidato a governador de São Paulo," AN-RJ, SNI, E0032104–1980, 26 June 1978, 8.

181. Maluf, interview with author.

182. "Crônica do dia em que a ARENA escolheu Salim Maluf."

183. "Incêndio e tumulto na convenção"; "Incêndio bloqueia apuração," *Folha*, 5 June 1978; "O fogo," *JT*, 5 June 1978.

184. "Maluf derrota Natel por 28 votos," *Folha*, 5 June 1978; "Incêndio e tumulto na convenção."

185. "Incêndio bloqueia apuração."

186. "A apuração."

187. "Incêndio bloqueia apuração."

188. "Ata da reunião da Convenção Regional da Aliança Renovadora Nacional."

189. "Frases," *Folha*, 6 June 1978.

190. "Crônica do dia em que a ARENA escolheu Salim Maluf."

191. "Convenção da ARENA à escolha do candidato a governador de São Paulo."

192. "Nos votos do Interior, a insatisfação," *O Estado*, 6 June 1978.

193. For more on ARENA's long-standing dissatisfaction with indirect elections, see Grinberg, *Partido político ou bode expiatório*, 156–57.

194. Antônio Salim Curiati (ARENA), *Diário Oficial: Estado de São Paulo*, 10 June 1978, 74.

195. Paulo Kobayashi (ARENA), *Diário Oficial: Estado de São Paulo*, 10 June 1978, 73.

196. Horácio Ortiz (MDB), *Diário Oficial: Estado de São Paulo*, 10 June 1978, 72.

197. "A derrota e as opções," *Folha*, 6 June 1978; "E agora?," *JT*, 6 June 1978.
198. "'Um acontecimento normal,'" *Folha*, 6 June 1978.
199. "Figueiredo pede todo apoio a Paulo Maluf," *Folha*, 8 June 1978.
200. "Confisco de bens poderia provocar inelegibilidade," *Folha*, 6 June 1978; "A CGI apressa sua ação no caso Lutfalla," *Veja*, 14 June 1978. The SNI had been collecting information on Maluf's financial dealings since the early 1970s. See "Antecedentes de Paulo Salim Maluf," AN-RJ, SNI, A1028820-1977, 29 Apr. 1977.
201. "'Confisco não envolve Maluf,'" *Folha*, 10 Aug. 1978.
202. A.T.C., "Ameaça persiste, adesismo começa," *O Estado*, 7 June 1978.
203. *Impugnação 877*, 56–59.
204. Ibid., 64–80, 141–61.
205. "Convenção da ARENA à escolha do candidato a governador de São Paulo," 12.
206. *Impugnação 877*, 408–47.
207. Ibid., 450–64.
208. "Maluf reafirma sua confiança na Justiça Eleitoral," *Folha*, 15 July 1978.
209. *Recurso 5046*, Tribunal Superior Eleitoral, in *Impugnação 877*, 516–26.
210. "No Diretório Estadual, garantia contra derrota," *Folha*, 15 July 1978.
211. "Procurador nega uma orientação de Geisel no parecer," *Folha*, 15 July 1978; "Com parecer, volta esperança de Natel," *O Estado*, 14 July 1978.
212. *Recurso 5046*, in *Impugnação 877*, 537–85.
213. "Natel desiste e aceita a derrota," *O Estado*, 20 July 1978.
214. Maluf, interview with author.
215. "Seguidores de Figueiredo não ocultam sua surpresa," *O Estado*, 6 June 1978.
216. Evandro Paranaguá, "O governo ficou em situação difícil," *JT*, 7 June 1978.

6. "WE CANNOT THINK ABOUT DEMOCRACY THE WAY WE USED TO": THE ABC STRIKES AND THE CHALLENGE OF POPULAR MOBILIZATION

1. "Todos do nosso lado, diz Lula," *Folha*, 2 May 1979.
2. French, *Lula and His Politics of Cunning*, 247–93.
3. On the Monteiro candidacy, see Chirio, *A política nos quartéis*, 205–30.
4. Angélica Muller, "A resistência do movimento estudantil brasileiro contra o regime ditatorial e o retorno da UNE à cena pública (1969–1979)" (PhD dissertation, Universidade de São Paulo, 2010), http://www.teses.usp.br/teses/disponiveis/8/8138/tde-06102010-161921/; Luiz Henrique Romagnoli and Tânia Gonçalves, *A volta da UNE, de Ibiúna a Salvador* (São Paulo: Alfa-Omega, 1979).
5. For the most complete discussion of the movement for amnesty, see Haike Kleber da Silva, ed., *A luta pela anistia* (São Paulo: Editora Unesp, Arquivo Público do Estado de São Paulo, Imprensa Oficial do Estado de São Paulo, 2009).
6. David Covin, *The Unified Black Movement in Brazil, 1978–2002* (Jefferson, NC: McFarland & Co., 2006); Michael George Hanchard, *Orpheus and Power: The Movimento Negro of Rio de Janeiro and São Paulo, Brazil, 1945–1988* (Princeton, NJ: Princeton University Press, 1994).
7. For studies of the rise of the LGBTQ+ movement, see James N. Green, *Beyond Carnival: Male Homosexuality in Twentieth-Century Brazil* (Chicago: University of Chicago Press, 1999), 242–77; Júlio Assis Simões and Regina Facchini, *Na trilha do arco-íris: Do*

movimento homossexual ao LGBT (São Paulo: Editora Fundação Perseu Abramo, 2009). For the best analysis of the women's movement, see Alvarez, *Engendering Democracy in Brazil*.

8. Luiz Carlos Bresser Pereira, "Os militares e a crise política," *Folha*, 7 May 1978.

9. For the authoritative history of the ferment of rapid industrialization, unchecked urbanization, migrant aspirations, and cultural transformation in suburban São Paulo during this time, see French, *Lula and His Politics of Cunning*.

10. Margaret E. Keck, "The New Unionism in the Brazilian Transition," in Stepan, *Democratizing Brazil*, 260–62.

11. S. L. Egerton to R. Bevan, British Embassy, Brasília, 15 Dec. 1978, BNA, FCO 7/3472.

12. Report from CENIMAR to Ministério da Justiça, 7 Oct. 1976, AN-RJ, DSI-MJ, Caixa 597/05263 MC, Dicom 60271; emphasis in original.

13. "Ata da 53a Sessão do Conselho de Segurança Nacional," 23 June 1978, ANB, 15. Available at http://www.an.gov.br/sian/inicial.asp.

14. "Severo defende a livre expressão para trabalhador," *Folha*, 10 May 1978.

15. "Em Santo André, debate livre e entusiasmado," *Folha*, 2 May 1978; "O MDB chega a Santo André sob vaias. E sai aplaudido," *JT*, 2 May 1978.

16. Miguel Reale, "Liberdade e participação," *Folha*, 17 May 1978.

17. "'Sabemos que só votar no MDB não resolverá,'" *Folha*, 7 May 1978.

18. "Sindicatos e política no Brasil hoje," *Folha*, 9 May 1978.

19. "Em Santo André, debate livre e entusiasmado."

20. "Discursos pedem justiça e liberdade," *Folha*, 2 May 1978.

21. "O MDB chega a Santo André sob vaias. E sai aplaudido."

22. "Em Osasco, a manifestação das oposições sindicais," *Folha*, 2 May 1978.

23. "800 operários participam de um 'ato cívico,'" *Folha*, 2 May 1978.

24. "Senadores defendem-se," *Folha*, 3 May 1978.

25. Melhem, *Política de botinas amarelas*, 163. Shortly before the coup, Montoro had spearheaded legislation establishing a "family salary" (*salário família*) that paid a small monthly supplement to certain low-income workers.

26. André Franco Montoro (MDB-SP), *DSF*, 5 May 1978, 1908–15.

27. Samuel Wainer, "Um alerta para o MDB," *Folha*, 4 May 1978. Wainer, founder of the newspaper *Ultima Hora*, had denounced the regime from the beginning, spent time in exile, and finally sold the paper due to his dissatisfaction with censorship.

28. "Operadores em S. Bernardo param e reclamam aumento," *Folha*, 13 May 1978.

29. "20 mil paralisados," *Folha*, 17 May 1978.

30. "TRT contra greve por 15 votos a 1," *Folha*, 19 May 1978; "50% dos trabalhadores da Scania paralisados," *Folha*, 20 May 1978; "Em Santo André, 15 mil em 12 empresas," *Folha*, 20 May 1978.

31. "Deslocada tropa de choque para o ABCD," "Prieto: decisão é dos empregados," *Folha*, 23 May 1978; "Intervir só com ordem escrita," *Folha*, 23 May 1978.

32. "Greve é sinal dos tempos," *Folha*, 22 May 1978.

33. "Que dizem o líder da Arena, o empresário, o deputado," *JT*, 18 May 1978.

34. Orestes Quércia (MDB-SP), *DSF*, 19 May 1978, 2293

35. André Franco Montoro (MDB-SP), *DSF*, 25 May 1978, 2478–82. See also Montoro, "Verdades sobre a política salarial," *Folha*, 17 May 1978.

36. "Dom Arns defende of movimento," *Folha*, 24 May 1978.

37. Eduardo Suplicy, "Greve e legitimidade," *Folha*, 21 May 1978.
38. Fernando Henrique Cardoso, "Os trabalhadores e a democracia," *Folha*, 28 May 1978.
39. Ibid.
40. "Um juiz votou pela absolvição da acusada. Um só," *JT*, 19 May 1978.
41. "O povo perguntou a Lula. Aqui estão as suas respostas," *JT*, 22 May 1978.
42. "Supensas todas as greves no ABC," *Folha*, 30 May 1978.
43. Fernando Henrique Cardoso and Ricardo A. Setti, *A arte da política: A história que vivi* (Rio de Janeiro: Civilização Brasileira, 2006), 85–86.
44. "Quércia quer que Lula seja filiado ao partido," *Folha*, 1 Apr. 1979.
45. Report from SNI to Ministério da Justiça, 23 Nov. 1978, AN-RJ, DSI-MJ, 8078, GAB 100.445
46. Mariana Viel and Aurélio Peres, "Aurélio Peres: É da luta de massas que saem os líderes do PCdoB," *Vermelho: A Esquerda Informada*, 14 Jan. 2011, http://www.vermelho.org.br/noticia.php?id_secao=1&id_noticia = 145476. Accessed 6 Mar. 2013.
47. Ricardo de Azevedo, "Memória: Geraldo Siqueira," *Teoria e Debate* 65 (2006), http://www2.fpa.org.br/o-que-fazemos/editora/teoria-e-debate/edicoes-anteriores/memoria-geraldo-siqueira.
48. Interview with Passoni, in Marieta de Moraes Ferreira and Alexandre Fortes, *Muitos caminhos, uma estrela: Memórias de militantes do PT* (São Paulo: Editora Fundação Perseu Abramo, 2008), 313–17.
49. Stanley Duncan to A. J. Collins, Latin America Department, 6 Aug. 1976, BNA, FCO 7/3405.
50. Norman Statham to J. B. Ure, South America Department, 17 Jan. 1978, BNA, FCO 7/3471.
51. "O que eu sou e o que eu penso," *Veja*, 12 Apr. 1978.
52. "O projeto e suas emendas," *Folha*, 21 Sept. 1978.
53. "São Bernardo fica fora de novo acordo salarial," *Folha*, 2 Mar. 1979; "Fiesp propõe reajustes de 44 a 58%," *Folha*, 9 Mar. 1979; "Metalúrgicos do ABC decretam greve geral," *Folha*, 10 Mar. 1979.
54. "Interior assina acordo, e o ABC vai à greve," *Folha*, 13 Mar. 1979; "Ferraz Torres encaminha processo para a Justiça," *Folha*, 14 Mar. 1979; "No ABC, param 154 mil," *Folha*, 14 Mar. 1979.
55. "No segundo dia, a greve ganha novas adesões," *Folha*, 15 Mar. 1979.
56. "Maluf: Parar é um direito democrata," *Folha*, 13 Mar. 1979.
57. "Novos ministros acham normais as manifestações," *Folha*, 16 Mar. 1979.
58. "Greve é assunto para o próximo governo," *JT*, 13 Mar. 1979.
59. "Intensificar os piquetes, a determinação para hoje," *Folha*, 19 Mar. 1979.
60. E.g., "Lula pede firmeza e calma aos operários," *Folha*, 15 Mar. 1979; "Operários recusam a proposta e mantém a greve," *Folha*, 23 Mar. 1979.
61. "As mulheres participam dos piquetes no ABCD," *JT*, 16 Mar. 1979; "Trabalhadores em dificuldades ameaçam retornar," *Folha*, 20 Mar. 1979; "Os alimentos doados somam mais de 2,4 toneladas," *Folha*, 21 Mar. 1979.
62. "MDB já arrecadou mais de Cr$ 150 mi," *Folha*, 21 Mar. 1979.
63. "Campanha nacional para sustentar o movimento do ABC," *Folha*, 21 Mar. 1979.

64. "A Fiesp mantém sua proposta, apesar do TRT," *JT*, 16 Mar. 1979; "Líder estranha rapidez no TRT," *Folha*, 16 Mar. 1979.
65. Antônio Lomanto Júnior (ARENA-BA), *DSF*, 21 Mar. 1979, 337.
66. Jarbas Passarinho (ARENA-PA), *DSF*, 22 Mar. 1979, 357.
67. "É assunto policial, diz Maluf," *Folha*, 20 Mar. 1979. Washington Luis, president from 1926 to 1930, was widely claimed to have stated, "The social question is a police question."
68. André Franco Montoro (MDB-SP), *DSF*, 22 Mar. 1979, 356–57.
69. Orestes Quércia (MDB-SP), *DSF*, 21 Mar. 1979, 336–38.
70. Marcos Freire (MDB-PE), *DSF*, 24 Mar. 1979, 402.
71. "Lula refuta infiltração ideológica no movimento," *Folha*, 18 Mar. 1979.
72. "Deops prende 24 e investiga denúncia," *Folha*, 20 Mar. 1979.
73. Aloysio Chaves (ARENA-PA), *DSF*, 20 Mar. 1979, 299–300.
74. Roberto Saturnino Braga (MDB-RJ), *DSF*, 20 Mar. 1979, 300.
75. Orestes Quércia (MDB-SP), *DSF*, 21 Mar. 1979, 337.
76. "Lula refuta infiltração ideológica no movimento," *Folha*, 18 Mar. 1979.
77. "Lula nega possibilidade de infiltração no movimento," *Folha*, 19 Mar. 1979.
78. Edson Flosi, "PM mobiliza toda a tropa de choque," *Folha*, 22 Mar. 1979; "PM dá trégua aos metalúrgicos," *Folha*, 23 Mar. 1979.
79. "Piquetes provocam incidentes," *Folha*, 14 Mar. 1979.
80. "Mobilizados 2 mil policiais," *Folha*, 15 Mar. 1979.
81. "Trabalhadores revoltados com ação policial," *Folha*, 16 Mar. 1979.
82. "Piquete foi reativado em Santo André," *Folha*, 17 Mar. 1979.
83. "Planalto examina as salvaguardas," *Folha*, 23 Mar. 1979; Carlos Chagas, "Medidas de emergência? Há desmentidos. Mas . . . ," *JT*, 24 Mar. 1979.
84. "Trabalhadores revoltados com ação policial."
85. "Parlamentares e Igreja vigiam ações policiais," *Folha*, 22 Mar. 1979.
86. "No ABC, apoio dos deputados aos piquetes," *JT*, 19 Mar. 1979.
87. "Parlamentares e Igreja vigiam ações policiais."
88. "Murilo Macedo em SP tenta acordo que suste a greve," *Folha*, 22 Mar. 1979.
89. "Operários recusam resposta e mantém a greve," *Folha*, 23 Mar. 1979.
90. "Governo diz que líderes incitaram," *Folha*, 24 Mar. 1979.
91. "Macedo garante que abertura não será prejudicada," *Folha*, 24 Mar. 1979.
92. "Sindicalistas reagem lembrando promessas de abertura no país," *Folha*, 24 Mar. 1979.
93. "As tropas chegam no ABC. E começam a bater nos operários," *JT*, 24 Mar. 1979.
94. "A notícia de intervenção chega com as tropas," *JT*, 24 Mar. 1979.
95. "A invasão," *JT*, 24 Mar. 1979.
96. "No ABC 25 mil aclamam a greve," *Folha*, 25 Mar. 1979.
97. "A volta na Missa dos Metalúrgicos," *Folha*, 26 Mar. 1979.
98. "Lideranças mantêm o comando da greve," *Folha*, 26 Mar. 1979.
99. "Greve persiste mas é menor e anima a Fiesp," *Folha*, 27 Mar. 1979.
100. "Operários voltam, sob condições," *Folha*, 28 Mar. 1979.
101. "A Igreja pede justiça," *Folha*, 2 May 1979.
102. "O 10 de Maio no Pacaembu vazio," *Folha*, 2 May 1979.
103. For "the social capital of Brazil," see "130 mil pessoas no 1o de Maio no ABC," *Folha*, 2 May 1979. For Guimarães, see "Marcílio defende autonomia," *Folha*, 2 May 1979.

104. "Todos do nosso lado, diz Lula."
105. "Duro e inábil," *Folha*, 3 May 1979.
106. "ABC não é Sierra Maestra, e o Brasil não é Cuba," *JT*, 4 May 1979.
107. "Acordo: 63% aos metalúrgicos do ABC," *Folha*, 12 May 1979; "Ratificado o acordo do ABC," *Folha*, 14 May 1979.
108. "Suspensa intervenção em sindicatos do ABC," *Folha*, 15 May 1979.
109. "'Sindicalismo deve ser ápolitico,'" *Folha*, 24 Apr. 1979.
110. "Maluf: Greve ameaça abertura," *Folha*, 5 May 1979.
111. "Manifesto de Fundação do Partido dos Trabalhadores," 10 Feb. 1980. Available at https://pt.org.br/manifesto-de-fundacao-do-partido-dos-trabalhadores/.
112. Cardoso and Setti, *A arte da política*, 85.
113. Fernando Henrique Cardoso, "Dependency and Development in Latin America," *New Left Review* 74 (1972): 83–95.
114. "A última proposta, de 5%, será levada às assembléias," *Folha*, 29 Mar. 1980.
115. "Metalúrgicos entram em greve," *Folha*, 31 Mar. 1980; "São Caetano também pára," *Folha*, 1 Apr. 1980.
116. "E veio a greve," *JT*, 31 Mar. 1980.
117. "Oposição unida em apoio ao ABC," *Folha*, 1 Apr. 1980.
118. "TRT dá 7% e não julga a greve," *Folha*, 2 Apr. 1980, 1.
119. Márcio Moreira Alves, *Teotônio, guerreiro da paz* (Petrópolis: Vozes, 1983), 202.
120. "ABC não aceita a proposta do TRT," *Folha*, 3 April 1980.
121. Moreira Alves, *Teotônio, guerreiro da paz*, 203. See also Fernando Henrique Cardoso and Brian Winter, *The Accidental President of Brazil: A Memoir* (New York: PublicAffairs, 2006), 138–40.
122. "Governo recorrerá da decisão do TRT," *Folha*, 9 Apr. 1980.
123. "Macedo prevê o fim da greve," *Folha*, 11 Apr. 1980.
124. "Os quatro partidos de oposição acusam Governo," *Folha*, 11 Apr. 1980.
125. "O TRT julgará novamente a greve," *Folha*, 12 Apr. 1980.
126. "TRT decide pela ilegalidade," *Folha*, 15 Apr. 1980; "CLT e ABC," *Folha*, 16 Apr. 1980.
127. "Macedo continua negando que planeja a intervenção," *Folha*, 17 Apr. 1980.
128. "Lula acusa TRT e diz que movimento continua," *Folha*, 16 Apr. 1980.
129. "Prisões e violência no ABC," *Folha*, 17 Apr. 1980.
130. "Ministério intervém nos dois sindicatos," *Folha*, 18 Apr. 1980.
131. "'Governo está forte para fazer cumprir a lei,'" *Folha*, 18 Apr. 1980.
132. "Revolta e choro na noite de vigília," *Folha*, 19 Apr. 1980.
133. "Muita violência na posse do interventor," *Folha*, 19 April 1980.
134. "Para Maluf, Lula é um líder morto," *Folha*, 19 Apr. 1980.
135. "Lula e mais 14 são presos por greve no ABC," *Folha*, 20 Apr. 1980. For the warning from Tuma, see Azevedo, "Memória: Geraldo Siqueira."
136. "Lula e mais 14 são presos por greve no ABC."
137. Ibid.
138. "Parlamentares no Deops," *Folha*, 21 Apr. 1980.
139. Pedro Simon (PMDB-RS), *DSF*, 25 Apr. 1980, 1105.
140. Evandro Carreira (PMDB-AM), *DSF*, 8 May 1980, 1424.

141. Francisco Leite Chaves (PTB-PR), *DSF*, 25 Apr. 1980, 1155.
142. "PDS considera urgente rever CLT," *Folha*, 1 May 1980.
143. Marcos Freire (PMDB-PE), *DSF*, 18 Apr. 1980, 994.
144. Henrique Santillo (PT-GO), *DSF*, 23 Apr. 1980, 1061.
145. Teotônio Vilela (PMDB-AL), *DSF*, 23 Apr. 1980, 1069.
146. "Teotônio Vilela," *DHBB*, http://www.fgv.br/cpdoc/busca/Busca/BuscaConsultar.aspx.
147. Moreira Alves, *Teotônio, guerreiro da paz*, 204.
148. Teotônio Viela (PMDB-AL), *DSF*, 23 Apr. 1980, 1067–68.
149. Moreira Alves, *Teotônio, guerreiro da paz*, 209–10.
150. Teotônio Vilela (PMDB-AL), *DSF*, 1 May 1980, 1297.
151. "S. Bernardo mantém greve, sob tensão," *Folha*, 23 Apr. 1980.
152. "Após a assembléia, incidentes e 3 prisões," *Folha*, 27 Apr. 1980; "Novas prisões provocam incidentes com políticos," *O Estado*, 27 Apr. 1980.
153. "Após a assembléia, incidentes e 3 prisões."
154. Ibid.
155. Ibid.
156. "A confusão geral se desloca para o Paço Municipal," *Folha*, 27 Apr. 1980; "Vilela relata os fatos ao Ministro da Justiça," *O Estado*, 27 Apr. 1980.
157. "A confusão geral se desloca para o Paço Municipal."
158. Ibid.
159. João Cunha (no party-SP), CD-COUAD, Arquivo Sonoro, 28 Apr. 1980.
160. "Assembléia na Matriz vaia proposta de volta," *Folha*, 29 Apr. 1980.
161. "Ninguém acreditava na festa," *Folha*, 2 May 1980.
162. "Da Matriz ao estádio, passeata de 100 mil para comemorar o 10 de maio," *Folha*, 2 May 1980.
163. "Assembléia decide retorno às fábricas," *Folha*, 12 May 1980.
164. José Álvaro Moisés, "Lições de liberdade e de opressão—2," *Folha*, 10 May 1980.
165. For a few representative examples, see Antonio Luigi Negro, *Linhas de montagem: Industrialismo nacional-desenvolvimentista e a sindicalização dos trabalhadores (1945–1978)* (São Paolo: Boitempo, 2004); Fernando Teixeira da Silva, *A carga e a culpa: Os operários das docas de Santos. Direitos e cultura de solidariedade, 1937–1968* (São Paulo: Editora Hucitec, 1995); Alexandre Fortes, *Nós do quarto distrito: A classe trabalhadora Porto-Alegrense e a era Vargas* (Caxias do Sul: EDUCS, 2004).
166. Paulo Fontes, *Migration and the Making of Industrial São Paulo* (Durham, NC: Duke University Press, 2016), 135.
167. John D. French, *The Brazilian Workers' ABC: Class Conflict and Alliances in Modern São Paulo* (Chapel Hill: University of North Carolina Press, 1992).
168. French, *Drowning in Laws*.
169. Marco Aurélio Santana, *Bravos companheiros: Comunistas e metalúrgicos no Rio de Janeiro (1945/1964)* (Rio de Janeiro: 7 Letras, 2012).
170. For a summary of the early years of this debate, see Marco Aurélio Santana, "Entre a ruptura e a continuidade: Visões da história do movimento sindical brasileiro," *Revista Brasileira de Ciências Sociais* 14 (1999): 103–20.

7 "I WANT TO VOTE FOR PRESIDENT": DIRETAS JÁ, THE POLITICAL CLASS, AND THE DEMISE OF THE MILITARY REGIME

An earlier version of the first half of this chapter was published as Bryan Pitts, "'Je veux élire mon président': Mobilisation populaire, classe politique, et chute du régime militaire (1984–1985)," in *1964: La dictature brésilienne et son legs*, ed. Monica Raisa Schpun and James N. Green (Paris: Le Poisson Volant, 2018). Reprinted with permission.

1. Ricardo Kotscho, "Todos sabiam aonde queriam chegar," *Folha*, 17 Apr. 1984; "São Paulo faz o maior comício," *Folha*, 17 Apr. 1984.
2. "Nove em cada dez brasileiros apóiam a direta, diz Gallup," *Folha*, 24 Jan. 1984.
3. Tel. A-2, Teixeira da Mota to MNE, 26 July 1982, AHD-MNE, 1982 Incoming Telegrams.
4. "Governo lança 'pacote de novembro,'" *Folha*, 26 Nov. 1981.
5. "O que muda na Carta," *Folha*, 25 June 1982.
6. Werner Baer, *The Brazilian Economy: Growth and Development*, 6th ed. (Boulder, CO: Lynne Rienner, 2008), 83–89, 405–411.
7. Kinzo, *Legal Opposition Politics*, 214.
8. "Montoro teve 5 milhões de votos," *Folha*, 25 Nov. 1982.
9. "Covas será o prefeito, anuncia Montoro," *Folha*, 20 Apr. 1983; "Covas toma posse 3a feira," *Folha*, 6 May 1983.
10. "Pedessistas exigem eleição direta para prefeito da Capital," *Folha*, 26 Nov. 1982.
11. "Painel: Sem consulta," *Folha*, 23 Nov. 1982.
12. "Painel: Na contramão," *Folha*, 29 Nov. 1982.
13. Roland Sierra, "Bancada federal preserva a linha do personalismo," *Folha*, 25 Nov. 1982.
14. "Painel: Estágio federal," *Folha*, 28 Nov. 1982.
15. Domingos Leonelli and Dante de Oliveira, *Diretas Já: 15 meses que abalaram a ditadura*, 2nd ed. (Rio de Janeiro: Editora Record, 2004), 77–78.
16. Ricardo Kotscho, "Manifestação pública reune sociedade civil e políticos," *Folha*, 25 Nov. 1983.
17. "Governadores oposicionistas oficializam campanha," *Folha*, 27 Nov. 1983.
18. Marcondes Sampaio, "Campanha divide pemedebistas," *Folha*, 27 Nov. 1983; "Ulisses promete todo o MDB na campanha por diretas," *Folha*, 27 Nov. 1983.
19. Plínio Fraga, *Tancredo Neves, o príncipe civil* (Rio de Janeiro: Objetiva, 2017), 370.
20. "Figueiredo devolve coordenação ao PDS," *Folha*, 30 Dec. 1983. Another possibility is that Figueiredo feared a repeat of the humiliation of 1978, when São Paulo arenistas had ignored his endorsement of Natel for the governorship. The thought of Maluf embarrassing him again may have been more than Figueiredo could bear.
21. Gaspari, *A ditadura acabada*, 256.
22. "Successão: Figueiredo desistiu," *JT*, 30 Dec. 1983.
23. "Maluf elogia e acha a decisão 'um grande avanço democrático,'" *Folha*, 30 Dec. 1983.
24. Bernado Braga Pasqualette, *Me esqueçam Figueiredo: A biografia de uma presidência* (Rio de Janeiro: Record, 2020), 543.
25. Regina Echeverria, *Sarney: A biografia* (São Paulo: LeYa, 2011), 273; quoted in Pasqualette, *Me esqueçam Figueiredo*, 543.

26. "Situação Política Nacional," AN-B, CSN, Série Análise da Situação Interna e Externa, Box 7, vol. D, 16. No date is included, but the context indicates that it dates from mid-1983. The CSN general secretariat was made up of high-ranking officers from all three military branches. See "Estudo no. 2—AJ/84: Análise da Conjuntura Política," 23 Oct. 1984, AN-B, CSN, Série Análise da Situação Interna e Externa, Box 8, vol. D, 7.

27. Maluf, interview with author; Jeffrey Lesser, "'Jews Are Arabs Who Sell on Credit': Elite Images of Arabs and Jews in Brazil," in *Arab and Jewish Immigrants in Latin America: Images and Realities*, ed. Jeffrey Lesser and Ignacio Klich (London: Frank Cass, 1998), 38–56. This is similar to what Cardoso pointed out in our 2007 interview: the worst thing about Maluf was not his alleged corruption but how brazen he was about it; a lack of discretion is another purported Syrian Lebanese characteristic. Fernando Henrique Cardoso, interview withauthor, Providence, RI, 14 Mar. 2007.

28. On perceptions of Arab Brazilians as corrupt in the early 2000s, see John Tofik Karam, *Another Arabesque: Syrian-Lebanese Ethnicity in Neoliberal Brazil* (Philadelphia, PA: Temple University Press, 2008), 46–70.

29. "Tendências dos convencionais do PDS," AN-RJ, SNI, ASP_ACE_15349_84, 1.

30. "Aureliano quer direta para sucessão de Figueiredo," *Folha*, 11 Feb. 1984.

31. "Tancredo tem boas chances no Colégio," *Folha*, 16 Jan. 1984.

32. Apreciação no. 003/15/AC/84, AN-RJ, SNI, BR_AN_BSB_N8_0_PSN_EST_424, 164.

33. Carlos Brickmann, "Comício pelas diretas reune 50 mil em Curitiba," *Folha*, 13 Jan. 1984.

34. "Comícios por bairros preparam o ato na Sé," *Folha*, 9 Jan. 1984.

35. The paper's position so irked some in the regime that the the SNI dedicated over half of a 59-page secret report on the paulista press to its "clearly contestatory" posture toward the "Revolution." See "Propaganda adversa: Imprensa escrita," AN-RJ, SNI, E0153473-1984, 29 Feb. 1984, 2.

36. "Montoro dedica todo o dia ao ato," *Folha*, 26 Jan. 1984.

37. "Na Sé, um brado retumbante pede eleições diretas," *Folha*, 26 Jan. 1984.

38. "Ulisses diz que a indireta já caiu," *Folha*, 26 Jan. 1984.

39. "Relatório sobre o comício realizado na Praça da Sé no dia 25 de janeiro de 1984," Departamento de Comunicação Social (DCS), APESP, 11-P-0, Pasta 2, Doc. 176, Feb. 1984.

40. Galeno de Freitas, "Pressionado, Congresso apóia direta, diz Montoro," *Folha*, 22 Jan. 1984.

41. Interview with Lula, in Ronaldo Costa Couto, *Memória viva do regime militar: O Brasil, 1964–1985* (Rio de Janeiro: Editora Record, 1999), 266.

42. "Presidente do PMDB vence pleito simulado para Presidência da República em Vila Prudente," *Folha*, 16 Jan. 1984.

43. "Diretas vencem jogo e torcida expulsa Indiretas do campo," *Folha*, 16 Jan. 1994.

44. "Festa pelas diretas no Bixiga," *Folha*, 13 Feb. 1984.

45. "Comícios por bairros preparam o ato na Sé," *Folha*, 9 Jan. 1984.

46. "Carta ao leitor," *Veja*, 18 April 1984.

47. "Prefeitos em 514 cidades apóiam direta," *Folha*, 12 Jan. 1984.

48. "Criado comitê supra-partidário nacional pró-diretas," *Folha*, 23 Feb. 1984.

49. "Executivo não fechará por indiretas, garante Sarnei," *Folha*, 1 Feb. 1984.

50. "Um milhão nas ruas do Rio," *JT*, 11 Apr. 1984.
51. Ibid.
52. "E o Rio amanhece em clima de Copa e Carnaval," *JT*, 11 Apr. 1984.
53. "Um milhão nas ruas do Rio."
54. Ricardo Kotscho, "O País grande reencontra a Nação," *Folha*, 11 Apr. 1984.
55. "Para Lula, muitas das 'marchadeiras' estavam lá," *JT*, 17 Apr. 1984.
56. "Um vale agitado, vivo, em festa," *JT*, 17 Apr. 1984; "O agitado QC dos políticos," *JT*, 17 Apr. 1984.
57. "Ferro, isopor, papel e tinta: um boneco de quatro metros que emociona todo o comício," *JT*, 17 Apr. 1984.
58. "'Foi a maior concentração cívica da história do país,'" *JT*, 17 Apr. 1984.
59. "Cansado, rouco, suado, Brizola garante: 'O Brasil mudou com a passeata,'" *JT*, 17 Apr. 1984.
60. "E a passeata carrega os líderes," *JT*, 17 Apr. 1984.
61. "Figueiredo reitera que Colégio indicará seu sucessor," *Folha*, 16 Feb. 1984.
62. "Nós queremos uma democracia estável," *Folha*, 16 Mar. 1984.
63. "Figueiredo: 'Se eu estivesse lá, seriam um milhão e um,'" *JT*, 11 Apr. 1984.
64. "Figueiredo propõe eleições diretas para 88 e apela ao diálogo," *Folha*, 17 Apr. 1984.
65. Ruy Lopes, "Indiretas sempre," *Folha*, 24 Apr. 1984.
66. Carlos Brickmann, "Tropa de oito mil homens isola a cidade proibida," *Folha*, 23 Apr. 1984.
67. "Esquema de segurança no aeroporto irrita políticos," *Folha*, 24 Apr. 1984.
68. Carlos Brickmann, "Votação é hoje, mas Brasília ontem aprovou as diretas," *Folha*, 25 Apr. 1984.
69. "Um dia nervoso no Planalto. Com Figueiredo irritado." *JT*, 17 Apr. 1984.
70. Laerte Rímoli, "Figueiredo conversa com 8 políticos e é apoiado por 5," *Folha*, 24 Apr. 1984.
71. "Rádio e TV proibidos de identificar os votantes," *Folha*, 26 Apr. 1984.
72. Ulysses Guimarães (PMDB-SP), *Diário da Câmara dos Deputados*, 25 Apr. 1984, 2407. For the audio, see CD-COAUD, Arquivo Sonoro, 24 Apr. 1984, 15:28:27.
73. "Votação é hoje, mas Brasília ontem aprovou as diretas."
74. Clovis Rossi, "Congresso cercado pelo Exército durante três horas," *Folha*, 25 Apr. 1984.
75. "Votação é hoje, mas Brasília ontem aprovou as diretas."
76. "Sem apoio do PDS, a emenda das diretas é rejeitada," *Folha*, 26 Apr. 1984.
77. Fraga, *Tancredo Neves, o príncipe civil*, 377.
78. "Comitê nacional decide prosseguir a campanha," *Folha*, 27 Apr. 1984.
79. "Ulisses rejeita mandato-tampinha e exige Diretas Já," *Folha*, 29 Apr. 1984.
80. Clovis Rossi, "Governadores podem perder entusiasmo pelas diretas," *Folha*, 19 Apr. 1984; "Brizola apóia proposta de Montoro, com ressalva," *Folha*, 9 May 1984. In Brazil holders of executive offices who wish to run for another office must resign six months before the election.
81. Tatiana Petit, "Montoro quer Tancredo no Colégio e Constituinte em 86," *Folha*, 5 July 1984.
82. "Levantamento de alternativas para o encaminhamento das conversações sobre a sucessão presidencial," AN-B, CSN, Série Análise da Situação Interna e Externa, Box 7, vol. D, 16, 2–4.

83. Gutemberg, *Moisés, codinome Ulysses Guimarães*, 193.
84. *Veja*, 6 Dec. 1984, cited in Fraga, *Tancredo Neves, o príncipe civil*, 379. The quip about *eleições* being a feminine word is a mildly homophobic joke. If *eleições* were masculine, his professed obsession could have been jokingly called homoerotic.
85. The glaring exception was Guimarães, who, despite his own "anti-candidacy" in 1973, was loath to accept winning power through the electoral college. It took two months of cajoling by Neves and Montoro to convince him to endorse an indirect election. Fraga, *Tancredo Neves, o príncipe civil*, 386.
86. "Estudo 005/1ª SC/84," 6 July 1984, AN-B, CSN, Série Análise da Situação Interna e Externa, Box 7, vol. D, 2.
87. Maluf, interview with author.
88. Marcondes Sampaio, "Recuos abrem caminho à negociação, *Folha*, 2 Apr. 1984.
89. Hudson Brandão and Octaviano Lage, "Tancredo e Figueiredo inciam diálogo em Minas," *Folha*, 4 May 1984.
90. "Tancredo e Aureliano conversam mas evitam falar em acordo," *Folha*, 2 July 1984.
91. Tancredo Neves, "A recuperação da liberdade," *Folha*, 17 June 1984.
92. Pasqualette, *Me esqueçam Figueiredo*, 546.
93. "Prévia escolherá candidato do PDS à Presidência," *Folha*, 7 June 1984.
94. Ruy Lopes, "O golpe de mestre," *Folha*, 8 June 1984.
95. "Maluf não quer a inclusão de seu nome na prévia," *Folha*, 8 June 1984.
96. Pasqualette, *Me esqueçam Figueiredo*, 547.
97. "Sob pressão malufistas, Sarnei deixa direção do PDS," *Folha*, 12 June 1984.
98. Roberto Stefanelli, "Sob tumulto malufista, Bornhausen também renuncia," *Folha*, 23 June 1984.
99. "Comitê espera 300 mil pessoas na manifestação de amanhã," *Folha*, 26 June 1984; José Roberto de Alencar, "Cem mil voltam à Sé para exigir as diretas-já," *Folha*, 27 June 1984.
100. "Decisão do PMDB de aceitar adiamento irrita oposicionistas," *Folha*, 28 June 1984.
101. André Singer, "Governadores indicam Tancredo e propõem programa," *Folha*, 20 June 1984.
102. "Figueiredo retira a emenda, o Congresso frustrado," *Folha*, 29 June 1984.
103. "Situação Política Nacional," AN-B, CSN, Série Análise da Situação Interna e Externa, Box 7, vol. D, 17.
104. Tão Gomes Pinto, "Tancredo acha que pode derrotar Maluf em indiretas," *Folha*, 1 Jan. 1984.
105. Gilberto Dimenstein, José Negreiros, Ricardo Noblat, Roberto Lopes, and Roberto Fernandes, *O complô que elegeu Tancredo* (Rio de Janeiro: Editora JB, 1985), 155.
106. "Frente defende governo de conciliação em manifesto," *Folha*, 6 July 1984.
107. Echeverria, *Sarney: A biografia*, 283.
108. Galeno de Freitas, "PMDB e Frente Liberal fecham em São Paulo o acordo," *Folha*, 20 July 1984.
109. "Presente conjuntura política e possíveis desdobramentos," 29 June 1984, AN-B, CSN, Série Análise da Situação Interna e Externa, Box 7, vol. D, 16, 3–4.
110. Flávio Bierrenbach, "Por que só diretas," *Folha*, 21 July 1984.
111. Ademir Malavazi and Haroldo Cerqueira Lima, "Itamar mantém resistência contra as eleições indiretas," *Folha*, 22 July 1984.
112. "Oposicionistas de Maranhão contra a indicação de Sarnei," *Folha*, 30 July 1984.
113. "Brizola critica acordo com a frente," *Folha*, 17 July 1984.

114. Francisco Weffort, "Não há como conciliar o inconciliável," *Folha*, 21 July 1984.
115. José Roberto de Alencar, "Petistas preferem errar com o povo, afirma Bittar," *Folha*, 23 July 1984.
116. "Vamos matar a cobra com o seu veneno, diz Ulisses," *Folha*, 15 July 1984.
117. Gutemberg, *Moisés, codinome Ulysses Guimarães*, 204.
118. Rubem de Azevedo Lima, "O adversário desejado," *Folha*, 11 Aug. 1984; Clóvis Rossi, "Pedessistas definem hoje o seu candidato ao Colégio," *Folha*, 11 Aug. 1984.
119. Nélio Lima, "Alegria pré-fabricada marca primeiro dia," *Folha*, 11 Aug. 1984.
120. "Pedessistas definem hoje o seu candidato ao Colégio."
121. "'O Brasil exige soluções ousadas,'" *Folha*, 12 Aug. 1984.
122. "PMDB confirma chapa Tancredo-Sarnei para o Colégio," *Folha*, 13 Aug. 1984.
123. "A causa do povo, se dispensa radicalismo, exige coragem," *Folha*, 13 Aug. 1984.
124. Echeverria, *Sarney: A biografia*, 284. Salim was Maluf's middle name.
125. "Andreazza recebe Maluf e emite uma fria nota manifestando apoio." *Folha*, 23 Aug. 1984; "Andreazza não vai subir em palanques," *Folha*, 14 Sept. 1984.
126. Luiz Ricardo Leitão, "Suruagi promete a Magalhães que apoiará chapa da oposição," *Folha*, 23 Aug. 1984.
127. "Figueiredo ameaça demitir quem estiver contra Maluf," *Folha*, 21 Aug. 1984.
128. "Governadores obtêm prazo para definição," *Folha*, 14 Aug. 1984.
129. Pasqualette, *Me esqueçam Figueiredo*, 566.
130. Dimenstein et al., *O complô que elegeu Tancredo*, 162.
131. Gaspari, *A ditadura acabada*, 289–92.
132. "Um alerta contra ambiciosos," *Folha*, 25 Aug. 1984.
133. "Délio acusa os dissidentes do PDS de traidores," *Folha*, 5 Sept. 1984.
134. "Maluf reage e remove suas armas," *Veja*, 26 Sept. 1984.
135. Pasqualette, *Me esqueçam Figueiredo*, 595.
136. Ruy Lopes, "Desestabilizando," *Folha*, 6 Sept. 1984.
137. Dimenstein et al., *O complô que elegeu Tancredo*, 177.
138. "'Fiel cumprimento da Constituição,'" *Folha*, 22 Sept. 1984.
139. "Successão presidencial—alternativas que visam a estabilidade política do País," AN-B, CSN, Série Análise da Situação Interna e Externa, Box 7, vol. D, 16, 7.
140. Fraga, *Tancredo Neves, o príncipe civil*, 375.
141. Pasqualette, *Me esqueçam Figueiredo*, 595.
142. Dimenstein et al., *O complô que elegeu Tancredo*, 181.
143. Maluf, interview with author. Maluf's position is corroborated by Delfim Neto, who insisted that Neves was "the chosen one," Figueiredo's preferred candidate, even before Andreazza lost at the PDS convention. Delfim Neto, interview with author.
144. "Constituição não prevê fidelidade no Colégio, vota TSE," *Folha*, 7 Nov. 1984; "Colégio Eleitoral não tem fidelidade, reafirma TSE," *Folha*, 28 Nov. 1984.
145. "Para Maluf, sua candidatura garantiu o processo," *Folha*, 16 Jan. 1984.
146. Agenor Maria (PMDB-RN), João Faustino (PDS-RN), Sebastião Néri (PDT-RJ), 15 Jan. 1985, CD-COAUD, Arquivo Sonoro, 15 Jan. 1985.
147. João Cunha (PMDB-SP), CD-COAUD, Arquivo Sonoro, 15 Jan. 1985.
148. Dimenstein et al., *O complô que elegeu Tancredo*, 23.
149. For an analysis of Maluf's political style and constituencies, see Mauricio Puls, *O malufismo* (São Paulo: Publifolha, 2000).
150. "Primeira tarefa será promover a organização institucional," *Folha*, 16 Jan. 1985.

CONCLUSION: FREEDOM, JUSTICE, AND SOLIDARITY FOR BRAZIL? THE POLITICAL CLASS UNDER DICTATORSHIP AND DEMOCRACY

1. For the most recent English edition, see Stefan Zweig, *Brazil: A Land of the Future* (Riverside, CA: Ariadne Press, 2018). For an analysis of Zweig's relationship with Brazil, see Harden Theo, "Stefan Zweig and the Land of the Future: The (His)story of an Uneasy Relationship," *Austrian Studies* 23 (2015): 72–87, https://dx.doi.org/10.5699/austrianstudies.23.2015.0072.

2. Cardoso, Covas, and other PMDB leaders had grown frustrated with Quércia's increasing influence in the party and left to found the PSDB in 1988.

3. For one of many analyses critical of Cardoso's privatizations, see Carlos Henrique Lopes Rodrigues and Vanessa Follmann Jurgenfeld, "Desnacionalização e financeirização: Um estudo sobre as privatizações brasileiras (de Collor ao primeiro governo FHC)," *Economia e Sociedade* 28 (2019): 393–420, https://dx.doi.org/10.1590/1982-3533.2019v28n2art05.

4. Sergio Tiezzi, "A organização da política social do governo Fernando Henrique," *São Paulo em Perspectiva* 18 (2004): 49–56, http://www.scielo.br/scielo.php?script=sci_arttext&pid=S0102-88392004000200006&nrm=iso.

5. Amy Stewart Nunn et al., "AIDS Treatment in Brazil: Impacts and Challenges," *Health Affairs (Project Hope)* 28:4 (July–Aug. 2009): 1103–13, https://dx.doi.org/10.1377/hlthaff.28.4.1103.

6. For a critique of US leftist media coverage of the PT governments, see Brian Mier, Sean Mitchell, and Bryan Pitts, "How the U.S. Left Failed Brasil," *Brasil Wire*, 12 Dec. 2018, https://www.brasilwire.com/how-the-us-left-failed-brasil/.

7. The preceding statistics were taken from Daniel Mariani, Bruno Lupion, and Rodolfo Almeida, "10 índices econômicos e sociais nos 13 anos de governo PT no Brasil," *Nexo Jornal*, 31 Aug. 2016, https://www.nexojornal.com.br/especial/2016/09/02/10-índices-econômicos-e-sociais-nos-13-anos-de-governo-PT-no-Brasil.

8. In recent years a growing number of political scientists and international relations scholars have critiqued the tendency of their disciplines to judge democracies in the Global South based on the extent to which they follow a northern ideal. See Amitav Acharya and Barry Buzan, "Why Is There No Non-Western International Relations Theory? An Introduction," *International Relations of the Asia-Pacific* 7:3 (2007): 287–312; Michael Coppedge et al., "Conceptualizing and Measuring Democracy: A New Approach," *Perspectives on Politics* 9:2 (2011): 247–67, https://dx.doi.org/10.1017/S1537592711000880; Sarah Sunn Bush, "The Politics of Rating Freedom: Ideological Affinity, Private Authority, and the Freedom in the World Ratings," *Perspectives on Politics* 15:3 (2017): 711–31, https://dx.doi.org/10.1017/S1537592717000925; Yong-Soo Eun, "Opening up the Debate over 'Non-Western' International Relations," *Politics* 39:1 (2018): 4–17, https://dx.doi.org/10.1177/0263395718805401. Thanks to Julia Payson for directing me to the second citation and Dat Nguyen for guiding me to the third.

9. For an analysis that emphasizes these continuities during the first decade after democratization, see Timothy J. Power, *The Political Right in Postauthoritarian Brazil: Elites, Institutions, and Democratization* (University Park: Pennsylvania State University Press, 2000).

10. On the centrality of families among the Brazilian elite, see Ricardo Costa de Oliveira et al., "Família, parentesco, instituições e poder no Brasil: Retomada e atualização de uma agenda de pesquisa," *Revista Brasileira de Sociologia* 5:11 (2017): 165–98, https://dx.doi.org/10.20336/rbs.225.

11. David Samuels and Fernando Luiz Abrucio, "Federalism and Democratic Transitions: The 'New' Politics of the Governors in Brazil," *Publius* 30:2 (2000): 43–61, https://dx.doi.org/10.2307/3331087.

12. For a scathing critique of the Brazilian elite's disdain for the popular classes, rooted in slavery, see Jessé Souza, *A elite do atraso da escravidão a Bolsonaro* (Rio de Janeiro: Estação Brasil, 2019).

13. Janaina Carvalho, "PMs vão presos após 5 jovens serem mortos em carro no subúrbio do Rio," *G1*, 29 Nov. 2015, http://g1.globo.com/rio-de-janeiro/noticia/2015/11/cinco-jovens-sao-mortos-no-rio-e-parentes-das-vitimas-culpam-pm.html.

14. On the growth of the *bancada da bala* (bullet caucus), see Marcos Paulo dos Reis Quadros and Rafael Machado Madeira, "Fim da direita envergonhada? Atuação da bancada evangélica e da bancada da bala e os caminhos da representação do conservadorismo no Brasil," *Opinião Pública* 24 (2018): 486–522, https://doi.org/10.1590/1807-019 12018243486. For Bolsonaro's call for more police killings, see Thiago de Araújo, "Bolsonaro defende que a PM mate mais no Brasil," *Exame*, 5 Oct. 2015, https://exame.com/brasil/bolsonaro-defende-que-a-pm-mate-mais-no-brasil/.

15. The protests that preceded Rousseff's impeachment exhibited a marked lack of representativity. The crowds that filled São Paulo's iconic Av. Paulista were whiter (69%), more male (57%), and older (45.5 years) than the average Brazilian. Most strikingly, 77% held a university degree. "Maior manifestação política da história de SP reúne 500 mil na Paulista," *Datafolha*, 14 Mar. 2016, https://datafolha.folha.uol.com.br/opiniaopublica/2016/03/1749713-maior-manifestacao-politica-da-historia-de-sp-reune-500-mil-na-paulista.shtml.

16. For more on the changing role of the Armed Forces since 1985, see Wendy Hunter, *Eroding Military Influence in Brazil: Politicians against Soldiers* (Chapel Hill: University of North Carolina Press, 1997), José Murilo de Carvalho, *Forças armadas e política no Brasil*, 2nd ed. (São Paulo: Todavia, 2019).

17. On the notion of development prior to the military coup, see Rafael R. Ioris, *Transforming Brazil: A History of National Development in the Postwar Era* (New York: Routledge, 2016).

18. Eduardo G. Noronha, "Ciclo de greves, transição política e estabilização: Brasil, 1978–2007," *Lua Nova: Revista de Cultura e Política* 76 (2009): 119–68, https://dx.doi.org/10.1590/S0102-64452009000100005.

19. The assertion that the political class's habitus changed departs from Bourdieu's description of habitus as highly durable. Indeed, one of the chief critiques of Bourdieu's use of the concept is that it is deterministic and static. Yang Yang, "Bourdieu, Practice and Change: Beyond the Critique of Determinism," *Educational Philosophy and Theory* 46:14 (2014): 1522–40, https://dx.doi.org/10.1080/00131857.2013.839375. Still, as Zander Navarro has pointed out, Bourdieu never intended to create a "formal and total theoretical model" but rather "a meta-theory that requires continuous adjustment to empirical conditions." The empirical conditions of the political class under military rule indicate that their habitus was changing in subtle but important ways. Zander Navarro, "In Search of a Cultural Interpretation of Power: The Contribution of Pierre Bourdieu," *IDS Bulletin* 37:6 (2006): 11–22.

20. Luiz Henrique Voguel, *A histórica sub-representação das mulheres na Câmara dos Deputados: Desigualdades e hierarquias sociais nas eleições de 2014* (Brasília: Câmara dos Deputados, 2019), 33.

21. Ollie A. Johnson, "Racial Representation and Brazilian Politics: Black Members of the National Congress, 1983–1999," *Journal of Interamerican Studies and World Affairs* 40:4 (1998): 104, https://dx.doi.org/10.2307/166456.

22. Daniela Amorim and Paulo Beraldo, "Apesar do alto número de candidaturas, negros são menos eleitos que brancos," *O Estado*, 13 Nov. 2019, https://politica.estadao.com.br/noticias/geral,apesar-do-alto-numero-de-candidaturas-negros-sao-menos-eleitos-que-brancos,70003087813.

23. Data from 1978 are taken from *Deputados brasileiros: Repertório biográfico dos membros da Câmara dos Deputados da oitava legislatura (1975–79)* (Brasília: Câmara dos Deputados, Centro de Documentação e Informação, 1979). The 2018 numbers are taken from "Conheça as profissões dos deputados federais eleitos," Federação dos Sindicatos dos Servidores Públicos no Estado de São Paulo, 26 Nov. 2018, https://www.fessp-esp.org.br/conheca-as-profissoes-dos-deputados-federais-eleitos/.

BIBLIOGRAPHY

ARCHIVES

Brasília, Brazil
Arquivo da Câmara dos Deputados
    Arquivo Sonoro
    Centro de Documentação e Informação
Arquivo Central da UnB
Arquivo Nacional—Brasília
    Conselho de Segurança Nacional
Secretaria de Arquivo, Senado Federal

Campinas, Brazil
Arquivo Edgard Leuenroth
    Instituto Brasileiro de Opinião Pública e Estatística

Rio de Janeiro, Brazil
Arquivo Nacional—Rio de Janeiro
    Divisão de Segurança e Informações—Ministério da Justiça
    Serviço Nacional de Informações (SNI)
Centro de Documentação da Rede Globo
Centro de Pesquisa e Documentação de História Contemporânea do Brasil
    Arquivo da Aliança Renovadora Nacional
    Arquivo Ernesto Geisel

São Paulo, Brazil
Arquivo Público do Estado de São Paulo
    Departamento de Ordem e Política Social (DOPS)

Departamento de Comunicação Social (DCS)
Biblioteca do Legislativo Paulista
Centro de Memória Eleitoral, Tribunal Regional Eleitoral—São Paulo
Fundação Mário Covas
Instituto Fernando Henrique Cardoso

Portugal
Ministério de Negócios Estrangeiros, Lisbon

Spain
Ministerio de Asuntos Exteriores, Madrid

United Kingdom
National Archives, London
   Foreign and Commonwealth Office

United States
Department of State, Washington, DC
National Archives and Records Administration, College Park, MD
   Department of State, Record Group 59

NEWSPAPERS AND MAGAZINES

Correio Braziliense
Correio da Manhã
Diário da Câmara dos Deputados
Diário do Congresso Nacional
Diário do Senado Federal
Diário Oficial—Estado de São Paulo
Diário Popular
O Estado de S. Paulo
Folha de S. Paulo
Jornal da Tarde
Jornal do Brasil
Tribuna de Santos
Veja

ORAL HISTORY INTERVIEWS

Almir Turisco d'Araújo
Antônio Delfim Neto
Fernando Henrique Cardoso
Gastone Righi and Luciene Prieto Cuoghi
José Alencar Furtado
José Bernardo Cabral
José Lurtz Sabiá
Léo de Almeida Neves

Marcos Tito
Osvaldo Martins
Paulo Salim Maluf
Rosa and Edgard Araújo
Vilma Pereira

PUBLISHED PRIMARY AND SECONDARY SOURCES

Acharya, Amitav, and Barry Buzan. "Why Is There No Non-Western International Relations Theory? An Introduction." *International Relations of the Asia-Pacific* 7:3 (2007): 287–312.
Ahn, Byong-Man. *Elites and Political Power in South Korea*. Cheltenham: Edward Elgar, 2003.
AI-5: O dia que não existiu. Dir. Paulo Markun. 2001. 180 min.
Alvarez, Sonia E. *Engendering Democracy in Brazil: Women's Movements in Transition Politics*. Princeton, NJ: Princeton University Press, 1990.
Alves, Maria Helena Moreira. *State and Opposition in Military Brazil*. Austin: University of Texas Press, 1985.
Aparecida de Aquino, Maria. *Censura, imprensa, estado autoritário (1968—1978): O exercício cotidiano da dominação e da resistência, o estado de São Paulo e movimento*. Bauru: Editora da Universidade do Sagrado Coração, 1999.
Araújo, Maria Paula Nascimento. *Memórias estudantis: Da fundação da UNE aos nossos dias*. Rio de Janeiro: Relume Dumará, Ediouro, 2007.
Azevedo, Ricardo de. "Memória: Geraldo Siqueira." *Teoria e Debate* 65 (2006). https://teoriaedebate.org.br/2006/02/10/geraldo-siqueira/.
Baer, Werner. *The Brazilian Economy: Growth and Development*. 6th ed. Boulder, CO: Lynne Rienner, 2008.
Barbosa, Leonardo Augusto de Andrade. "The Ballot under the Bayonet: Election Law in the First Years of the Brazilian Civil-Military Regime (1964–1967)." *Revista Direito GV* 13 (2017): 145–70. https://dx.doi.org/10.1590/2317-6172201707.
Barra 68: Sem perder a ternura. Europa Filmes, 2002. 85 min.
Barreira, Irlys. *Chuva de papeis: Ritos e símbolos de campanhas eleitorais no Brasil*. Rio de Janeiro: Relume Dumará; Núcleo de Antropologia da Política, 1998.
Bethell, Leslie, and Celso Castro. "Politics in Brazil under Military Rule, 1964–1985." In *Brazil since 1930*, edited by Leslie Bethell, 165–230. Cambridge History of Latin America 9. Cambridge: Cambridge University Press, 2008.
Bieber, Judy. *Power, Patronage, and Political Violence: State Building on a Brazilian Frontier, 1822–1889*. Lincoln: University of Nebraska Press, 1999.
Bottomore, Tom. *Élites and Society*. 2nd ed. New York: Routledge, 1993.
Bourdieu, Pierre. *Distinction: A Social Critique of the Judgment of Taste*. Cambridge, MA: Harvard University Press, [1979] 2004.
———. *Outline of a Theory of Practice*. Cambridge: Cambridge University Press, 1977.
Bush, Sarah Sunn. "The Politics of Rating Freedom: Ideological Affinity, Private Authority, and the Freedom in the World Ratings." *Perspectives on Politics* 15:3 (2017): 711–31. https://dx.doi.org/10.1017/S1537592717000925.

Campos, Milton, and Antônio Gontijo de Carvalho. *Testemunhos e ensinamentos*. Rio de Janeiro: Livraria José Olympio, 1972.
Campos, Pedro Henrique Pedreira. *"Estranhas Catedrais": As empreiteiras brasileiras e a ditadura civil-militar, 1964–1988*. Niterói: EdUFF, 2014.
Capistrano Filho, David, and Antonio Roque Citadini. *PMDB no poder*. São Paulo: CERI-FA, Oboré Editorial, 1982.
Cardoso, Fernando Henrique. "Associated-Dependent Development: Theoretical and Practical Implications." In *Authoritarian Brazil: Origins, Policies, and Future*, edited by Alfred Stepan, 142–76. New Haven, CT: Yale University Press, 1973.
———. "Dependency and Development in Latin America." *New Left Review* 74 (1972): 83–95.
———. "Partidos e deputados em São Paulo: Passado e presente." In *Os partidos e as eleições no Brasil*, edited by Bolivar Lamounier and Fernando Henrique Cardoso. 45–75. Rio de Janeiro: Paz e Terra, 1975.
Cardoso, Fernando Henrique, and Bolivar Lamounier, eds. *Os partidos e as eleições no Brasil*. Rio de Janeiro: Paz e Terra, 1975.
Cardoso, Fernando Henrique, and Ricardo A. Setti. *A arte da política: A história que vivi*. Rio de Janeiro: Civilização Brasileira, 2006.
Cardoso, Fernando Henrique, and Brian Winter. *The Accidental President of Brazil: A Memoir*. New York: PublicAffairs, 2006.
Carneiro, Glauco. *Cunha Bueno: História de um político*. São Paulo: Livraria Pioneira Editora, 1982.
Carvalho, Alessandra. "Elites políticas durante o regime militar: Um estudo sobre os parlamentares da ARENA e do MDB." PhD dissertation, Universidade Federal do Rio de Janeiro, 2008.
Carvalho, José Murilo de. *Forças armadas e política no Brasil*. 2nd ed. São Paulo: Todavia, 2019.
Chagas, Carlos. *113 dias de angústia: Impedimento e morte de um presidente*. 2nd ed. Porto Alegre: L&PM Editores, 1979.
Chirio, Maud. *A política nos quartéis: Revoltas e protestos de oficiais na ditadura militar brasileira*. Translated by André Telles. Rio de Janeiro: Zahar, 2012.
Coelho, Edmundo Campos. *Em busca de identidade: O exército e a política na sociedade brasileira*. 2nd ed. Rio de Janeiro: Editora Record, 2000.
Coelho, Marco Antônio Tavares. *Herança de um sonho: As memórias de um comunista*. Rio de Janeiro: Editora Record, 2000.
Coppedge, Michael, John Gerring, David Altman, Michael Bernhard, Steven Fish, Allen Hicken, Matthew Kroenig, Staffan I. Lindberg, Kelly McMann, Pamela Paxton, Holli A. Semetko, Svend-Erik Skaaning, Jeffrey Staton, and Jan Teorell. "Conceptualizing and Measuring Democracy: A New Approach." *Perspectives on Politics* 9:2 (2011): 247–67. https://dx.doi.org/10.1017/S1537592711000880.
Costa, Célia, and Juliana Gagliardi. "Lysâneas: Um autêntico do MDB." *Revista de Estudos Históricos* 37 (2006): 201–12.
Costa, Emilia Viotti da. *The Brazilian Empire: Myths and Histories*. Rev. ed. Chapel Hill: University of North Carolina Press, 2000.
Cotton, James. "From Authoritarianism to Democracy in South Korea." *Political Studies* 37:2 (1989): 244–59. https://dx.doi.org/10.1111/j.1467-9248.1989.tb01481.x.

Couloumbis, Theodore A. "The Greek Junta Phenomenon." *Polity* 6 (1974): 345–74.
Couto, Ronaldo Costa. *Memória viva do regime militar: O Brasil, 1964–1985*. Rio de Janeiro: Editora Record, 1999.
Covas, Lila, and Luci Molina. *Lila Covas: Histórias e receitas de uma vida*. São Paulo: Global Editora, 2007.
Covin, David. *The Unified Black Movement in Brazil, 1978–2002*. Jefferson, NC: McFarland & Co., 2006.
Cowan, Benjamin A. *Securing Sex: Morality and Repression in the Making of Cold War Brazil*. Chapel Hill: University of North Carolina Press, 2016.
Cruz, Sebastião C. Velasco e. *Empresariado e estado na transição brasileira: Um estudo sobre a economia política do autoritarismo (1974–1977)*. Campinas: Editora da UNICAMP, 1995.
Cruz, Sebastião Carlos Velasco e, and Carlos Estevam Martins. "De Castello a Figueiredo: Uma incursão na pre-história da 'abertura.'" In *Sociedade e política no Brasil pós-64*, edited by Bernardo Sorj and Maria Hermínia Tavares de Almeida. São Paulo: Editora Brasiliense, 1984.
d'Araújo, Maria Celina Soares. *O Partido Trabalhista Brasileiro e os dilemas dos partidos classistas*. Rio de Janeiro: Fundação Getúlio Vargas, Centro de Pesquisa e Documentação de História Contemporânea do Brasil, 1991.
d'Araújo, Maria Celina Soares, and Celso Castro. *Ernesto Geisel*. Rio de Janeiro: Editora Fundação Getúlio Vargas, 1997.
Dahl, Robert A. *Who Governs? Democracy and Power in an American City*. New Haven, CT: Yale University Press, 1961.
Deputados brasileiros: Repertório biográfico dos membros da Câmara dos Deputados, Oitava Legislatura (1979–1983). Brasília: Câmara dos Deputados, Centro de Documentação e Informação, 1979.
Dimenstein, Gilberto, José Negreiros, Ricardo Noblat, Roberto Lopes, and Roberto Fernandes. *O complô que elegeu Tancredo*. Rio de Janeiro: Editora JB, 1985.
Diniz, Eli. *Voto e máquina política: Patronagem e clientelismo no Rio de Janeiro*. Rio de Janeiro: Paz e Terra, 1982.
dos Santos, Elizabeth Paes. "A palavra como arma: Análise do discurso do Deputado Mário Covas em defesa da imunidade parlamentar." Monograph, Curso de Especialização em Processo Legislativo da Câmara dos Deputados, Cefor, 2007. https://doi.org/10.51206/e-legis.v4i4.36.
Doukas, George. "Party Elites and Democratization in Greece." *Parliamentary Affairs* 46 (1993): 506–16.
Dreifuss, René Armand. *1964, a conquista do estado: Ação política, poder e golpe de classe*. Petrópolis: Editora Vozes, 1981.
Dulles, John W. F. *Resisting Brazil's Military Regime: An Account of the Battles of Sobral Pinto*. Austin: University of Texas Press, 2007.
———. *The São Paulo Law School and the Anti-Vargas Resistance (1938–1945)*. Austin: University of Texas Press, 1986.
Echeverria, Regina. *Sarney: A biografia*. São Paulo: LeYa, 2011.
Eun, Yong-Soo. "Opening up the Debate over 'Non-Western' International Relations." *Politics* 39:1 (2018): 4–17. https://dx.doi.org/10.1177/0263395718805401.

Ferreira, Marieta de Moraes, and Alexandre Fortes. *Muitos caminhos, uma estrela: Memórias de militantes do PT*. São Paulo: Editora Fundação Perseu Abramo, 2008.

Ferreira, Marieta de Moraes, Dora Rocha, and Américo Freire, eds. *Vozes da oposição*. Rio de Janeiro: Grafline Editora, 2001.

Fico, Carlos. *Como eles agiam. Os subterrâneos da ditadura militar: Espionagem e polícia política*. Rio de Janeiro: Editora Record, 2001.

———. "Ditadura militar brasileira: Aproximações teóricas e historiográficas." *Tempo e Argumento* 9:20 (2017): 5–74. https://dx.doi.org/10.5965/2175180309202017005.

———. "Versões e controvérsias sobre 1964 e a ditadura militar." *Revista Brasileira de História* 24:47 (2004): 29–60.

Fleischer, David V. *Thirty Years of Legislative Recruitment in Brazil*. Washington, DC: Center of Brazilian Studies, 1976.

Fontes, Paulo. *Migration and the Making of Industrial São Paulo*. Durham, NC: Duke University Press, 2016.

Fortes, Alexandre. *Nós do quarto distrito: A classe trabalhadora Porto-Alegrense e a era Vargas*. Caxias do Sul: EDUCS, 2004.

Fraga, Plínio. *Tancredo Neves, o príncipe civil*. Rio de Janeiro: Objetiva, 2017.

French, John D. *The Brazilian Workers' ABC: Class Conflict and Alliances in Modern São Paulo*. Chapel Hill: University of North Carolina Press, 1992.

———. *Drowning in Laws: Labor Law and Brazilian Political Culture*. Chapel Hill: University of North Carolina Press, 2004.

———. *Lula and His Politics of Cunning: From Metalworker to President of Brazil*. Chapel Hill: University of North Carolina Press, 2020.

Gaspari, Elio. *A ditadura acabada*. São Paulo: Companhia das Letras, 2016.

———. *A ditadura derrotada: O sacerdote e o feiticeiro*. São Paulo: Companhia das Letras, 2003.

———. *A ditadura encurralada*. São Paulo: Companhia de Letras, 2004.

———. *A ditadura escancarada: As ilusões armadas*. São Paulo: Companhia das Letras, 2002.

———. *A ditadura envergonhada: As ilusões armadas*. São Paulo: Companhia das Letras, 2002.

Gazzotti, Juliana. "Jornal da Tarde (1966–75): Ideologia liberal e ditadura militar." PhD dissertation, Universidade Federal de São Carlos, 2004

Geisel, Ernesto. *Discursos*. Vol. 1. Brasília: Assessoria de Imprensa e Relações Públicas da Presidência da República, 1975.

Goldman, Marcio, and Moacir Palmeira. *Antropologia, voto e representação política*. Rio de Janeiro: Contra Capa, 1996.

Gould, Jeffrey L. "Solidarity under Siege: The Latin American Left, 1968." *American Historical Review* 114:2 (2009): 348–75. https://dx.doi.org/10.1086/ahr.114.2.348.

Green, James N. *Beyond Carnival: Male Homosexuality in Twentieth-Century Brazil*. Chicago: University of Chicago Press, 1999.

———. *We Cannot Remain Silent: Opposition to the Brazilian Military Dictatorship in the United States*. Radical Perspectives. Durham, NC: Duke University Press, 2010.

Grinberg, Lucia. *Partido político ou bode expiatório: Um estudo sobre a Aliança Renovadora Nacional, ARENA (1965–1979)*. Rio de Janeiro: Mauad X, 2009.

Gurgel, Antonio de Padua. *A rebelião dos estudantes: Brasília, 1968*. Brasília: Editora UnB, 2002.

Gutemberg, Luiz. *Moisés, codinome Ulysses Guimarães: Uma biografia.* São Paulo: Companhia das Letras, 1994.
Hagopian, Frances. *Traditional Politics and Regime Change in Brazil.* Cambridge: Cambridge University Press, 1996.
Hanchard, Michael George. *Orpheus and Power: The Movimento Negro of Rio de Janeiro and São Paulo, Brazil, 1945–1988.* Princeton, NJ: Princeton University Press, 1994.
Hartmann, Michael. *The Sociology of Elites.* London: Routledge, 2012.
Higley, John, and Michael G. Burton. *Elite Foundations of Liberal Democracy.* Lanham, MD: Rowman & Littlefield, 2006.
Hippolito, Lucia. *De raposas e reformistas: O PSD e a experiência democrática brasileira (1945–1964).* Rio de Janeiro: Paz e Terra, 1985.
Hoeveler, Rejane Carolina. "Ditadura e democracia restrita: A elaboração do projeto de descompressão controlada no Brasil, 1972–1973." Thesis, Universidade Federal do Rio de Janeiro, 2012.
Holston, James. *Insurgent Citizenship: Disjunctions of Democracy and Modernity in Brazil.* Princeton, NJ: Princeton University Press, 2008.
Hunter, Wendy. *Eroding Military Influence in Brazil: Politicians against Soldiers.* Chapel Hill: University of North Carolina Press, 1997.
Ioris, Rafael R. *Transforming Brazil: A History of National Development in the Postwar Era.* New York: Routledge, 2016.
Jenks, Margaret Sarles. "Political Parties in Authoritarian Brazil." PhD dissertation, Duke University, 1979.
Jobim, Nelson, and Walter Costa Porto, eds. *Legislação eleitoral no Brasil: Do século XVI aos nossos dias.* Vol. 3. Brasília: Senado Federal, Secretaria de Documentação e Informação, Subsecretaria de Biblioteca, 1996.
Johnson, Ollie A. "Racial Representation and Brazilian Politics: Black Members of the National Congress, 1983–1999." *Journal of Interamerican Studies and World Affairs* 40:4 (1998): 97–118. https://dx.doi.org/10.2307/166456.
Karam, John Tofik. *Another Arabesque: Syrian-Lebanese Ethnicity in Neoliberal Brazil.* Philadelphia, PA: Temple University Press, 2008.
Keck, Margaret E. "The New Unionism in the Brazilian Transition." In *Democratizing Brazil: Problems of Transition and Consolidation,* edited by Alfred Stepan. 252–96. Oxford: Oxford University Press, 1989.
———. *The Workers' Party and Democratization in Brazil.* New Haven, CT: Yale University Press, 1992.
Kim, Sŏn-hyŏk. *The Politics of Democratization in Korea: The Role of Civil Society.* Pittsburgh, PA: University of Pittsburgh Press, 2000.
Kinzo, Maria D'Alva Gil. *Legal Opposition Politics under Authoritarian Rule in Brazil: The Case of the MDB, 1966–79.* New York: St. Martin's Press, 1988.
Kirkendall, Andrew J. *Class Mates: Male Student Culture and and the Making of a Political Class in Nineteenth-Century Brazil.* Lincoln: University of Nebraska Press, 2002.
Klein, Lucia, and Marcus Faria Figueiredo. *Legitimidade e coação no Brasil pos-64.* Rio de Janeiro: Forense-Universitária, 1978.
Knack, Diego. "O combate à corrupção durante a Ditadura Militar por meio da Comissão Geral de Investigações (1968–1978)." Thesis, Universidade Federal do Rio de Janeiro, 2014.

Krieger, Daniel. *Desde as Missões... : Saudades, lutas, esperanças*. Rio de Janeiro: J. Olympio Editora, 1977.

Kushnir, Beatriz. *Cães de guarda: Jornalistas e censores, do AI-5 à constituição de 1988*. São Paulo: FAPESP and Boitempo Editorial, 2004.

Lacerda, Claudio. *Carlos Lacerda e os anos sessenta: Oposição*. Rio de Janeiro: Editora Nova Fronteira, 1998.

Lamounier, Bolivar. "Authoritarian Brazil Revisited: The Impact of Elections on the Abertura." In *Democratizing Brazil: Problems of Transition and Consolidation*, edited by Alfred Stepan, 15–44. New York: Oxford University Press, 1989.

Lamounier, Bolivar, ed. *Voto de desconfiança: Eleições e mudança política no Brasil: 1970–1979*. Petrópolis: Editora Vozes, 1980.

Langland, Victoria. *Speaking of Flowers: Student Movements and the Making and Remembering of 1968 in Military Brazil*. Durham, NC: Duke University Press, 2013.

Lasswell, Harold D., and Abraham Kaplan. *Power and Society: A Framework for Political Inquiry*. New Haven, CT: Yale University Press, 1950.

Leonelli, Domingos, and Dante de Oliveira. *Diretas Já: 15 meses que abalaram a ditadura*. 2nd ed. Rio de Janeiro: Editora Record, 2004.

Lesser, Jeffrey. "'Jews Are Arabs Who Sell on Credit': Elite Images of Arabs and Jews in Brazil." In *Arab and Jewish Immigrants in Latin America: Images and Realities*, edited by Jeffrey Lesser and Ignacio Klich, 38–56. London: Frank Cass, 1998.

Linz, Juan J. "The Future of an Authoritarian Situation or the Institutionalization of a Military Regime: The Case of Brazil." In *Authoritarian Brazil: Origins, Policies, and Future*, edited by Alfred C. Stepan, 233–54. New Haven, CT: Yale University Press, 1973.

Lopes, João Herculino de Souza. *Minhas melhores lembranças*. Brasília: Dom Quixote Editora.

Mainwaring, Scott. *The Catholic Church and Politics in Brazil, 1916–1985*. Stanford, CA: Stanford University Press, 1986.

Maluf, Paulo Salim, and Tão Gomes Pinto. *Ele: Paulo Maluf, trajetória da audácia*. São Paulo: Ediouro, 2008.

Martins, Carlos Estevam. "O balanço da campanha." In *Os partidos e as eleições no Brasil*, edited by Bolivar Lamounier and Fernando Henrique Cardoso, 77–125. Rio de Janeiro: Paz e Terra, 1975.

Martins Filho, João Roberto. *Movimento estudantil e ditadura militar: 1964–1968*. São Paulo: Papirus, 1987.

———. *O palácio e a caserna: A dinâmica militar das crises políticas na ditadura, 1964–1969*. São Carlos: Editora da Universidade Federal de São Carlos, 1995.

Martins, Osvaldo. "Surge um líder." In *Mario Covas, democracia: Defender, conquistar, praticar*, edited by Osvaldo Martins, 11–71. São Paulo: Fundação Mario Covas, 2011.

Martins, Paulo Egydio, Verena Alberti, Ignez Cordeiro de Farias, and Dora Rocha. *Paulo Egydio conta: Depoimento ao CPDOC-FGV*. São Paulo: Imprensa Oficial do Estado, 2007.

Mattos, Sérgio. *História da televisão brasileira: Uma visão econômica, social e política*. Petrópolis: Editora Vozes, 2002.

McCann, Frank Daniel. *Soldiers of the Pátria: A History of the Brazilian Army, 1889–1937*. Stanford, CA: Stanford University Press, 2004.

Médici, Roberto Nogueira, Maria Celina Soares d'Araújo, and Gláucio Ary Dillon Soares. *Médici, o depoimento*. Rio de Janeiro: Mauad, 1995.

Melhem, Célia Soibelmann. *Política de botinas amarelas: O MDB-PMDB paulista de 1965 a 1988*. São Paulo: Editora Hucitec, 1998.

Melhem, Célia Soibelmann, and Sonia Morgenstern Russo. *Dr. Ulysses, o homem que pensou o Brasil. 39 depoimentos sobre a trajetória do Sr. Diretas*. São Paulo: Premio, 2004.

Meneguello, Rachel. *PT: A formação de um partido, 1979-1982*. São Paulo: Paz e Terra, 1989.

Mesquita Benevides, Maria Victoria de. *A UDN e o udenismo: Ambiguïdades do liberalismo brasileiro (1945-1965)*. Rio de Janeiro: Paz e Terra, 1981.

Michels, Robert. *Political Parties: A Sociological Study of the Oligarchical Tendencies of Modern Democracy*. Glencoe, IL: Free Press, [1911] 1958.

Mills, C. Wright. *The Power Elite*. New York: Oxford University Press, 1956.

Montoro, André Franco, and Pedro Rodrigues de Albuquerque Cavalcanti. *Memórias em linha reta*. São Paulo: Editora SENAC, 2000.

Moraes, João Quartim de. *A esquerda militar no Brasil: Da coluna a comuna*. São Paulo: Editora Siciliano, 1994.

_____. *A esquerda militar no Brasil: Da conspiração republicana à guerrilha dos tenentes*. São Paulo: Editora Siciliano, 1991.

Moreira Alves, Márcio. *68 mudou o mundo*. Rio de Janeiro: Editora Nova Fronteira, 1993.

_____. *A Grain of Mustard Seed: The Awakening of the Brazilian Revolution*. Garden City, NY: Anchor Books, 1973.

_____. *Teotônio, guerreiro da paz*. Petrópolis: Vozes, 1983.

_____. *Torturas e torturados*. Rio de Janeiro: Empresa Jornalística, 1967.

_____. *A velha classe*. Rio de Janeiro: Editora Arte Nova, 1964.

Mosca, Gaetano. *The Ruling Class (Elementi di scienza politica)*. Translated by Hannah D. Kahn. New York: McGraw-Hill, [1896] 1939.

Motta, Rodrigo Patto Sá, ed. *Ditaduras militares: Brasil, Argentina, Chile e Uruguai*. Belo Horizonte: Editora UFMG, 2015.

Mourão Filho, Olympio, and Hélio Silva. *Memórias, a verdade de um revolucionário*. Porto Alegre: L&PM Editores, 1978.

Muller, Angélica. "A resistência do movimento estudantil brasileiro contra o regime ditatorial e o retorno da UNE à cena pública (1969-1979)." PhD dissertation, Universidade de São Paulo, 2010. https://teses.usp.br/teses/disponiveis/8/8138/tde-06102010-161921/en.php.

Nader, Ana Beatriz. *Autênticos do MDB, semeadores da democracia: História oral de vida política*. São Paulo: Paz e Terra, 1998.

Navarro, Zander. "In Search of a Cultural Interpretation of Power: The Contribution of Pierre Bourdieu." *IDS Bulletin* 37:6 (2006): 11-22.

Negro, Antonio Luigi. *Linhas de montagem: Industrialismo nacional-desenvolvimentista e a sindicalização dos trabalhadores (1945-1978)*. São Paulo: Boitempo, 2004.

Nery, Sebastião. *As 16 derrotas que abalaram o Brasil*. Rio de Janeiro: F. Alves Editora, 1975.

_____. *Grandes pecados da imprensa*. São Paulo: Geração Editorial, 2000.

Nicolau, Jairo. "O sistema eleitoral de lista aberta no Brasil." *Dados* 49:4 (2006): 689-720. https://doi.org/10.1590/S0011-52582006000400002.

Noronha, Eduardo G. "Ciclo de greves, transição política e estabilização: Brasil, 1978-2007." *Lua Nova: Revista de Cultura e Política* 76 (2009): 119-68. https://dx.doi.org/10.1590/S0102-64452009000100005.

Nunn, Amy Stewart, Elize Massard da Fonseca, Francisco I. Bastos, and Sofia Gruskin. "AIDS Treatment in Brazil: Impacts and Challenges." *Health Affairs (Project Hope)* 28:4 (2009): 1103–13. https://dx.doi.org/10.1377/hlthaff.28.4.1103.

Oliveira, Jorge. *Curral da morte: O impeachment de sangue, poder e política no Nordeste*. Rio de Janeiro: Editora Record, 2010.

Oliveira, Paulo Adolfo Martins de. *Atos Institucionais: Sanções políticas*. Brasília: Câmara dos Deputados, Centro de Documentação e Informação, 2000.

Oliveira, Ricardo Costa de, Mônica Helena Harrich Silva Goulart, Ana Christina Vanali, and José Marciano Monteiro. "Família, parentesco, instituições e poder no Brasil: Retomada e atualização de uma agenda de pesquisa." *Revista Brasileira de Sociologia* 5:11 (2017): 165–98. https://dx.doi.org/10.20336/rbs.225.

Pagliarini, André. "'De onde? Para onde?' The Continuity Question and the Debate over Brazil's 'Civil'-Military Dictatorship." *Latin American Research Review* 52:5 (2016): 760–74. https://dx.doi.org/10.25222/larr.216.

Pareto, Vilfredo. *A Treatise on General Sociology*. Translated by Arthur Livingston. New York: Dover, [1915–19] 1963.

Pasqualette, Bernado Braga. *Me esqueçam Figueiredo: A biografia de uma presidência*. Rio de Janeiro: Record, 2020.

Payne, Leigh A. *Brazilian Industrialists and Democratic Change*. Baltimore: Johns Hopkins University Press, 1994.

Pereira, Anthony W. *Political (In)justice: Authoritarianism and the Rule of Law in Brazil, Chile, and Argentina*. Pitt Latin American Series. Pittsburgh: University of Pittsburgh Press, 2005.

Pimentel, Carlos Henrique Lopes. "O anticomunismo e a esquerda militar no Brasil: Uma análise historiográfica." *História em Reflexão* 5:10 (2011): 1–12.

Pitts, Bryan. "The Audacity to Strong-Arm the Generals: Paulo Maluf and the 1978 São Paulo Gubernatorial Contest." *Hispanic American Historical Review* 92:3 (2012): 471–505.

———. "'Je veux élire mon président': Mobilisation populaire, classe politique, et chute du régime militaire (1984–1985)." In *1964: La dictature brésilienne et son legs*, edited by Monica Raisa Schpun and James N. Green. 399–415. Paris: Le Poisson Volant, 2018.

———. "'O funeral da democracia': O caso Moreira Alves, a cultura política das elites e o estabelecimento de uma ditadura no Brasil." In *Paulistânia eleitoral: Ensaios, imagens, dados*. Edited by José D'Amico Bauab. São Paulo: TRE-SP, Imprensa Oficial, 2011.

———. "'O sangue da mocidade está correndo': A classe política e seus filhos enfrentam os militares em 1968." *Revista Brasileira de História* 34:67 (2014): 39–65. https://dx.doi.org/10.1590/S0102-01882014000100003.

Pitts, Bryan, Yahn Wagner, and Madeleine Roberts. "Sound and Politics: The Audio Archive of Brazil's Chamber of Deputies." *Latin American Research Review* 55:1 (2020): 135–47.

Poerner, Artur José. *O poder jovem: História da participação política dos estudantes brasileiros*. 4th ed. Rio de Janeiro: Fundação Biblioteca Nacional, 1995.

Portella de Mello, Jayme. *A Revolução e o governo Costa e Silva*. Rio de Janeiro: Guavira Editores, 1979.

Power, Timothy J. *The Political Right in Postauthoritarian Brazil: Elites, Institutions, and Democratization*. University Park: Pennsylvania State University Press, 2000.

Puls, Mauricio. *O malufismo*. São Paulo: Publifolha, 2000.

Quadros, Marcos Paulo dos Reis, and Rafael Machado Madeira. "Fim da direita envergonhada? Atuação da bancada evangélica e da bancada da bala e os caminhos da representação do conservadorismo no Brasil." *Opinião Pública* 24 (2018): 486–522. https://doi.org/10.1590/1807-01912018243486.

Recording of the 43rd Meeting of the CSN. "1968: Ato Institucional No. 5. A reunião." *Folha de S. Paulo*, 13 December 2008. https://www1.folha.uol.com.br/folha/treinamento/hotsites/ai5/reuniao/index.html.

Rego, Antônio Carlos Pojo do. *O congresso brasileiro e o regime militar (1964–1985)*. Rio de Janeiro: FGV Editora, 2008.

Reis, Fábio Wanderley, ed. *Os partidos e o regime: A lógica do processo eleitoral brasileiro*. São Paulo: Edições Símbolo, 1978.

Rial, Juan. *Partidos políticos, democracia y autoritarismo*. Vol. 2. Montevideo: Ediciones de la Banda Oriental, 1984.

Rodrigues, Carlos Henrique Lopes, and Vanessa Follmann Jurgenfeld. "Desnacionalização e financeirização: Um estudo sobre as privatizações brasileiras (de Collor ao primeiro governo FHC)." *Economia e Sociedade* 28 (2019): 393–420. https://dx.doi.org/10.1590/1982-3533.2019v28n2art05.

Rodrigues, Leôncio Martins. *Partidos, ideologia e composição social: Um estudo das bancadas partidárias na Câmara dos Deputados*. São Paulo: Edusp, 2002.

Romagnoli, Luiz Henrique, and Tânia Gonçalves. *A volta da UNE, de Ibiúna a Salvador*. São Paulo: Alfa-Omega, 1979.

Rossiaud, Jean, and Ilse Scherer-Warren. *A democracia inacabável: Memórias do futuro*. Florianópolis: Universidade Federal de Santa Catarina, 2000.

Russo, Sonia Morgenstern, and Celia Soibelmann Melhem. *PMDB, democracia sempre*. São Paulo: Global, 1987.

Samuels, David. *Ambassadors of the State: Federalism, Ambition, and Congressional Politics in Brazil*. New York: Cambridge University Press, 2002.

Samuels, David, and Fernando Luiz Abrucio. "Federalism and Democratic Transitions: The 'New' Politics of the Governors in Brazil." *Publius* 30:2 (2000): 43–61. https://dx.doi.org/10.2307/3331087.

Santana, Marco Aurélio. *Bravos companheiros: Comunistas e metalúrgicos no Rio de Janeiro (1945/1964)*. Rio de Janeiro: 7 Letras, 2012.

———. "Entre a ruptura e a continuidade: Visões da história do movimento sindical brasileiro." *Revista Brasileira de Ciências Sociais* 14 (1999): 103–20.

Sarmento, Carlos Eduardo. *O espelho partido da metrópole: Chagas Freitas e o campo político carioca (1950–1983). Liderança, voto e estruturas clientelistas*. Rio de Janeiro: Folha Seca/FAPERJ, 2008.

Scartezini, A. C. *Dr. Ulysses: Uma biografia*. São Paulo: Marco Zero, 1993.

Schmitter, Philippe C. "The 'Portugalization' of Brazil?" In *Authoritarian Brazil: Origins, Policies, and Future*, edited by Alfred Stepan, 179–232. New Haven, CT: Yale University Press, 1973.

Serbin, Kenneth P. *From Revolution to Power in Brazil: How Radical Leftists Embraced Capitalism and Struggled with Leadership*. South Bend, IN: University of Notre Dame Press, 2019.

Silva, Haike Kleber da, ed. *A luta pela anistia*. São Paulo: Editora Unesp, Arquivo Público do Estado de São Paulo, Imprensa Oficial do Estado de São Paulo, 2009.

Silva, Hélio. *1933—A crise do tenentismo: O ciclo de Vargas*. Rio de Janeiro: Civilização Brasileira, 1968.

Silva, Marcos, ed., *Brasil 1964/1968: A ditadura já era ditadura*. São Paulo: LCTE Editora, 2006.

Simões, Júlio Assis, and Regina Facchini. *Na trilha do arco-íris: Do movimento homossexual ao LGBT*. São Paulo: Editora Fundação Perseu Abramo, 2009.

Skidmore, Thomas E. "Brazil's Slow Road to Democratization: 1974–1985." In *Democratizing Brazil: Problems of Transition and Consolidation*, edited by Alfred Stepan, 5–42. New York: Oxford University Press, 1989.

———. "Politics and Economic Policy Making in Authoritarian Brazil, 1937–71." In *Authoritarian Brazil: Origins, Policies, and Future*, edited by Alfred Stepan, 7–46. New Haven, CT: Yale University Press, 1973.

———. *The Politics of Military Rule in Brazil, 1964–85*. New York: Oxford University Press, 1988.

Smith, Anne-Marie. *A Forced Agreement: Press Acquiescence to Censorship in Brazil*. Pittsburgh: University of Pittsburgh Press, 1997.

Soares, Gláucio Ary Dillon. "As políticas de cassações." *Dados* 21 (1977): 69–85.

Sodré, Roberto de Abreu. *No espelho do tempo: Meio século de política*. São Paulo: Best Seller, 1995.

Souza, Jessé. *A elite do atraso: Da escravidão a Bolsonaro*. Rio de Janeiro: Estação Brasil, 2019.

Stepan, Alfred, ed., *Authoritarian Brazil: Origins, Policies, and Future*. New Haven, CT: Yale University Press, 1973.

———, ed., *Democratizing Brazil: Problems of Transition and Consolidation*. New York: Oxford University Press, 1993.

———. *The Military in Politics: Changing Patterns in Brazil*. Princeton, NJ: Princeton University Press, 1971.

Sydow, Evanize, and Marilda Ferri. *Dom Paulo Evaristo Arns: Um homem amado e perseguido*. Petrópolis: Editora Vozes, 1999.

Teixeira da Silva, Fernando. *A carga e a culpa: Os operários das docas de Santos. Direitos e cultura de solidariedade, 1937–1968*. São Paulo: Editora Hucitec, 1995.

Teixeirense, Pedro Ivo Carneiro. "Reinventando o inimigo: História, política e memória na montagem dos dossiês e contra-dossiês da ditadura militar brasileira (1964–2001)." PhD dissertation, Universidade Federal do Rio de Janeiro, 2017.

Theo, Harden. "Stefan Zweig and the Land of the Future: The (His)story of an Uneasy Relationship." *Austrian Studies* 23 (2015): 72–87. https://dx.doi.org/10.5699/austrianstudies.23.2015.0072.

Tiezzi, Sergio. "A organização da política social do governo Fernando Henrique." *São Paulo em Perspectiva* 18 (2004): 49–56. http://www.scielo.br/scielo.php?script=sci_arttext&pid=S0102-88392004000200006&nrm=iso.

Tzortzis, Ioannis. *Greek Democracy and the Junta: Regime Crisis and the Failed Transition of 1973*. London: Bloomsbury, 2020.

Verner, Joel G. "The Structure of the Public Careers of Brazilian Legislators, 1963–1970." *International Journal of Comparative Sociology* 16:1–2 (1975): 64–80.

Viel, Mariana, and Aurélio Peres. "Aurélio Peres: É da luta de massas que saem os líderes do PCdoB." *Vermelho: A Esquerda Informada*, January 14, 2011. https://vermelho.org.br/2011/01/14/aurelio-peres-e-da-luta-de-massas-que-saem-os-lideres-do-pcdob/.

Villa, Marco Antônio. *Ditadura à brasileira: A democracia golpeada à esquerda e à direita*. São Paulo: Leya, 2014.

Viveiros, Ricardo. *Laudo Natel: Um bandeirante.* São Paulo: Imprensa Oficial do Estado de São Paulo, 2010.

Voguel, Luiz Henrique. *A histórica sub-representação das mulheres na Câmara dos Deputados: Desigualdades e hierarquias sociais nas eleições de 2014.* Brasília: Câmara dos Deputados, Consultoria Legislativa, 2019.

Weinstein, Barbara. *The Color of Modernity: São Paulo and the Making of Race and Nation in Brazil.* Durham, NC: Duke University Press, 2015.

Woodard, James P. *A Place in Politics: São Paulo, Brazil, from Seigneurial Republicanism to Regionalist Revolt.* Durham, NC: Duke University Press, 2009.

Yang, Yang. "Bourdieu, Practice and Change: Beyond the Critique of Determinism." *Educational Philosophy and Theory* 46:14 (2014): 1522–40. https://dx.doi.org/10.1080/001318 57.2013.839375.

Yannuzzi, María de los Angeles. *Política y dictadura: Los partidos políticos y el "proceso de reorganización nacional" 1976-1982.* Rosario: Editorial Fundación Ross, 1996.

Yocelevzky R., Ricardo A. *Chile: Partidos políticos, democracia y dictadura: 1970-1990.* Mexico City: Fondo de Cultura Económica, 2002.

Zuckerman, Alan. "The Concept 'Political Elite': Lessons from Mosca and Pareto." *Journal of Politics* 39:2 (1977): 324–44.

Zweig, Stefan. *Brazil: A Land of the Future.* Riverside, CA: Ariadne Press, 2018.

INDEX

abertura, 132, 136, 139, 143
Abi-Ackel, Ibrahim, 144, 146
AI-5: as a punishment of the political class, 51–52, 60–61, 69, 74, 76, 121; as a way to intimidate the political class, 78, 94, 113–114; decree of, 50, 56–60; politicians' attitudes toward, 60, 63–64, 75, 77, 87, 103, 144; relationship to Moreira Alves case, 51–52, 60; revocation of, 94–96, 116, 132, 144
AI-1, 15, 37, 68
AI-3, 17
AI-2, 16–18, 35, 38, 68
Aleixo, Pedro, 57–60, 67–69, 75–77, 114
Alemão, o. *See* Moura, Enilson Simões de
Alfonsín, Raúl, 154
Aliança Renovadora Nacional (ARENA), 17; and conservative ideology, 26; defense of student movement, 24, 26–28; dissatisfaction with military regime, 18, 60, 64, 97, 108–109, 114–115, 120–121, 124; lack of internal coherence, 93–94, 108; military distrust of, 32, 51–52, 60, 74–75, 108–110, 114–115, 120; role of personal rivalries, 89–90, 97, 99–100, 104–105, 108–109; tendency toward opportunism, 90, 105; tension between support for military and obligation to voters, 105
amnesty, 139
Andrade, Joaquim dos Santos, 128–129
Andreazza, Mário, 38, 154, 163, 166–167

anti-candidacy. *See* Guimarães, Ulysses
April Package, 114–116, 123, 126, 151
Arns, Paulo Evaristo, 96, 130, 144
autênticos 81, 83–89, 96–97, 114, 126, 171, 176

Barros, Adhemar de, 15–17, 67, 90
Barros Filho, Adhemar de, 104, 158
Bolsonaro, Jair 1, 175–177, 180
Bourdieu, Pierre, 5, 226n19
Braga, Roberto Saturnino, 106, 134
Brizola, Leonel, 139, 149, 151, 155–158, 162

Cabral, Bernardo, 45–46
Cardoso, Fernando Henrique, 98, 207n1; presidency of, 174, 178; role in ABC strikes, 127, 130–131, 136, 140–141; role in 1984–85 presidential succession, 151–152, 157, 165, 167
Carone, Nísia, 42–43, 46, 74
Carvalho Pinto, Carlos, 18, 100, 103–106, 108
cassação, 15–16, 65, 74, 187n7, 199n62; arbitrary nature of, 54, 66–71; as a badge of honor, 53, 71; as a tool to threaten political class, 36, 38, 49; as punishment for political class, 52–53; lived experience of, 71–74; use against regime allies, 17, 63, 67, 71
Castelo Branco, Humberto, 15–17, 37–38
Centro Brasileiro de Análise e Planejamento (CEBRAP), 98, 100, 102, 140
Chagas Freitas, Antônio, 83, 85
Chaves, Aureliano, 153–154, 158, 162–165

Chaves, Francisco Leite, 143
civil society, 3, 7–10, 94, 124, 137, 147, 171, 174
Congress: as a rubber stamp for the military, 17, 21, 44–45, 79, 81–82; closure of, 2, 4, 50, 53–54, 59, 61–64, 74, 80, 114; curtailment of powers, 18, 36, 89; defense of prerogatives, 41–46; defense of student movement, 18–32; role in presidential elections, 15–17, 77, 86–89, 169–170; vote on Diretas Já, 157–161
Conselho de Segurança Nacional (CSN), 127, 153, 162, 165, 168; role in cassações, 65–72, 74, 77; role in decree of AI-5 56–60
Constitutionalist Revolution, 15, 118, 152, 157
corruption: accusations against military, 146, 169; instrumental use of accusations of, 54–55, 66, 71, 122–123, 197n6; military claims to oppose, 2, 4, 62, 66, 76, 100, 170, 182n8
Costa, Tito, 136–137, 146,
Costa e Silva, Artur da, 17–18, 31; and the decree of AI-5, 49–52, 56–60; as a relative "moderate," 38, 41, 61, 64; attitudes toward legality, 60; position on Moreira Alves case, 34, 38, 40; post-AI-5 reforms, 74–77; relationship with ARENA, 51, 57, 60–61, 67; role in cassações ,54, 65–71; stroke and incapacitation, 76, 79
Coup of 1964. *See* "Revolution" of 1964
Covas, Lila, 53, 56, 71–72, 202–203n125
Covas, Mário: career after 1979 amnesty, 144, 151, 157, 160; cassação and imprisonment, 53, 55–56, 67–69, 71–72; role in Moreira Alves case, 36, 40–41, 43, 47–50; support for student movement, 19, 21, 23, 27
Cunha, João, 143, 146, 170
Cunha Bueno, Antônio, 20, 72–74

Delfim Neto, Antônio, 58, 68–69, 74, 81, 99, 115, 117, 200n82
détente, 95–96, 104, 206–207n97; disillusionment with, 113–114, 124
Diretas Já, 152–161
distensão. *See* détente
Dória, Carlos Sampaio, 118–119

Elections: as only channel for opposition to the regime, 89, 112, 171; indirect, 16–18, 84, 88, 95, 114, 162–163; 169–170; 208n12; military refusal to abolish, 4, 80, 92, 171–172; of 1968, 70, 90; of 1970, 78, 82; of 1978, 114, 117, 126, 131–132; of 1974, 98–110, 207n5; of 1976, 114; of 1972, 82; sublegenda system, 89–90, 176
elite theory, 4–5, 79–80

Empire, Brazilian, 177
Estado Novo, 37–38, 53, 79

Figueiredo, João Batista, 107, 115, 126, 132–133, 139; attempts to preserve the regime, 150–152; attitude toward Maluf candidacy, 153, 164, 167; attitude toward Neves candidacy, 169; opposition to Diretas Já, 158–159, 164–165; refusal to endorse successor, 153; role in ABC strikes, 135, 142; role in abertura 132, 139; role in 1978 São Paulo gubernatorial contest, 116, 120–121, 123
Franco, Itamar, 165, 174
Freire, Geraldo, 36, 38, 42, 48, 50
Freire, Marcos, 134, 143
Freitas Nobre, José de, 113, 143–145
Frente Liberal (FL), 165–167
Furtado, José Alencar, 83, 101, 114. 201n113, 208n20

Gama e Silva, Luis Antônio da, 26, 34–35, 38, 49–50, 59–60, 65–66, 68, 74–75
Gato, Alberto Marcelo, 110–111, 114
Geisel, Ernesto, 7, 53, 99–100, 115–118, 121, 123, 132, 153; commitment to controlled liberalization, 94- 97, 99, 110; election of, 81, 84, 88, 86–89, 94; repressive tendencies, 100, 110, 113–115
Goldman, Alberto, 110–111, 135
Gomes, Severo, 144, 157
Gonzaga Júnior, Otávio, 134, 144, 146
Goulart, João, 2, 4, 15–16, 18, 61, 68, 125, 148, 157
Guimarães, Honestino, 19, 23, 32
Guimarães, Ulysse,s 96, 113; anti-candidacy of, 81, 83–89; attitude toward democracy, 160; initial timidity toward regime, 15, 84–85; role in Diretas Já, 154–157, 159–160; role in indirect election of Neves, 162–163, 166; role in 1974 elections, 98, 100–102, 105, 109

Herzog, Vladimir, 112–113, 124
honor: of military, 31–32, 37, 39, 43, 51, 58; of political class, 30, 38, 42, 44–48, 50, 53, 60, 71, 171
Hummes, Cláudio, 133, 135–136
Huntington, Samuel, 93–94

immunity, parliamentary 35; as protection against arrest, 23, 44, 53, 145; as protection for criticizing the regime, 39–40, 42, 44; historical attitudes toward, 38, 47; limits of, 35, 48, 77; military views of, 61; restoration of, 132

Krieger, Daniel, 37–38, 60, 63–64, 66
Kubitschek, Juscelino, 15–16, 20, 22, 55–56, 61, 63, 68

Lacerda, Carlos, 54, 65
Lembo, Cláudio, 118–120, 129, 139
Lerer, David, 26–27, 65, 73
Lima, Alfonso Albuquerque, 39, 77
Lula. *See* Silva, Luis Inácio Lula da

Macedo, Murilo, 133, 135, 138, 141–143
Maluf, Paulo, 71–72; accusations of corruption, 121–123, 153–154, 167, 221n27; candidacy for governor of São Paulo, 115–124; candidacy for presidency, 151, 153–154, 163–170; reaction to ABC strikes, 133–134, 138, 142–143
Marcílio, Benedito, 131, 135–136, 140, 142
Marinho, Djalma, 39–41, 101
Marinho, Roberto, 117
Martins, Paulo Egydio, 15–16, 69, 73, 99–100, 104, 117
masculinity, 30, 37, 44–45, 53, 60, 83, 187n17
Matos, Délio Jardim de, 168–169
Médici, Emílio Garrastazu, 77–79, 82, 92–94
military: anti-communism of, 15, 32, 39, 56, 110–112, 151; attempts to reform political class, 2, 62, 74–76, 79–80, 108, 171; divisions within; need for collaboration of political class, 4, 18, 80, 97, 99, 172; social composition, 4; suspicion of political class, 2, 4, 6, 32, 51–54; 61–62, 123–124, 153, 170, 175; views concerning legality and legitimacy, 4, 18, 34, 60, 65, 75, 79
Moises, José Álvaro, 140, 146
Montoro, André Franco, 16, 151, 203n8; as MDB coordinator of 1974 electoral campaign, 100–102, 109, 112; initial timidity, 15; relationship with labor movement, 127–130, 134, 140, 145; role in Diretas Já, 152, 157, 162.
Moreira Alves, Márcio, 54; defense of student movement, 20, 26–31; regime's attempt to prosecute, 34–35, 39–41, 46–50; threats against, 35–36; unpopularity among deputies, 30, 36
Moura, Enilson Simões de, 144–146
Movimento Democrático Brasileiro (MDB), 17; conflict between moderados and autênticos, 83–84, 89; defense of civil liberties, 17, 90, 98, 103, 114; difficulty attracting members, 17, 73, 82, 89, 91–92, 101, 111; military vision of its role, 78–79, 95, 97, 99, 101, 110; relationship with labor movement, 128–131, 135–136; shift to targeting working-class voters, 92, 98, 100–102, 104–105, 124; ties to communists, 111–112

Natel, Laudo, 104, 115–123, 166
Neves, Léo de Almeida, 19, 71
Neves, Tancredo, 81, 109, 139, 153; presidential campaign and election, 162–172; role in Diretas Já, 155–157, 161

Partido Comunista Brasileiro (PCB), 91, 148, 173; persecution under military the regime, 111–113; preference for working within the system rather than armed revolution, 147–148; relationship with the legal opposition, 110.
Partido Comunista do Brasil (PCdoB), 110, 131, 172
Partido Democrático Social (PDS), 139, 149; attempts by regime to help win elections, 150–151; attitudes toward Diretas Já, 155–156. 159, 161; inability to agree on presidential candidate, 153–154, 158, 162, 166–167; split over Maluf candidacy, 163–166; willingness to abandon regime, 156, 168, 170–171
Partido Democrático Trabalhista (PDT), 152
Partido do Movimento Democrático Brasileiro (PMDB), 139; and Diretas Já 152, 154; attitudes toward labor movement, 140; participation in indirect elections, 151, 162, 164–167, 160–170.
Partido dos Trabalhadores (PT), 139–141, 148, 152, 154, 166, 174
Partido Social Democrático (PSD), 16, 83, 108, 187n17
Partido Social Progressista (PSP), 15
Passarinho, Jarbas, 59, 66–67, 72, 74, 134
Passoni, Irma, 132, 135, 140, 147
Pazzianoto, Almir, 134, 141–142
Peres, Aurélio, 131, 137
Pinto, Francisco, 81, 84, 100, 157, 208n20
Pires, Walter, 152, 168–169
political class: as part of socioeconomic elite, 4–6, 31–32, 55; at state and local level, 6, 8, 75, 89–90, 115, 176; attitudes toward democracy, 3, 43–44, 150; attitudes toward working class and mass mobilization, 4, 144, 148, 156, 160, 169, 173; decisive role in democratic transition, 1 3, 7 8, 13, 170; defense of prerogatives, 18, 44, 46, 52, 171; definition, 2, 5–6; discontent with two-party system 17–18; disregard for ideology, 10,

42, 64, 176; hereditary nature of, 2, 4, 5–6, 46, 74, 175; legitimization of rule through liberal democracy, 44, 46–47; relationship with military, 4, 6, 60–62, 97, 109; social ties among, 5, 10, 42, 56, 138; transformation under military rule, 177–180
political culture, 8–10, 42, 46, 94
political opening. *See* abertura
Populist Republic, 107, 147–148
Portella de Mello, Jayme, 21, 37, 51
Portella, Petrônio, 64, 86, 88, 99–100, 105, 107

Quadros, Jânio, 56, 68, 90, 104
Quércia, Orestes, 82, 89–92, 151; 1974 Senate candidacy, 100, 102–104, 106–107, 109, 111–112; role in ABC strikes, 127–129, 131, 134, 145

Rademaker, Augusto, 57–58
Ramalho, Thales, 91, 96
Reale, Miguel, 128
regionalism, 6, 15
"Revolution" of 1964: objectives of, 2, 32, 59, 96, 151; political class's acceptance of, 14, 89, 96–97, 101; relationship with democracy, 4, 34, 93; relationship with law, 39, 42–43, 51; targeting of political class, 2, 14, 54, 67–68
Righi Cuoghi, Gastone, 26, 55, 65, 71, 73
rivalries: among politicians, 4, 17, 89–90, 94, 97, 99–100; 105, 165–166; role in cassações, 69, 70–71; within the military, 10
Rodrigues, José Martins, 17, 23–24, 26, 28, 55
Rousseff, Dilma, 3, 32, 157, 174–175

Sabiá, José Lurtz, 17, 66–67, 70, 72, 84
Santilli Sobrinho, José, 24–25, 136
Santillo, Henrique, 143
Santos, Osmar, 154–155
São Paulo (state), 6–7; 9; as center of opposition, 6–7, 65, 121, 124, 127, 157, 170; as target of regime repression, 65, 112–114; 1978 gubernatorial contest, 114–123; 1974 Senate election, 99–107; regional identity, 15; role in 1964 coup, 7
Sarney, José, 109, 133, 156, 163, 173; falling out with regime, 164–167
Sátiro, Ernani, 24, 27–28, 31, 38
Serviço Nacional de Informações (SNI), 11, 77, 107; confidential and secret reports, 96, 99, 108, 111, 119–120, 154, 166, 168; role in political repression, 23–24, 59, 65, 70
Silva, Golbery do Couto e, 94–96, 108, 111, 114, 141
Silva, Luiz Inácio Lula da: as a union leader, 125, 127, 131, 133–138, 141–142; attitude toward student movement, 130–131; attitude toward workers' political role, 131, 137–140; imprisonment of, 142–145, 147, 179; presidency of, 1, 174; role in Diretas Já, 152, 155–158;
Simon, Pedro, 143
Siqueira Filho, Geraldo, 131, 135–136, 140, 142, 145
Soares, Airton, 135, 140, 142–143
Sobral Pinto, Heráclito, 55
Southern Cone military dictatorships, 4, 76, 168, 202n138 and 139, 206n88, 211n114
student movement: eventual careers in politics, 32, 149, 171; military repression of, 18–23; scorn for the political class, 21–22, 31; social composition, 20; ties to political class, 14, 19, 22–23, 26, 31–32.
Stenzel, Clovis, 24, 36, 41, 49, 79
Suplicy, Eduardo, 130, 132, 135

Tarquínio, Esmeraldo, 70–71
Tavares, Lyra, 31, 34
Tavares Coelho, Marco Antônio, 110–113
Tiradentes, 46, 172, 180
tutelage, military: as an objective of the military regime, 4, 54, 74, 76–79, 151, 171; resentment of political class toward, 1–4, 8, 52, 97, 144, 174, 177
Tuma, Romeu, 134, 142–143, 145

União Democrática Nacional (UDN), 15–16, 18, 108, 187n17
União Nacional dos Estudantes (UNE), 19
Universidade de Brasília (UnB), 22–23; invasion of, 14, 23–26
Universidade de São Paulo (USP), 34, 73, 98

Vargas, Getúlio, 15, 19–20, 29, 38, 53, 94, 147–148, 170–171, 182n9
Vargas, Ivette, 30, 139
Vilela, Teotônio, 56, 143–147, 157

Wainer, Samuel, 129, 215n27
Weffort, Francisco, 140, 166

Founded in 1893,
UNIVERSITY OF CALIFORNIA PRESS
publishes bold, progressive books and journals
on topics in the arts, humanities, social sciences,
and natural sciences—with a focus on social
justice issues—that inspire thought and action
among readers worldwide.

The UC PRESS FOUNDATION
raises funds to uphold the press's vital role
as an independent, nonprofit publisher, and
receives philanthropic support from a wide
range of individuals and institutions—and from
committed readers like you. To learn more, visit
ucpress.edu/supportus.